Shojo Beat

27

Story & Art by
Taeko Watanabe

Contents

Story Thus Far

It is the end of the Bakufu era, the third year of Bunkyu (1863) in Kyoto. The Shinsengumi is a band of warriors formed to protect the shogun.

Tominaga Sei, the daughter of a former Bakufu *bushi*, joined the Shinsengumi disguised as a boy by the name of Kamiya Seizaburo to avenge her father and brother. She has continued her training under the only person in the Shinsengumi who knows her true identity, Okita Soji, and she aspires to become a true *bushi*.

The Choshu and Satsuma Hans sign a secret agreement, and the two regions begin to build up an anti-Bakufu front. Under orders from the Bakufu, Kondo goes on a mission to spy on Choshu but returns to Kyoto in despair after witnessing Choshu's commitment to its position and the miserable state of the weakened Bakufu. Oko, the former courtesan, comforts Kondo in his moment of weakness. Meanwhile, councilor Ito, who once schemed to assassinate Kondo, is still operating within the Shinsengumi…

Characters

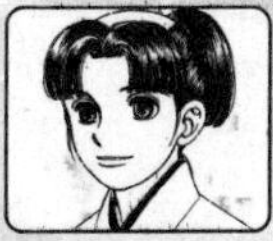

Tominaga Sei

She disguises herself as a boy to enter the Mibu-Roshi. She trains under Soji, aspiring to become a true *bushi*. But secretly, she is in love with Soji.

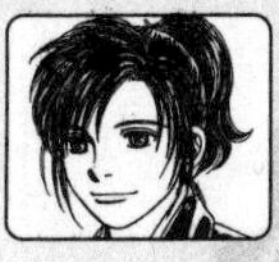

Okita Soji

Assistant vice captain of the Shinsengumi and licensed master of the Ten'nen Rishin-ryu. He supports the troop alongside Kondo and Hijikata and guides Seizaburo with a kind yet firm hand.

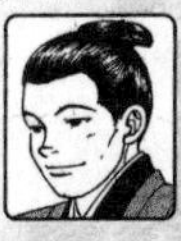

Kondo Isami

Captain of the Shinsengumi and fourth grandmaster of the Ten'nen Rishin-ryu. A passionate, warm and well-respected leader.

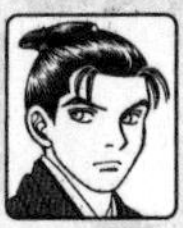

Hijikata Toshizo

Vice captain of the Shinsengumi. He commands both the group and himself with a rigid strictness. He is also known as the "Oni vice captain."

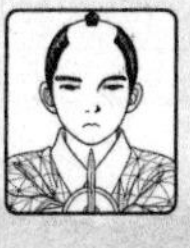

Saito Hajime

Assistant vice captain. He was a friend of Sei's older brother. Sei is attached to him in place of her lost brother.

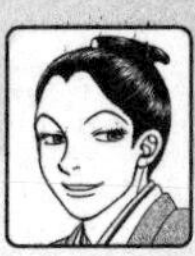

Ito Kashitaro

Councilor of the Shinsengumi. A skilled swordsman and an academic with anti-Bakufu sentiments, he plots to sway the direction of the troop.

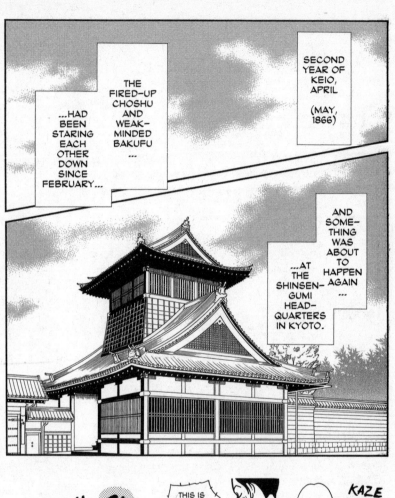

SECOND YEAR OF KEIO, APRIL
(MAY, 1866)
THE FIRED-UP CHOSHU AND WEAK-MINDED BAKUFU...
...HAD BEEN STARING EACH OTHER DOWN SINCE FEBRUARY...
AND SOME-THING WAS ABOUT TO HAPPEN AGAIN...
...AT THE SHINSEN-GUMI HEAD-QUARTERS IN KYOTO.

KAZE HIKARU IROHA KARUTA
Would you rub it on me.. Hijikata-kun? ♥
THIS IS MEANT TO BE SWAL-LOWED!!
stop stripping!!
"HI" ひ
HIJI, KATA, KOSHI NI ISHIDA SANYAKU.
"ISHIDA'S POWDERED MEDICINE FOR YOUR ELBOWS, SHOULDERS AND WAIST."
by Asuka-san from Fukuoka

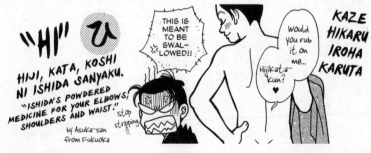

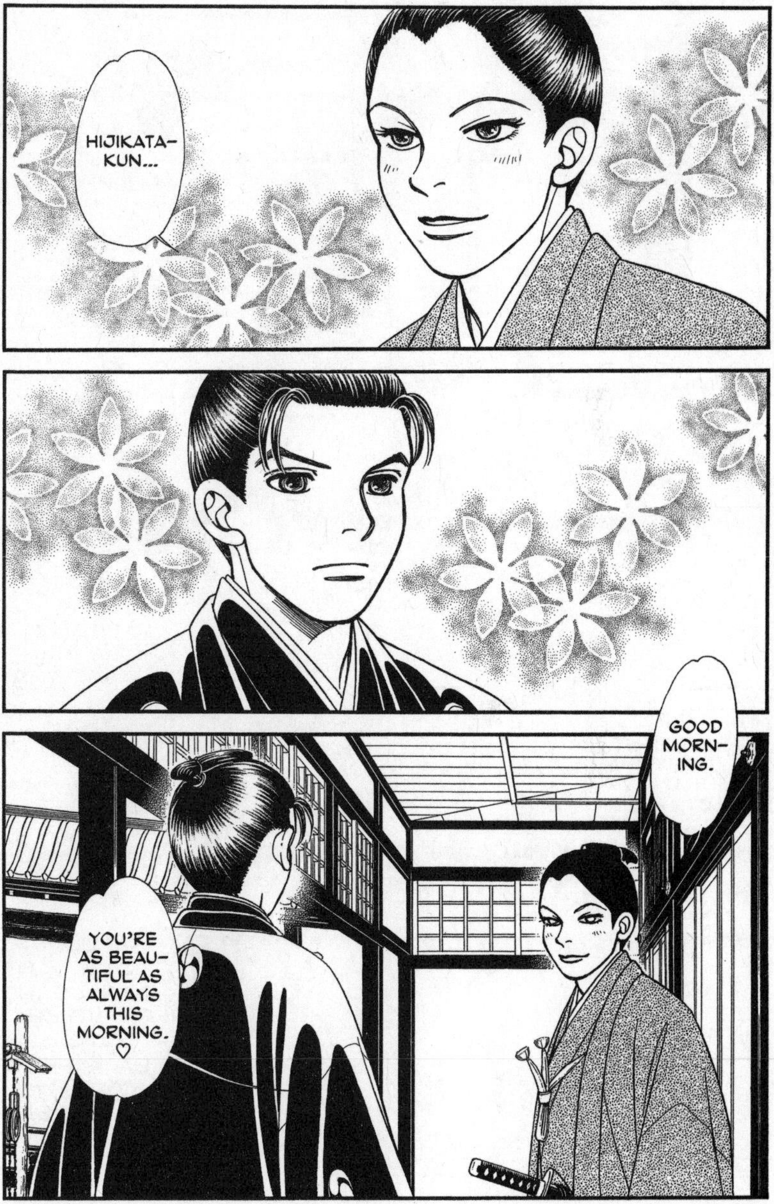
HIJIKATA-KUN...
GOOD MORNING.
YOU'RE AS BEAUTIFUL AS ALWAYS THIS MORNING. ♡

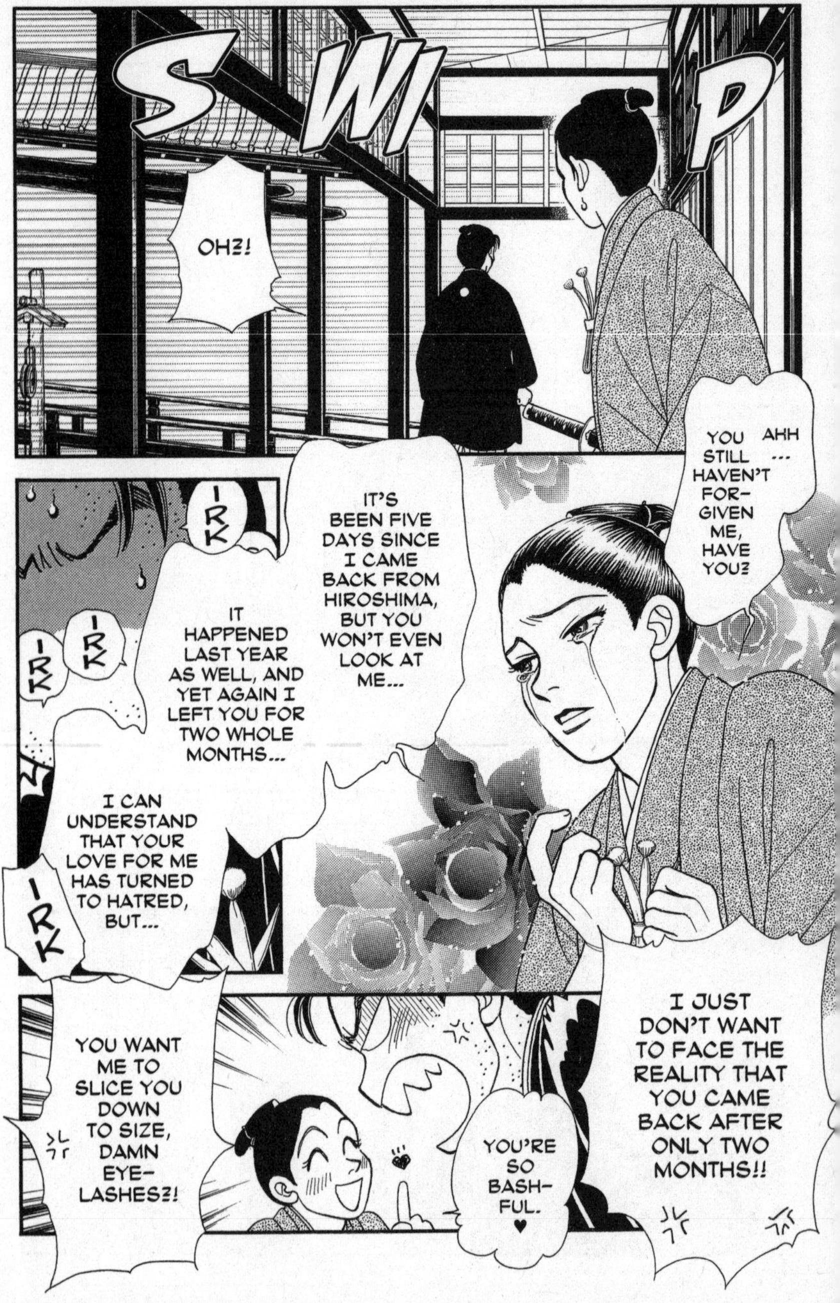
SWIP
OH?!
AHH...
YOU STILL HAVEN'T FORGIVEN ME, HAVE YOU?
IRK
IT'S BEEN FIVE DAYS SINCE I CAME BACK FROM HIROSHIMA, BUT YOU WON'T EVEN LOOK AT ME...
IRK
IRK
IT HAPPENED LAST YEAR AS WELL, AND YET AGAIN I LEFT YOU FOR TWO WHOLE MONTHS...
I CAN UNDERSTAND THAT YOUR LOVE FOR ME HAS TURNED TO HATRED, BUT...
IRK
I JUST DON'T WANT TO FACE THE REALITY THAT YOU CAME BACK AFTER ONLY TWO MONTHS!!
YOU'RE SO BASHFUL. ♥
YOU WANT ME TO SLICE YOU DOWN TO SIZE, DAMN EYELASHES?!

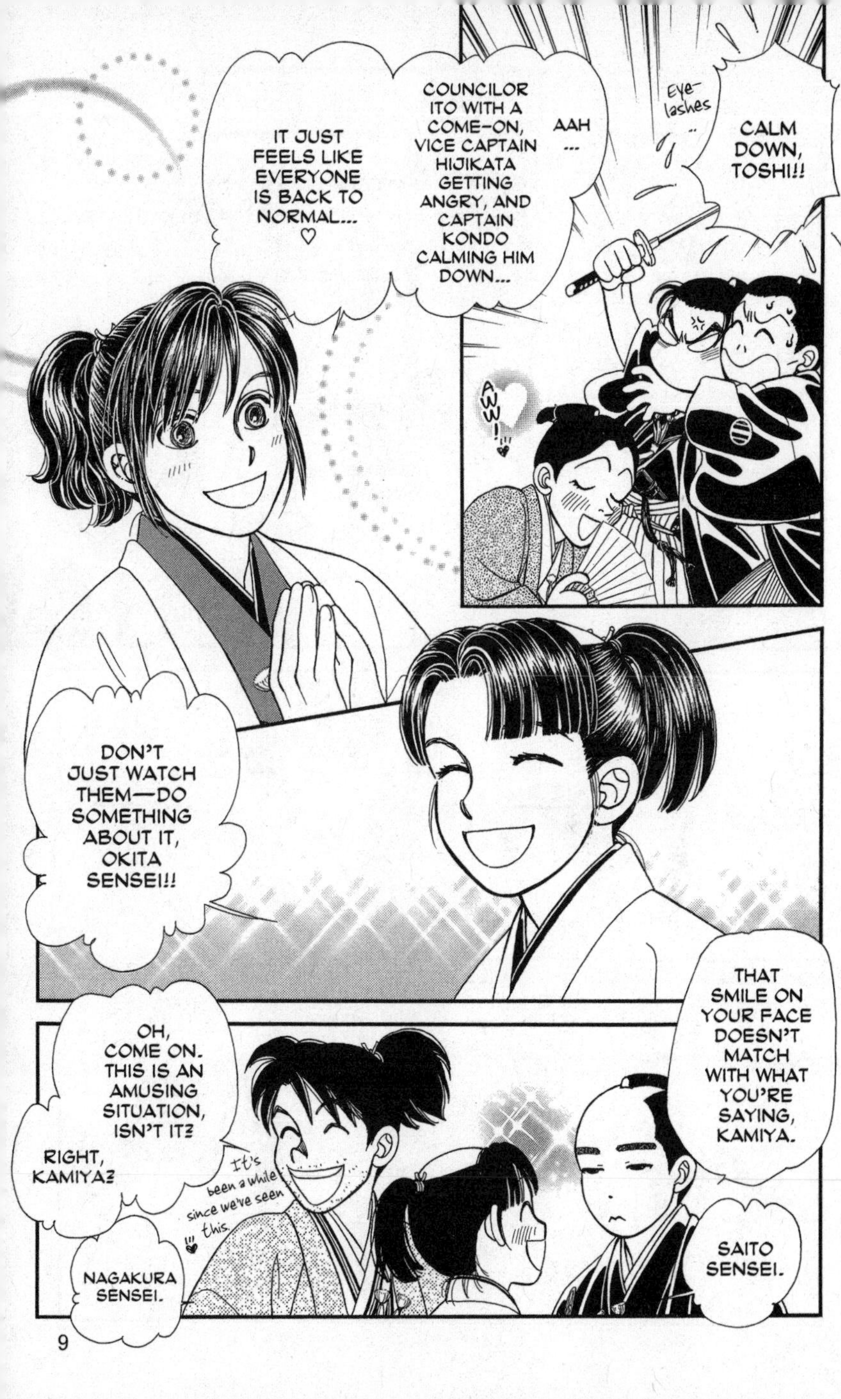
CALM DOWN, TOSHI!!
Eye-lashes ..
AAH ...
AWW!!!
COUNCILOR ITO WITH A COME-ON, VICE CAPTAIN HIJIKATA GETTING ANGRY, AND CAPTAIN KONDO CALMING HIM DOWN...
IT JUST FEELS LIKE EVERYONE IS BACK TO NORMAL... ♡
DON'T JUST WATCH THEM—DO SOMETHING ABOUT IT, OKITA SENSEI!!
THAT SMILE ON YOUR FACE DOESN'T MATCH WITH WHAT YOU'RE SAYING, KAMIYA.
SAITO SENSEI.
OH, COME ON. THIS IS AN AMUSING SITUATION, ISN'T IT?
RIGHT, KAMIYA?
It's been a while since we've seen this.
NAGAKURA SENSEI.

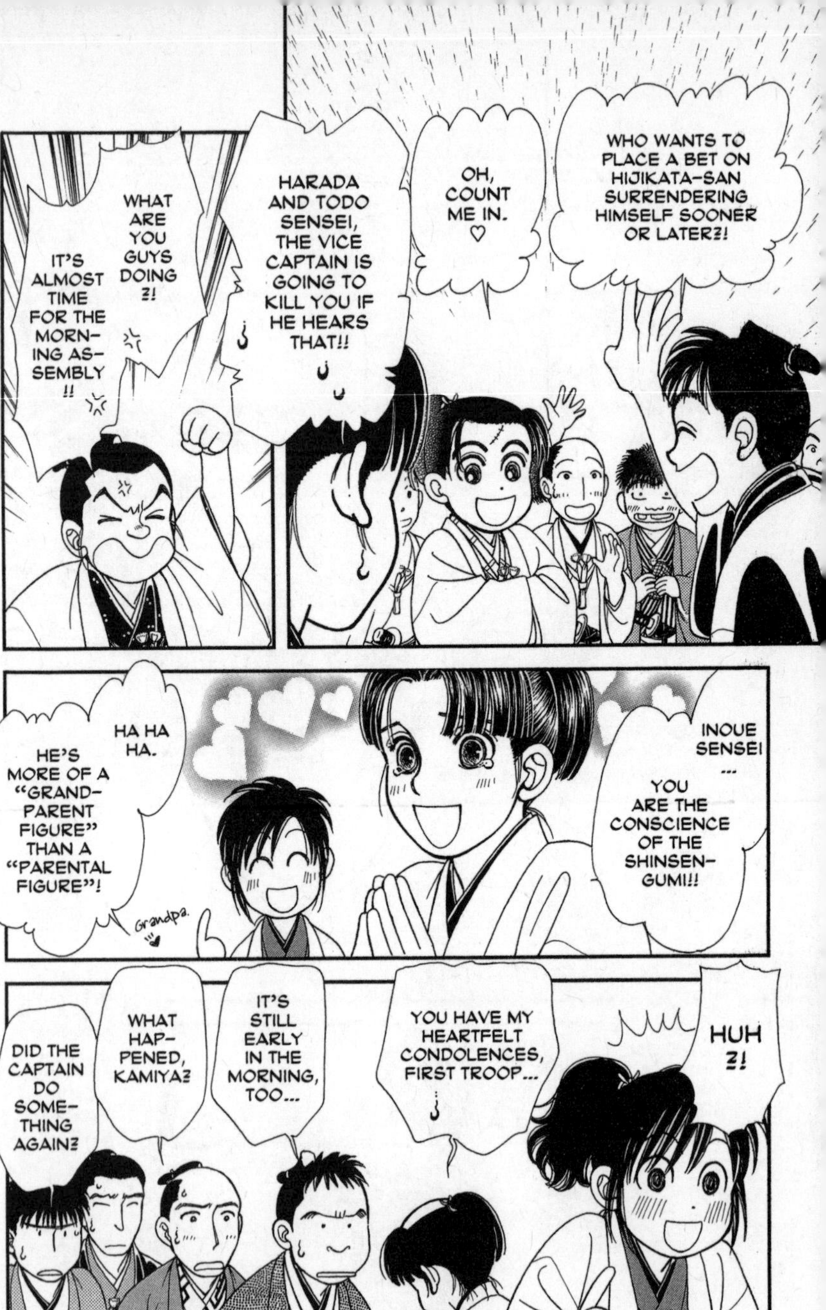
WHO WANTS TO PLACE A BET ON HIJIKATA-SAN SURRENDERING HIMSELF SOONER OR LATER?!
OH, COUNT ME IN. ♡
HARADA AND TODO SENSEI, THE VICE CAPTAIN IS GOING TO KILL YOU IF HE HEARS THAT!!
WHAT ARE YOU GUYS DOING?!
IT'S ALMOST TIME FOR THE MORNING ASSEMBLY!!
INOUE SENSEI...
YOU ARE THE CONSCIENCE OF THE SHINSENGUMI!!
HA HA HA.
HE'S MORE OF A "GRANDPARENT FIGURE" THAN A "PARENTAL FIGURE"!
Grandpa.
HUH?!
YOU HAVE MY HEARTFELT CONDOLENCES, FIRST TROOP...
IT'S STILL EARLY IN THE MORNING, TOO...
WHAT HAPPENED, KAMIYA?
DID THE CAPTAIN DO SOMETHING AGAIN?

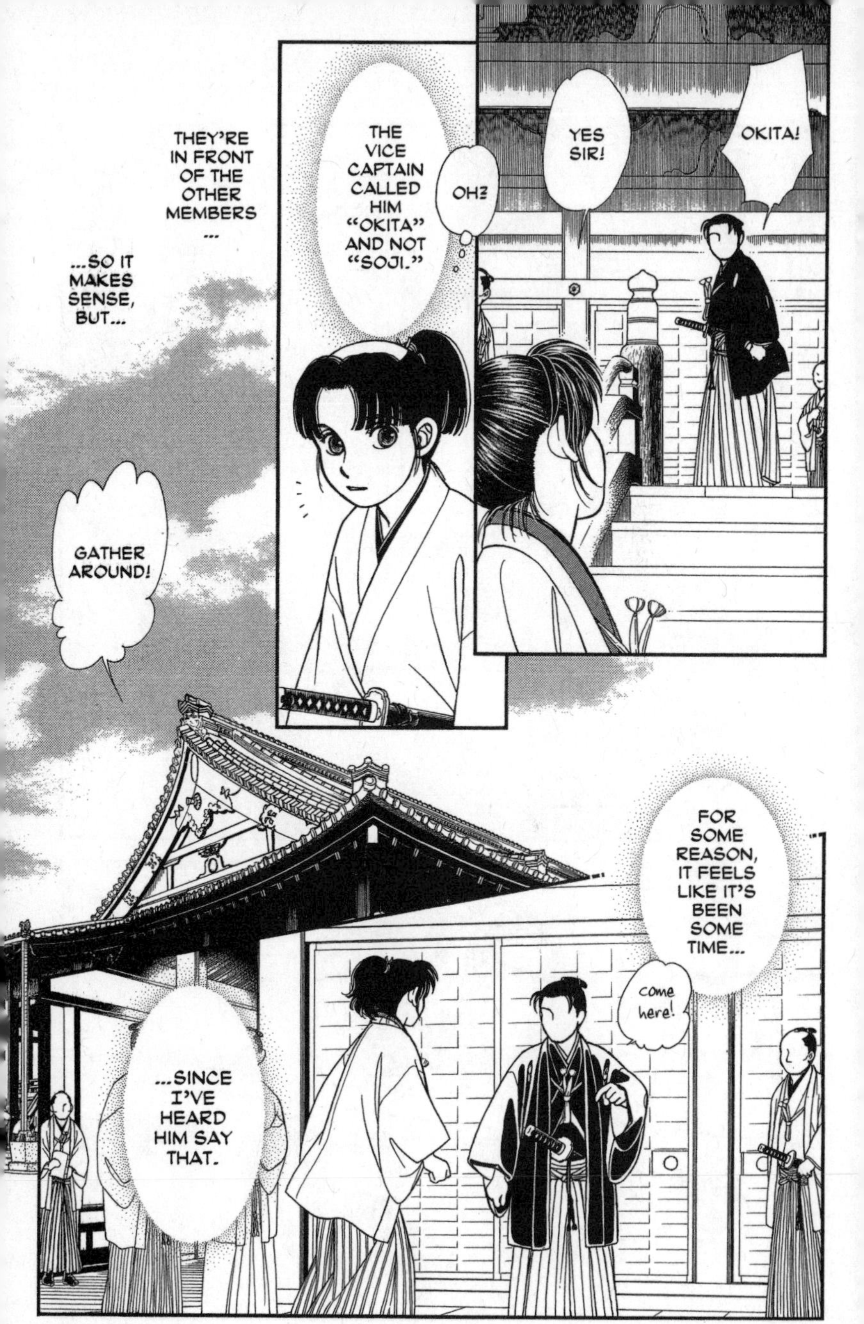
OKITA!
YES SIR!
OH?
THE VICE CAPTAIN CALLED HIM “OKITA” AND NOT “SOJI.”
THEY’RE IN FRONT OF THE OTHER MEMBERS...
...SO IT MAKES SENSE, BUT...
GATHER AROUND!
FOR SOME REASON, IT FEELS LIKE IT’S BEEN SOME TIME...
Come here!
...SINCE I’VE HEARD HIM SAY THAT.

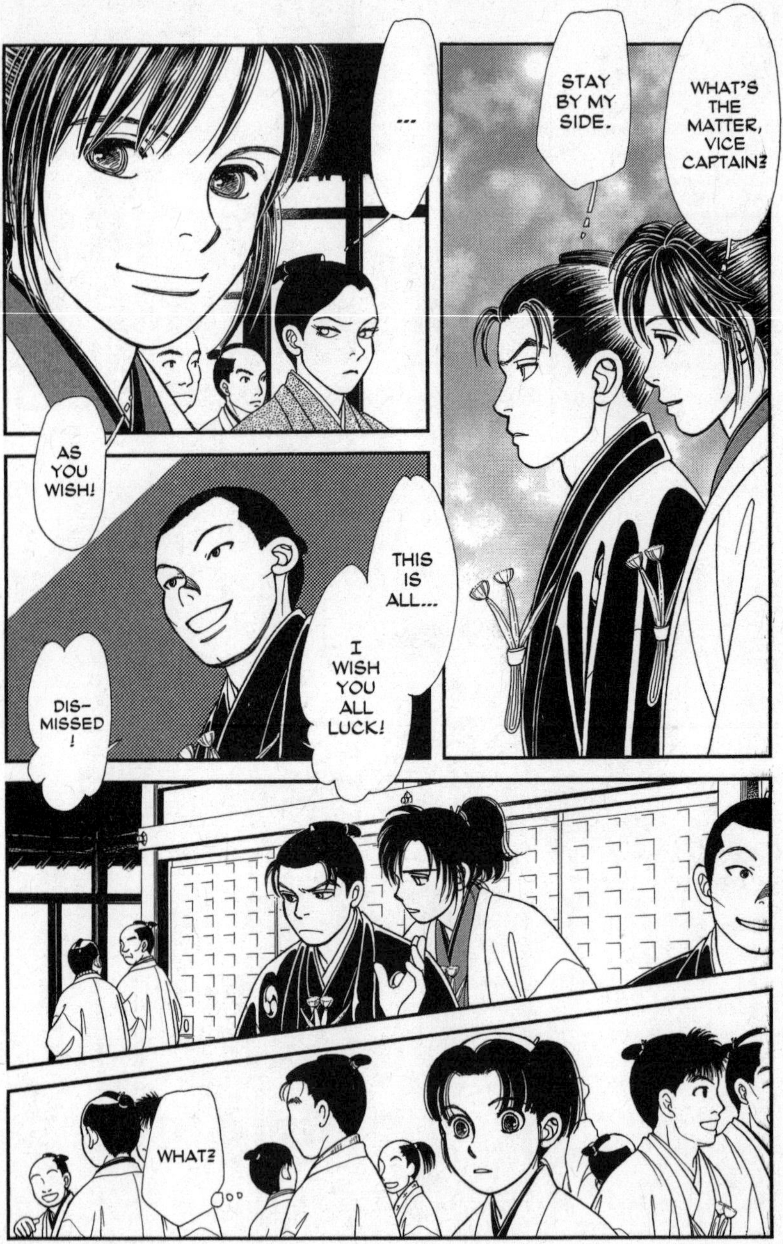
WHAT'S THE MATTER, VICE CAPTAIN?
STAY BY MY SIDE.
...
AS YOU WISH!
THIS IS ALL...
I WISH YOU ALL LUCK!
DIS-MISSED!
WHAT?

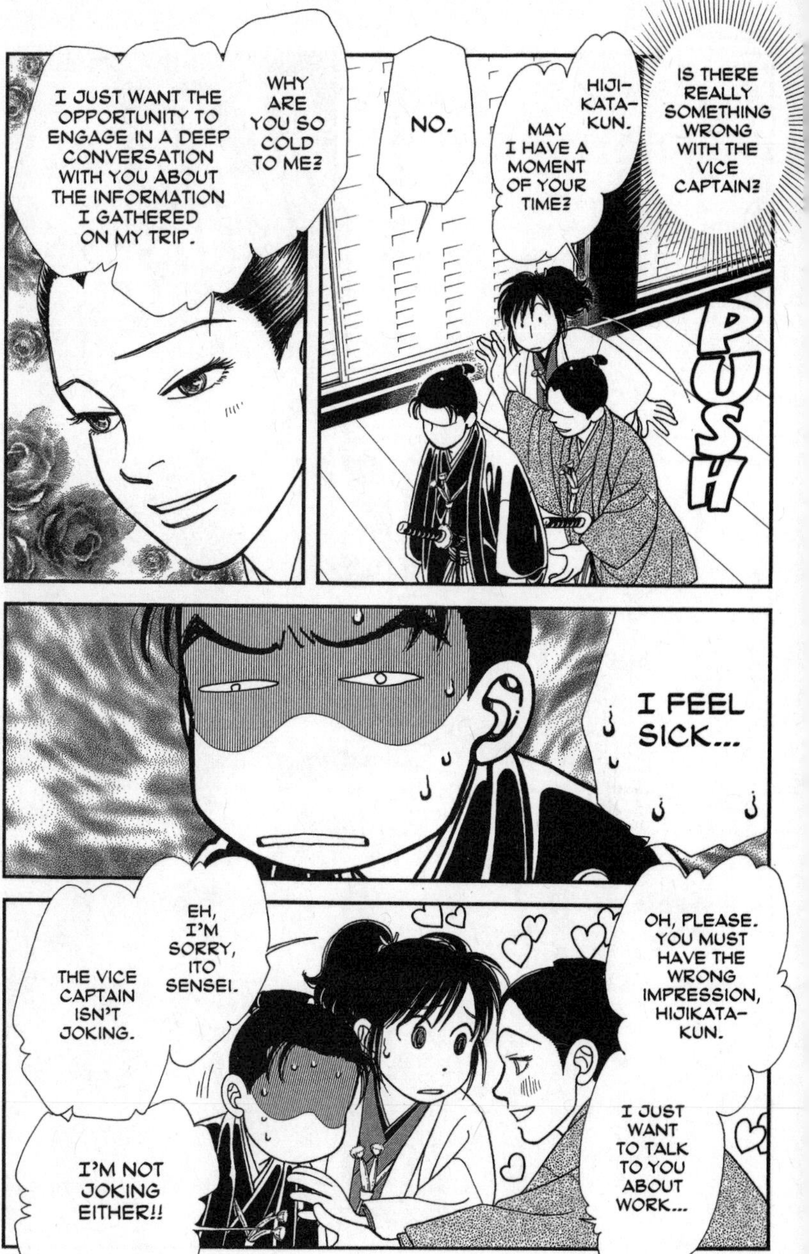
IS THERE REALLY SOMETHING WRONG WITH THE VICE CAPTAIN?
HIJI-KATA-KUN.
MAY I HAVE A MOMENT OF YOUR TIME?
NO.
PUSH
WHY ARE YOU SO COLD TO ME?
I JUST WANT THE OPPORTUNITY TO ENGAGE IN A DEEP CONVERSATION WITH YOU ABOUT THE INFORMATION I GATHERED ON MY TRIP.
I FEEL SICK...
OH, PLEASE. YOU MUST HAVE THE WRONG IMPRESSION, HIJIKATA-KUN.
I JUST WANT TO TALK TO YOU ABOUT WORK...
EH, I'M SORRY, ITO SENSEI.
THE VICE CAPTAIN ISN'T JOKING.
I'M NOT JOKING EITHER!!

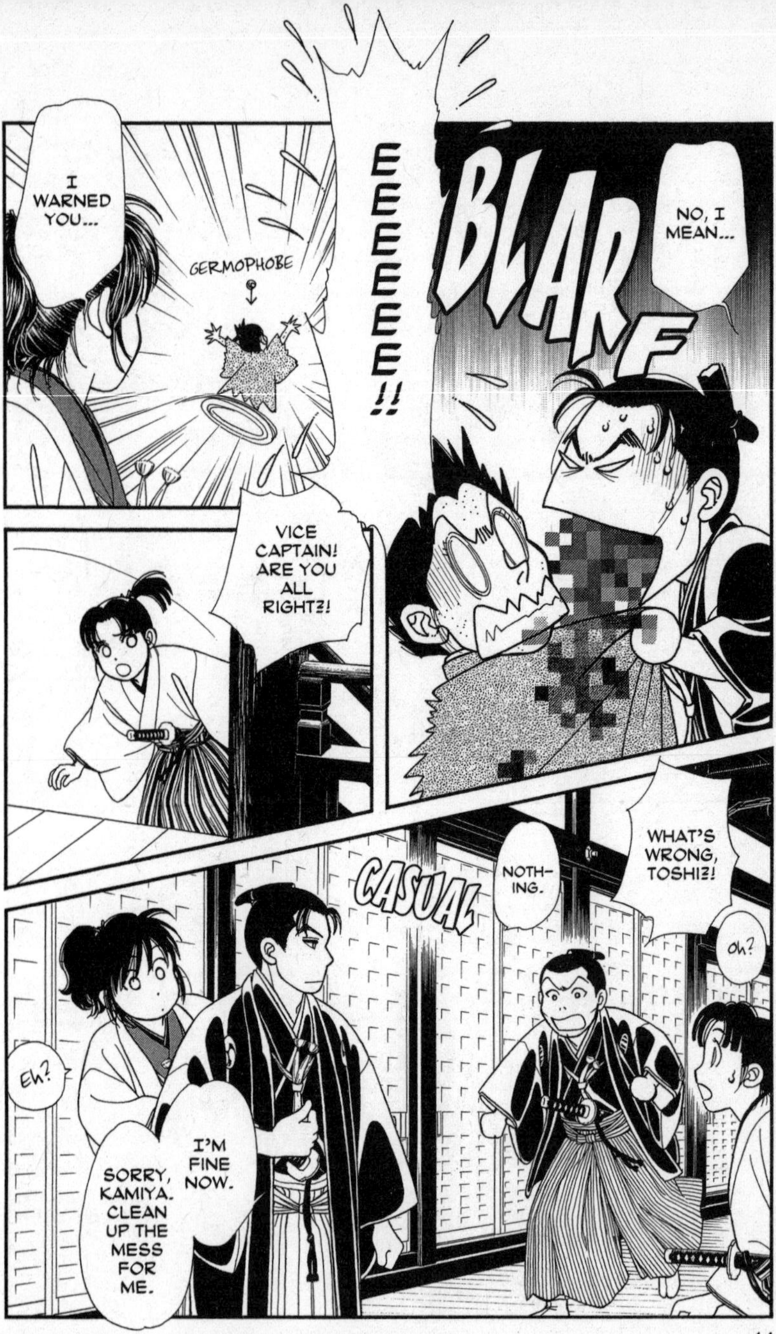
NO, I MEAN...
BLARF
EEEEEEE!!
I WARNED YOU...
GERMOPHOBE
VICE CAPTAIN! ARE YOU ALL RIGHT?!
WHAT'S WRONG, TOSHI?!
Oh?
NOTH-ING.
CASUAL
Eh?
I'M FINE NOW.
SORRY, KAMIYA. CLEAN UP THE MESS FOR ME.

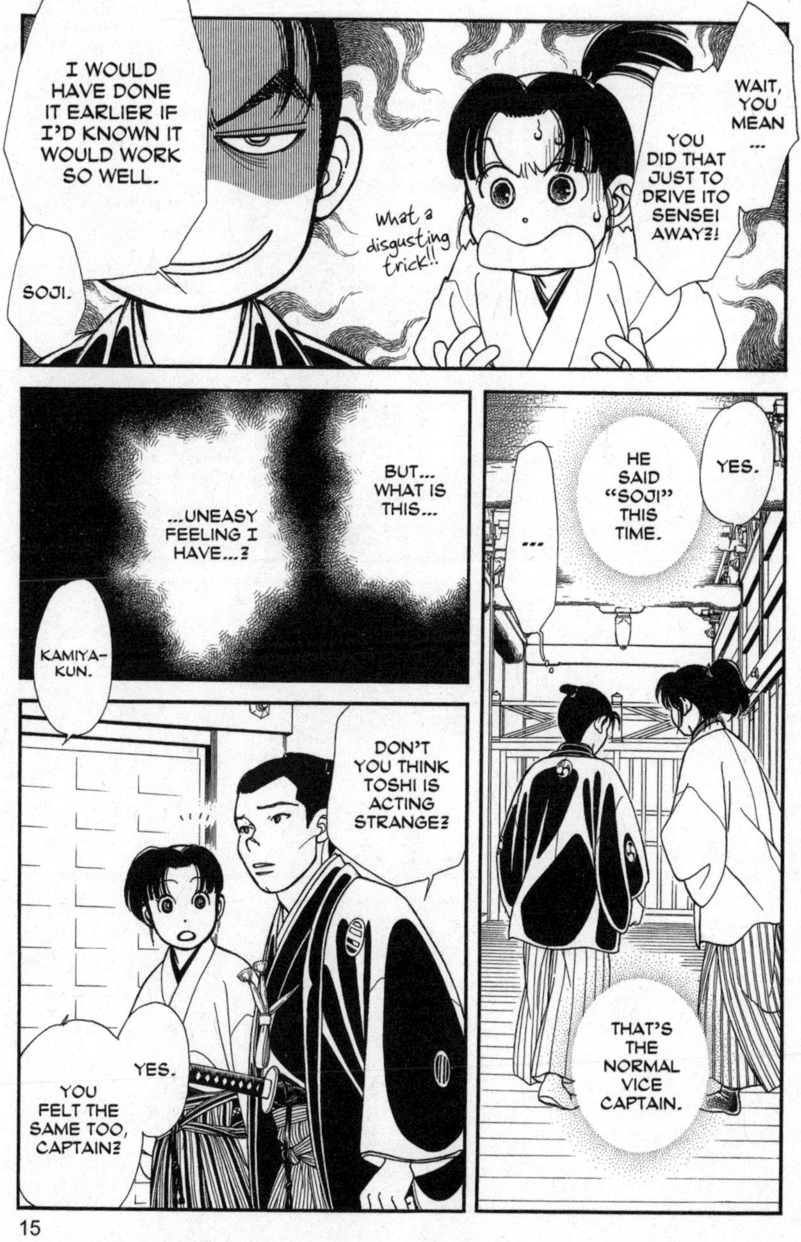
WAIT, YOU MEAN ...
YOU DID THAT JUST TO DRIVE ITO SENSEI AWAY?!
What a disgusting trick!!
I WOULD HAVE DONE IT EARLIER IF I'D KNOWN IT WOULD WORK SO WELL.
SOJI.
YES.
HE SAID "SOJI" THIS TIME.
...
THAT'S THE NORMAL VICE CAPTAIN.
BUT... WHAT IS THIS...
...UNEASY FEELING I HAVE...?
KAMIYA-KUN.
DON'T YOU THINK TOSHI IS ACTING STRANGE?
YES.
YOU FELT THE SAME TOO, CAPTAIN?

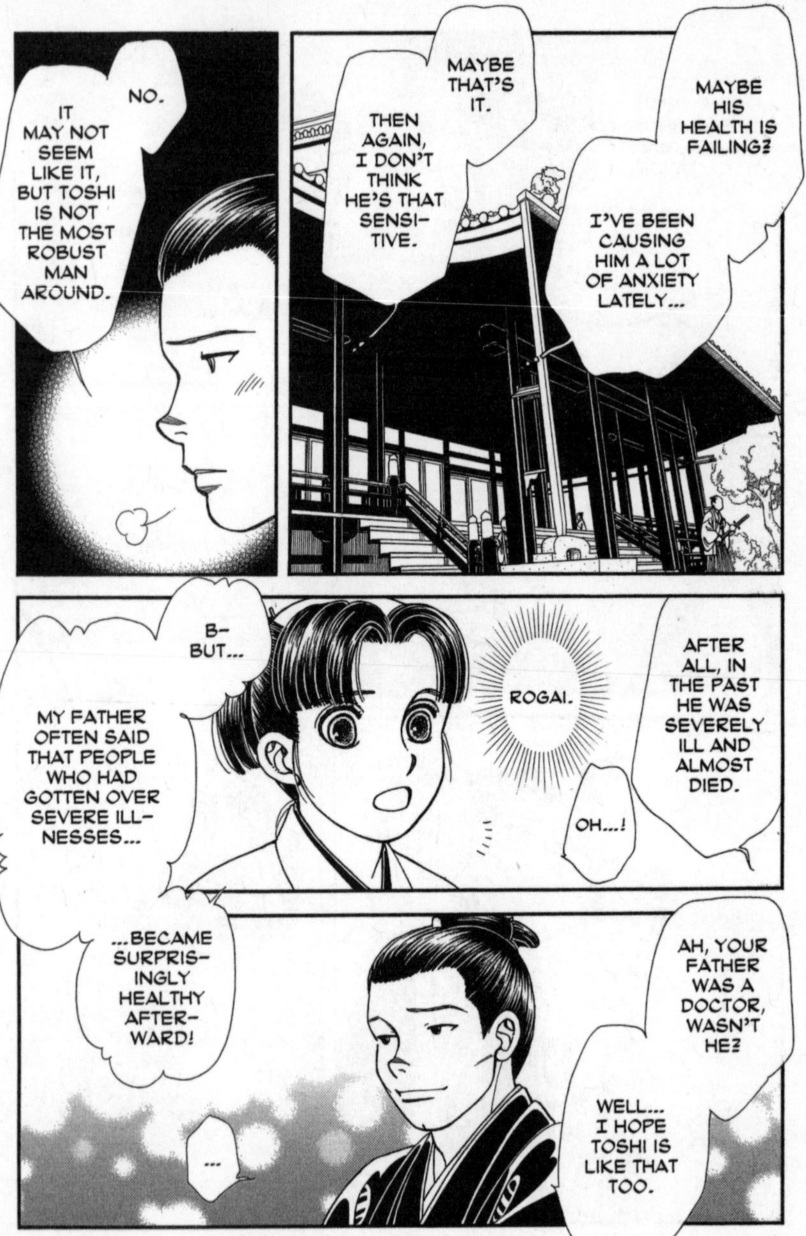
MAYBE HIS HEALTH IS FAILING?
I'VE BEEN CAUSING HIM A LOT OF ANXIETY LATELY...
MAYBE THAT'S IT.
THEN AGAIN, I DON'T THINK HE'S THAT SENSI-TIVE.
NO.
IT MAY NOT SEEM LIKE IT, BUT TOSHI IS NOT THE MOST ROBUST MAN AROUND.
AFTER ALL, IN THE PAST HE WAS SEVERELY ILL AND ALMOST DIED.
OH...!
ROGAI.
B-BUT...
MY FATHER OFTEN SAID THAT PEOPLE WHO HAD GOTTEN OVER SEVERE ILL-NESSES...
...BECAME SURPRIS-INGLY HEALTHY AFTER-WARD!
AH, YOUR FATHER WAS A DOCTOR, WASN'T HE?
WELL... I HOPE TOSHI IS LIKE THAT TOO.
...

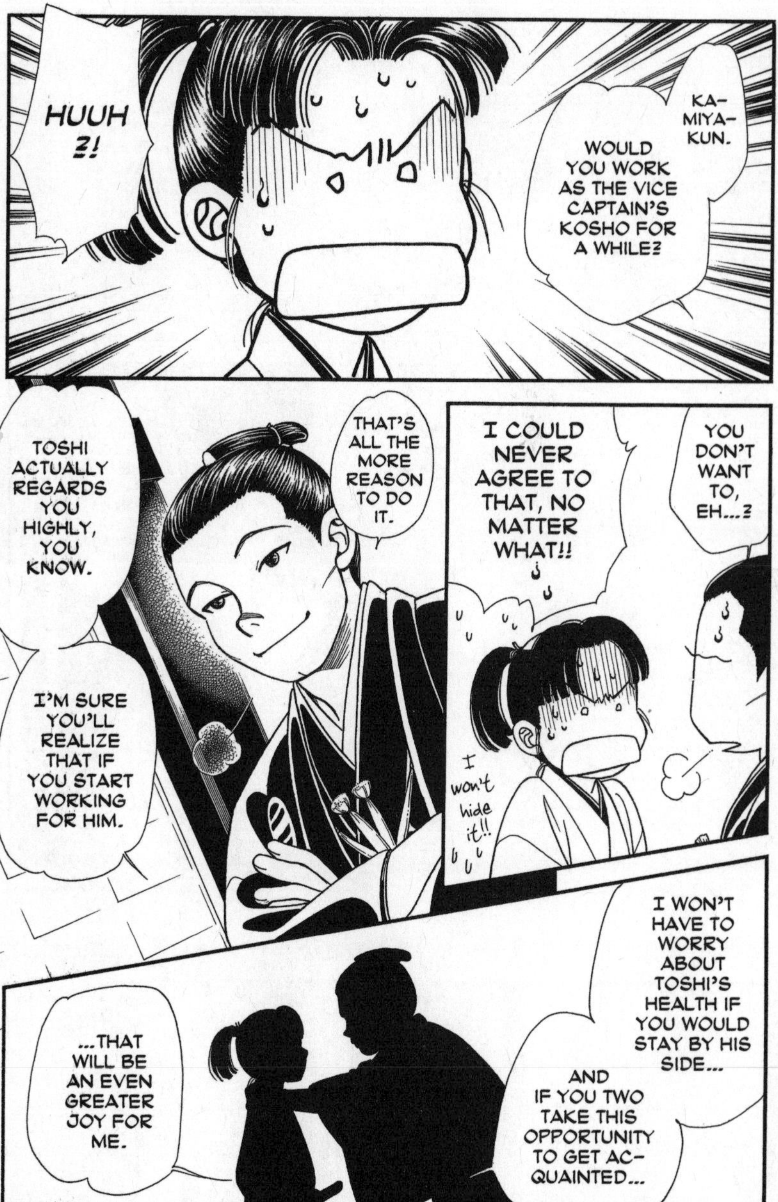
KA-MIYA-KUN.
WOULD YOU WORK AS THE VICE CAPTAIN'S KOSHO FOR A WHILE?
HUUH?!
YOU DON'T WANT TO, EH...?
I COULD NEVER AGREE TO THAT, NO MATTER WHAT!!
I won't hide it!!
THAT'S ALL THE MORE REASON TO DO IT.
TOSHI ACTUALLY REGARDS YOU HIGHLY, YOU KNOW.
I'M SURE YOU'LL REALIZE THAT IF YOU START WORKING FOR HIM.
I WON'T HAVE TO WORRY ABOUT TOSHI'S HEALTH IF YOU WOULD STAY BY HIS SIDE...
AND IF YOU TWO TAKE THIS OPPORTUNITY TO GET AC-QUAINTED...
...THAT WILL BE AN EVEN GREATER JOY FOR ME.

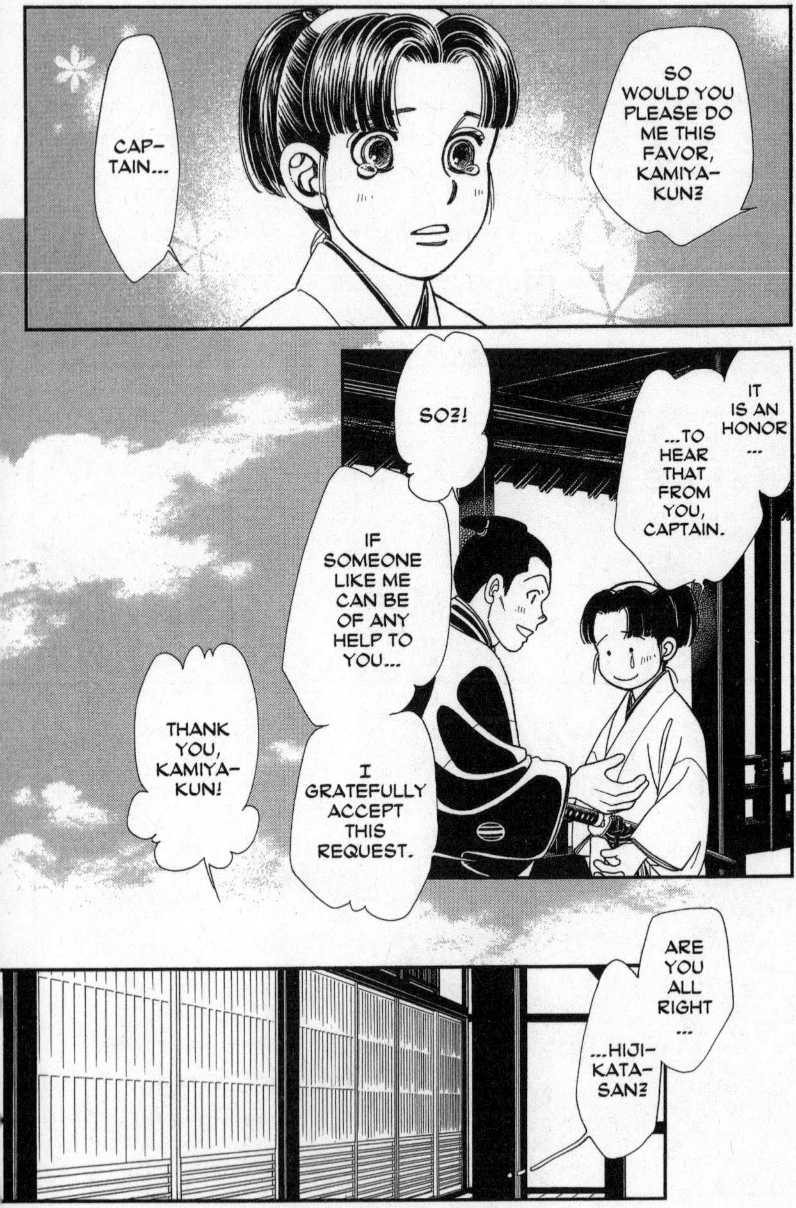
SO WOULD YOU PLEASE DO ME THIS FAVOR, KAMIYA-KUN?
CAP-TAIN...
IT IS AN HONOR...
...TO HEAR THAT FROM YOU, CAPTAIN.
SO?!
IF SOMEONE LIKE ME CAN BE OF ANY HELP TO YOU...
I GRATEFULLY ACCEPT THIS REQUEST.
THANK YOU, KAMIYA-KUN!
ARE YOU ALL RIGHT...
...HIJI-KATA-SAN?

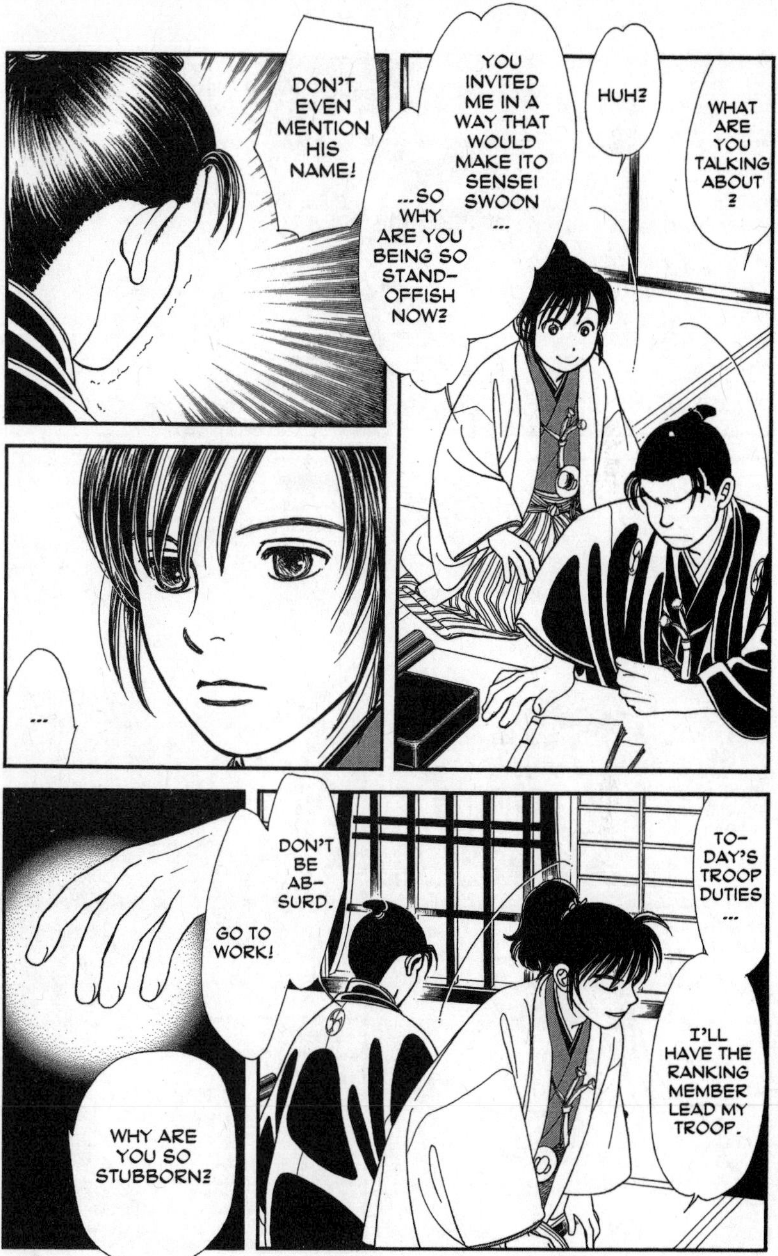

WHAT ARE YOU TALKING ABOUT?
HUH?
YOU INVITED ME IN A WAY THAT WOULD MAKE ITO SENSEI SWOON...
...SO WHY ARE YOU BEING SO STAND-OFFISH NOW?
DON'T EVEN MENTION HIS NAME!
...
TO-DAY'S TROOP DUTIES...
I'LL HAVE THE RANKING MEMBER LEAD MY TROOP.
DON'T BE AB-SURD.
GO TO WORK!
WHY ARE YOU SO STUBBORN?

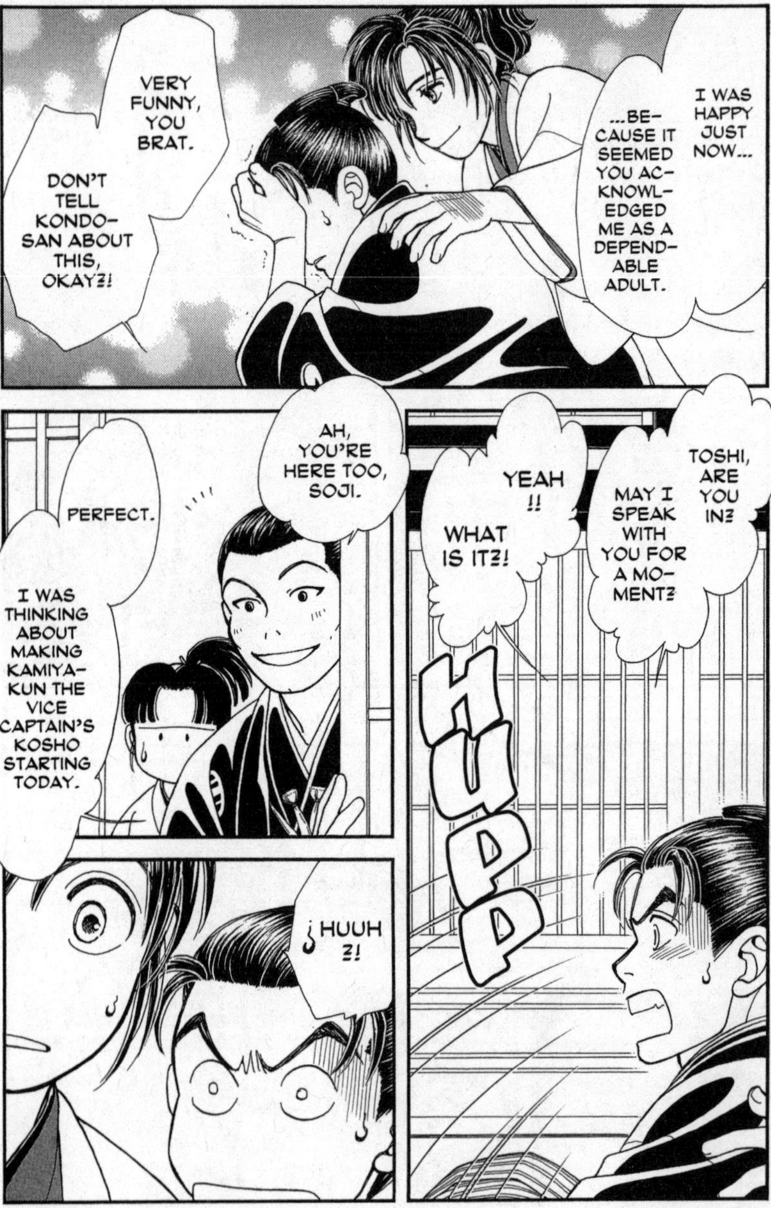
I WAS HAPPY JUST NOW...
...BE-CAUSE IT SEEMED YOU AC-KNOWL-EDGED ME AS A DEPEND-ABLE ADULT.
VERY FUNNY, YOU BRAT.
DON'T TELL KONDO-SAN ABOUT THIS, OKAY?!
TOSHI, ARE YOU IN?
MAY I SPEAK WITH YOU FOR A MO-MENT?
YEAH!!
WHAT IS IT?!
HUPP
AH, YOU'RE HERE TOO, SOJI.
PERFECT.
I WAS THINKING ABOUT MAKING KAMIYA-KUN THE VICE CAPTAIN'S KOSHO STARTING TODAY.
¿HUUH?!

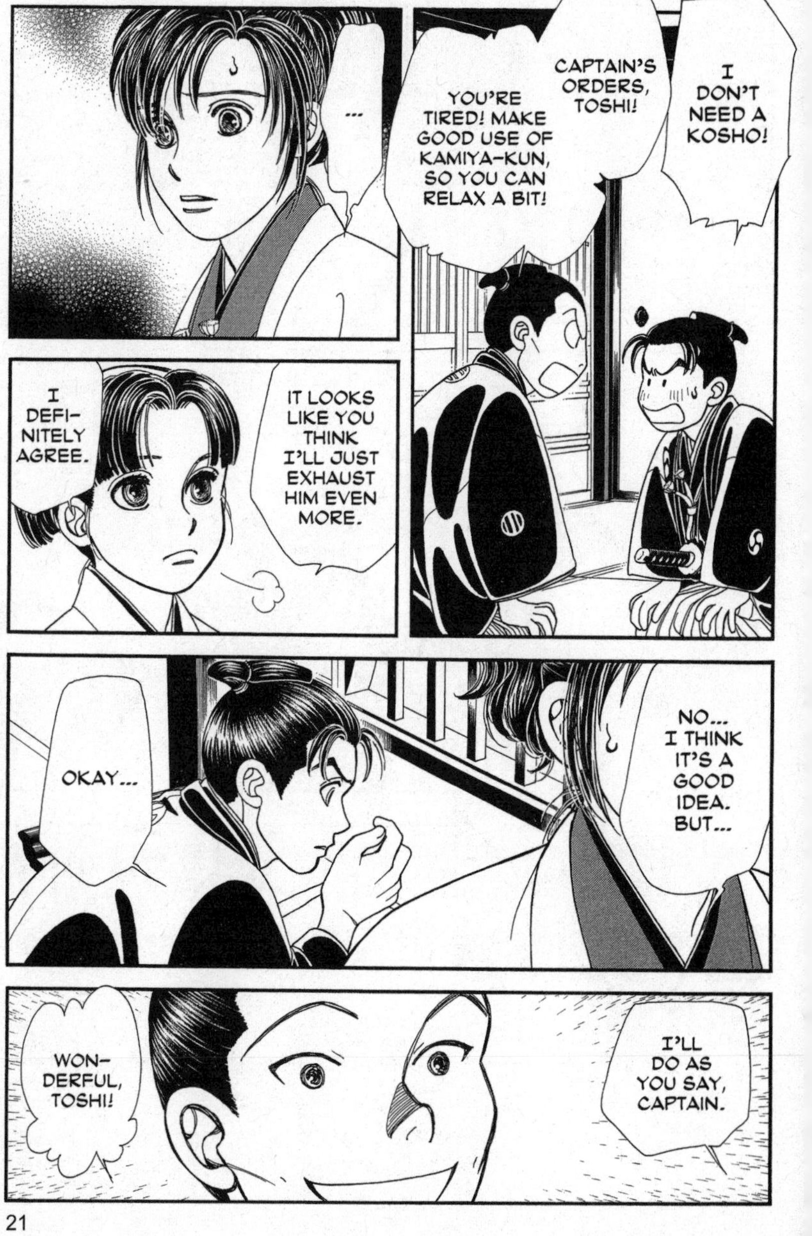
I DON'T NEED A KOSHO!
CAPTAIN'S ORDERS, TOSHI!
YOU'RE TIRED! MAKE GOOD USE OF KAMIYA-KUN, SO YOU CAN RELAX A BIT!
...
IT LOOKS LIKE YOU THINK I'LL JUST EXHAUST HIM EVEN MORE.
I DEFI-NITELY AGREE.
NO... I THINK IT'S A GOOD IDEA. BUT...
OKAY...
I'LL DO AS YOU SAY, CAPTAIN.
WON-DERFUL, TOSHI!

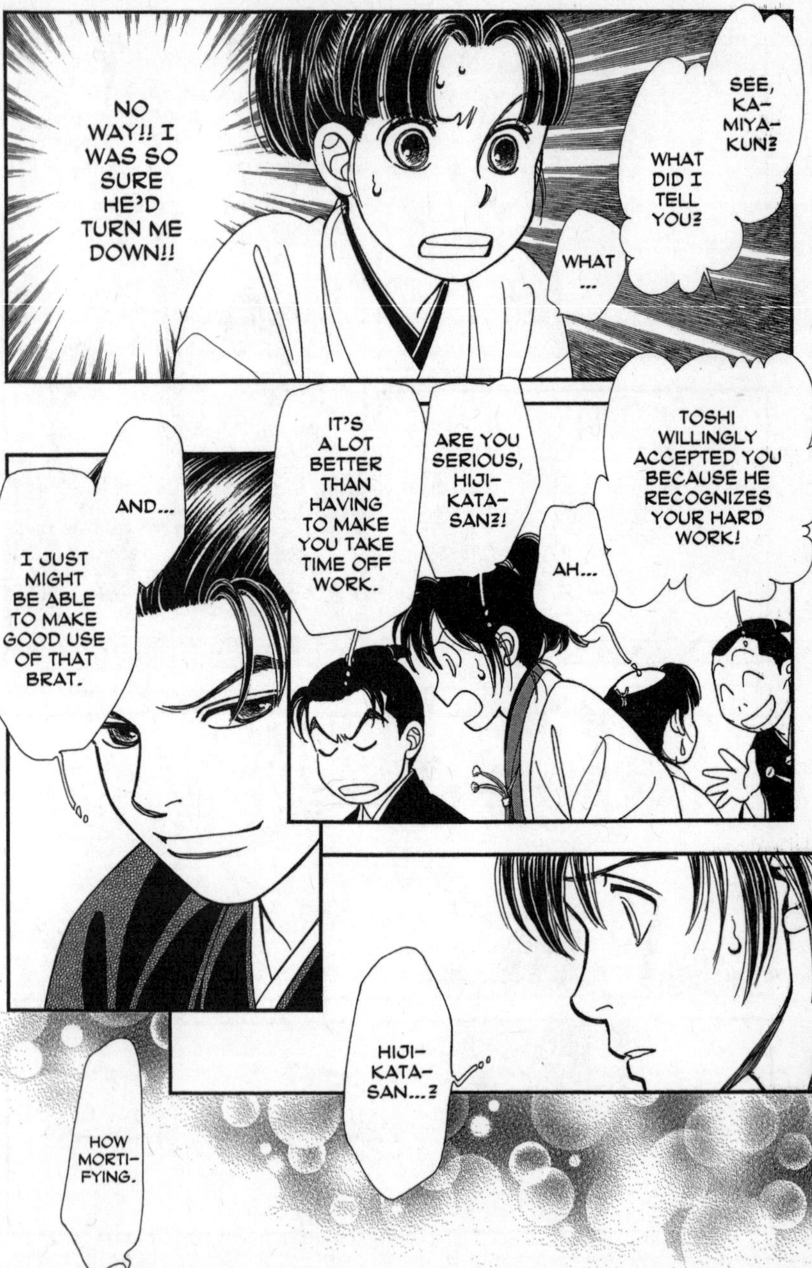
SEE, KAMIYA-KUN?
WHAT DID I TELL YOU?
WHAT...
NO WAY!! I WAS SO SURE HE'D TURN ME DOWN!!
TOSHI WILLINGLY ACCEPTED YOU BECAUSE HE RECOGNIZES YOUR HARD WORK!
AH...
ARE YOU SERIOUS, HIJI-KATA-SAN?!
IT'S A LOT BETTER THAN HAVING TO MAKE YOU TAKE TIME OFF WORK.
AND...
I JUST MIGHT BE ABLE TO MAKE GOOD USE OF THAT BRAT.
HIJI-KATA-SAN...?
HOW MORTI-FYING.

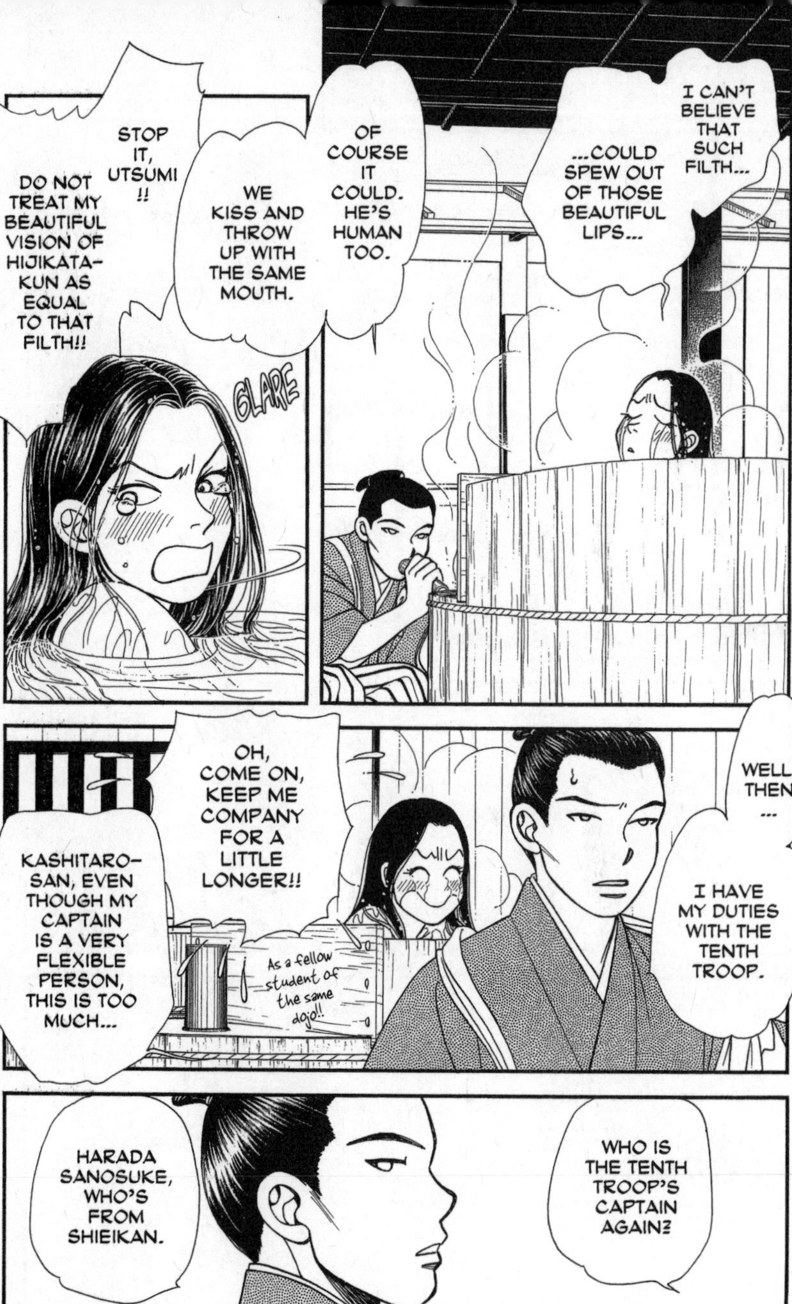
I CAN'T BELIEVE THAT SUCH FILTH...
...COULD SPEW OUT OF THOSE BEAUTIFUL LIPS...
OF COURSE IT COULD. HE'S HUMAN TOO.
WE KISS AND THROW UP WITH THE SAME MOUTH.
STOP IT, UTSUMI!!
DO NOT TREAT MY BEAUTIFUL VISION OF HIJIKATA-KUN AS EQUAL TO THAT FILTH!!
GLARE
WELL, THEN ...
I HAVE MY DUTIES WITH THE TENTH TROOP.
OH, COME ON, KEEP ME COMPANY FOR A LITTLE LONGER!!
As a fellow student of the same dojo!!
KASHITARO-SAN, EVEN THOUGH MY CAPTAIN IS A VERY FLEXIBLE PERSON, THIS IS TOO MUCH...
WHO IS THE TENTH TROOP'S CAPTAIN AGAIN?
HARADA SANOSUKE, WHO'S FROM SHIEIKAN.

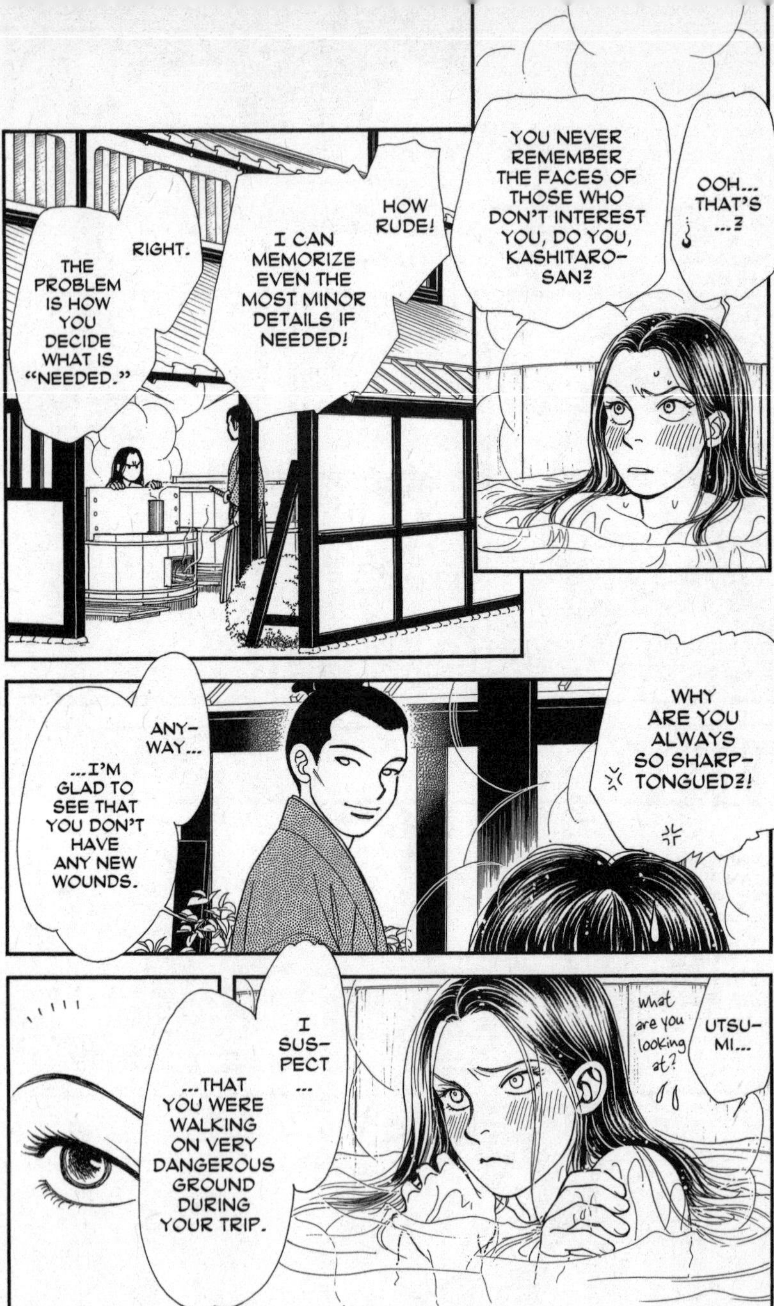
OOH... THAT'S ...?
YOU NEVER REMEMBER THE FACES OF THOSE WHO DON'T INTEREST YOU, DO YOU, KASHITARO-SAN?
HOW RUDE!
I CAN MEMORIZE EVEN THE MOST MINOR DETAILS IF NEEDED!
RIGHT.
THE PROBLEM IS HOW YOU DECIDE WHAT IS "NEEDED."
WHY ARE YOU ALWAYS SO SHARP-TONGUED?!
ANY-WAY...
...I'M GLAD TO SEE THAT YOU DON'T HAVE ANY NEW WOUNDS.
UTSU-MI...
What are you looking at?
I SUS-PECT ...
...THAT YOU WERE WALKING ON VERY DANGEROUS GROUND DURING YOUR TRIP.

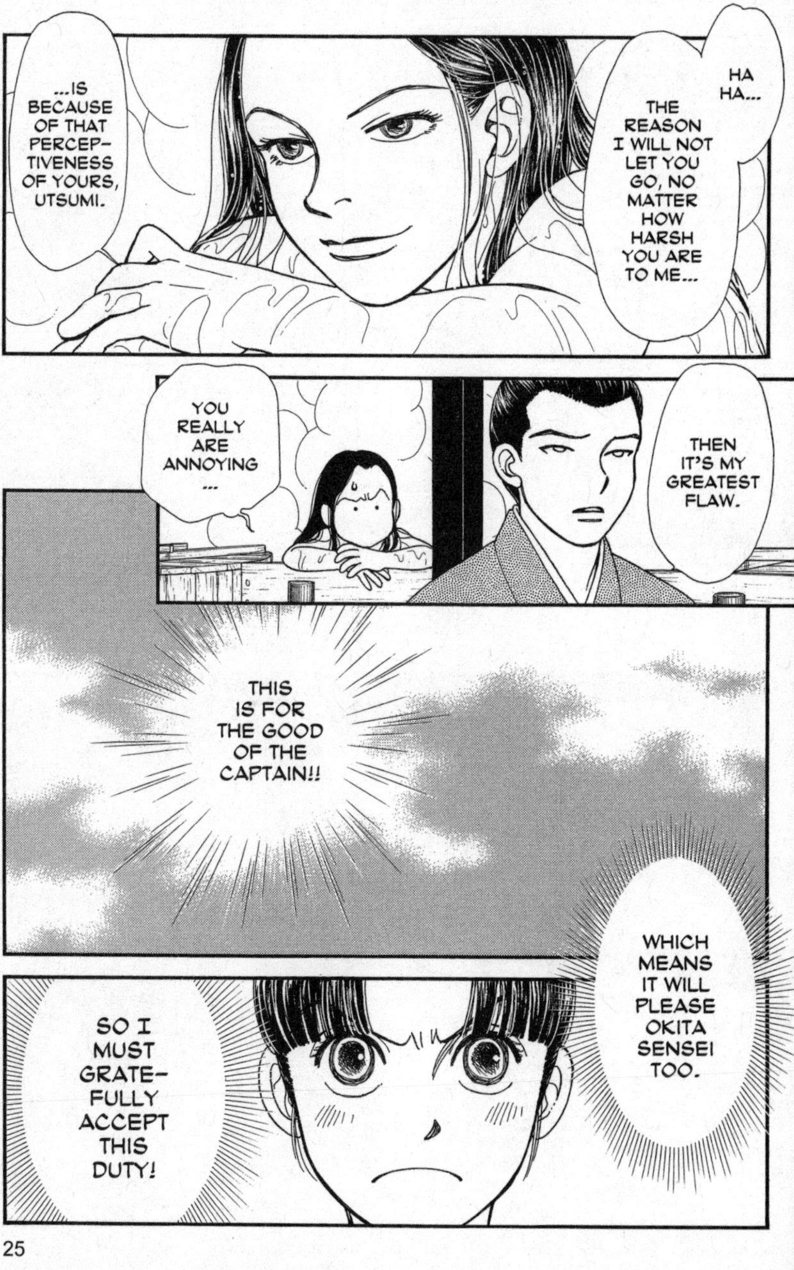
HA HA... THE REASON I WILL NOT LET YOU GO, NO MATTER HOW HARSH YOU ARE TO ME...
...IS BECAUSE OF THAT PERCEP-TIVENESS OF YOURS, UTSUMI.
THEN IT'S MY GREATEST FLAW.
YOU REALLY ARE ANNOYING ...
THIS IS FOR THE GOOD OF THE CAPTAIN!!
WHICH MEANS IT WILL PLEASE OKITA SENSEI TOO.
SO I MUST GRATE-FULLY ACCEPT THIS DUTY!

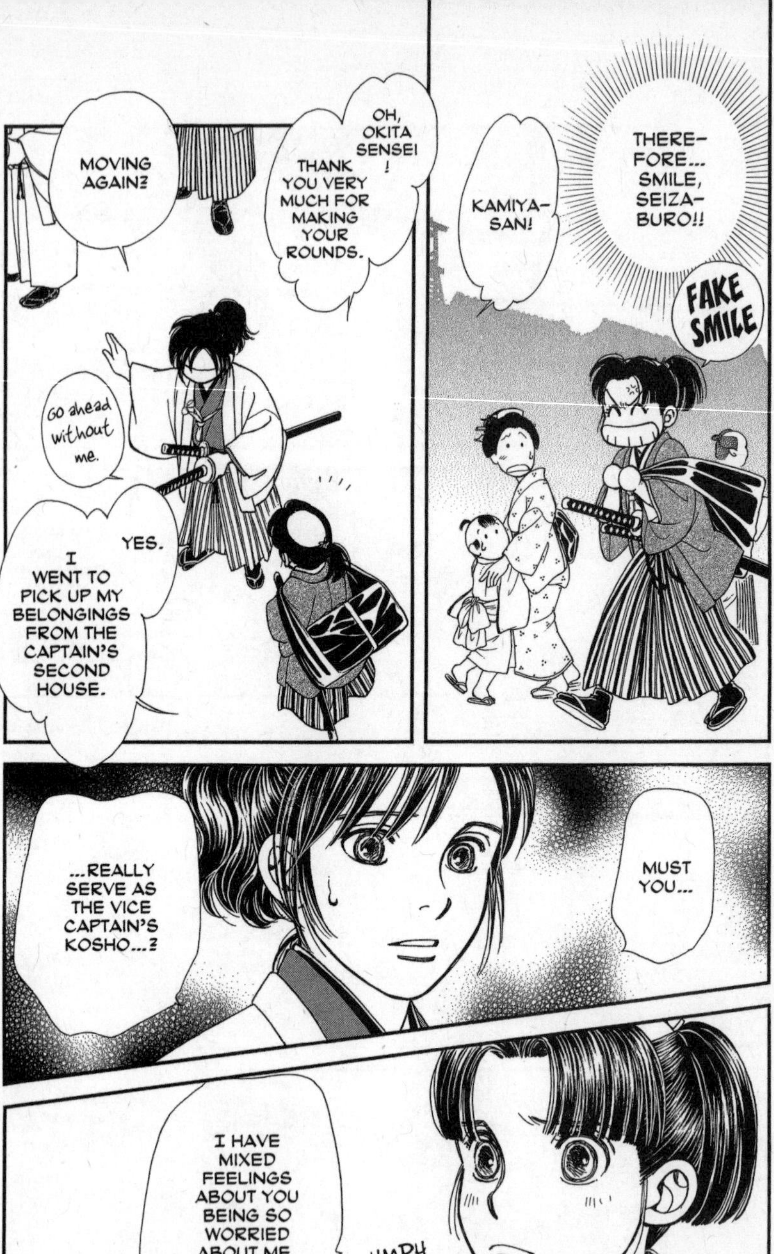
THEREFORE... SMILE, SEIZABURO!!
FAKE SMILE
KAMIYA-SAN!
OH, OKITA SENSEI!
THANK YOU VERY MUCH FOR MAKING YOUR ROUNDS.
MOVING AGAIN?
Go ahead without me.
YES.
I WENT TO PICK UP MY BELONGINGS FROM THE CAPTAIN'S SECOND HOUSE.
MUST YOU...
...REALLY SERVE AS THE VICE CAPTAIN'S KOSHO...?
I HAVE MIXED FEELINGS ABOUT YOU BEING SO WORRIED ABOUT ME.
HMPH

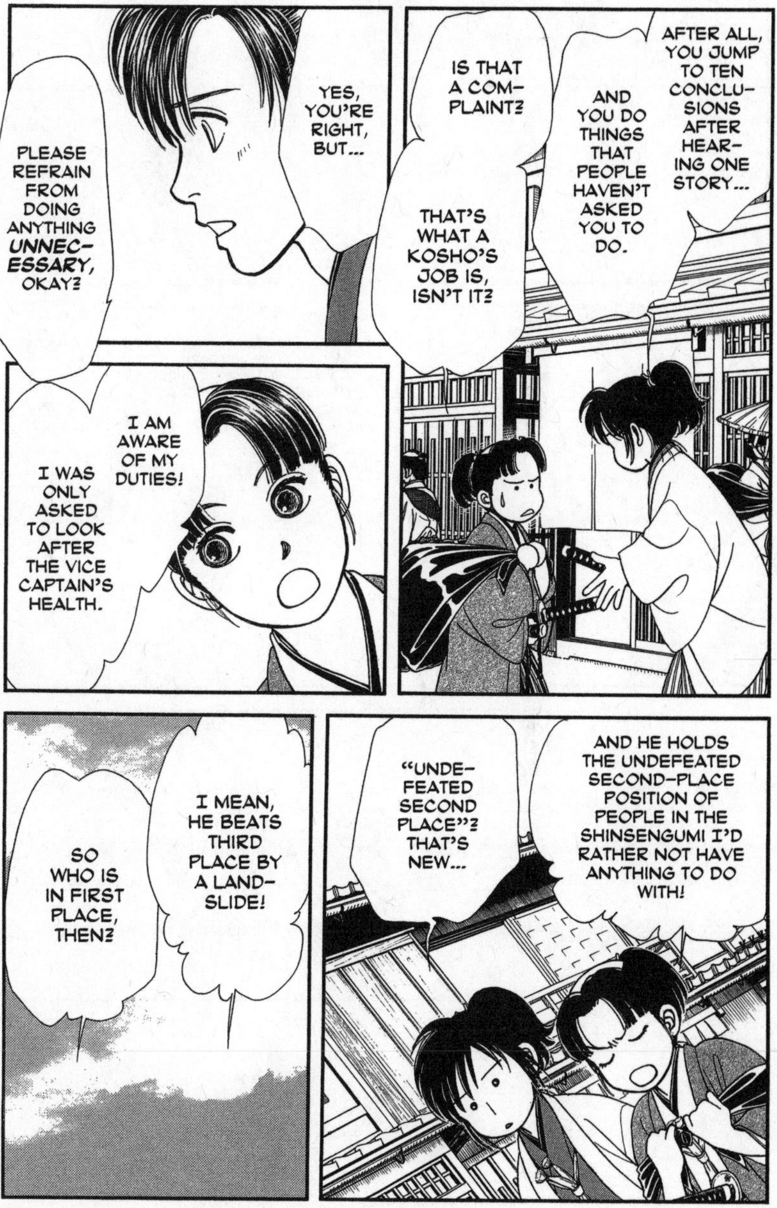
AFTER ALL, YOU JUMP TO TEN CONCLUSIONS AFTER HEARING ONE STORY...
AND YOU DO THINGS THAT PEOPLE HAVEN'T ASKED YOU TO DO.
IS THAT A COMPLAINT?
THAT'S WHAT A KOSHO'S JOB IS, ISN'T IT?
YES, YOU'RE RIGHT, BUT...
PLEASE REFRAIN FROM DOING ANYTHING *UNNECESSARY*, OKAY?
I AM AWARE OF MY DUTIES!
I WAS ONLY ASKED TO LOOK AFTER THE VICE CAPTAIN'S HEALTH.
AND HE HOLDS THE UNDEFEATED SECOND-PLACE POSITION OF PEOPLE IN THE SHINSENGUMI I'D RATHER NOT HAVE ANYTHING TO DO WITH!
"UNDEFEATED SECOND PLACE"? THAT'S NEW...
I MEAN, HE BEATS THIRD PLACE BY A LANDSLIDE!
SO WHO IS IN FIRST PLACE, THEN?

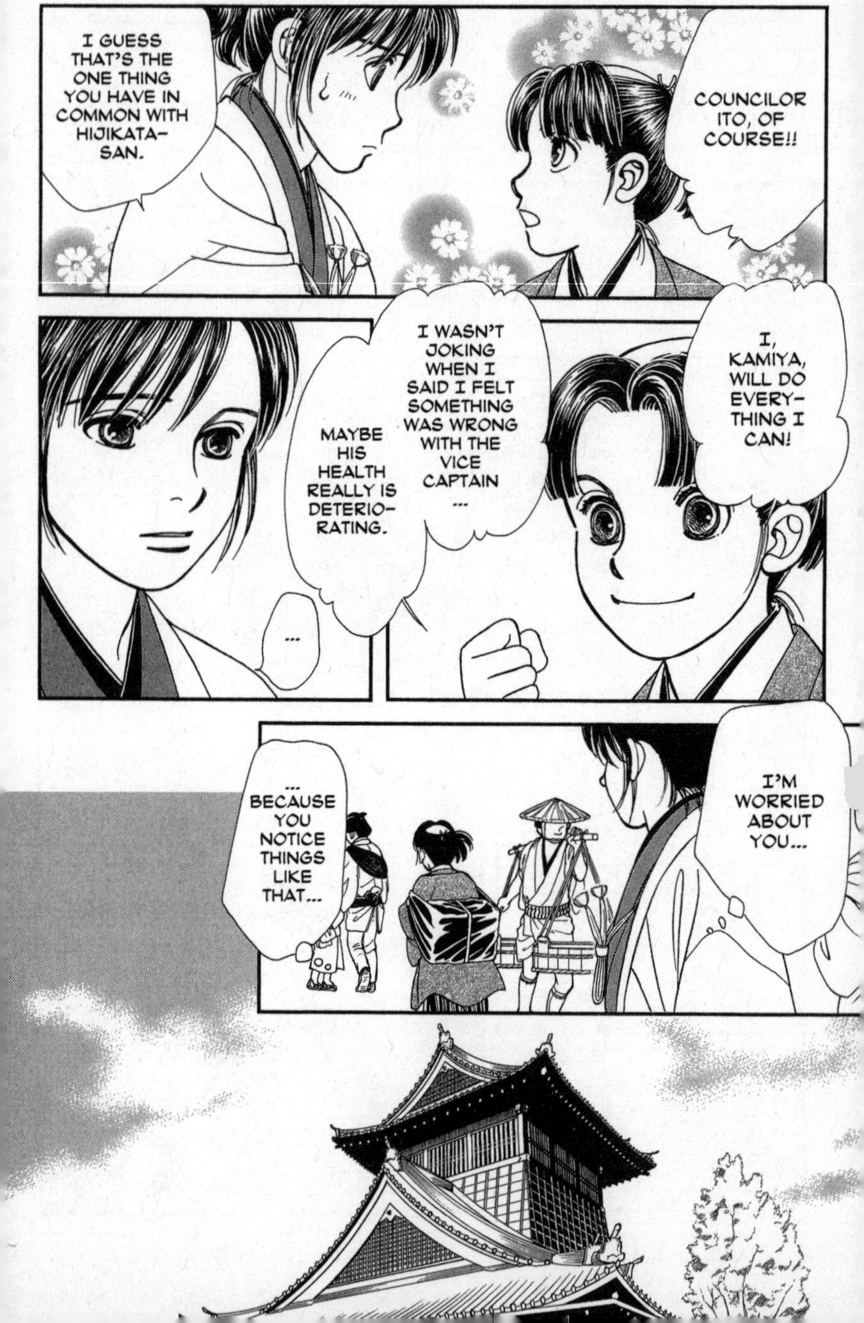
COUNCILOR ITO, OF COURSE!!
I GUESS THAT'S THE ONE THING YOU HAVE IN COMMON WITH HIJIKATA-SAN.
I, KAMIYA, WILL DO EVERY-THING I CAN!
I WASN'T JOKING WHEN I SAID I FELT SOMETHING WAS WRONG WITH THE VICE CAPTAIN ...
MAYBE HIS HEALTH REALLY IS DETERIO-RATING.
...
I'M WORRIED ABOUT YOU...
... BECAUSE YOU NOTICE THINGS LIKE THAT...

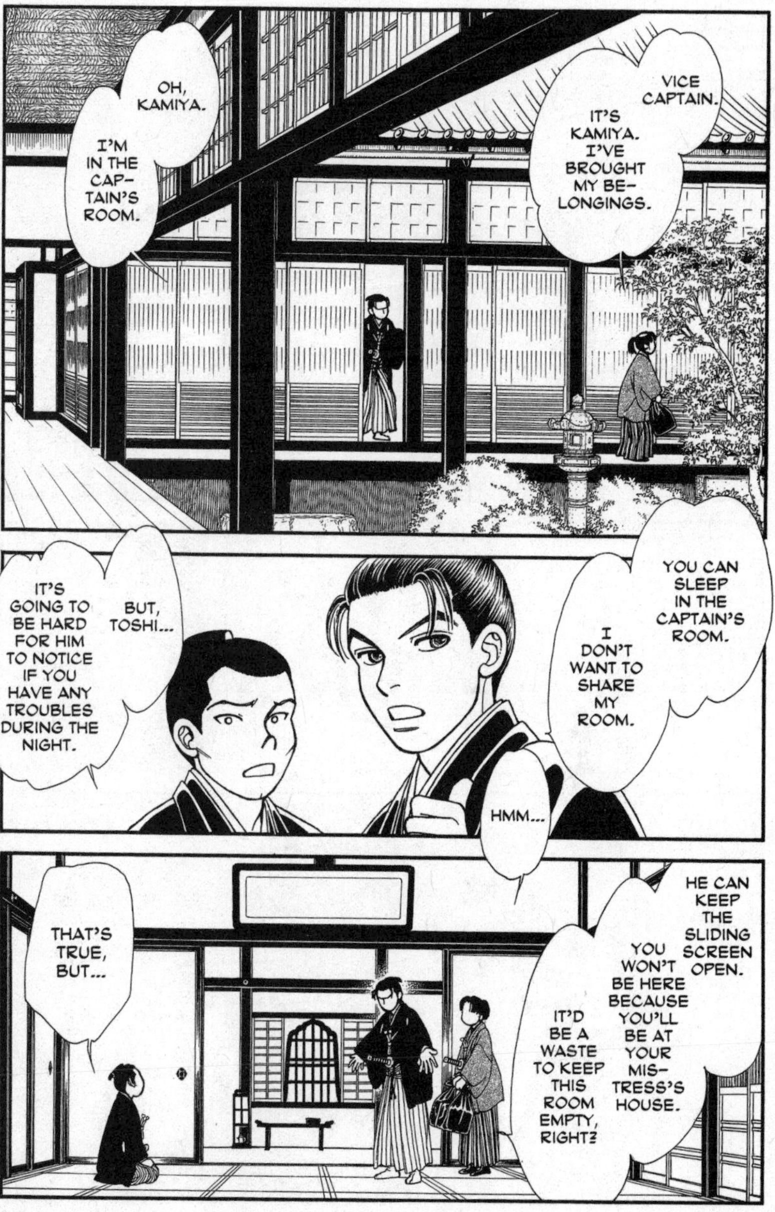
VICE CAPTAIN.
IT'S KAMIYA. I'VE BROUGHT MY BELONGINGS.
OH, KAMIYA.
I'M IN THE CAPTAIN'S ROOM.
YOU CAN SLEEP IN THE CAPTAIN'S ROOM.
I DON'T WANT TO SHARE MY ROOM.
BUT, TOSHI...
IT'S GOING TO BE HARD FOR HIM TO NOTICE IF YOU HAVE ANY TROUBLES DURING THE NIGHT.
HMM...
HE CAN KEEP THE SLIDING SCREEN OPEN.
YOU WON'T BE HERE BECAUSE YOU'LL BE AT YOUR MISTRESS'S HOUSE.
IT'D BE A WASTE TO KEEP THIS ROOM EMPTY, RIGHT?
THAT'S TRUE, BUT...

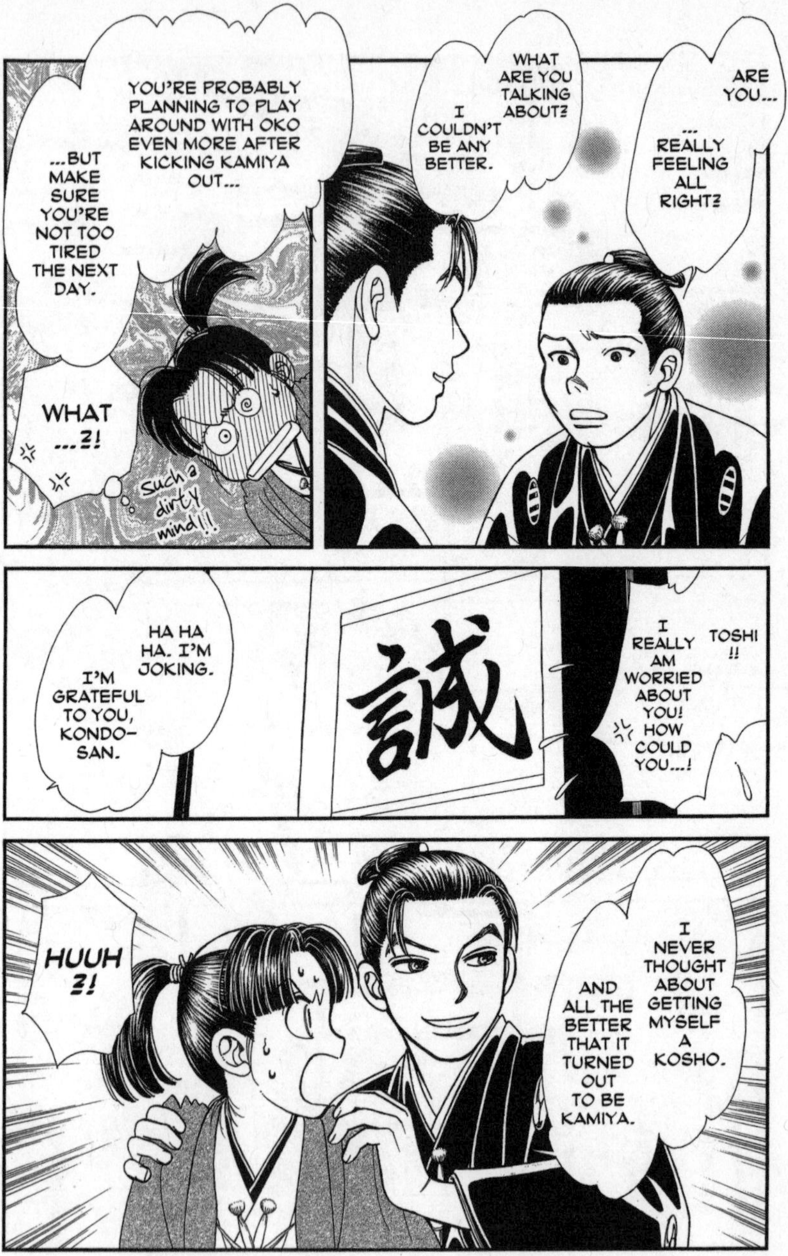
ARE YOU...
...REALLY FEELING ALL RIGHT?
WHAT ARE YOU TALKING ABOUT?
I COULDN'T BE ANY BETTER.
YOU'RE PROBABLY PLANNING TO PLAY AROUND WITH OKO EVEN MORE AFTER KICKING KAMIYA OUT...
...BUT MAKE SURE YOU'RE NOT TOO TIRED THE NEXT DAY.
WHAT...?!
Such a dirty mind!!
TOSHI!!
I REALLY AM WORRIED ABOUT YOU! HOW COULD YOU...!
誠
HA HA HA. I'M JOKING.
I'M GRATEFUL TO YOU, KONDO-SAN.
I NEVER THOUGHT ABOUT GETTING MYSELF A KOSHO.
AND ALL THE BETTER THAT IT TURNED OUT TO BE KAMIYA.
HUUH?!

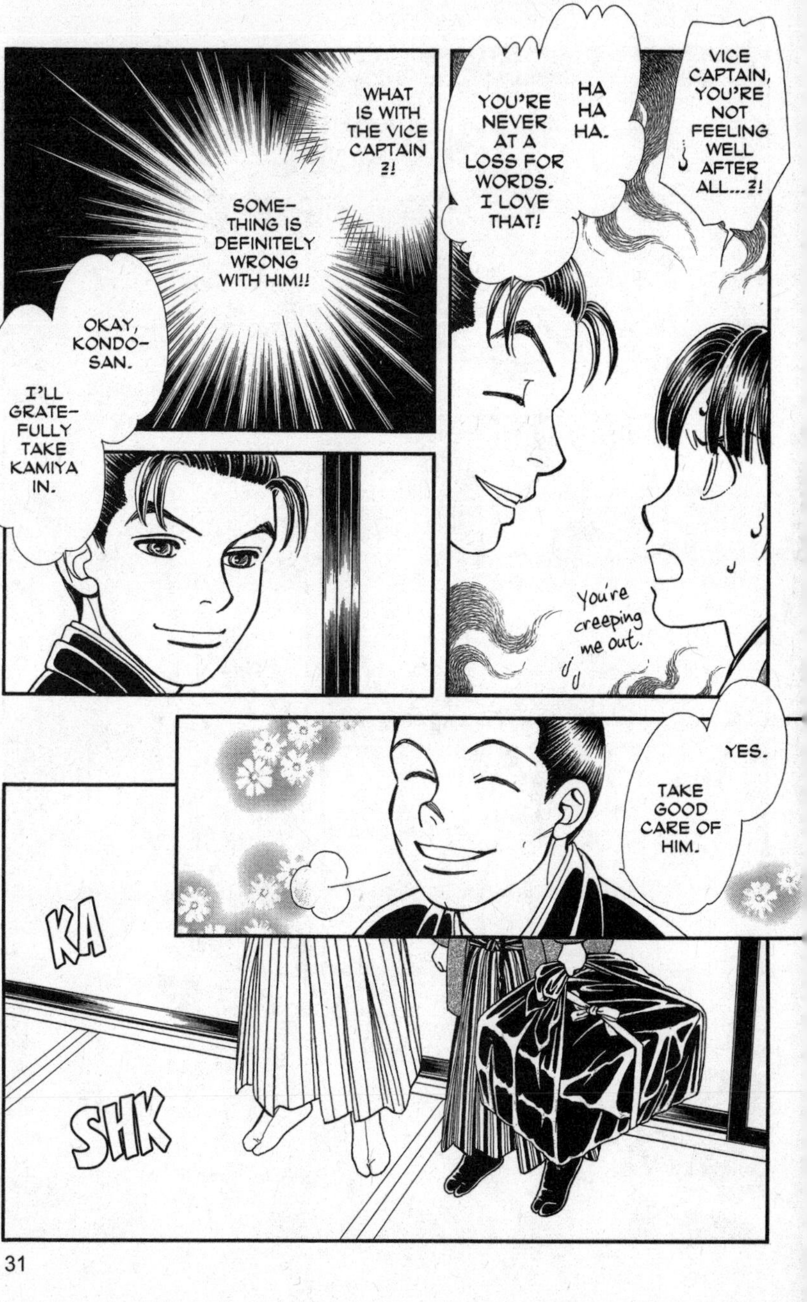
VICE CAPTAIN, YOU'RE NOT FEELING WELL AFTER ALL...?!
HA HA HA.
YOU'RE NEVER AT A LOSS FOR WORDS. I LOVE THAT!
You're creeping me out.
WHAT IS WITH THE VICE CAPTAIN ?!
SOME-THING IS DEFINITELY WRONG WITH HIM!!
OKAY, KONDO-SAN.
I'LL GRATE-FULLY TAKE KAMIYA IN.
YES.
TAKE GOOD CARE OF HIM.
KA
SHK

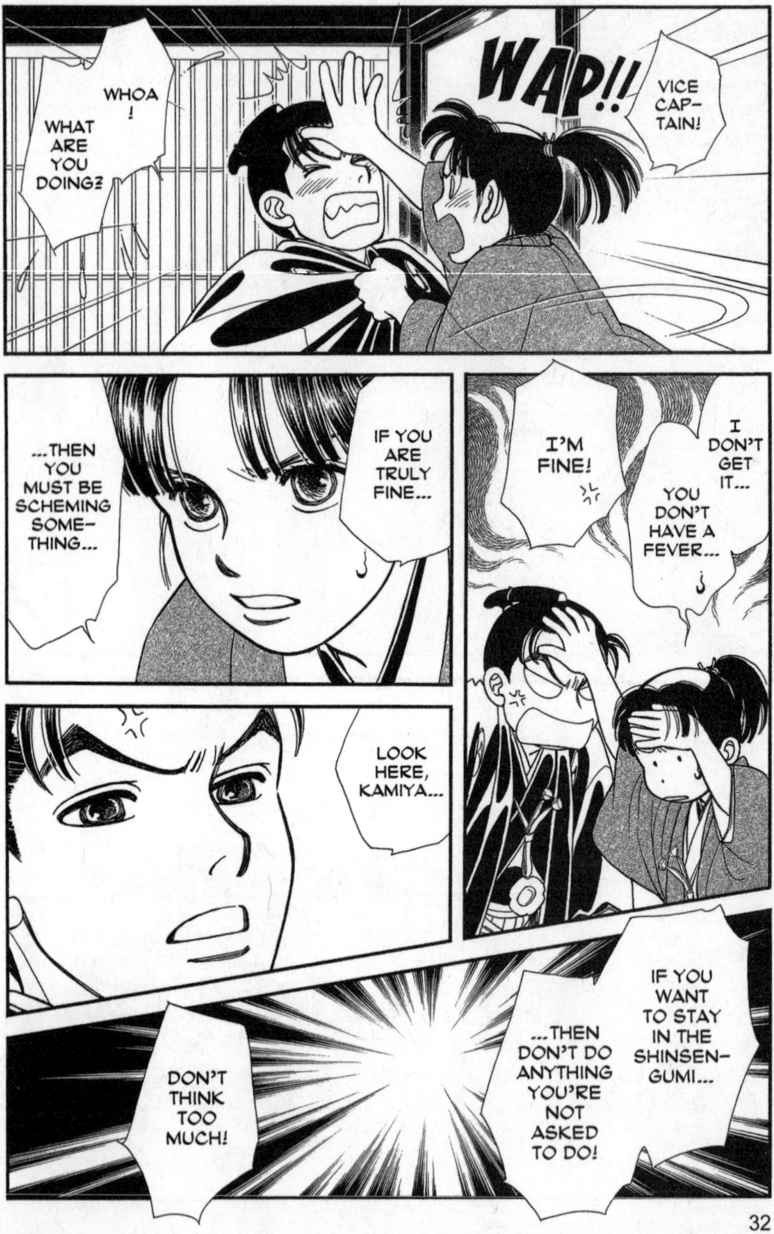
VICE CAPTAIN!
WAP!!
WHOA! WHAT ARE YOU DOING?
I DON'T GET IT... YOU DON'T HAVE A FEVER...
I'M FINE!
IF YOU ARE TRULY FINE...
...THEN YOU MUST BE SCHEMING SOMETHING...
LOOK HERE, KAMIYA...
IF YOU WANT TO STAY IN THE SHINSENGUMI...
...THEN DON'T DO ANYTHING YOU'RE NOT ASKED TO DO!
DON'T THINK TOO MUCH!

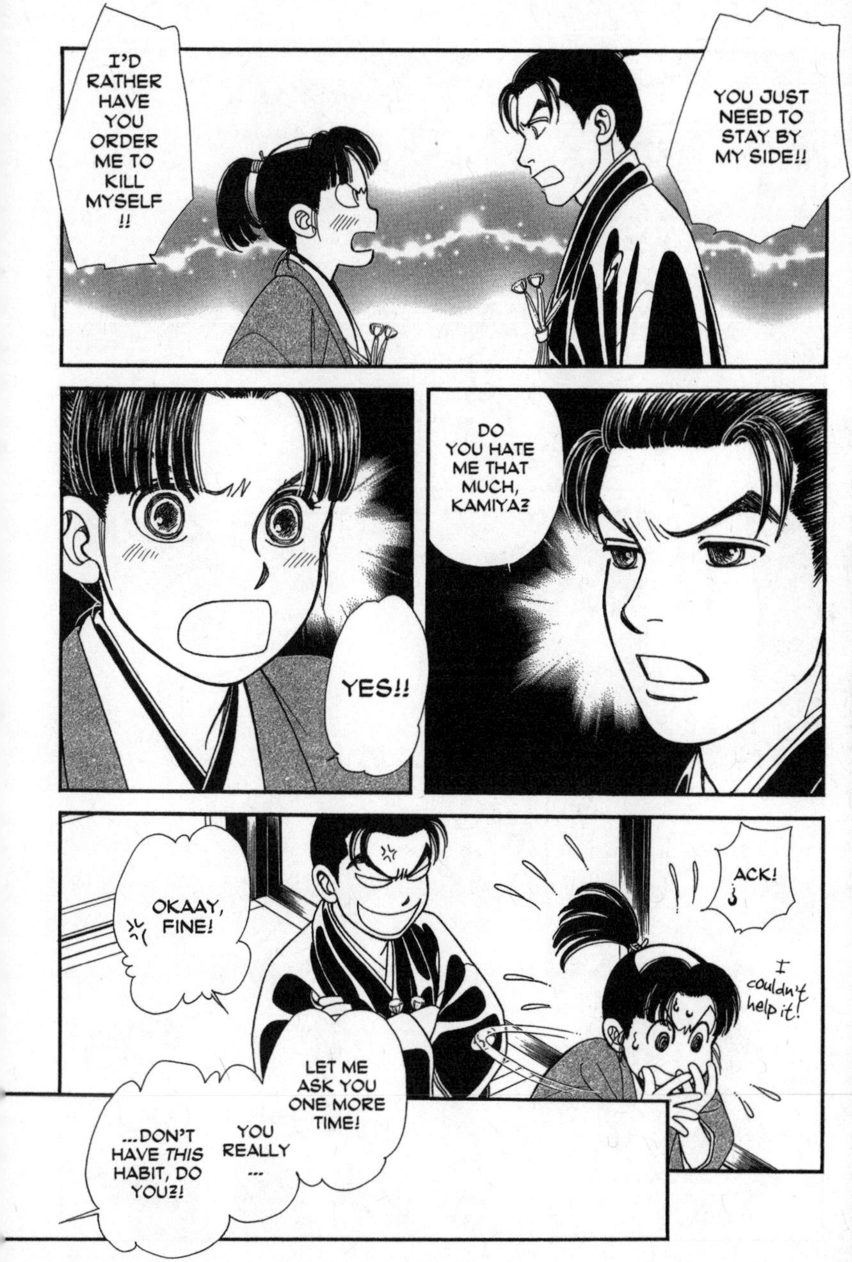
YOU JUST NEED TO STAY BY MY SIDE!!
I'D RATHER HAVE YOU ORDER ME TO KILL MYSELF!!
DO YOU HATE ME THAT MUCH, KAMIYA?
YES!!
ACK!
I couldn't help it!
OKAAY, FINE!
LET ME ASK YOU ONE MORE TIME!
YOU REALLY...
...DON'T HAVE *THIS* HABIT, DO YOU?!

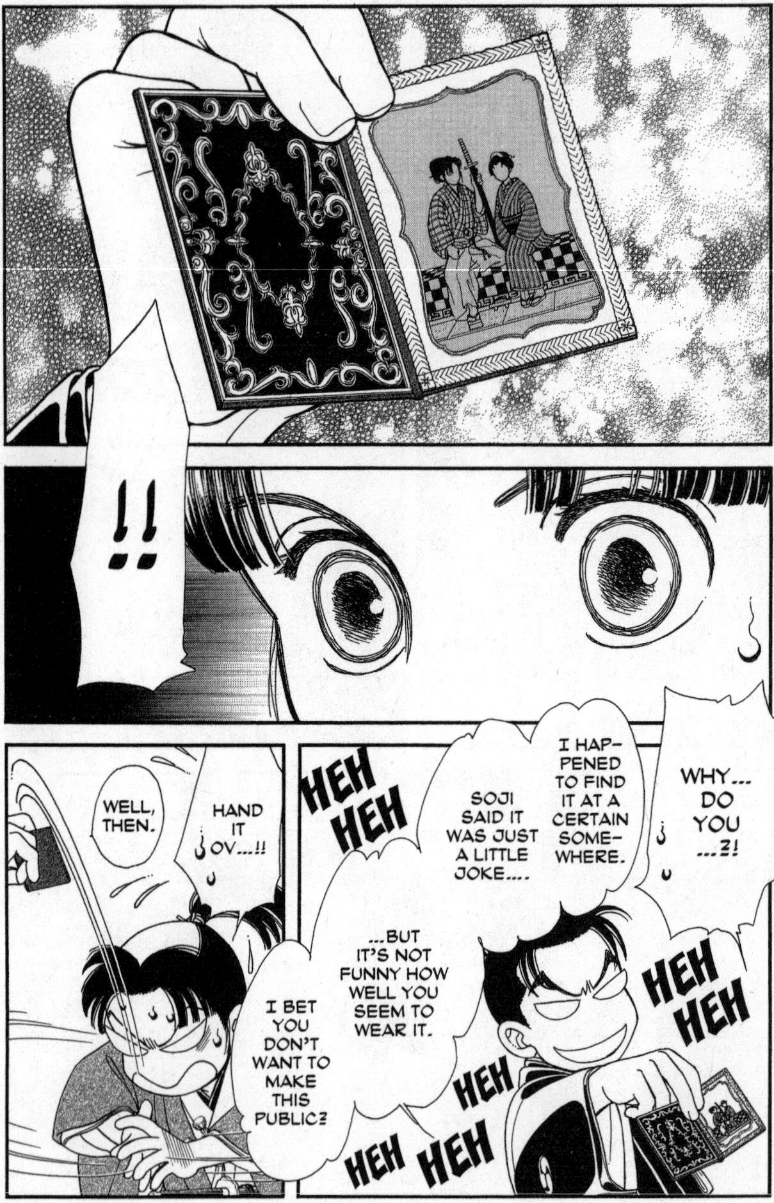
!!
WHY... DO YOU ...?!
I HAP-PENED TO FIND IT AT A CERTAIN SOME-WHERE.
SOJI SAID IT WAS JUST A LITTLE JOKE....
HEH HEH
...BUT IT'S NOT FUNNY HOW WELL YOU SEEM TO WEAR IT.
HEH HEH
I BET YOU DON'T WANT TO MAKE THIS PUBLIC?
HEH HEH HEH HEH
HAND IT OV...!!
WELL, THEN.

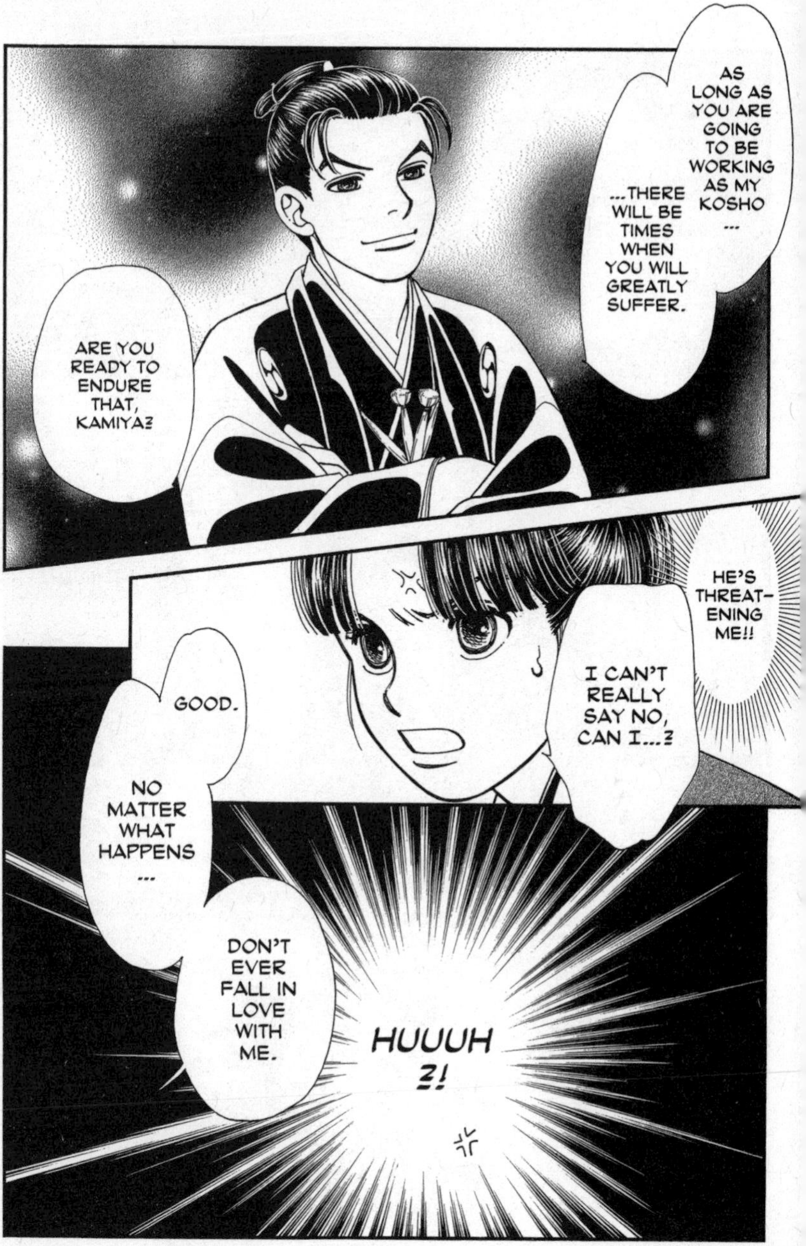
AS LONG AS YOU ARE GOING TO BE WORKING AS MY KOSHO ...
...THERE WILL BE TIMES WHEN YOU WILL GREATLY SUFFER.
ARE YOU READY TO ENDURE THAT, KAMIYA?
HE'S THREAT-ENING ME!!
I CAN'T REALLY SAY NO, CAN I...?
GOOD.
NO MATTER WHAT HAPPENS ...
DON'T EVER FALL IN LOVE WITH ME.
HUUUH ?!

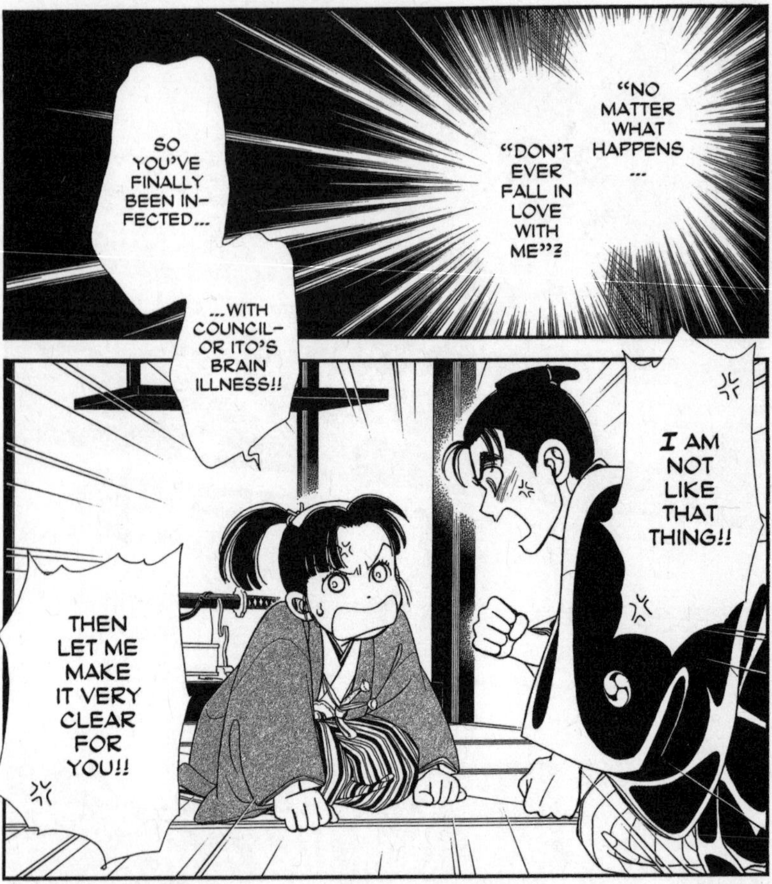
"NO MATTER WHAT HAPPENS ...
"DON'T EVER FALL IN LOVE WITH ME"?
SO YOU'VE FINALLY BEEN INFECTED...
...WITH COUNCILOR ITO'S BRAIN ILLNESS!!
I AM NOT LIKE THAT THING!!
THEN LET ME MAKE IT VERY CLEAR FOR YOU!!

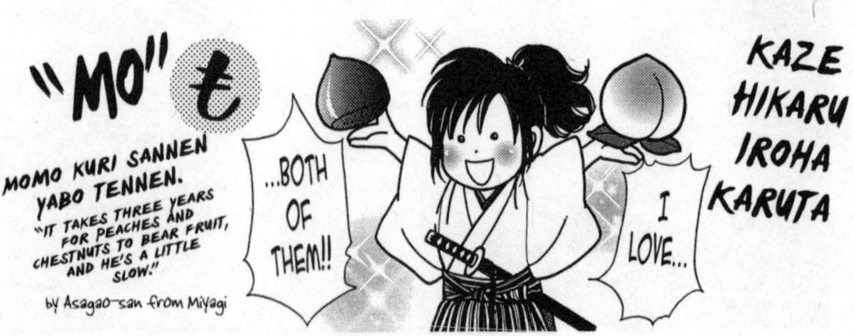
KAZE HIKARU IROHA KARUTA
"MO" も
MOMO KURI SANNEN YABO TENNEN.
"IT TAKES THREE YEARS FOR PEACHES AND CHESTNUTS TO BEAR FRUIT, AND HE'S A LITTLE SLOW."
by Asagao-san from Miyagi
I LOVE...
...BOTH OF THEM!!

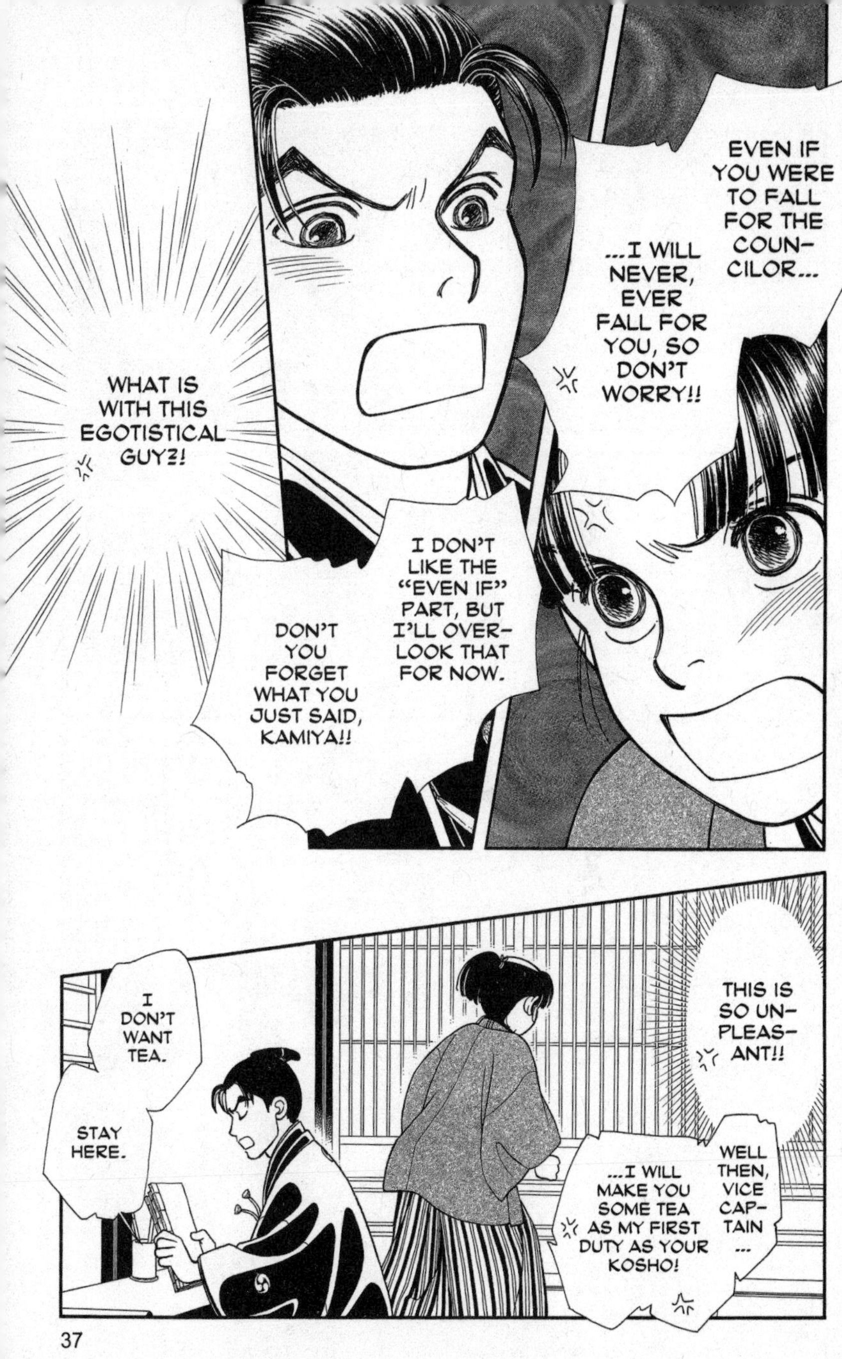
EVEN IF YOU WERE TO FALL FOR THE COUNCILOR...
...I WILL NEVER, EVER FALL FOR YOU, SO DON'T WORRY!!
WHAT IS WITH THIS EGOTISTICAL GUY?!
I DON'T LIKE THE "EVEN IF" PART, BUT I'LL OVERLOOK THAT FOR NOW.
DON'T YOU FORGET WHAT YOU JUST SAID, KAMIYA!!
THIS IS SO UNPLEASANT!!
WELL THEN, VICE CAPTAIN ...
...I WILL MAKE YOU SOME TEA AS MY FIRST DUTY AS YOUR KOSHO!
I DON'T WANT TEA.
STAY HERE.

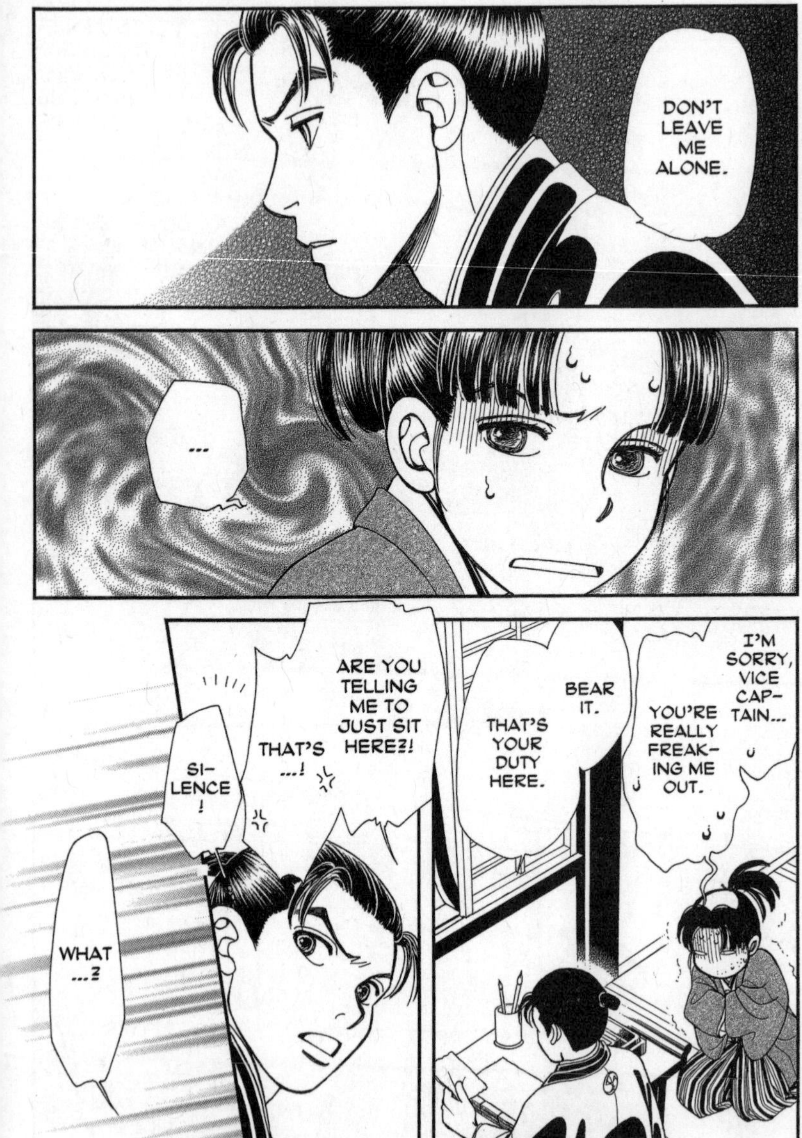
DON'T LEAVE ME ALONE.
...
I'M SORRY, VICE CAP-TAIN...
YOU'RE REALLY FREAK-ING ME OUT.
BEAR IT.
THAT'S YOUR DUTY HERE.
ARE YOU TELLING ME TO JUST SIT HERE?!
THAT'S ...!
SI-LENCE!
WHAT ...?

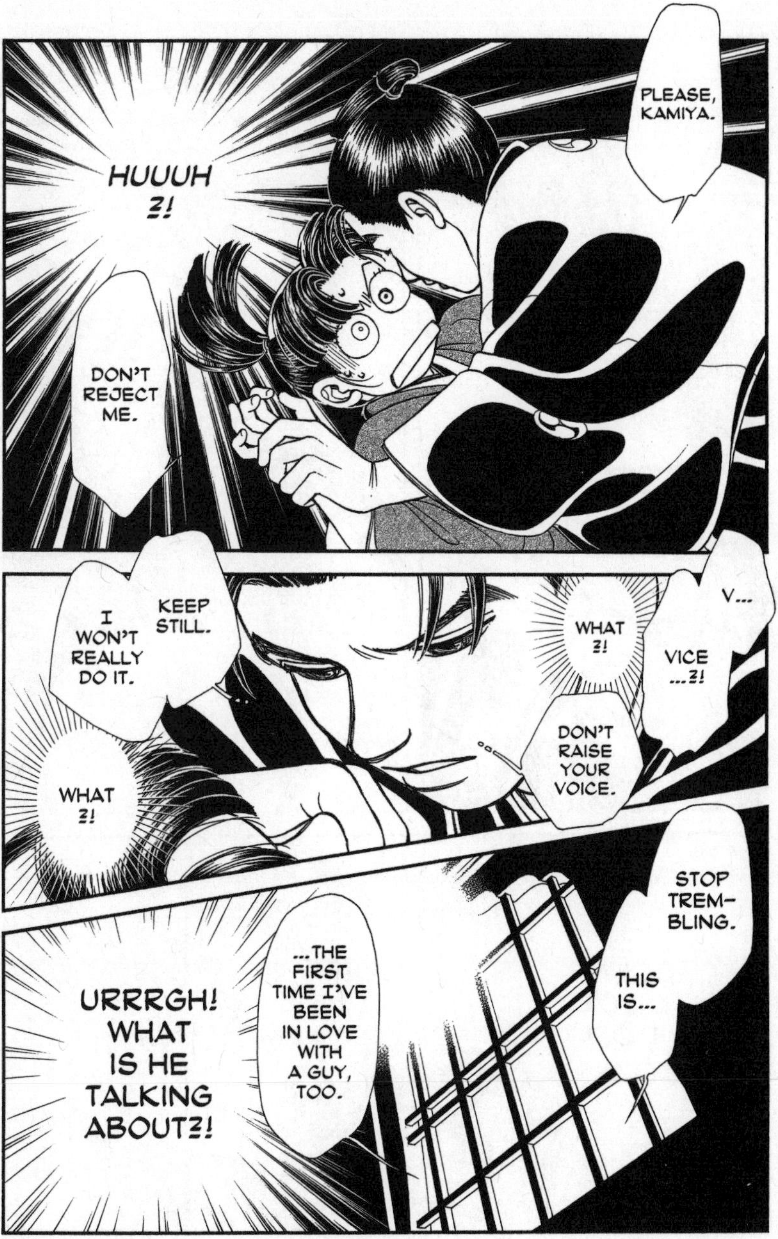
PLEASE, KAMIYA.
HUUUH ?!
DON'T REJECT ME.
V...
VICE ...?!
WHAT ?!
DON'T RAISE YOUR VOICE.
KEEP STILL.
I WON'T REALLY DO IT.
WHAT ?!
STOP TREMBLING.
THIS IS...
...THE FIRST TIME I'VE BEEN IN LOVE WITH A GUY, TOO.
URRRGH! WHAT IS HE TALKING ABOUT?!

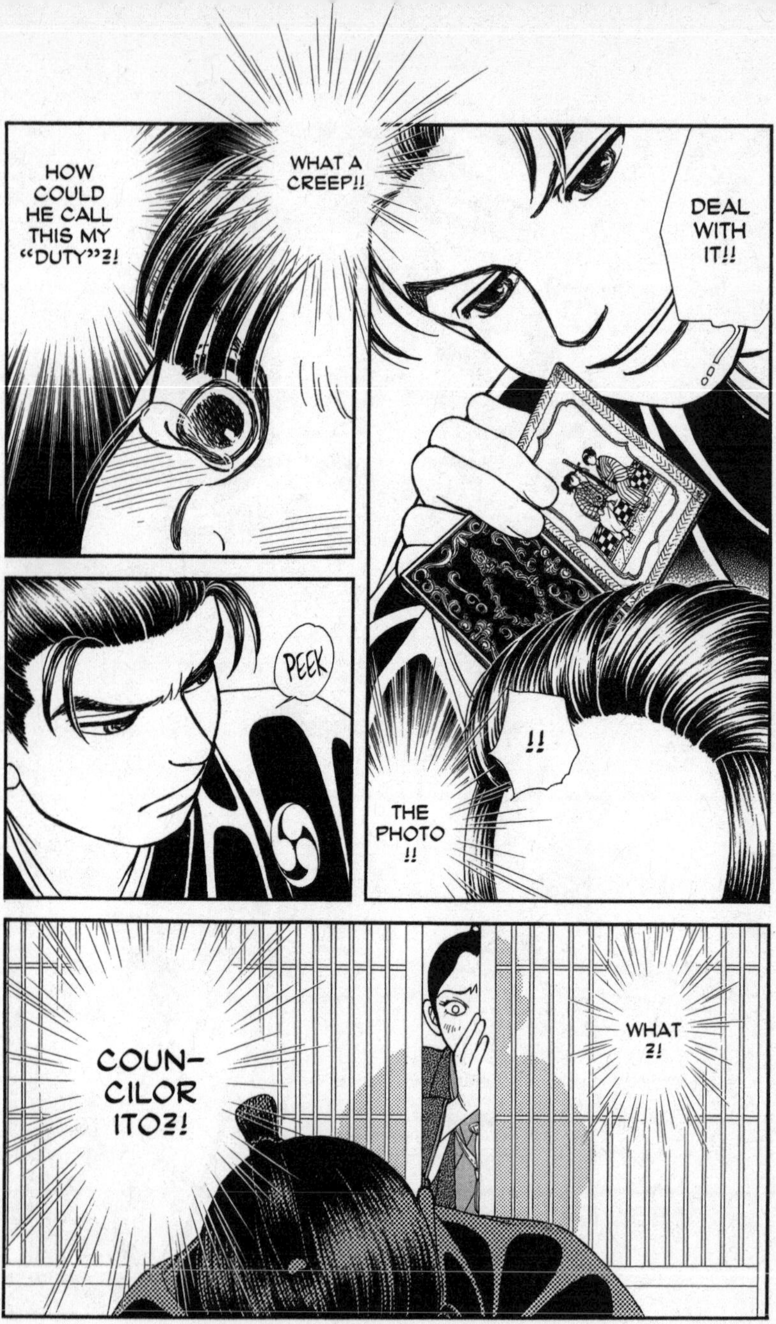

DEAL WITH IT!!
!!
THE PHOTO!!
WHAT A CREEP!!
HOW COULD HE CALL THIS MY "DUTY"?!
PEEK
WHAT?!
COUN-CILOR ITO?!

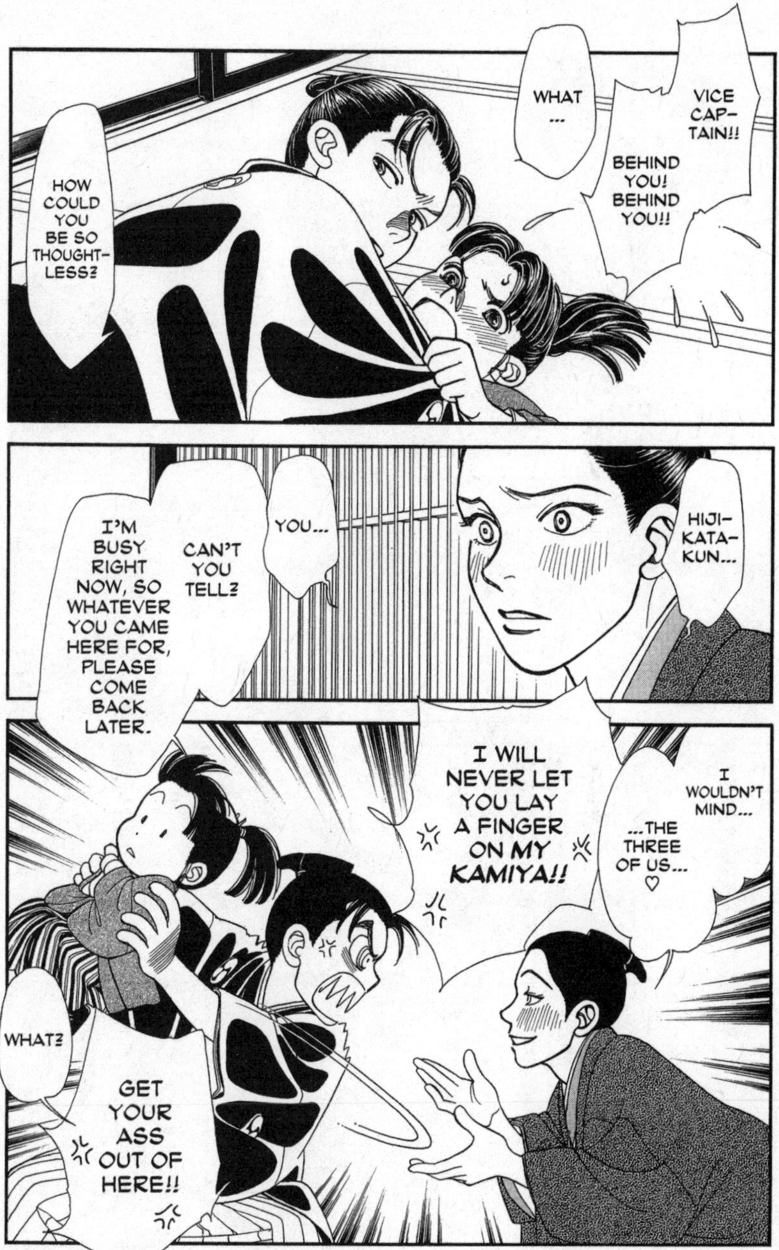
VICE CAP-TAIN!!
BEHIND YOU! BEHIND YOU!!
WHAT ...
HOW COULD YOU BE SO THOUGHT-LESS?
HIJI-KATA-KUN...
YOU...
CAN'T YOU TELL?
I'M BUSY RIGHT NOW, SO WHATEVER YOU CAME HERE FOR, PLEASE COME BACK LATER.
I WOULDN'T MIND...
...THE THREE OF US... ♡
I WILL NEVER LET YOU LAY A FINGER ON MY KAMIYA!!
WHAT?
GET YOUR ASS OUT OF HERE!!

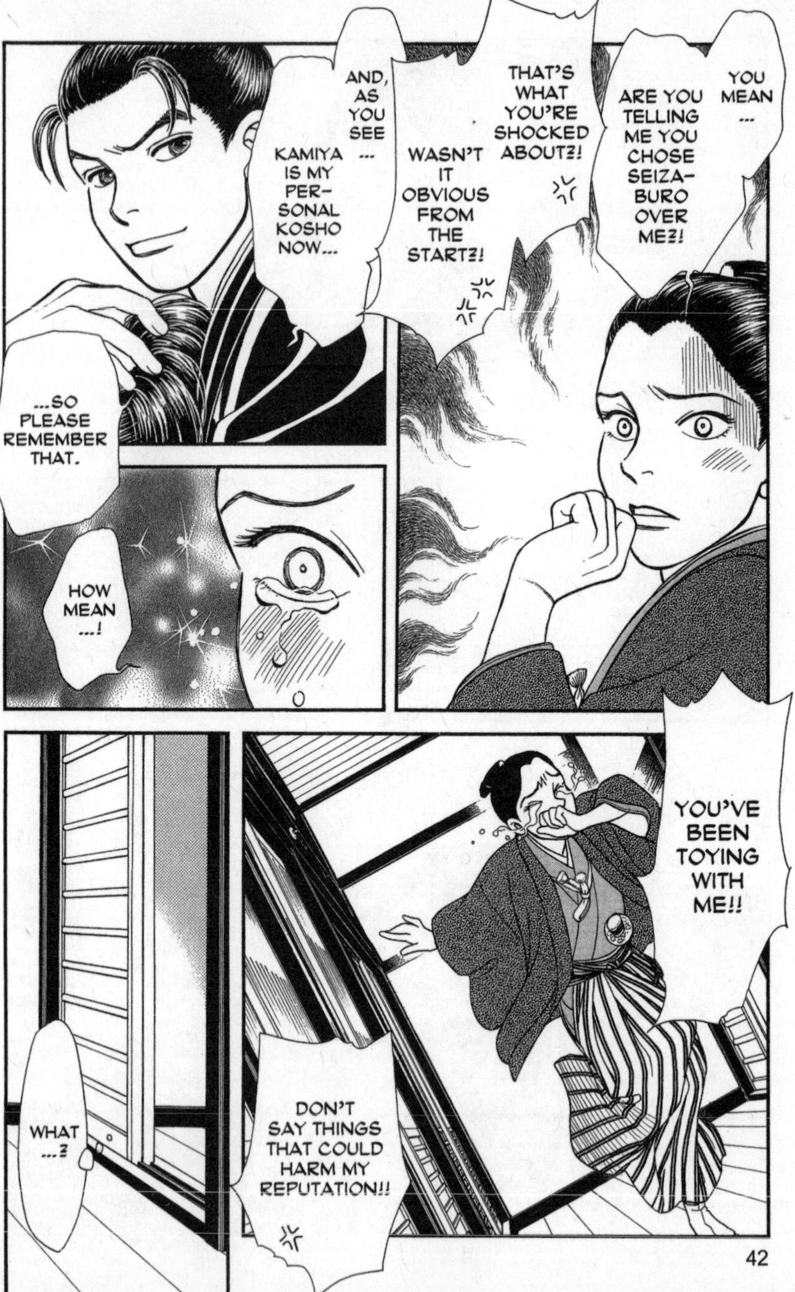

YOU MEAN ...
ARE YOU TELLING ME YOU CHOSE SEIZABURO OVER ME?!
THAT'S WHAT YOU'RE SHOCKED ABOUT?!
WASN'T IT OBVIOUS FROM THE START?!
AND, AS YOU SEE ...
KAMIYA IS MY PERSONAL KOSHO NOW...
...SO PLEASE REMEMBER THAT.
HOW MEAN ...!
YOU'VE BEEN TOYING WITH ME!!
DON'T SAY THINGS THAT COULD HARM MY REPUTATION!!
WHAT ...?

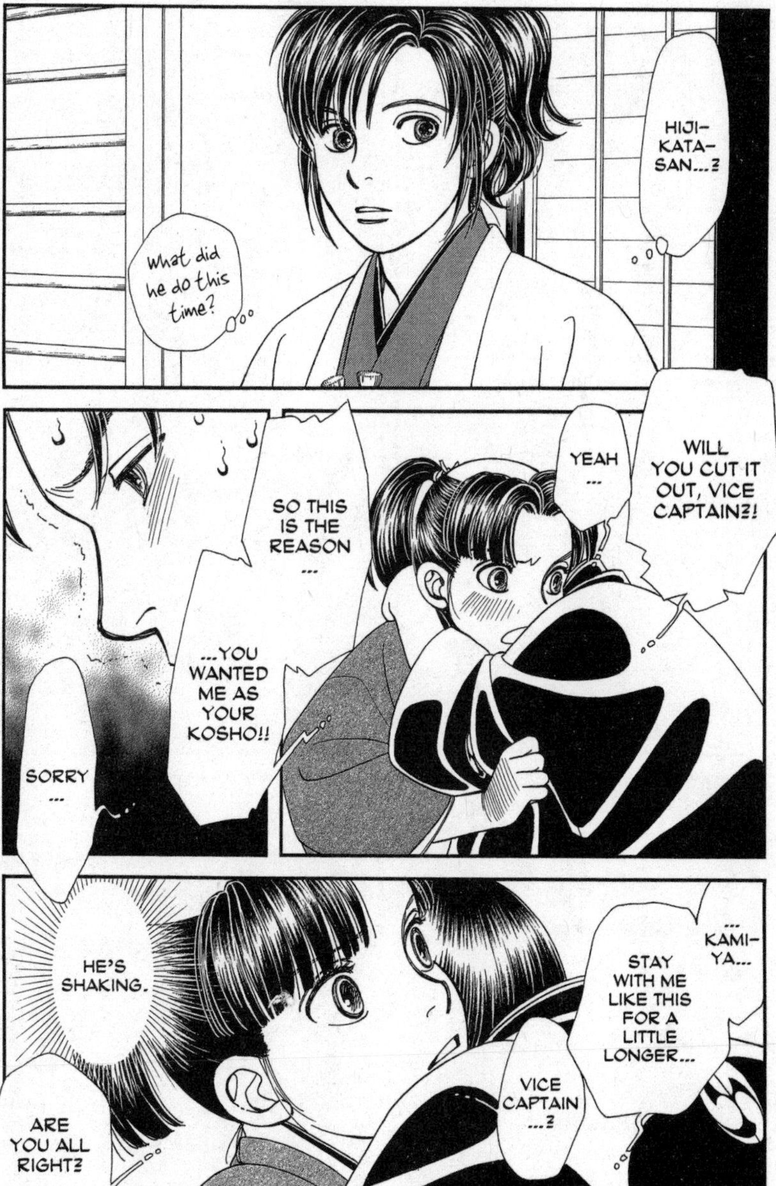
HIJI-KATA-SAN...?
What did he do this time?
WILL YOU CUT IT OUT, VICE CAPTAIN?!
YEAH ...
SO THIS IS THE REASON ...
...YOU WANTED ME AS YOUR KOSHO!!
SORRY ...
...KAMI-YA...
STAY WITH ME LIKE THIS FOR A LITTLE LONGER...
VICE CAPTAIN ...?
HE'S SHAKING.
ARE YOU ALL RIGHT?

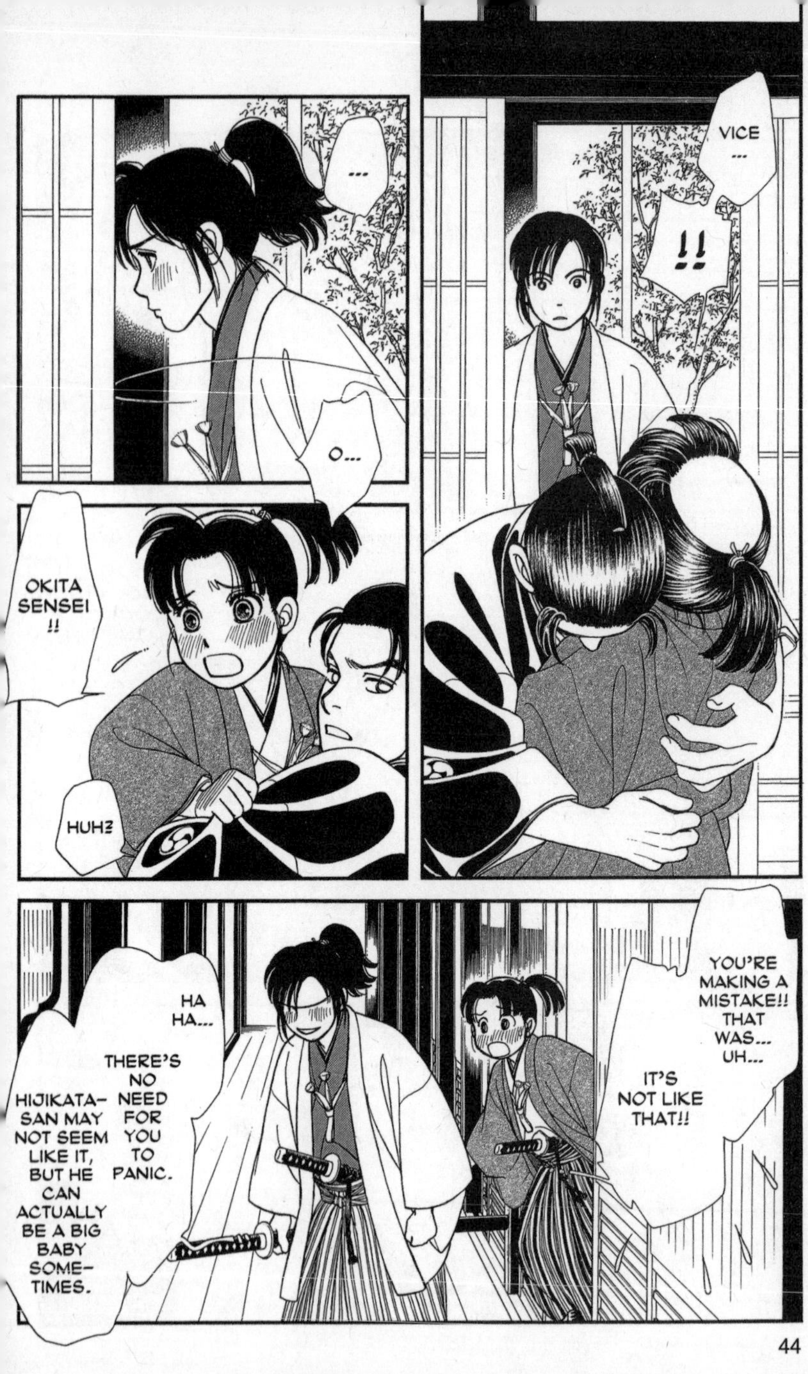
VICE ...
!!
...
O...
OKITA SENSEI !!
HUH?
YOU'RE MAKING A MISTAKE!! THAT WAS... UH...
IT'S NOT LIKE THAT!!
HA HA...
THERE'S NO NEED FOR YOU TO PANIC.
HIJIKATA-SAN MAY NOT SEEM LIKE IT, BUT HE CAN ACTUALLY BE A BIG BABY SOME-TIMES.

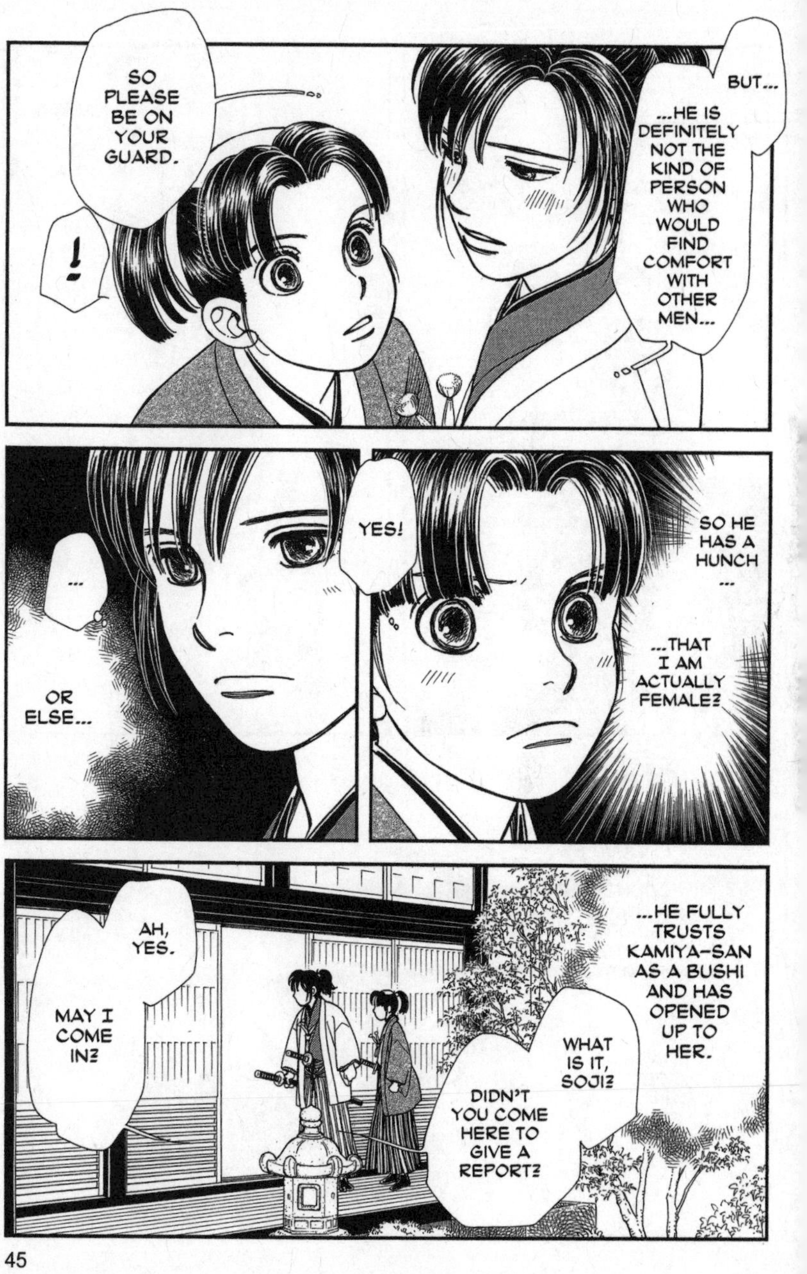
BUT...
...HE IS DEFINITELY NOT THE KIND OF PERSON WHO WOULD FIND COMFORT WITH OTHER MEN...
SO PLEASE BE ON YOUR GUARD.
!
SO HE HAS A HUNCH...
YES!
...THAT I AM ACTUALLY FEMALE?
...
OR ELSE...
...HE FULLY TRUSTS KAMIYA-SAN AS A BUSHI AND HAS OPENED UP TO HER.
WHAT IS IT, SOJI?
DIDN'T YOU COME HERE TO GIVE A REPORT?
AH, YES.
MAY I COME IN?

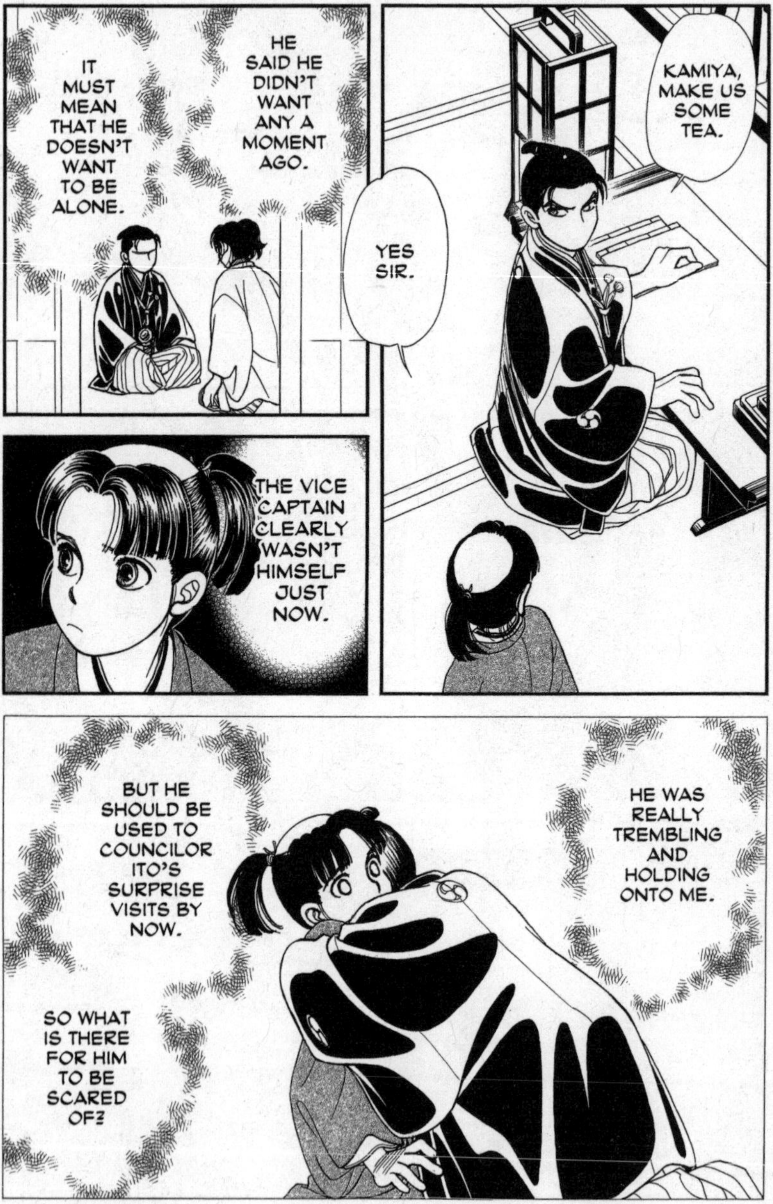
KAMIYA, MAKE US SOME TEA.
YES SIR.
HE SAID HE DIDN'T WANT ANY A MOMENT AGO.
IT MUST MEAN THAT HE DOESN'T WANT TO BE ALONE.
THE VICE CAPTAIN CLEARLY WASN'T HIMSELF JUST NOW.
HE WAS REALLY TREMBLING AND HOLDING ONTO ME.
BUT HE SHOULD BE USED TO COUNCILOR ITO'S SURPRISE VISITS BY NOW.
SO WHAT IS THERE FOR HIM TO BE SCARED OF?

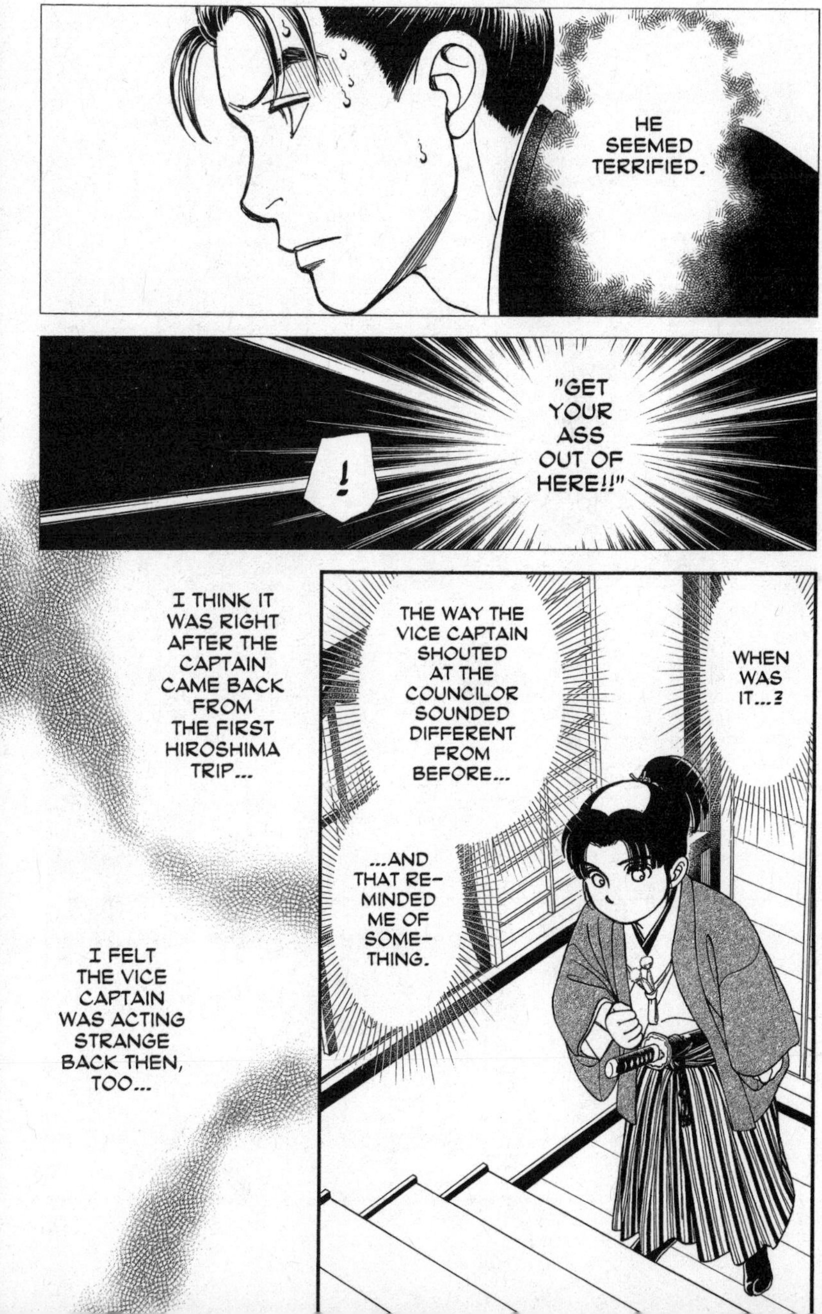
HE SEEMED TERRIFIED.
"GET YOUR ASS OUT OF HERE!!"
!
WHEN WAS IT...?
THE WAY THE VICE CAPTAIN SHOUTED AT THE COUNCILOR SOUNDED DIFFERENT FROM BEFORE...
...AND THAT RE-MINDED ME OF SOME-THING.
I THINK IT WAS RIGHT AFTER THE CAPTAIN CAME BACK FROM THE FIRST HIROSHIMA TRIP...
I FELT THE VICE CAPTAIN WAS ACTING STRANGE BACK THEN, TOO...

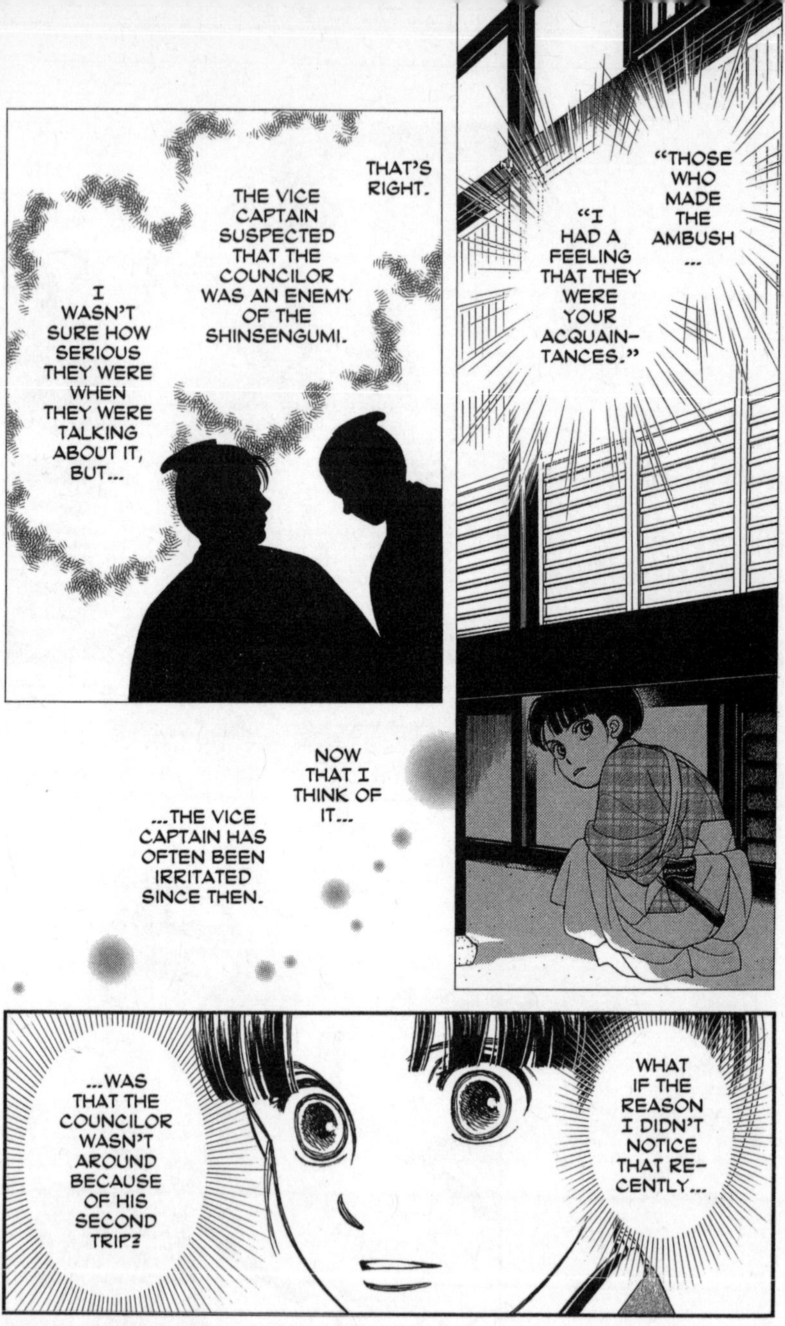
"THOSE WHO MADE THE AMBUSH...
"I HAD A FEELING THAT THEY WERE YOUR ACQUAIN-TANCES."
THAT'S RIGHT.
THE VICE CAPTAIN SUSPECTED THAT THE COUNCILOR WAS AN ENEMY OF THE SHINSENGUMI.
I WASN'T SURE HOW SERIOUS THEY WERE WHEN THEY WERE TALKING ABOUT IT, BUT...
NOW THAT I THINK OF IT...
...THE VICE CAPTAIN HAS OFTEN BEEN IRRITATED SINCE THEN.
WHAT IF THE REASON I DIDN'T NOTICE THAT RE-CENTLY...
...WAS THAT THE COUNCILOR WASN'T AROUND BECAUSE OF HIS SECOND TRIP?

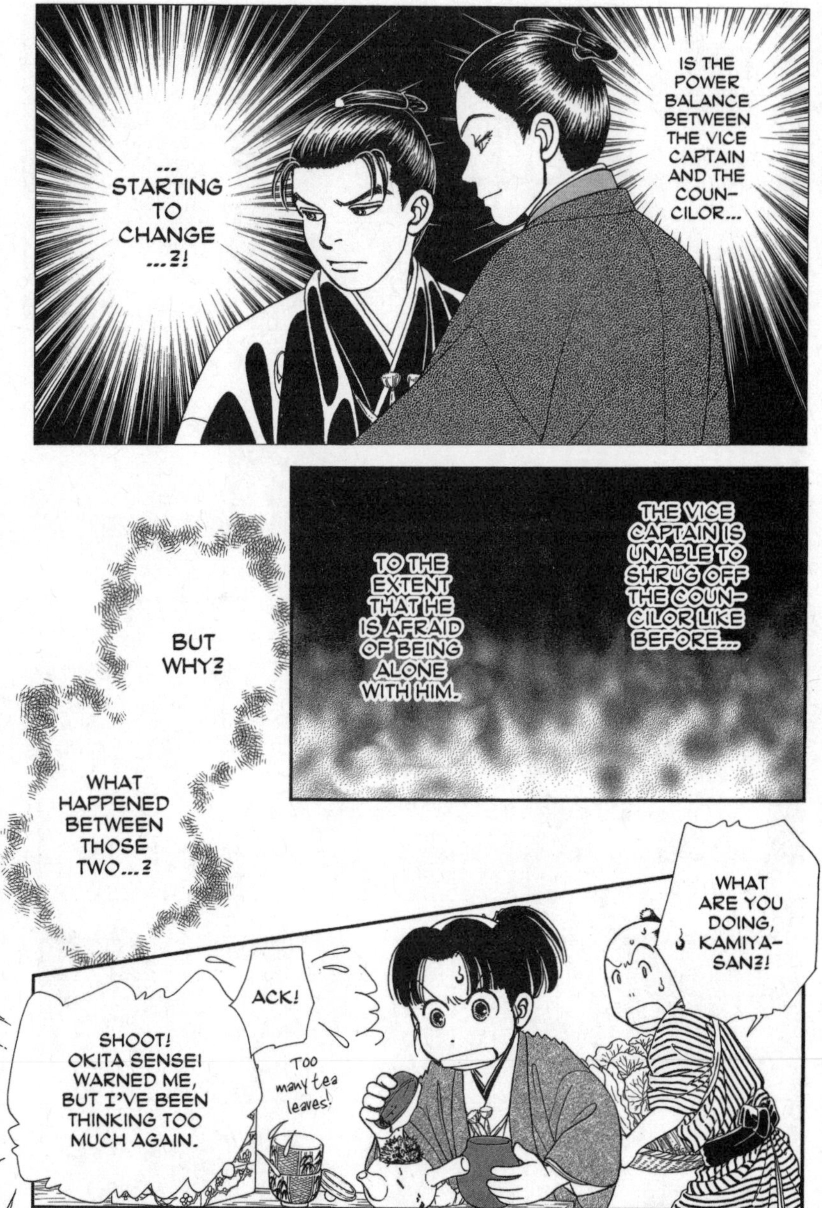
IS THE POWER BALANCE BETWEEN THE VICE CAPTAIN AND THE COUNCILOR...
...STARTING TO CHANGE ...?!
THE VICE CAPTAIN IS UNABLE TO SHRUG OFF THE COUNCILOR LIKE BEFORE...
TO THE EXTENT THAT HE IS AFRAID OF BEING ALONE WITH HIM.
BUT WHY?
WHAT HAPPENED BETWEEN THOSE TWO...?
WHAT ARE YOU DOING, KAMIYA-SAN?!
ACK!
Too many tea leaves!
SHOOT! OKITA SENSEI WARNED ME, BUT I'VE BEEN THINKING TOO MUCH AGAIN.

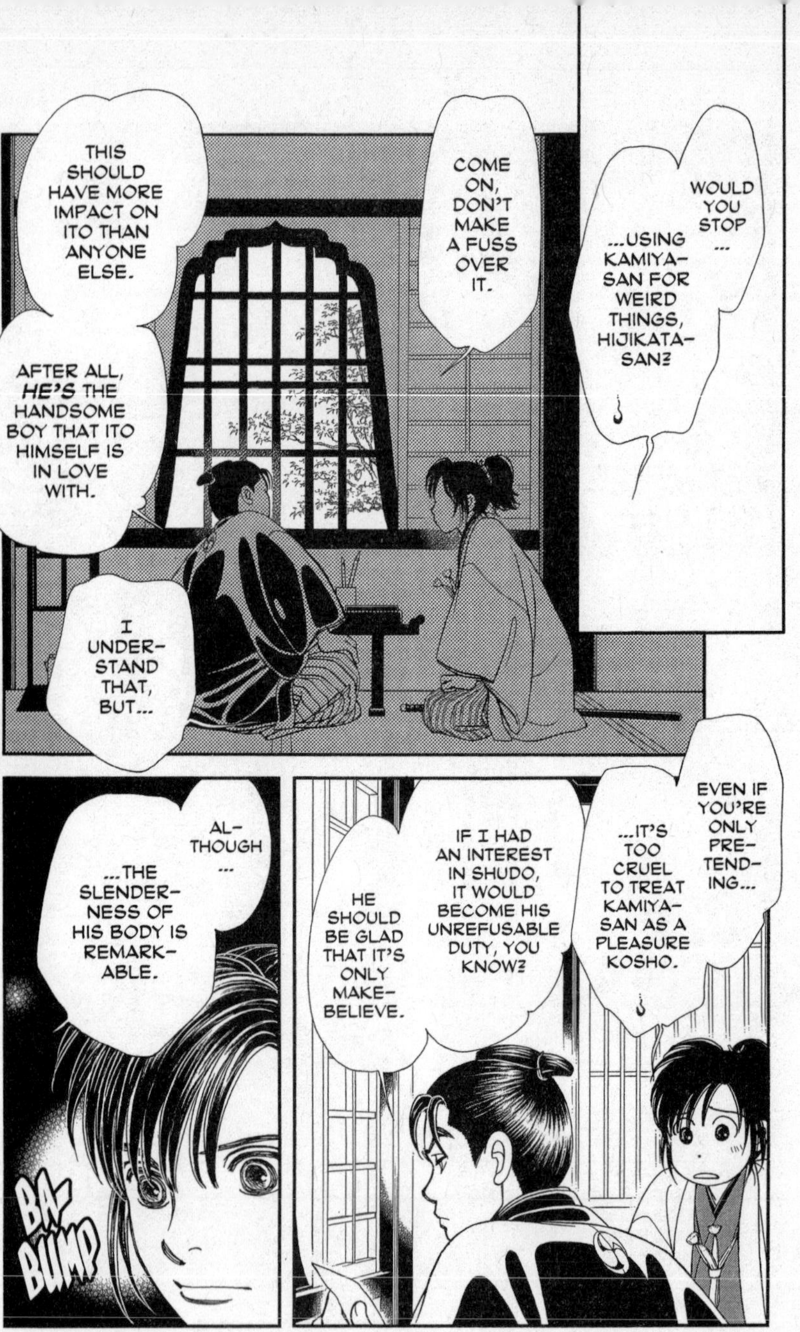
WOULD YOU STOP ...
...USING KAMIYA-SAN FOR WEIRD THINGS, HIJIKATA-SAN?
COME ON, DON'T MAKE A FUSS OVER IT.
THIS SHOULD HAVE MORE IMPACT ON ITO THAN ANYONE ELSE.
AFTER ALL, *HE'S* THE HANDSOME BOY THAT ITO HIMSELF IS IN LOVE WITH.
I UNDER-STAND THAT, BUT...
EVEN IF YOU'RE ONLY PRE-TEND-ING...
...IT'S TOO CRUEL TO TREAT KAMIYA-SAN AS A PLEASURE KOSHO.
IF I HAD AN INTEREST IN SHUDO, IT WOULD BECOME HIS UNREFUSABLE DUTY, YOU KNOW?
HE SHOULD BE GLAD THAT IT'S ONLY MAKE-BELIEVE.
AL-THOUGH ...
...THE SLENDER-NESS OF HIS BODY IS REMARK-ABLE.
BA-BUMP

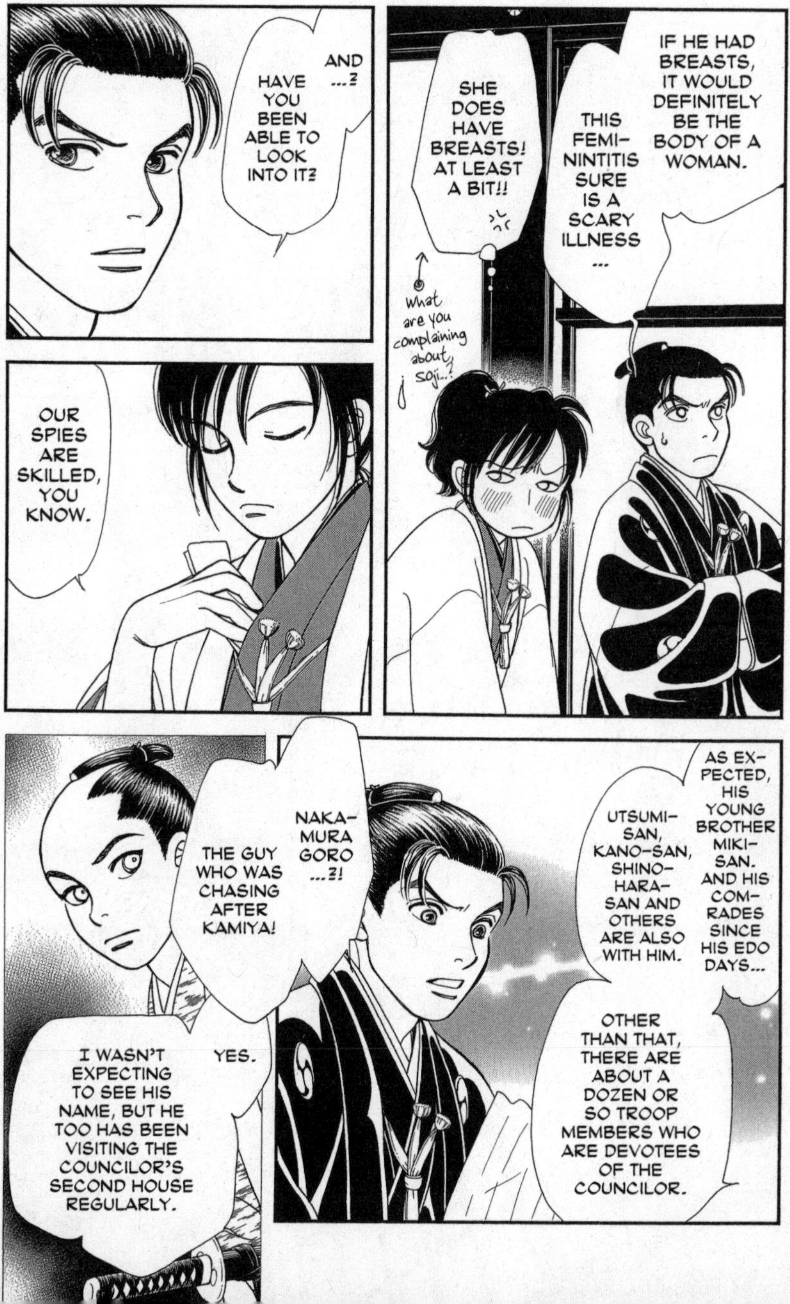
IF HE HAD BREASTS, IT WOULD DEFINITELY BE THE BODY OF A WOMAN.
THIS FEMININTITIS SURE IS A SCARY ILLNESS...
SHE DOES HAVE BREASTS! AT LEAST A BIT!!
What are you complaining about, Soji...?
AND ...?
HAVE YOU BEEN ABLE TO LOOK INTO IT?
OUR SPIES ARE SKILLED, YOU KNOW.
AS EXPECTED, HIS YOUNG BROTHER MIKI-SAN. AND HIS COMRADES SINCE HIS EDO DAYS...
UTSUMI-SAN, KANO-SAN, SHINOHARA-SAN AND OTHERS ARE ALSO WITH HIM.
OTHER THAN THAT, THERE ARE ABOUT A DOZEN OR SO TROOP MEMBERS WHO ARE DEVOTEES OF THE COUNCILOR.
NAKAMURA GORO...?!
THE GUY WHO WAS CHASING AFTER KAMIYA!
YES.
I WASN'T EXPECTING TO SEE HIS NAME, BUT HE TOO HAS BEEN VISITING THE COUNCILOR'S SECOND HOUSE REGULARLY.

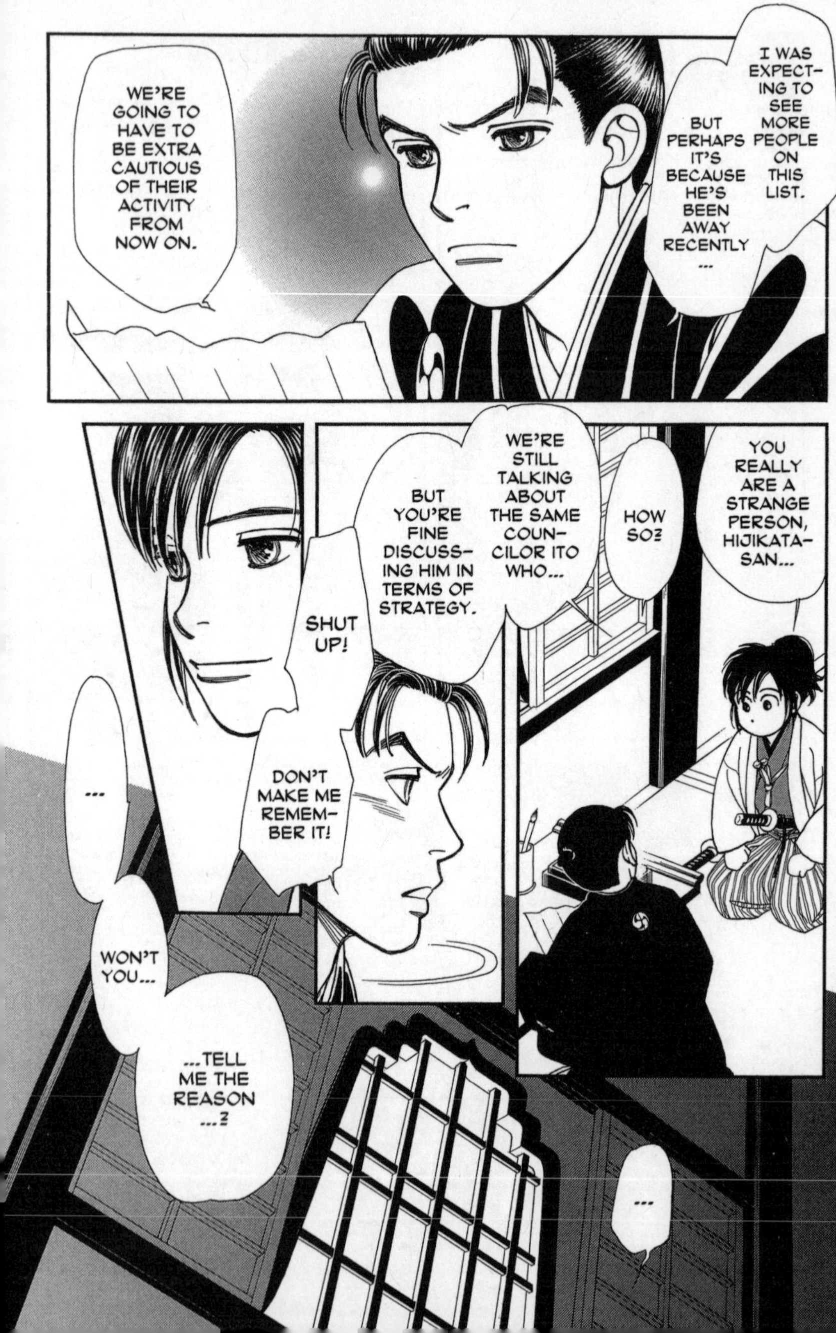

I WAS EXPECTING TO SEE MORE PEOPLE ON THIS LIST.
BUT PERHAPS IT'S BECAUSE HE'S BEEN AWAY RECENTLY...
WE'RE GOING TO HAVE TO BE EXTRA CAUTIOUS OF THEIR ACTIVITY FROM NOW ON.
YOU REALLY ARE A STRANGE PERSON, HIJIKATA-SAN...
HOW SO?
WE'RE STILL TALKING ABOUT THE SAME COUNCILOR ITO WHO...
BUT YOU'RE FINE DISCUSSING HIM IN TERMS OF STRATEGY.
SHUT UP!
DON'T MAKE ME REMEMBER IT!
...
...
WON'T YOU...
...TELL ME THE REASON...?

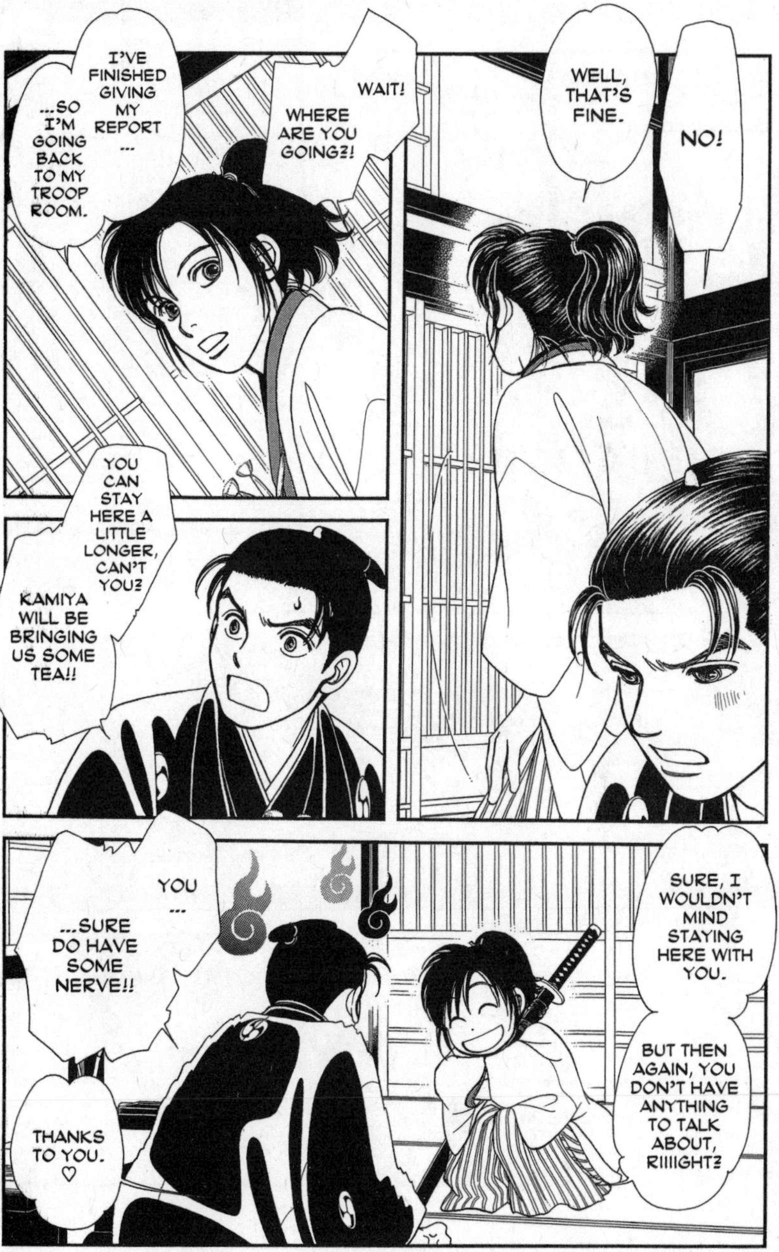
NO!
WELL, THAT'S FINE.
I'VE FINISHED GIVING MY REPORT ...
...SO I'M GOING BACK TO MY TROOP ROOM.
WAIT!
WHERE ARE YOU GOING?!
YOU CAN STAY HERE A LITTLE LONGER, CAN'T YOU?
KAMIYA WILL BE BRINGING US SOME TEA!!
SURE, I WOULDN'T MIND STAYING HERE WITH YOU.
BUT THEN AGAIN, YOU DON'T HAVE ANYTHING TO TALK ABOUT, RIIIIGHT?
YOU ...
...SURE DO HAVE SOME NERVE!!
THANKS TO YOU. ♡

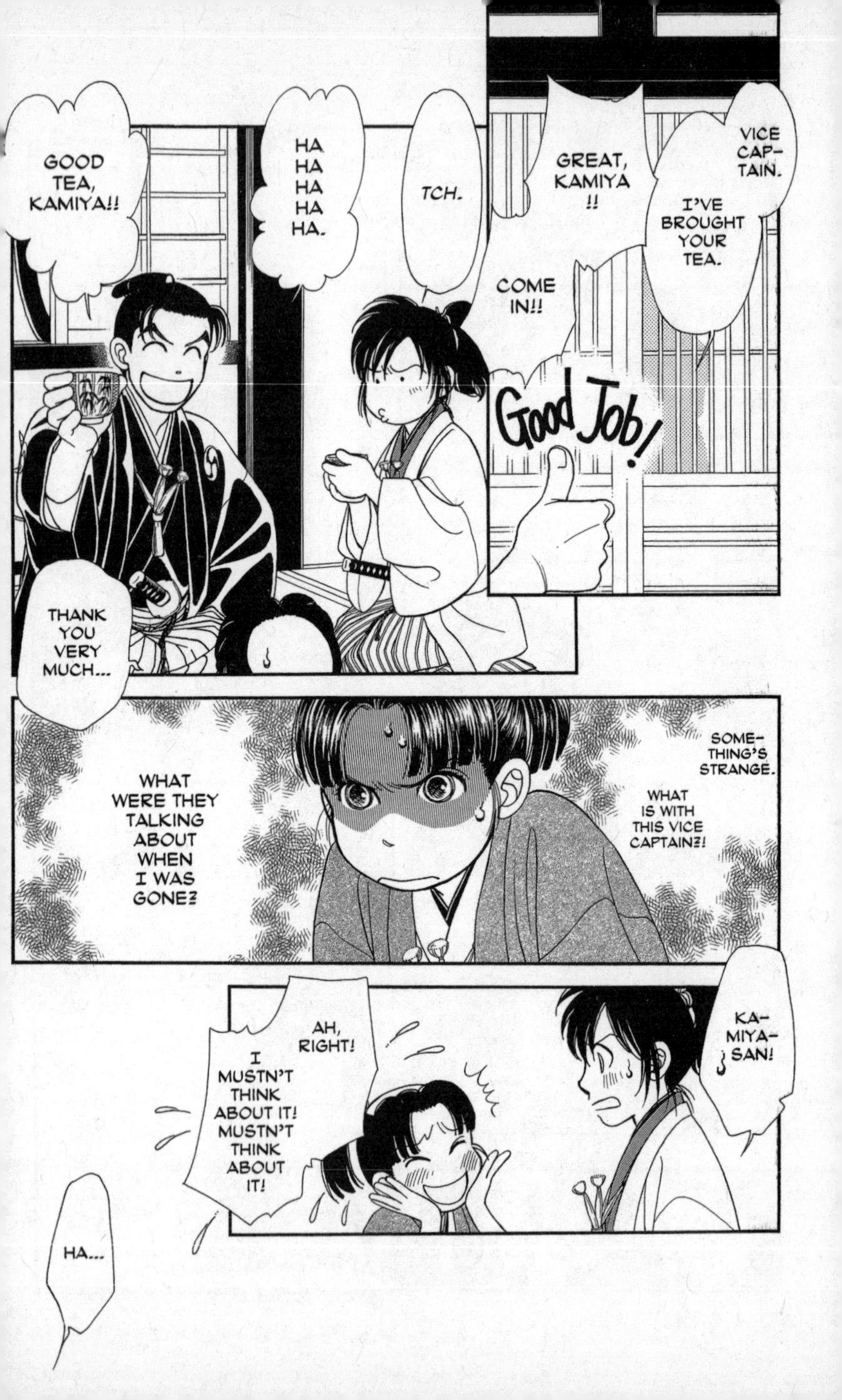
VICE CAPTAIN.
I'VE BROUGHT YOUR TEA.
GREAT, KAMIYA!!
COME IN!!
Good Job!
TCH.
HA HA HA HA HA.
GOOD TEA, KAMIYA!!
THANK YOU VERY MUCH...
SOMETHING'S STRANGE.
WHAT IS WITH THIS VICE CAPTAIN?!
WHAT WERE THEY TALKING ABOUT WHEN I WAS GONE?
KAMIYA-SAN!
AH, RIGHT!
I MUSTN'T THINK ABOUT IT! MUSTN'T THINK ABOUT IT!
HA...

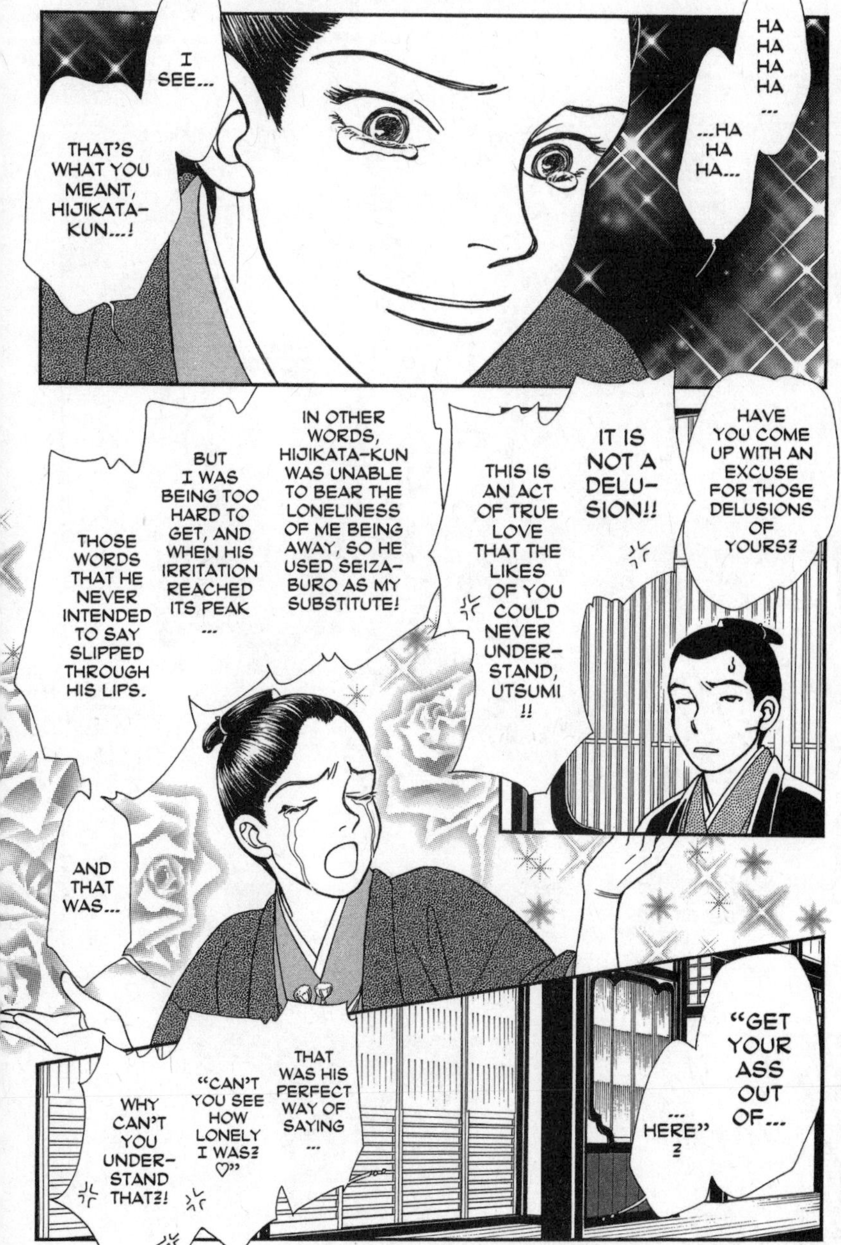
HA HA HA HA ... ...HA HA HA...
I SEE... THAT'S WHAT YOU MEANT, HIJIKATA-KUN...!
HAVE YOU COME UP WITH AN EXCUSE FOR THOSE DELUSIONS OF YOURS?
IT IS NOT A DELUSION!!
THIS IS AN ACT OF TRUE LOVE THAT THE LIKES OF YOU COULD NEVER UNDERSTAND, UTSUMI!!
IN OTHER WORDS, HIJIKATA-KUN WAS UNABLE TO BEAR THE LONELINESS OF ME BEING AWAY, SO HE USED SEIZABURO AS MY SUBSTITUTE!
BUT I WAS BEING TOO HARD TO GET, AND WHEN HIS IRRITATION REACHED ITS PEAK...
THOSE WORDS THAT HE NEVER INTENDED TO SAY SLIPPED THROUGH HIS LIPS.
AND THAT WAS...
"GET YOUR ASS OUT OF... ...HERE"?
THAT WAS HIS PERFECT WAY OF SAYING...
"CAN'T YOU SEE HOW LONELY I WAS? ♡"
WHY CAN'T YOU UNDERSTAND THAT?!

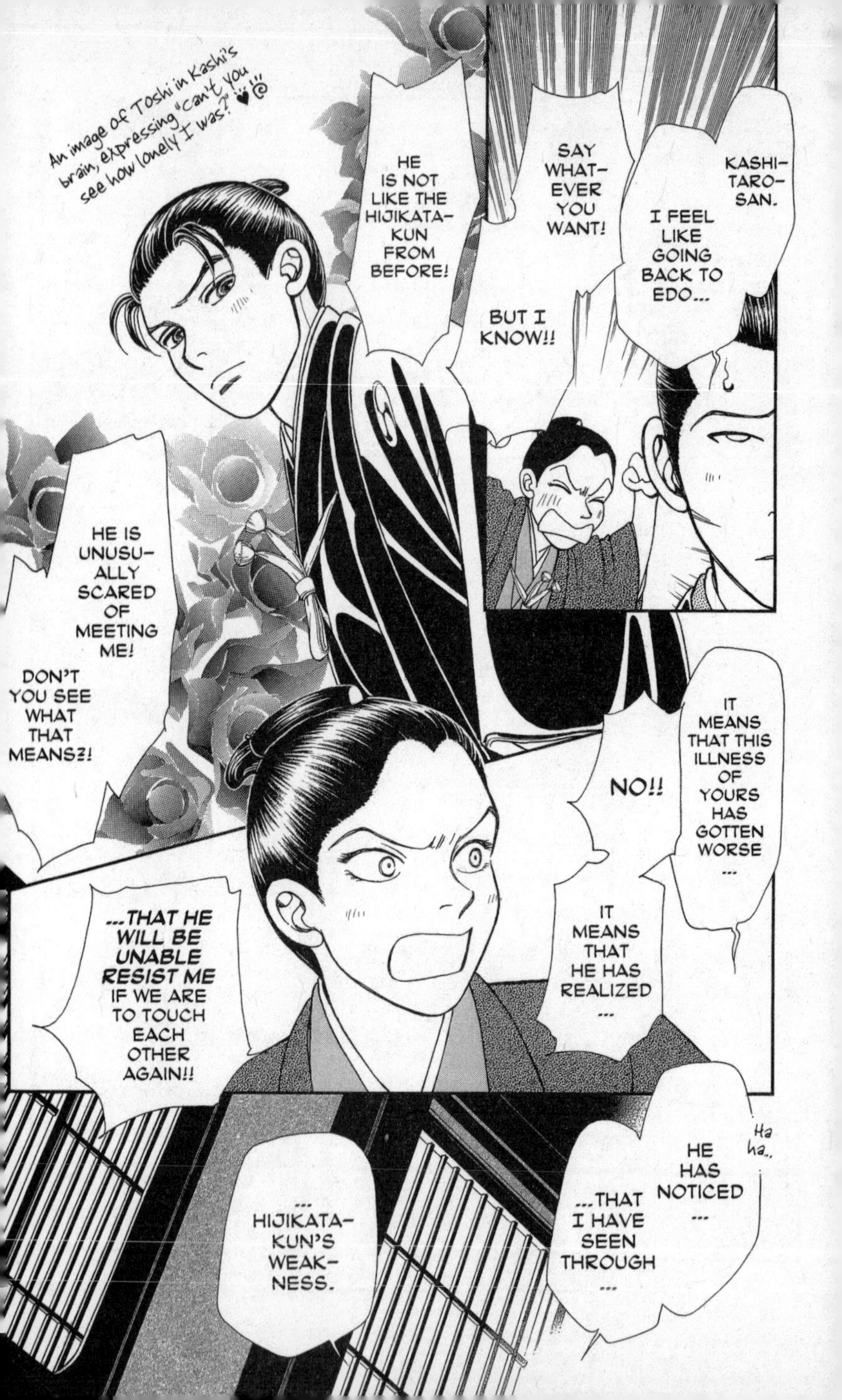
KASHI-TARO-SAN.
I FEEL LIKE GOING BACK TO EDO...
SAY WHAT-EVER YOU WANT!
BUT I KNOW!!
HE IS NOT LIKE THE HIJIKATA-KUN FROM BEFORE!
An image of Toshi in Kashi's brain, expressing "can't you see how lonely I was?" ♥
HE IS UNUSU-ALLY SCARED OF MEETING ME!
DON'T YOU SEE WHAT THAT MEANS?!
IT MEANS THAT THIS ILLNESS OF YOURS HAS GOTTEN WORSE...
NO!!
IT MEANS THAT HE HAS REALIZED...
...THAT HE WILL BE UNABLE RESIST ME IF WE ARE TO TOUCH EACH OTHER AGAIN!!
Ha ha..
HE HAS NOTICED...
...THAT I HAVE SEEN THROUGH...
...HIJIKATA-KUN'S WEAK-NESS.

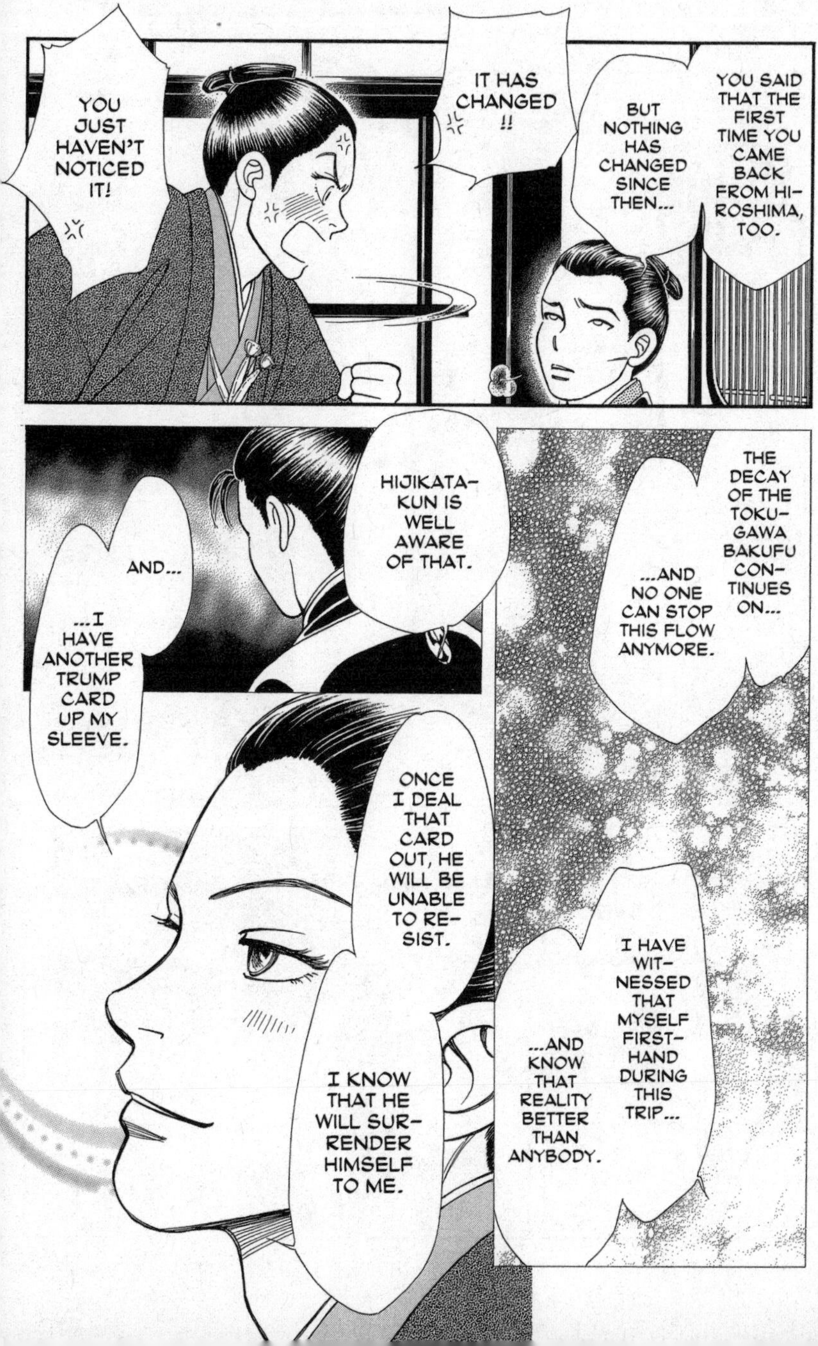
YOU SAID THAT THE FIRST TIME YOU CAME BACK FROM HIROSHIMA, TOO.
BUT NOTHING HAS CHANGED SINCE THEN...
IT HAS CHANGED!!
YOU JUST HAVEN'T NOTICED IT!
THE DECAY OF THE TOKUGAWA BAKUFU CONTINUES ON...
...AND NO ONE CAN STOP THIS FLOW ANYMORE.
I HAVE WITNESSED THAT MYSELF FIRST-HAND DURING THIS TRIP...
...AND KNOW THAT REALITY BETTER THAN ANYBODY.
HIJIKATA-KUN IS WELL AWARE OF THAT.
AND...
...I HAVE ANOTHER TRUMP CARD UP MY SLEEVE.
ONCE I DEAL THAT CARD OUT, HE WILL BE UNABLE TO RESIST.
I KNOW THAT HE WILL SURRENDER HIMSELF TO ME.

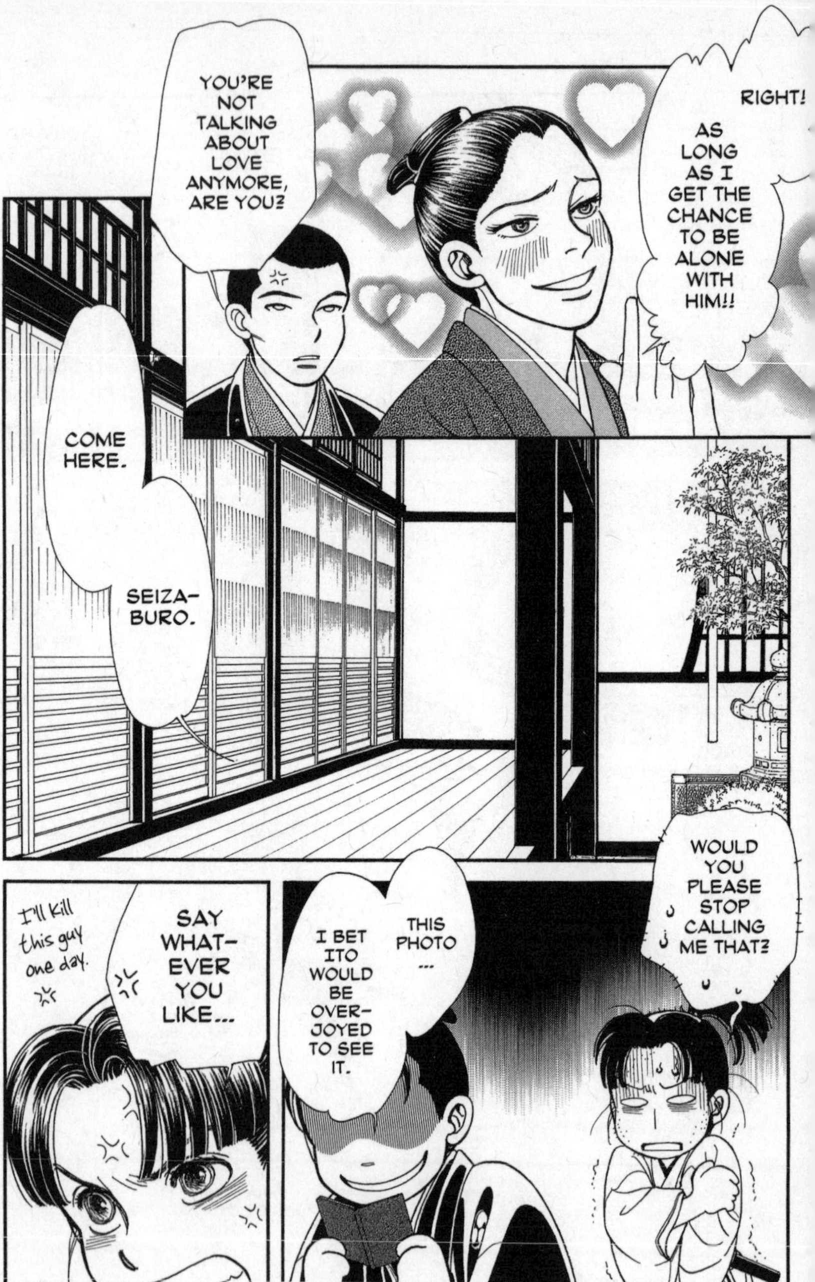
RIGHT!
AS LONG AS I GET THE CHANCE TO BE ALONE WITH HIM!!
YOU'RE NOT TALKING ABOUT LOVE ANYMORE, ARE YOU?
COME HERE.
SEIZABURO.
WOULD YOU PLEASE STOP CALLING ME THAT?
THIS PHOTO...
I BET ITO WOULD BE OVERJOYED TO SEE IT.
SAY WHATEVER YOU LIKE...
I'll kill this guy one day.

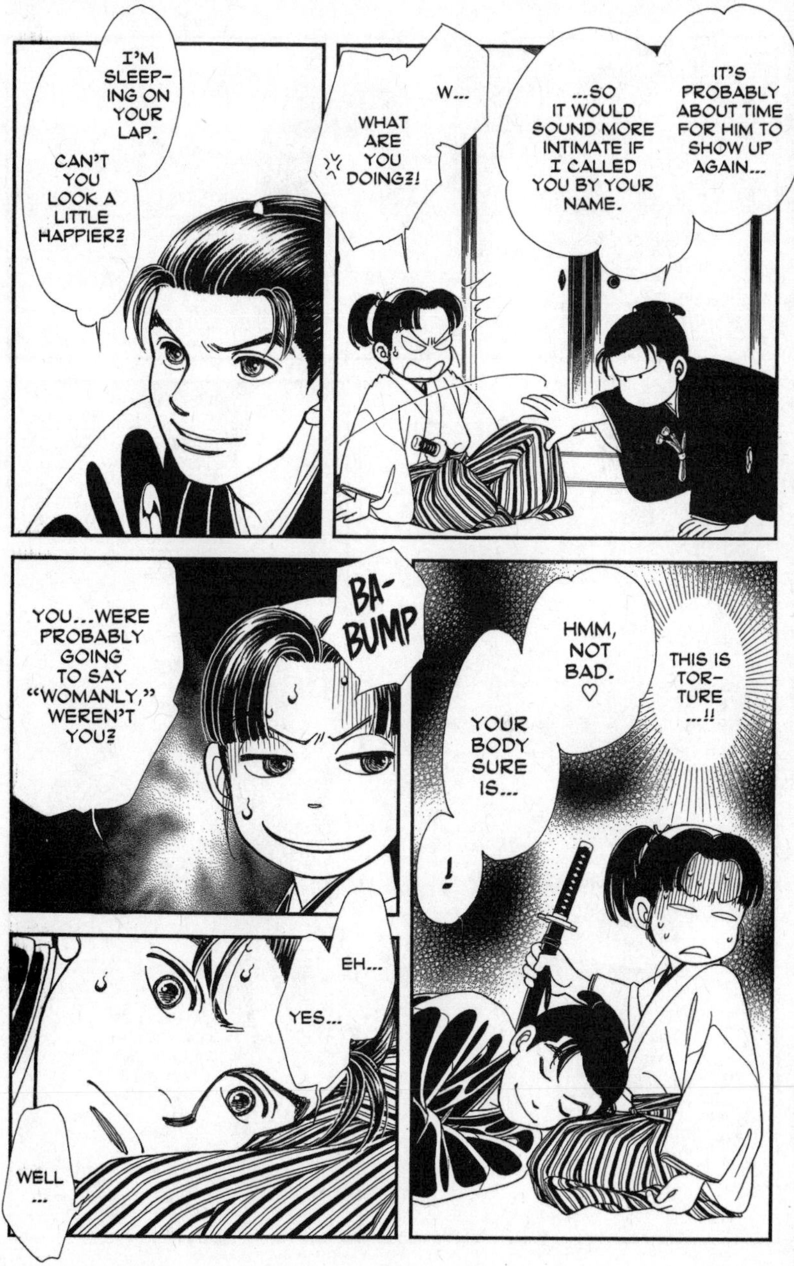
IT'S PROBABLY ABOUT TIME FOR HIM TO SHOW UP AGAIN...
...SO IT WOULD SOUND MORE INTIMATE IF I CALLED YOU BY YOUR NAME.
W...
WHAT ARE YOU DOING?!
I'M SLEEPING ON YOUR LAP.
CAN'T YOU LOOK A LITTLE HAPPIER?
THIS IS TORTURE...!!
HMM, NOT BAD. ♡
YOUR BODY SURE IS...
!
BA-BUMP
YOU...WERE PROBABLY GOING TO SAY "WOMANLY," WEREN'T YOU?
EH...
YES...
WELL...

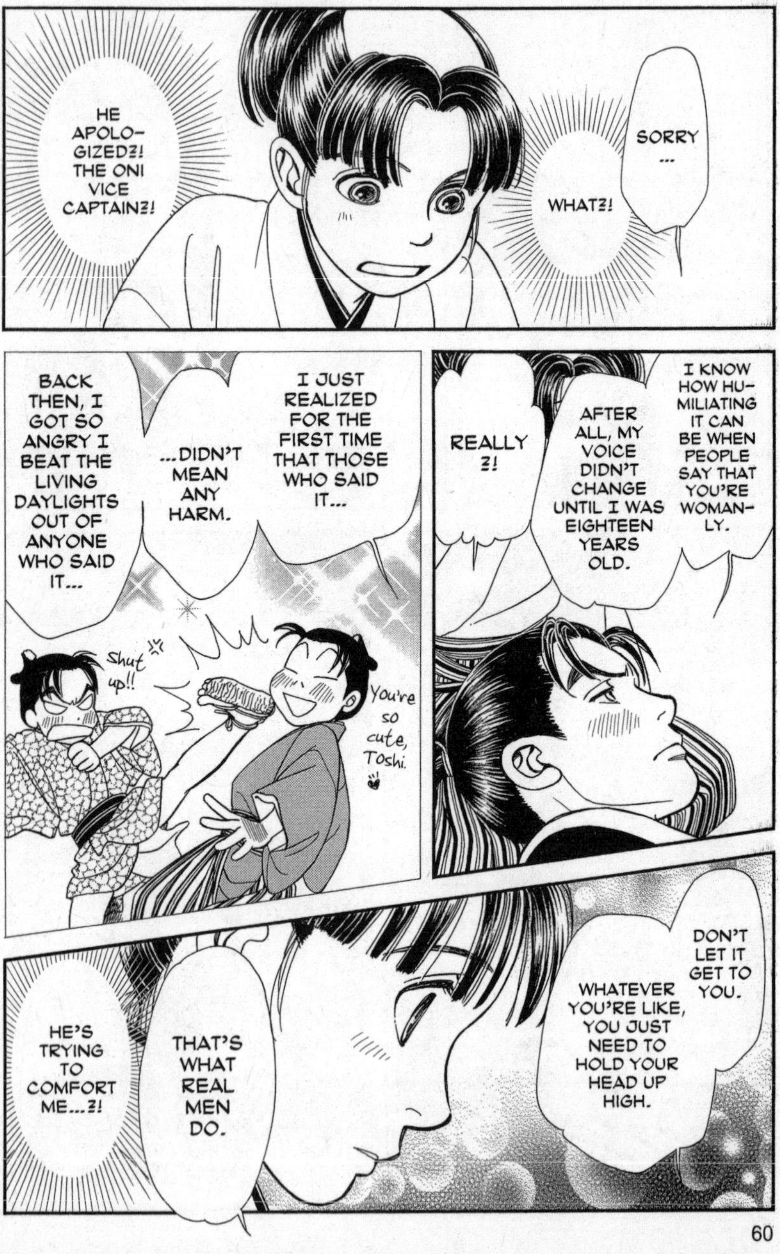
SORRY ...
WHAT?!
HE APOLOGIZED?! THE ONI VICE CAPTAIN?!
I KNOW HOW HUMILIATING IT CAN BE WHEN PEOPLE SAY THAT YOU'RE WOMANLY.
AFTER ALL, MY VOICE DIDN'T CHANGE UNTIL I WAS EIGHTEEN YEARS OLD.
REALLY?!
I JUST REALIZED FOR THE FIRST TIME THAT THOSE WHO SAID IT...
...DIDN'T MEAN ANY HARM.
BACK THEN, I GOT SO ANGRY I BEAT THE LIVING DAYLIGHTS OUT OF ANYONE WHO SAID IT...
You're so cute, Toshi.
Shut up!!
DON'T LET IT GET TO YOU.
WHATEVER YOU'RE LIKE, YOU JUST NEED TO HOLD YOUR HEAD UP HIGH.
THAT'S WHAT REAL MEN DO.
HE'S TRYING TO COMFORT ME...?!

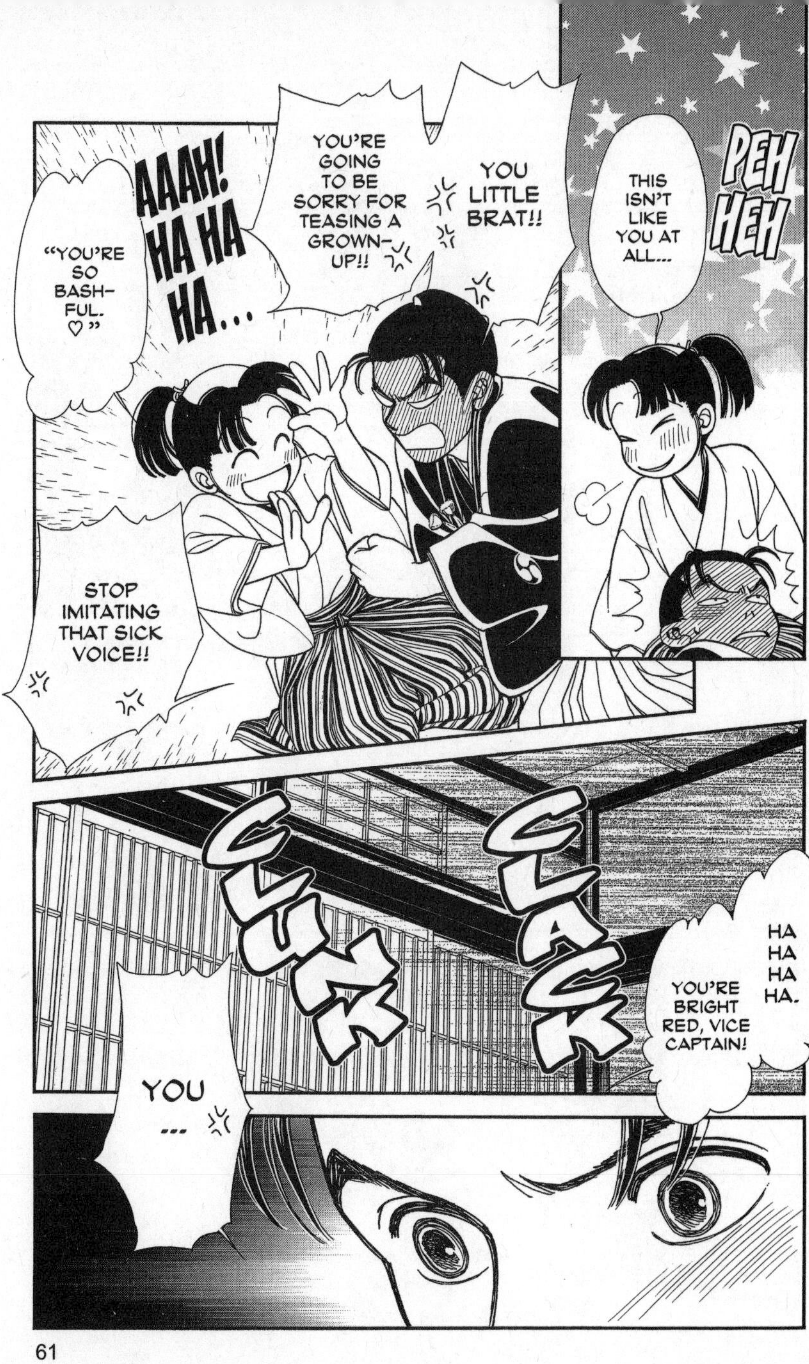
PEH HEH
THIS ISN'T LIKE YOU AT ALL...
YOU LITTLE BRAT!!
YOU'RE GOING TO BE SORRY FOR TEASING A GROWN-UP!!
AAAH! HA HA HA...
"YOU'RE SO BASH-FUL. ♡"
STOP IMITATING THAT SICK VOICE!!
CLACK
CLUNK
HA HA HA HA.
YOU'RE BRIGHT RED, VICE CAPTAIN!
YOU...

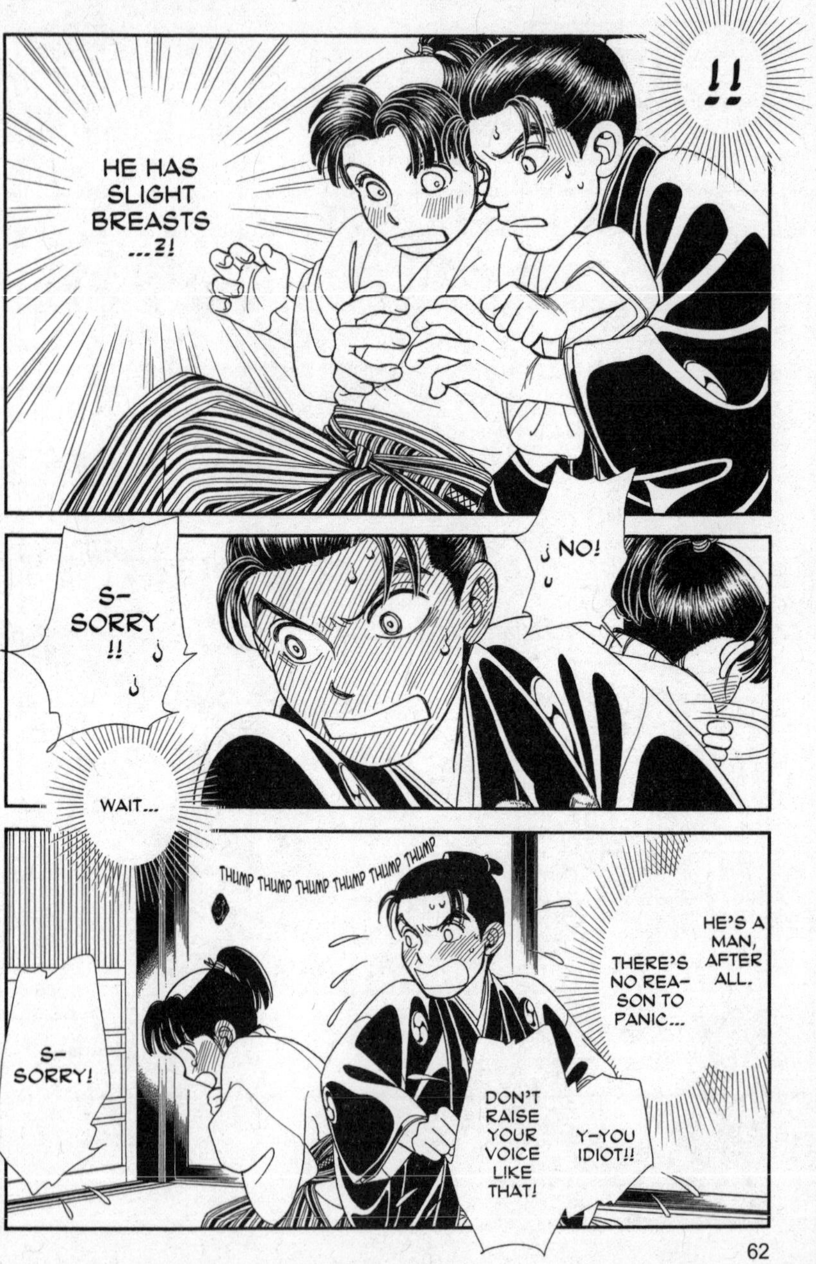
!!
HE HAS SLIGHT BREASTS ...?!
NO!
S-SORRY!!
HE'S A MAN, AFTER ALL.
THERE'S NO REA-SON TO PANIC...
WAIT...
THUMP THUMP THUMP THUMP THUMP THUMP
Y-YOU IDIOT!!
DON'T RAISE YOUR VOICE LIKE THAT!
S-SORRY!

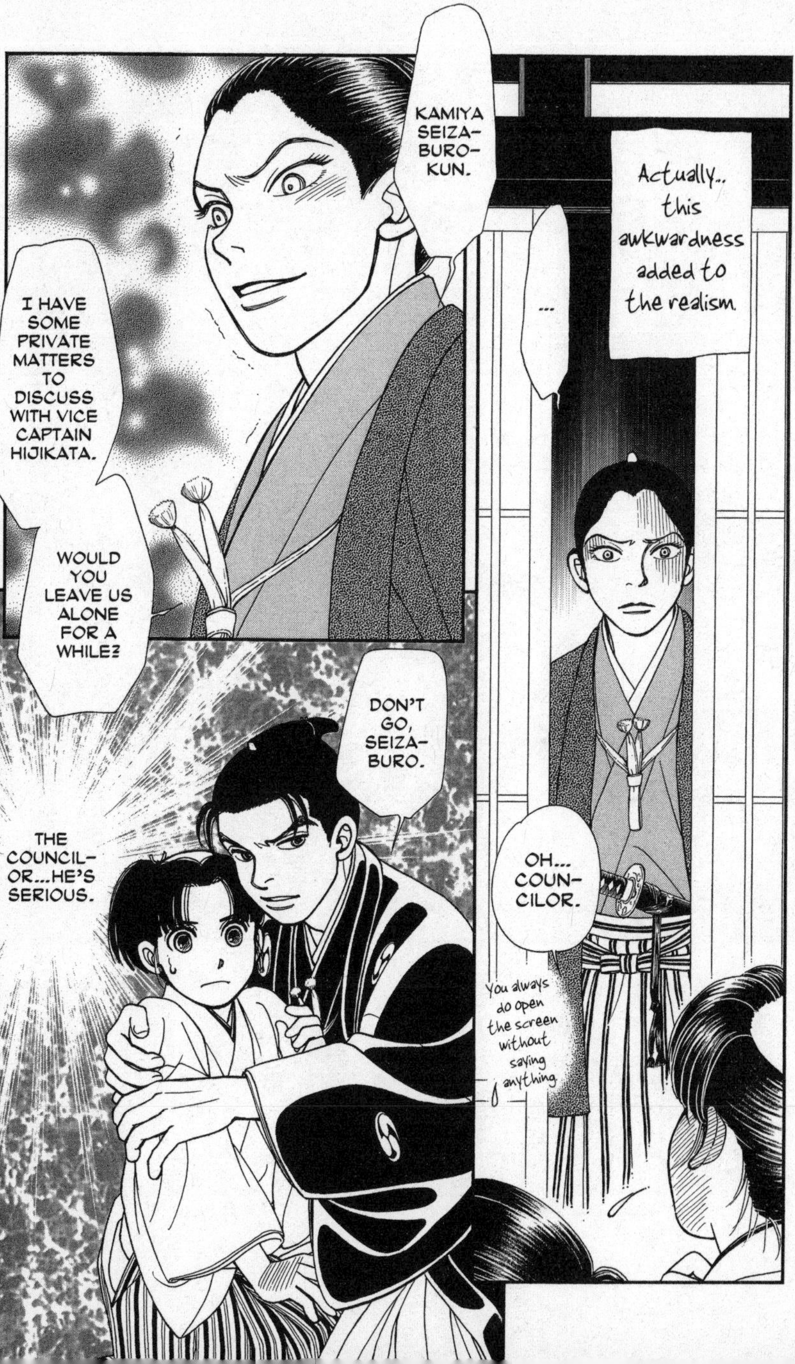
Actually.. this awkwardness added to the realism.
...
OH... COUNCILOR.
You always do open the screen without saying anything.
KAMIYA SEIZABURO-KUN.
I HAVE SOME PRIVATE MATTERS TO DISCUSS WITH VICE CAPTAIN HIJIKATA.
WOULD YOU LEAVE US ALONE FOR A WHILE?
DON'T GO, SEIZABURO.
THE COUNCILOR...HE'S SERIOUS.

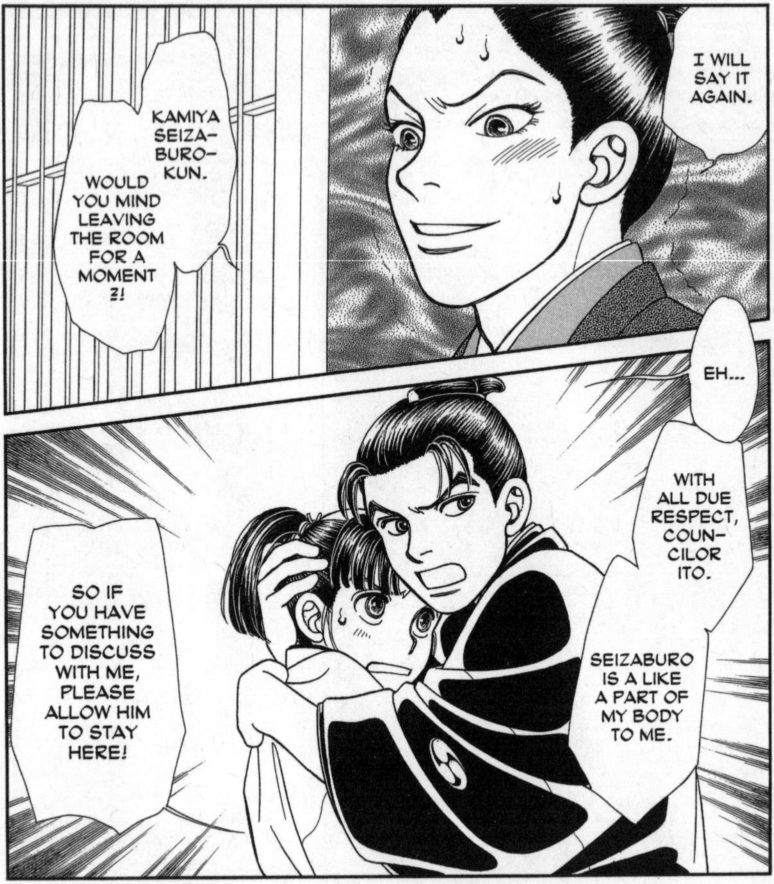
I WILL SAY IT AGAIN.
KAMIYA SEIZABURO-KUN.
WOULD YOU MIND LEAVING THE ROOM FOR A MOMENT?!
EH...
WITH ALL DUE RESPECT, COUNCILOR ITO.
SEIZABURO IS A LIKE A PART OF MY BODY TO ME.
SO IF YOU HAVE SOMETHING TO DISCUSS WITH ME, PLEASE ALLOW HIM TO STAY HERE!

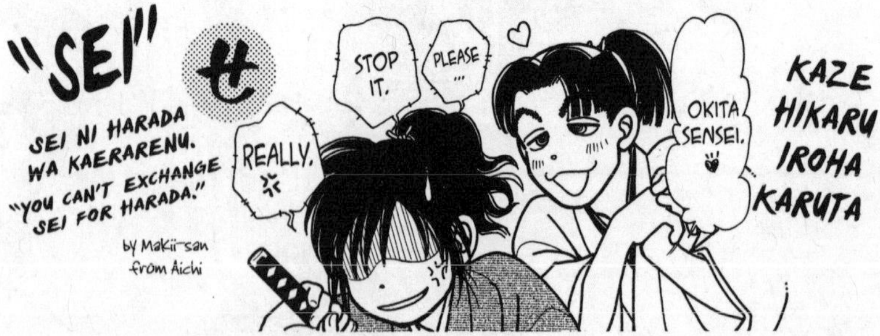
KAZE HIKARU IROHA KARUTA
OKITA SENSEI.
PLEASE...
STOP IT.
REALLY.
"SEI"
せ
SEI NI HARADA WA KAERARENU.
"YOU CAN'T EXCHANGE SEI FOR HARADA."
by Makii-san from Aichi

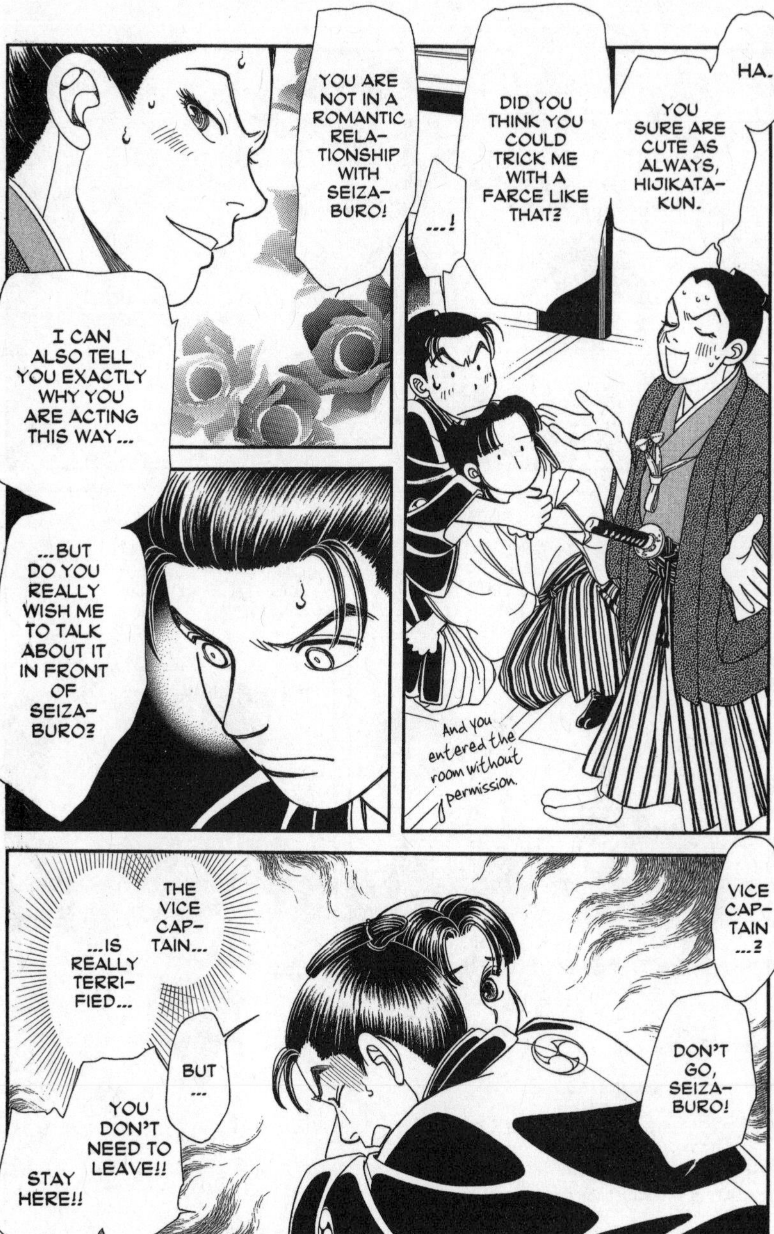
HA.
YOU SURE ARE CUTE AS ALWAYS, HIJIKATA-KUN.
DID YOU THINK YOU COULD TRICK ME WITH A FARCE LIKE THAT?
...!
And you entered the room without permission.
YOU ARE NOT IN A ROMANTIC RELATIONSHIP WITH SEIZABURO!
I CAN ALSO TELL YOU EXACTLY WHY YOU ARE ACTING THIS WAY...
...BUT DO YOU REALLY WISH ME TO TALK ABOUT IT IN FRONT OF SEIZABURO?
VICE CAPTAIN...?
DON'T GO, SEIZABURO!
THE VICE CAPTAIN...
...IS REALLY TERRIFIED...
BUT...
YOU DON'T NEED TO LEAVE!!
STAY HERE!!

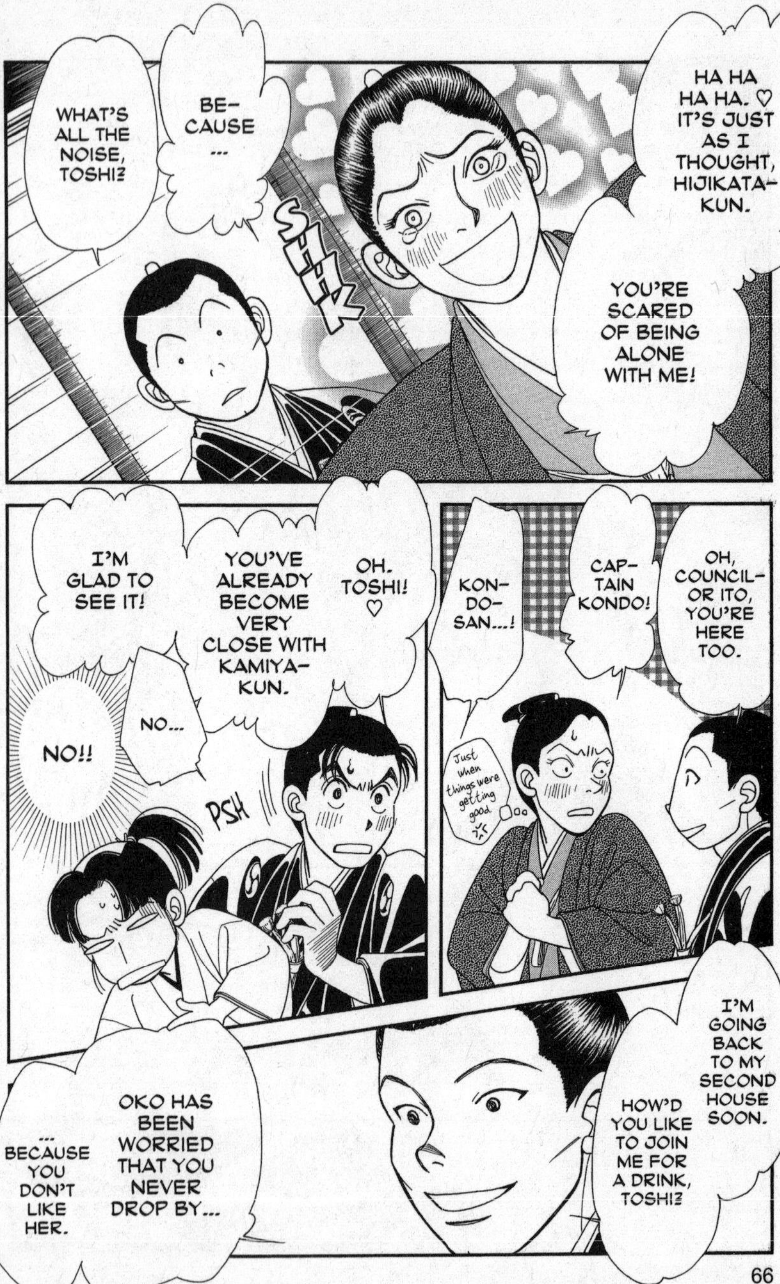
HA HA HA HA. ♡ IT'S JUST AS I THOUGHT, HIJIKATA-KUN.
YOU'RE SCARED OF BEING ALONE WITH ME!
SHHK
BE-CAUSE ...
WHAT'S ALL THE NOISE, TOSHI!?
OH, COUNCIL-OR ITO, YOU'RE HERE TOO.
CAP-TAIN KONDO!
KON-DO-SAN...!
Just when things were getting good
OH. TOSHI! ♡
YOU'VE ALREADY BECOME VERY CLOSE WITH KAMIYA-KUN.
I'M GLAD TO SEE IT!
NO...
PSH
NO!!
I'M GOING BACK TO MY SECOND HOUSE SOON.
HOW'D YOU LIKE TO JOIN ME FOR A DRINK, TOSHI!?
OKO HAS BEEN WORRIED THAT YOU NEVER DROP BY...
... BECAUSE YOU DON'T LIKE HER.

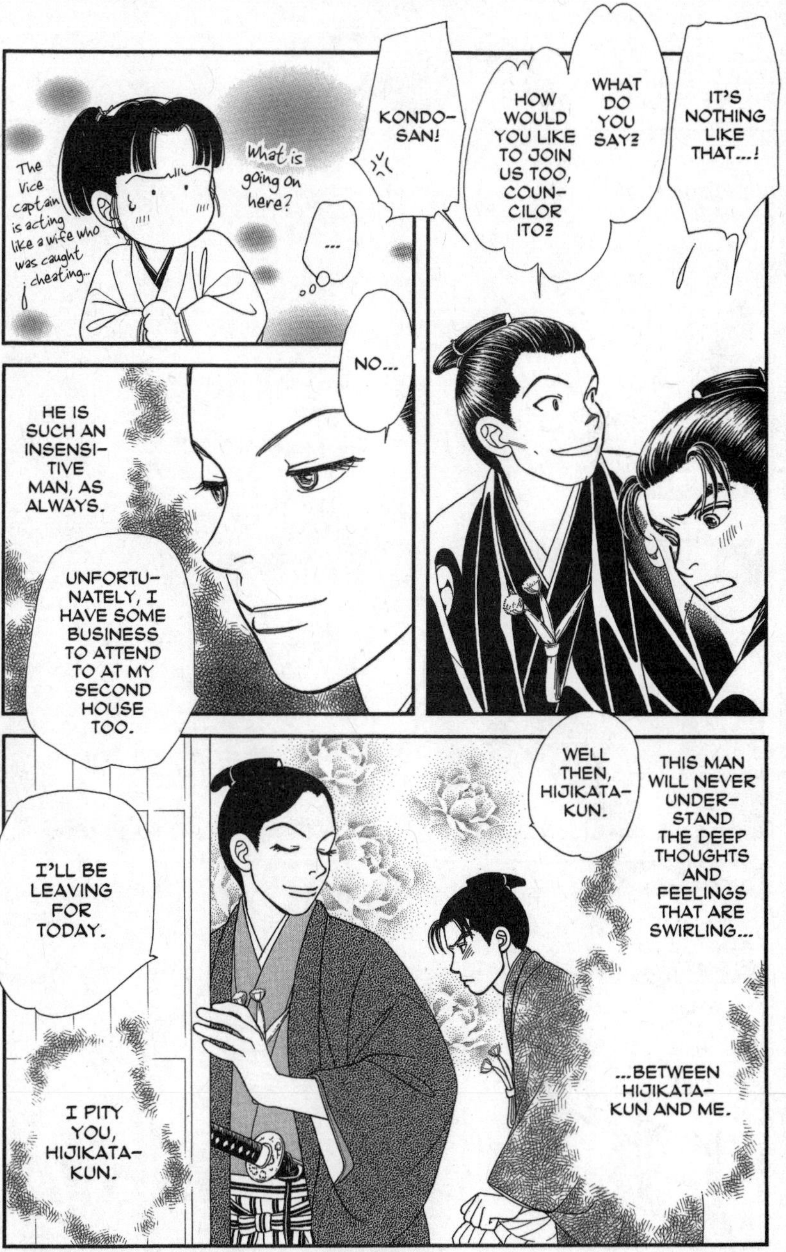
IT'S NOTHING LIKE THAT...!
WHAT DO YOU SAY?
HOW WOULD YOU LIKE TO JOIN US TOO, COUNCILOR ITO?
KONDO-SAN!
What is going on here?
...
The Vice captain is acting like a wife who was caught cheating...
NO...
HE IS SUCH AN INSENSITIVE MAN, AS ALWAYS.
UNFORTUNATELY, I HAVE SOME BUSINESS TO ATTEND TO AT MY SECOND HOUSE TOO.
THIS MAN WILL NEVER UNDERSTAND THE DEEP THOUGHTS AND FEELINGS THAT ARE SWIRLING...
WELL THEN, HIJIKATA-KUN.
I'LL BE LEAVING FOR TODAY.
...BETWEEN HIJIKATA-KUN AND ME.
I PITY YOU, HIJIKATA-KUN.

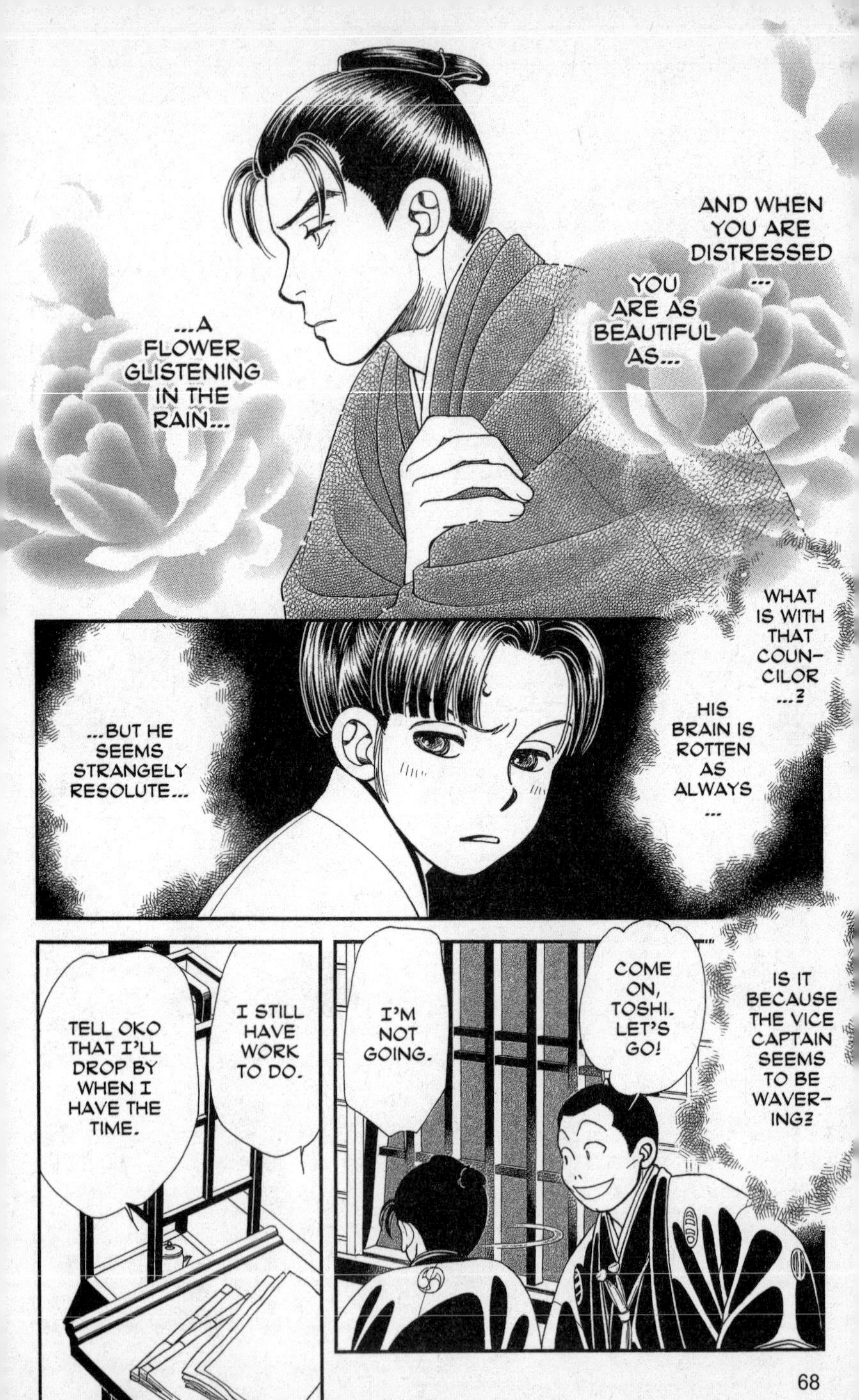
AND WHEN YOU ARE DISTRESSED...
YOU ARE AS BEAUTIFUL AS...
...A FLOWER GLISTENING IN THE RAIN...
WHAT IS WITH THAT COUNCILOR...?
HIS BRAIN IS ROTTEN AS ALWAYS...
...BUT HE SEEMS STRANGELY RESOLUTE...
IS IT BECAUSE THE VICE CAPTAIN SEEMS TO BE WAVERING?
COME ON, TOSHI. LET'S GO!
I'M NOT GOING.
I STILL HAVE WORK TO DO.
TELL OKO THAT I'LL DROP BY WHEN I HAVE THE TIME.

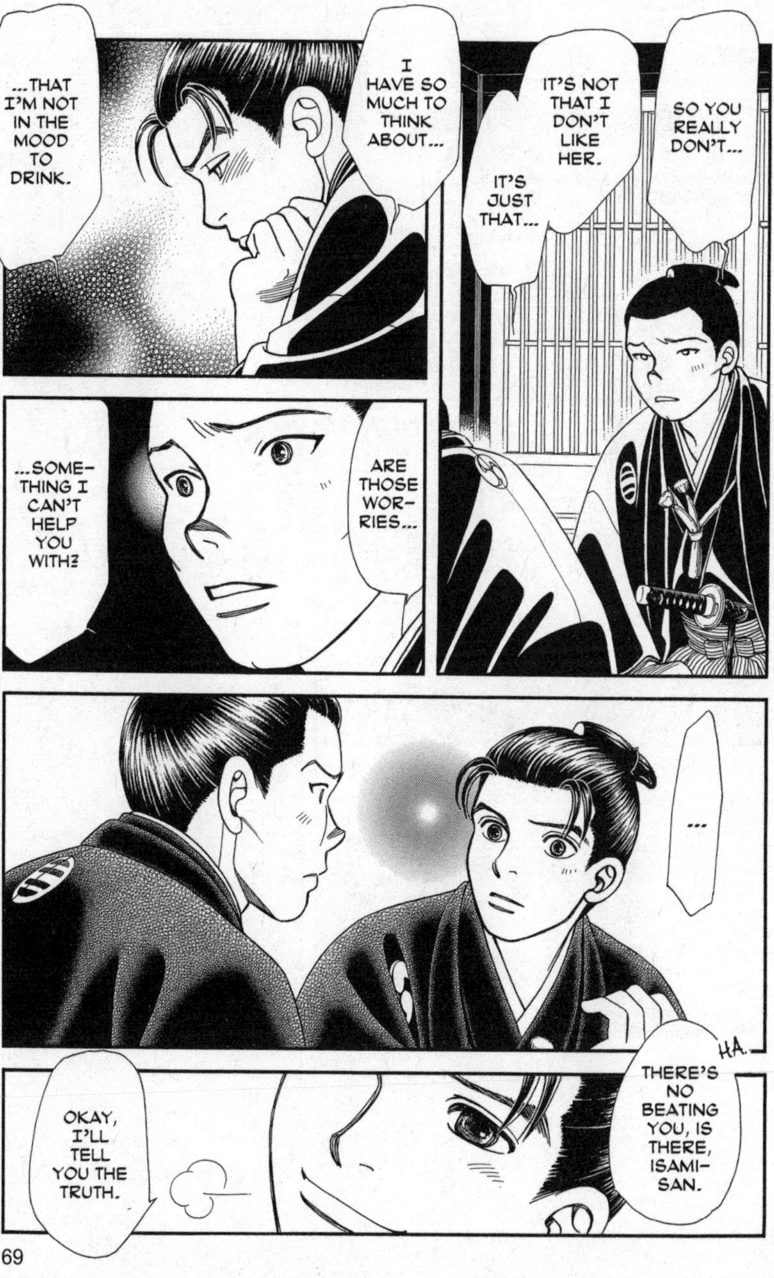
SO YOU REALLY DON'T...
IT'S NOT THAT I DON'T LIKE HER.
IT'S JUST THAT...
I HAVE SO MUCH TO THINK ABOUT...
...THAT I'M NOT IN THE MOOD TO DRINK.
ARE THOSE WORRIES...
...SOMETHING I CAN'T HELP YOU WITH?
...
HA.
THERE'S NO BEATING YOU, IS THERE, ISAMI-SAN.
OKAY, I'LL TELL YOU THE TRUTH.

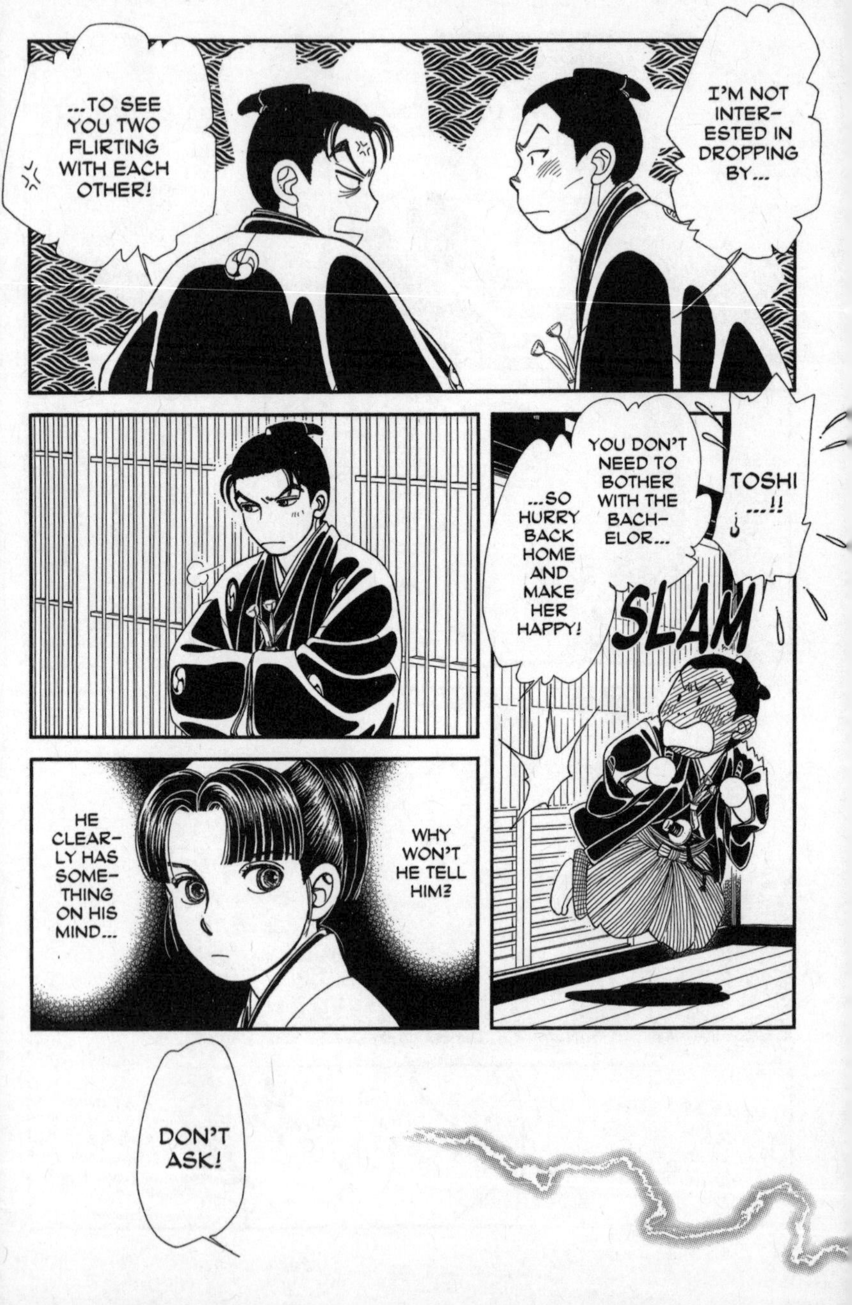
I'M NOT INTERESTED IN DROPPING BY...
...TO SEE YOU TWO FLIRTING WITH EACH OTHER!
YOU DON'T NEED TO BOTHER WITH THE BACHELOR...
...SO HURRY BACK HOME AND MAKE HER HAPPY!
SLAM
TOSHI ...!!
WHY WON'T HE TELL HIM?
HE CLEARLY HAS SOMETHING ON HIS MIND...
DON'T ASK!

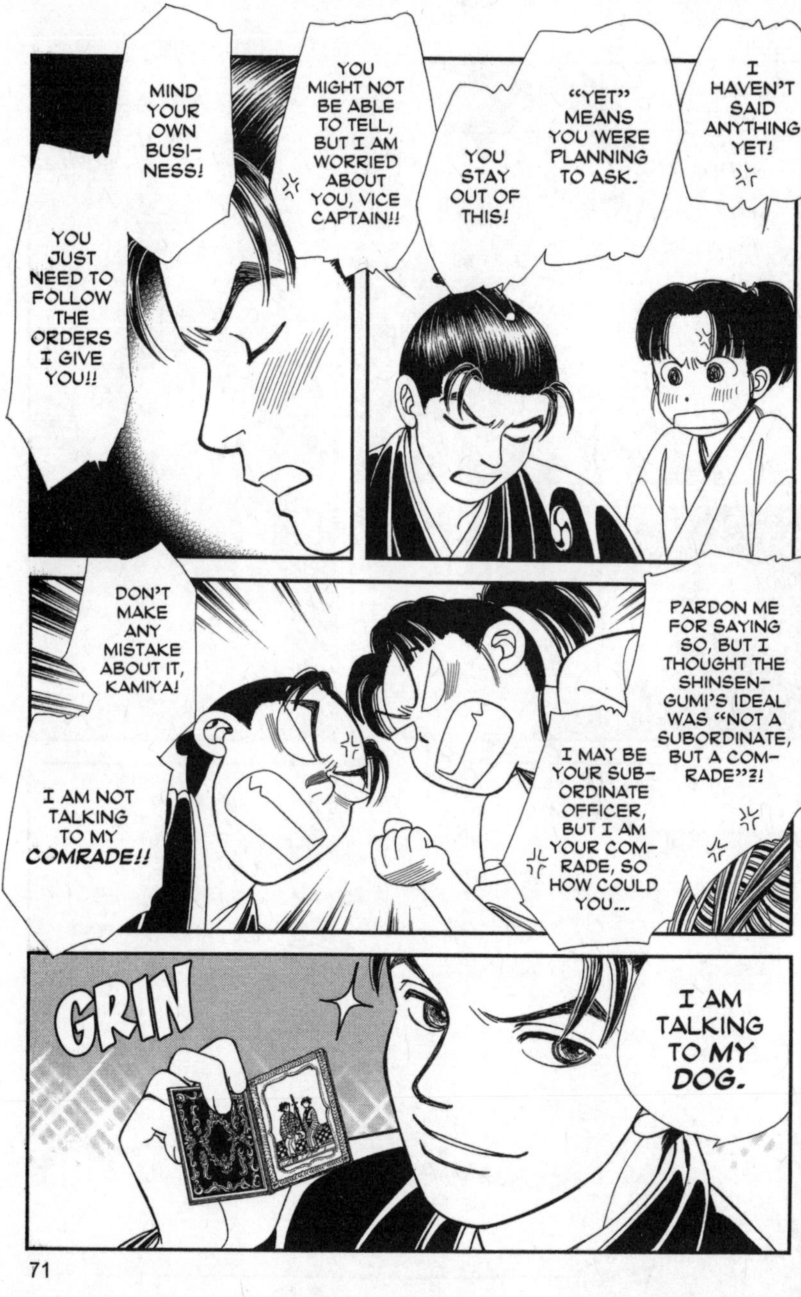
I HAVEN'T SAID ANYTHING YET!
"YET" MEANS YOU WERE PLANNING TO ASK.
YOU STAY OUT OF THIS!
YOU MIGHT NOT BE ABLE TO TELL, BUT I AM WORRIED ABOUT YOU, VICE CAPTAIN!!
MIND YOUR OWN BUSI-NESS!
YOU JUST NEED TO FOLLOW THE ORDERS I GIVE YOU!!
PARDON ME FOR SAYING SO, BUT I THOUGHT THE SHINSEN-GUMI'S IDEAL WAS "NOT A SUBORDINATE, BUT A COM-RADE"?!
I MAY BE YOUR SUB-ORDINATE OFFICER, BUT I AM YOUR COM-RADE, SO HOW COULD YOU...
DON'T MAKE ANY MISTAKE ABOUT IT, KAMIYA!
I AM NOT TALKING TO MY ***COMRADE!!***
I AM TALKING TO ***MY DOG.***
GRIN

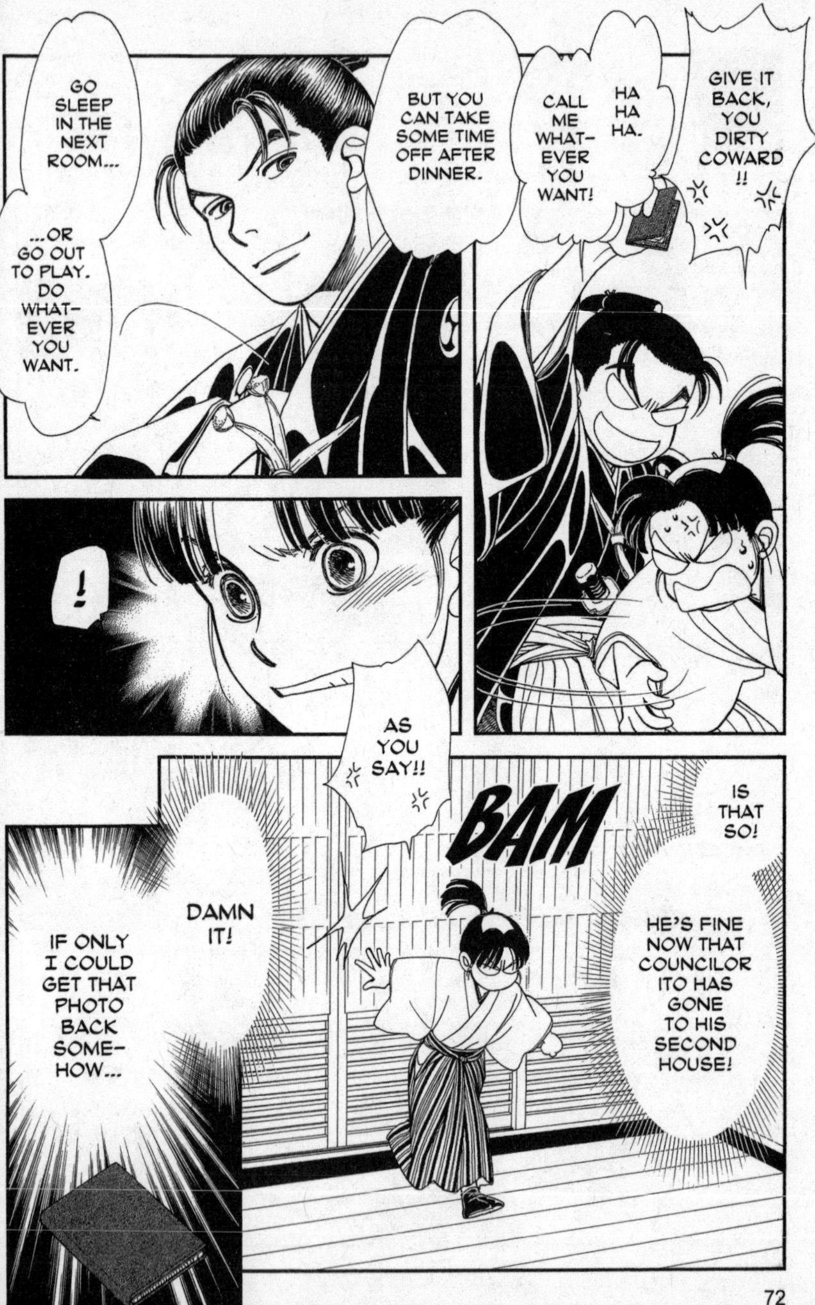
GIVE IT BACK, YOU DIRTY COWARD!!
HA HA HA.
CALL ME WHATEVER YOU WANT!
BUT YOU CAN TAKE SOME TIME OFF AFTER DINNER.
GO SLEEP IN THE NEXT ROOM...
...OR GO OUT TO PLAY. DO WHATEVER YOU WANT.
!
AS YOU SAY!!
BAM
IS THAT SO!
HE'S FINE NOW THAT COUNCILOR ITO HAS GONE TO HIS SECOND HOUSE!
DAMN IT!
IF ONLY I COULD GET THAT PHOTO BACK SOMEHOW...

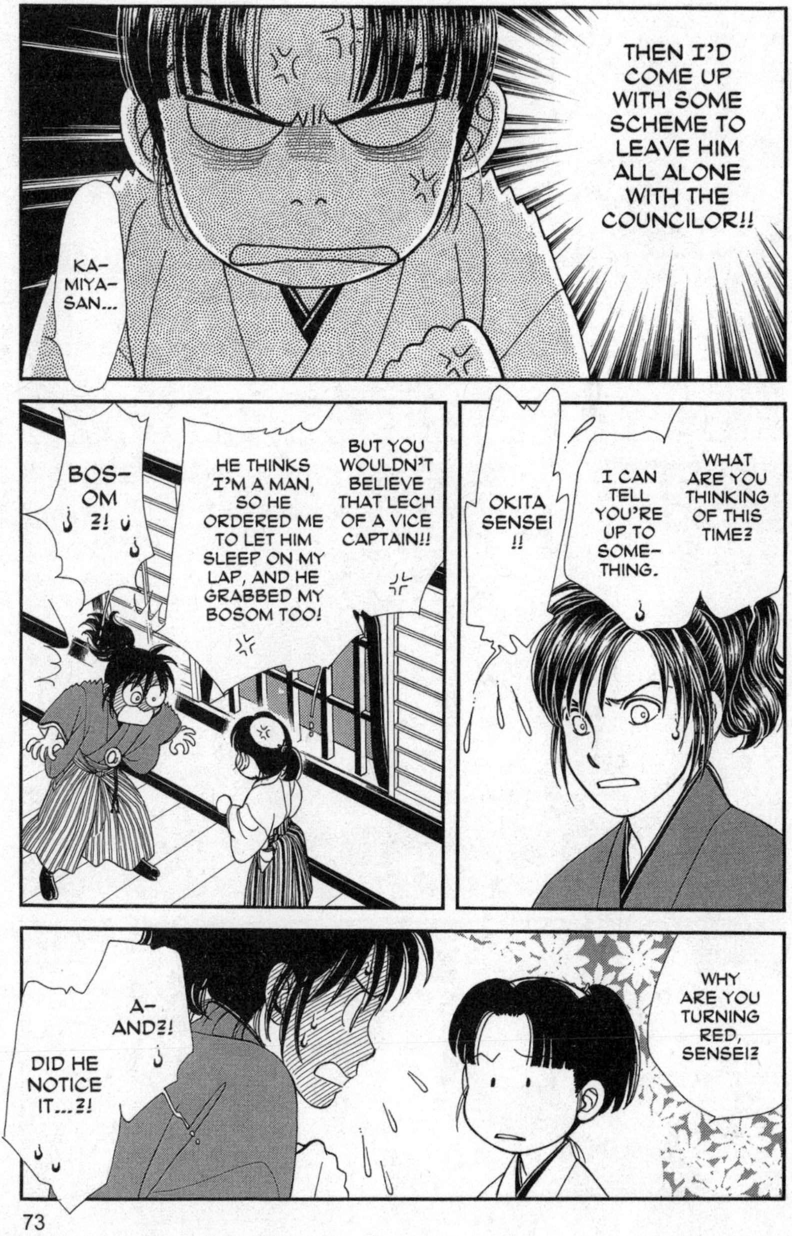
THEN I'D COME UP WITH SOME SCHEME TO LEAVE HIM ALL ALONE WITH THE COUNCILOR!!
KA-MIYA-SAN...
WHAT ARE YOU THINKING OF THIS TIME?
I CAN TELL YOU'RE UP TO SOME-THING.
OKITA SENSEI!!
BUT YOU WOULDN'T BELIEVE THAT LECH OF A VICE CAPTAIN!!
HE THINKS I'M A MAN, SO HE ORDERED ME TO LET HIM SLEEP ON MY LAP, AND HE GRABBED MY BOSOM TOO!
BOS-OM?!
WHY ARE YOU TURNING RED, SENSEI?
A-AND?!
DID HE NOTICE IT...?!

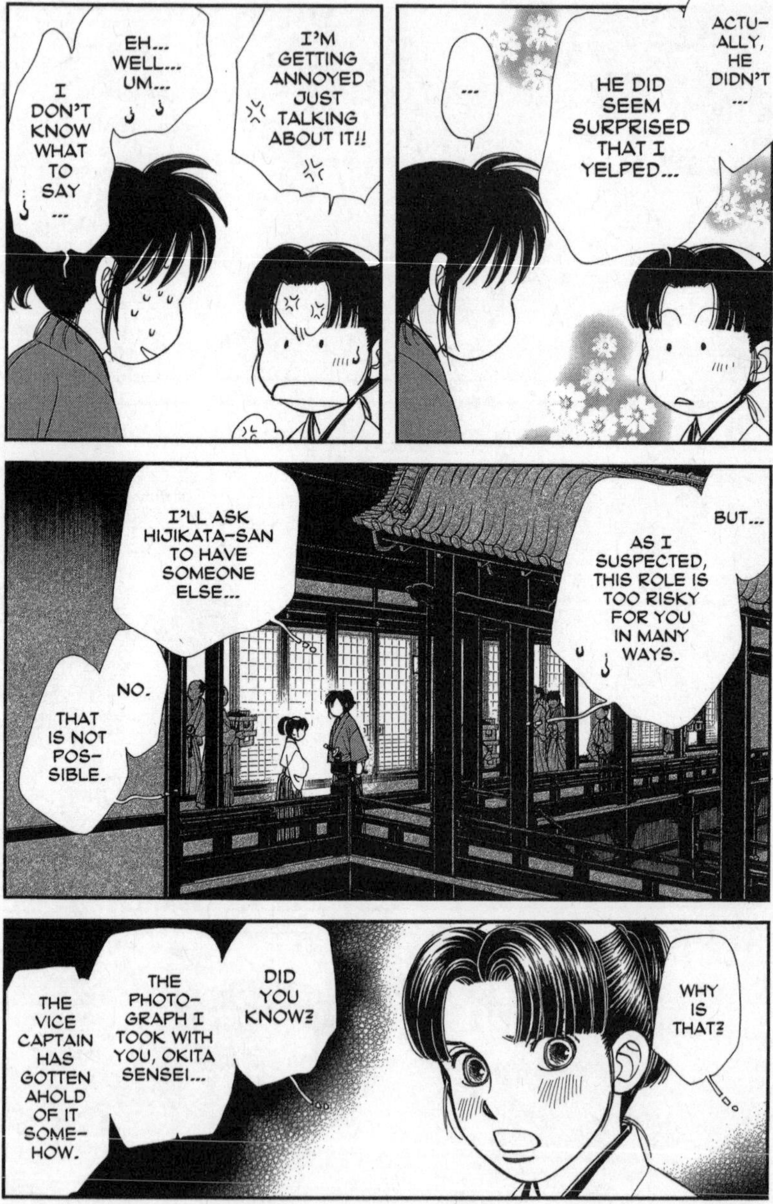
ACTUALLY, HE DIDN'T ...
HE DID SEEM SURPRISED THAT I YELPED...
...
I'M GETTING ANNOYED JUST TALKING ABOUT IT!!
EH... WELL... UM...
I DON'T KNOW WHAT TO SAY ...
BUT...
AS I SUSPECTED, THIS ROLE IS TOO RISKY FOR YOU IN MANY WAYS.
I'LL ASK HIJIKATA-SAN TO HAVE SOMEONE ELSE...
NO.
THAT IS NOT POSSIBLE.
WHY IS THAT?
DID YOU KNOW?
THE PHOTOGRAPH I TOOK WITH YOU, OKITA SENSEI...
THE VICE CAPTAIN HAS GOTTEN AHOLD OF IT SOMEHOW.

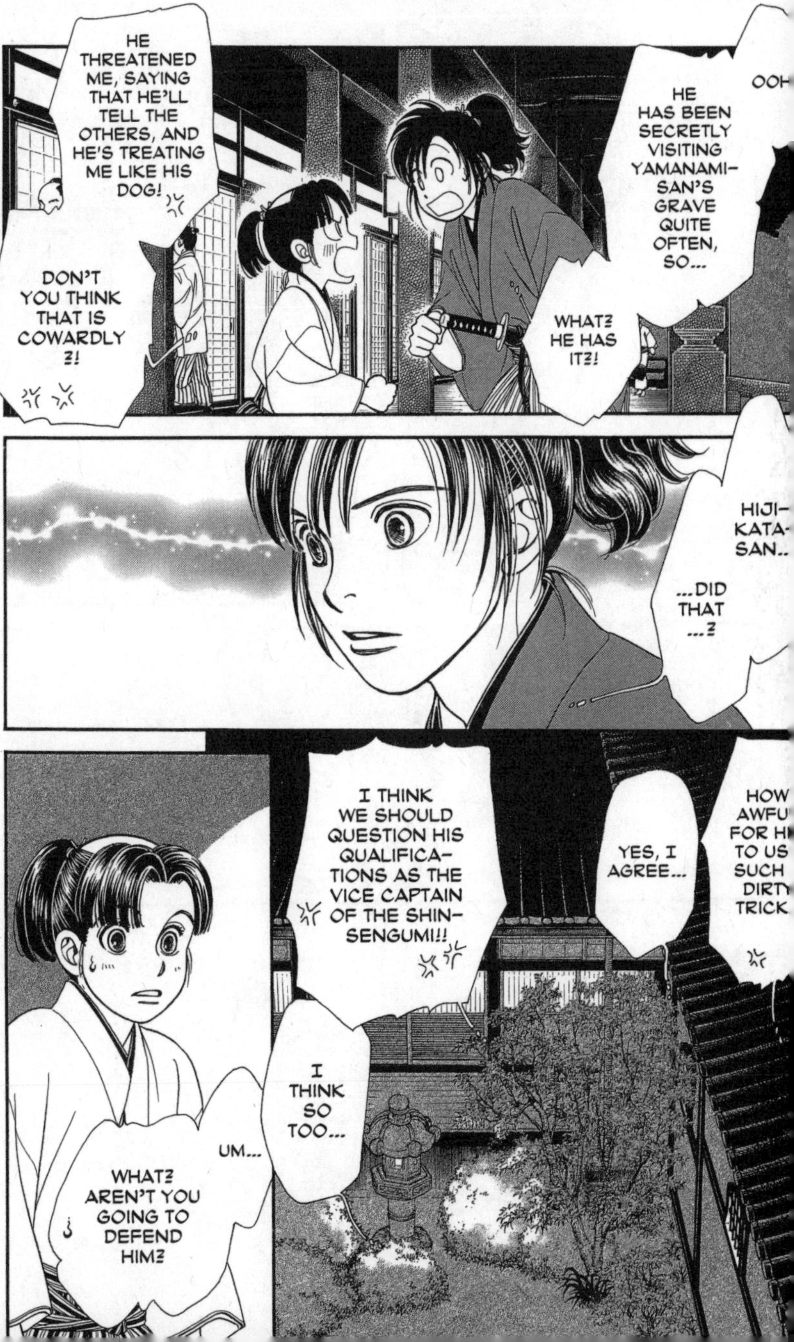
OOH
HE HAS BEEN SECRETLY VISITING YAMANAMI-SAN'S GRAVE QUITE OFTEN, SO...
WHAT? HE HAS IT?!
HE THREATENED ME, SAYING THAT HE'LL TELL THE OTHERS, AND HE'S TREATING ME LIKE HIS DOG!
DON'T YOU THINK THAT IS COWARDLY?!
HIJI-KATA-SAN...
...DID THAT ...?
HOW AWFU FOR H TO US SUCH DIRT TRICK
YES, I AGREE...
I THINK WE SHOULD QUESTION HIS QUALIFICA-TIONS AS THE VICE CAPTAIN OF THE SHIN-SENGUMI!!
I THINK SO TOO...
UM...
WHAT? AREN'T YOU GOING TO DEFEND HIM?

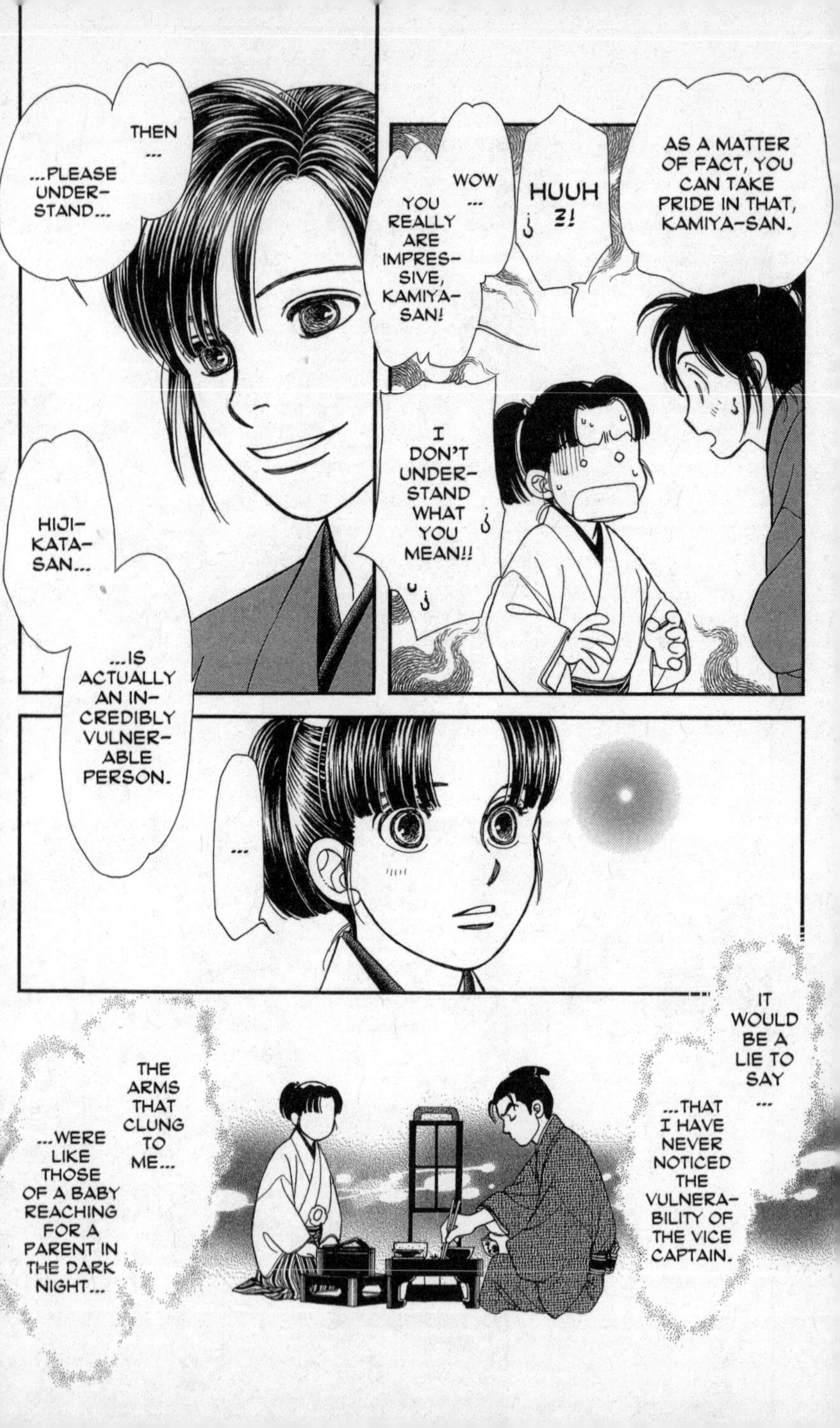
AS A MATTER OF FACT, YOU CAN TAKE PRIDE IN THAT, KAMIYA-SAN.
HUUH ?!
WOW... YOU REALLY ARE IMPRESSIVE, KAMIYA-SAN!
I DON'T UNDERSTAND WHAT YOU MEAN!!
THEN...
...PLEASE UNDERSTAND...
HIJIKATA-SAN...
...IS ACTUALLY AN INCREDIBLY VULNERABLE PERSON.
...
IT WOULD BE A LIE TO SAY...
...THAT I HAVE NEVER NOTICED THE VULNERABILITY OF THE VICE CAPTAIN.
THE ARMS THAT CLUNG TO ME...
...WERE LIKE THOSE OF A BABY REACHING FOR A PARENT IN THE DARK NIGHT...

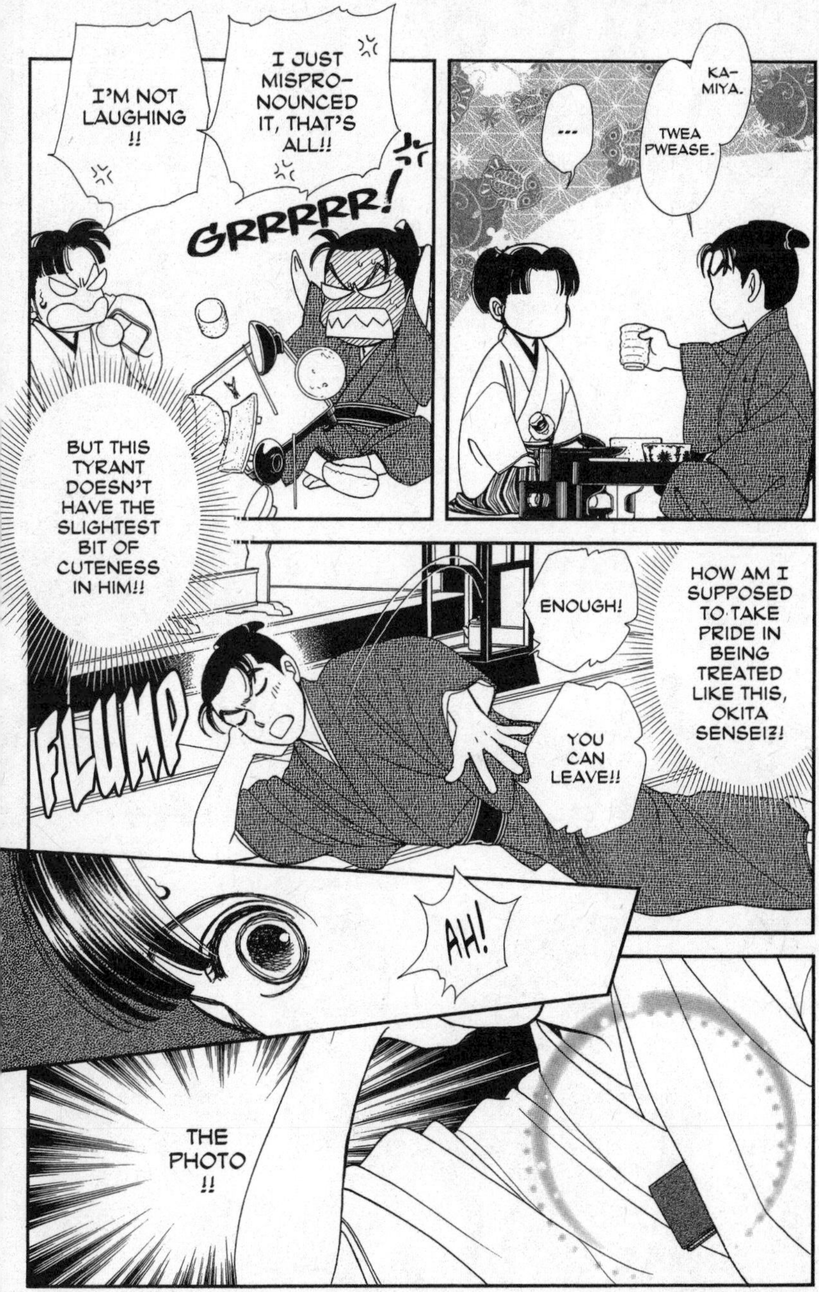
KA-
MIYA.
TWEA PWEASE.
...
I JUST MISPRO-NOUNCED IT, THAT'S ALL!!
I'M NOT LAUGHING !!
GRRRRR!
BUT THIS TYRANT DOESN'T HAVE THE SLIGHTEST BIT OF CUTENESS IN HIM!!
HOW AM I SUPPOSED TO TAKE PRIDE IN BEING TREATED LIKE THIS, OKITA SENSEI?!
ENOUGH!
YOU CAN LEAVE!!
FLUMP
AH!
THE PHOTO !!

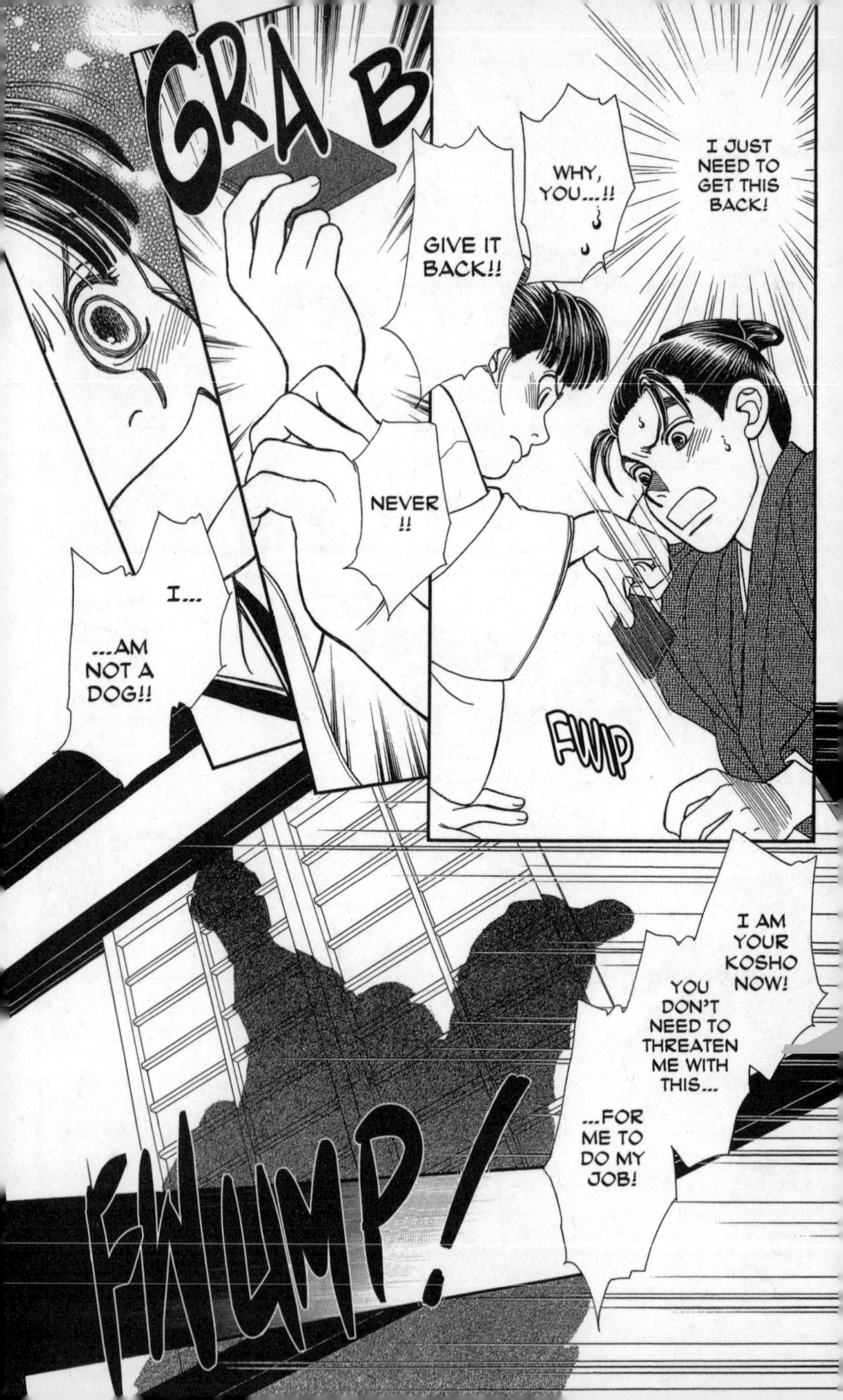
I JUST NEED TO GET THIS BACK!
WHY, YOU...!!
GIVE IT BACK!!
NEVER !!
FWIP
GRAB
I...
...AM NOT A DOG!!
I AM YOUR KOSHO NOW!
YOU DON'T NEED TO THREATEN ME WITH THIS...
...FOR ME TO DO MY JOB!
FWUMP!

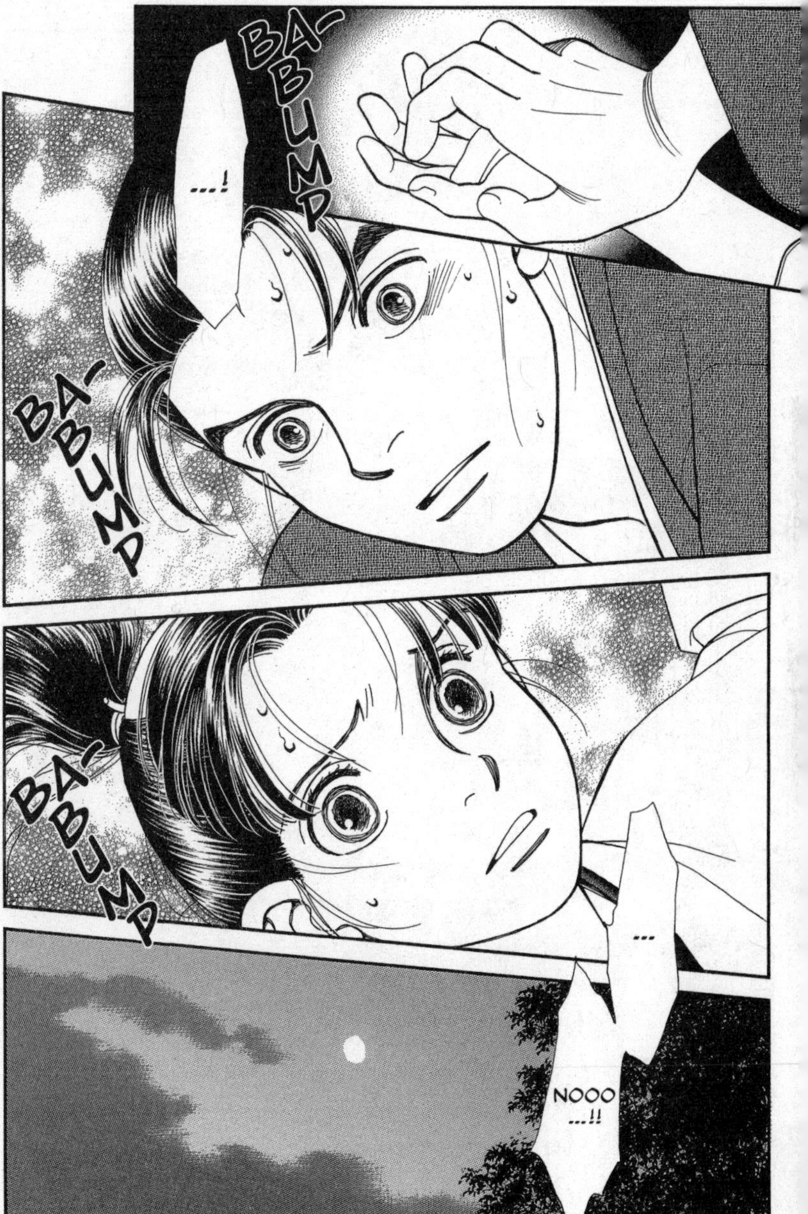
BA-BUMP
...!
BA-BUMP
BA-BUMP
...
NOOO ...!!

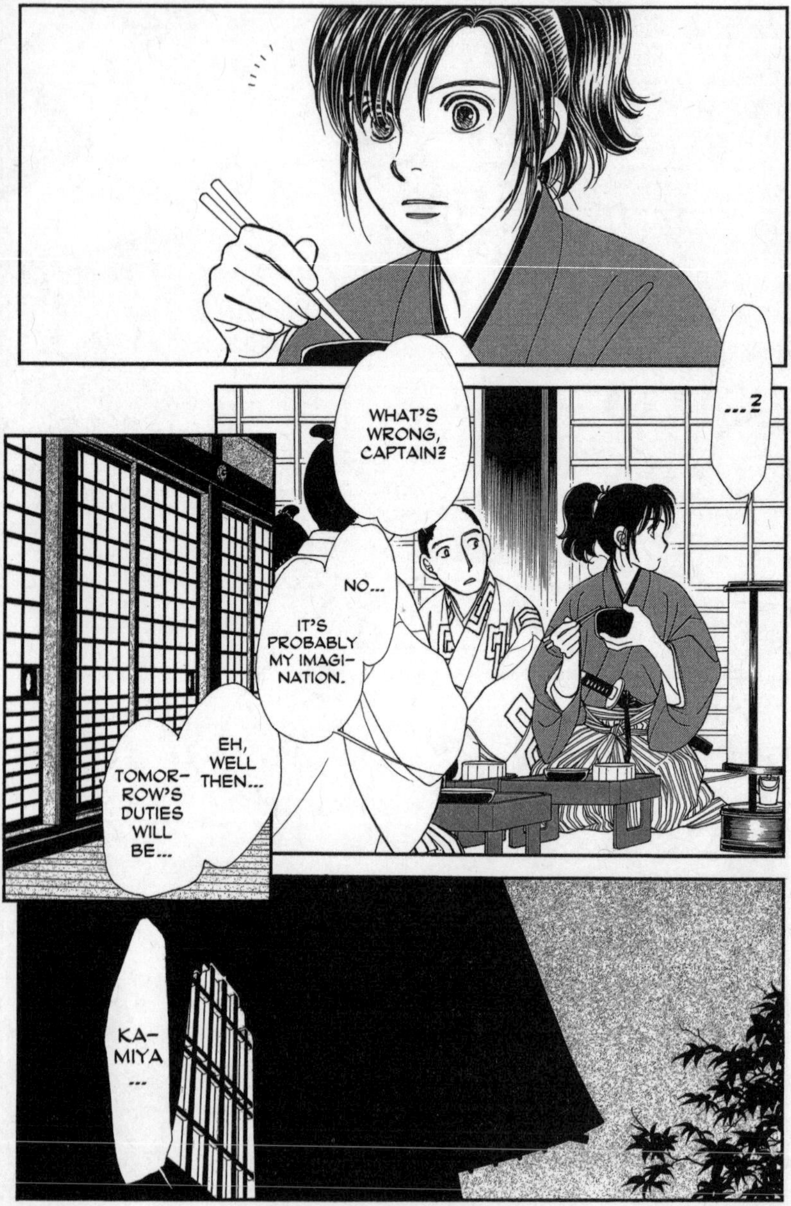
...?
WHAT'S WRONG, CAPTAIN?
NO...
IT'S PROBABLY MY IMAGINATION.
EH, WELL THEN...
TOMORROW'S DUTIES WILL BE...
KAMIYA...

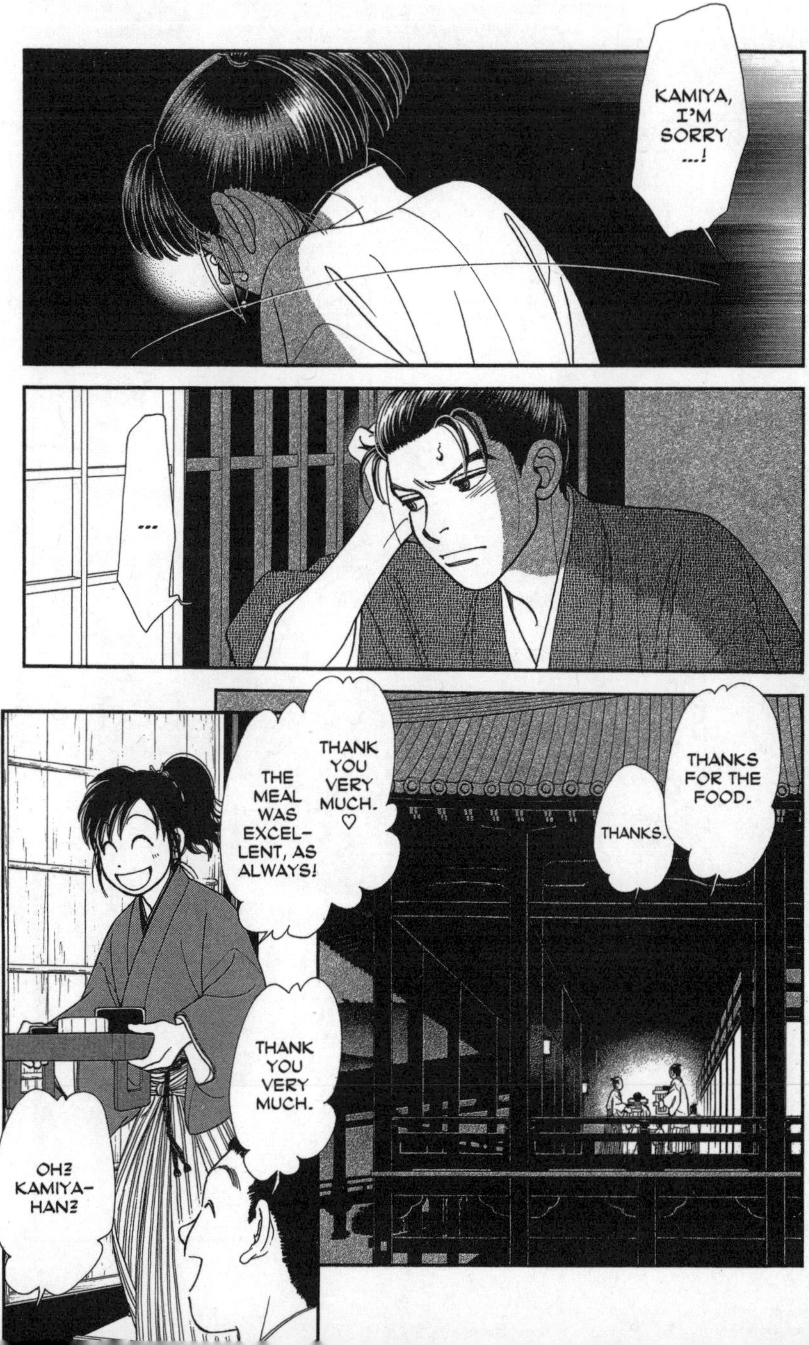

KAMIYA, I'M SORRY ...!
...
THANKS FOR THE FOOD.
THANKS.
THANK YOU VERY MUCH. ♡
THE MEAL WAS EXCEL-LENT, AS ALWAYS!
THANK YOU VERY MUCH.
OH? KAMIYA-HAN?

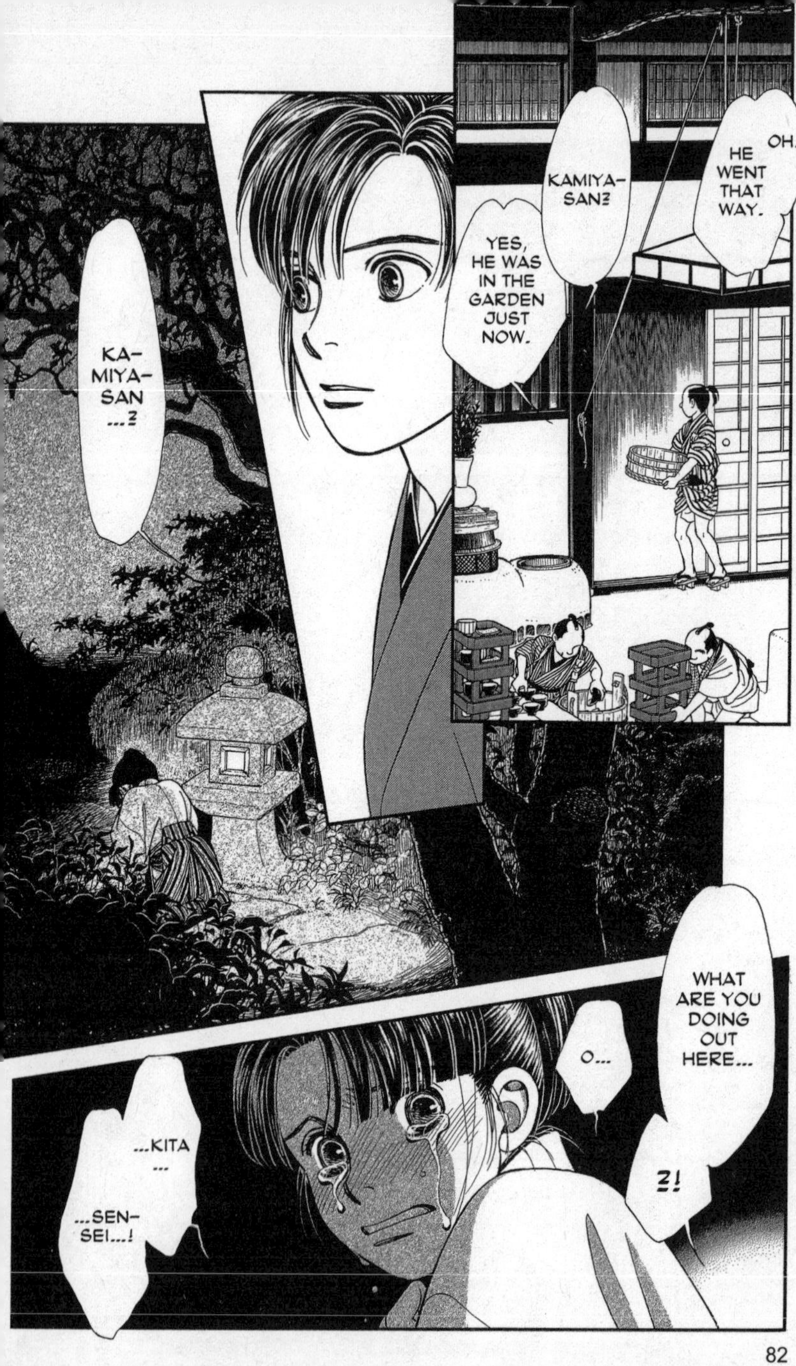
KAMIYA-SAN?
YES, HE WAS IN THE GARDEN JUST NOW.
OH. HE WENT THAT WAY.
KA-MIYA-SAN ...?
WHAT ARE YOU DOING OUT HERE...
O...
?!
...KITA ... ...SEN-SEI...!

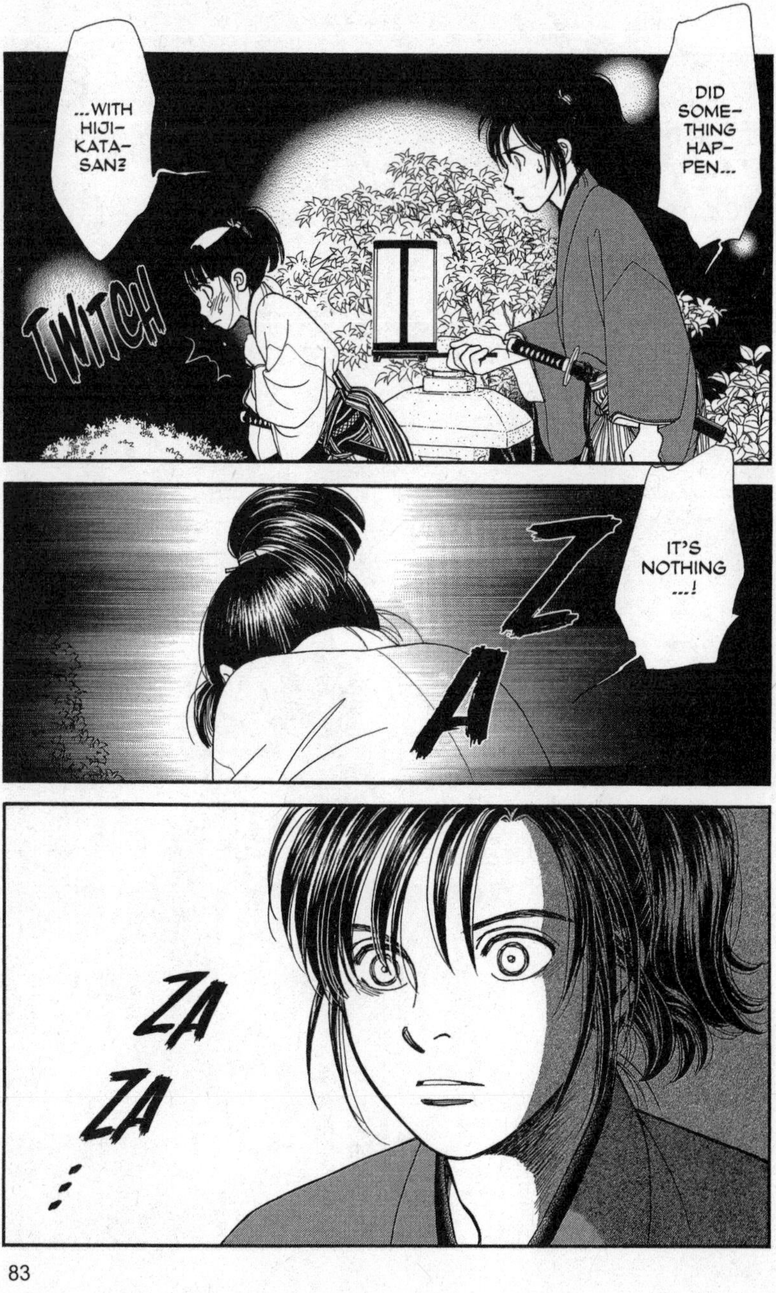
DID SOME-THING HAP-PEN...
...WITH HIJI-KATA-SAN?
TWITCH
IT'S NOTHING ...!
ZA
ZA ZA...

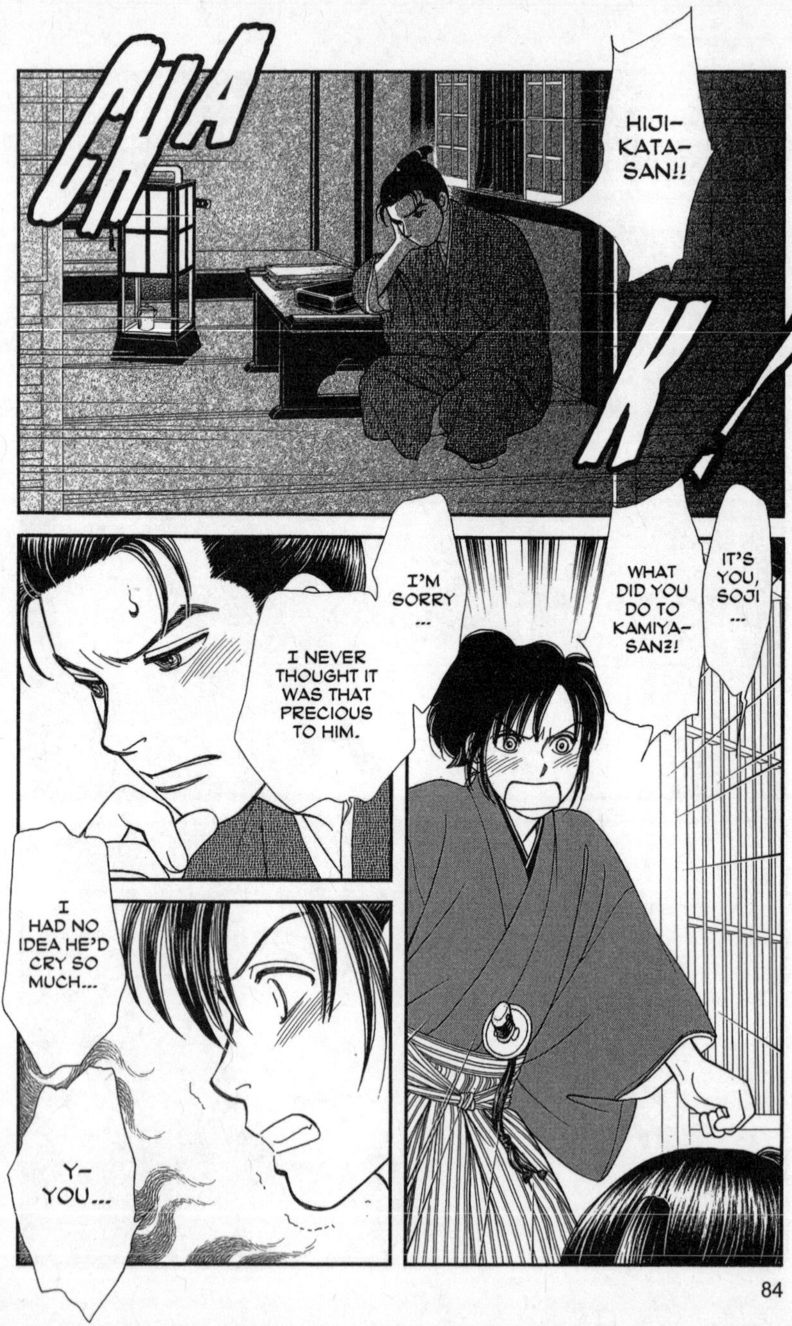
HIJI-KATA-SAN!!
CHIA
K!
IT'S YOU, SOJI...
WHAT DID YOU DO TO KAMIYA-SAN?!
I'M SORRY...
I NEVER THOUGHT IT WAS THAT PRECIOUS TO HIM.
I HAD NO IDEA HE'D CRY SO MUCH...
Y-YOU...

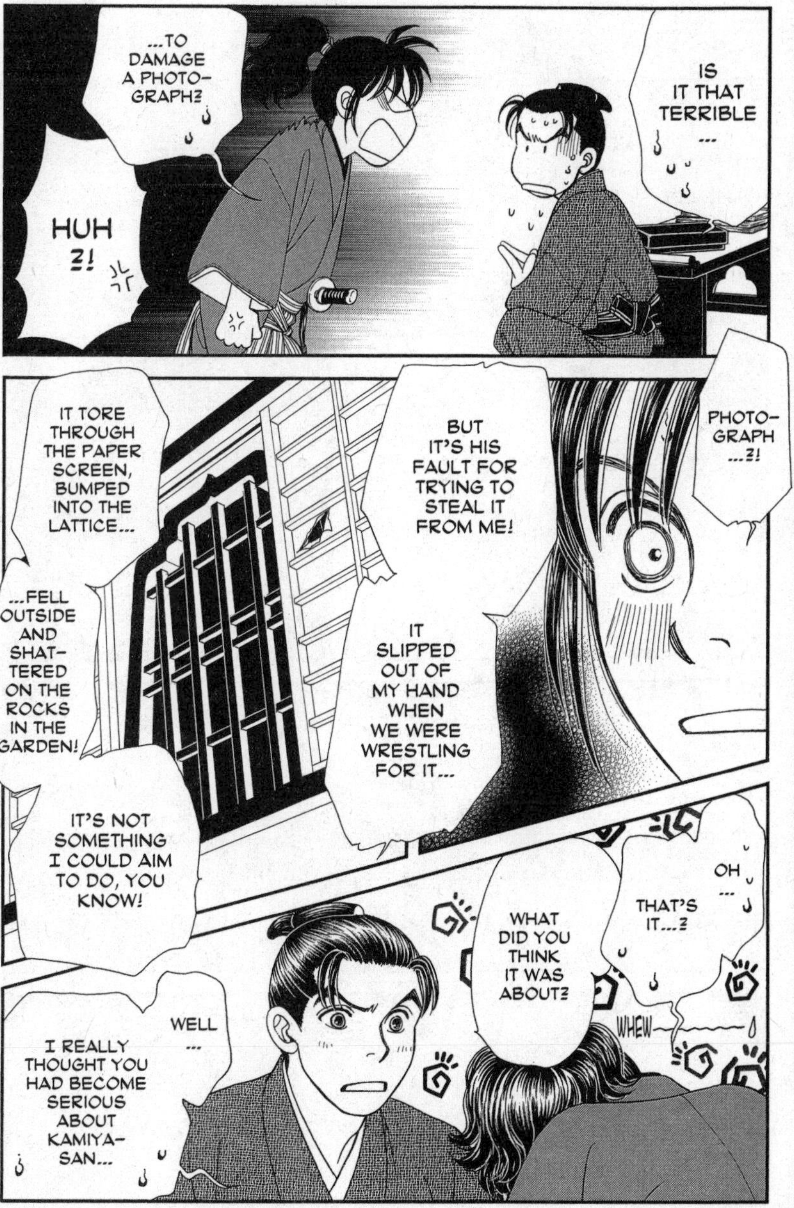

IS IT THAT TERRIBLE...
...TO DAMAGE A PHOTOGRAPH?
HUH?!
PHOTOGRAPH...?!
BUT IT'S HIS FAULT FOR TRYING TO STEAL IT FROM ME!
IT SLIPPED OUT OF MY HAND WHEN WE WERE WRESTLING FOR IT...
IT TORE THROUGH THE PAPER SCREEN, BUMPED INTO THE LATTICE...
...FELL OUTSIDE AND SHATTERED ON THE ROCKS IN THE GARDEN!
IT'S NOT SOMETHING I COULD AIM TO DO, YOU KNOW!
OH...
THAT'S IT...?
WHAT DID YOU THINK IT WAS ABOUT?
WHEW
WELL...
I REALLY THOUGHT YOU HAD BECOME SERIOUS ABOUT KAMIYA-SAN...

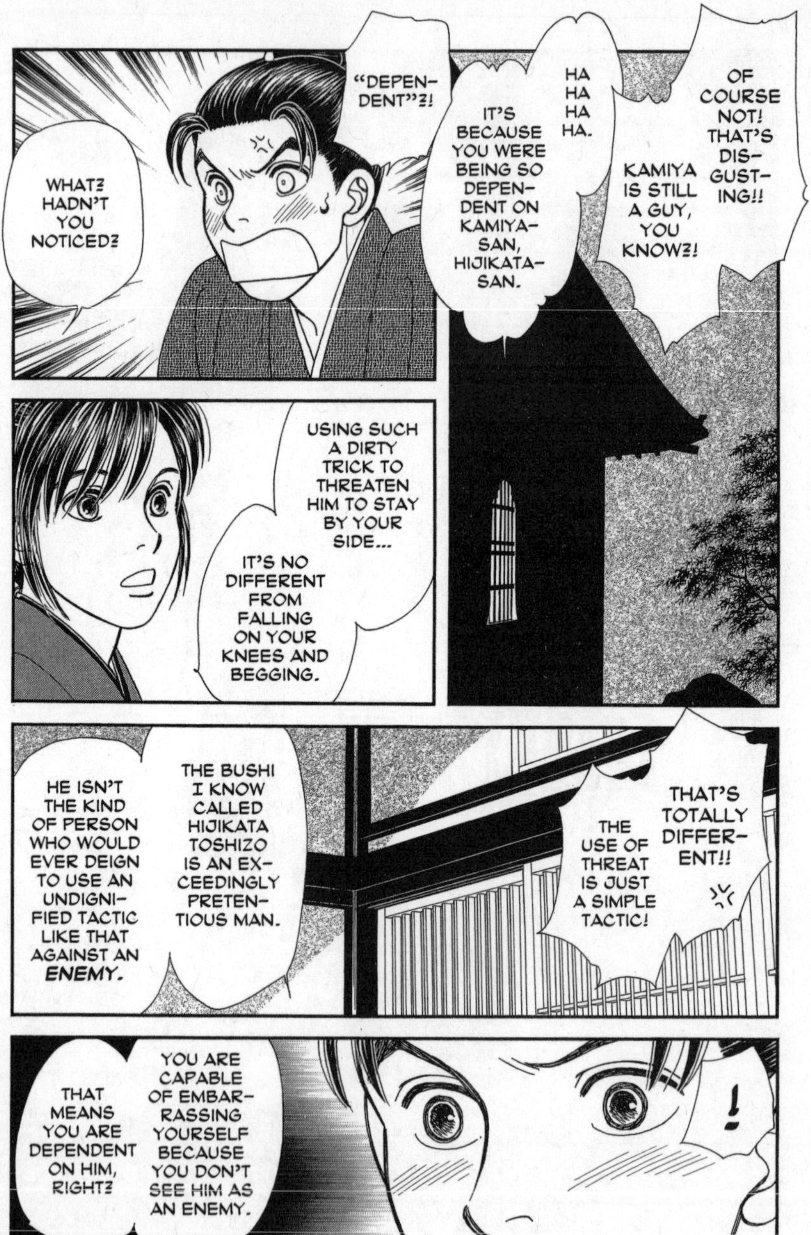
OF COURSE NOT! THAT'S DISGUSTING!!
KAMIYA IS STILL A GUY, YOU KNOW?!
HA HA HA HA.
IT'S BECAUSE YOU WERE BEING SO DEPENDENT ON KAMIYA-SAN, HIJIKATA-SAN.
"DEPENDENT"?!
WHAT? HADN'T YOU NOTICED?
USING SUCH A DIRTY TRICK TO THREATEN HIM TO STAY BY YOUR SIDE...
IT'S NO DIFFERENT FROM FALLING ON YOUR KNEES AND BEGGING.
THAT'S TOTALLY DIFFERENT!!
THE USE OF THREAT IS JUST A SIMPLE TACTIC!
THE BUSHI I KNOW CALLED HIJIKATA TOSHIZO IS AN EXCEEDINGLY PRETENTIOUS MAN.
HE ISN'T THE KIND OF PERSON WHO WOULD EVER DEIGN TO USE AN UNDIGNIFIED TACTIC LIKE THAT AGAINST AN *ENEMY*.
YOU ARE CAPABLE OF EMBARRASSING YOURSELF BECAUSE YOU DON'T SEE HIM AS AN ENEMY.
THAT MEANS YOU ARE DEPENDENT ON HIM, RIGHT?
!

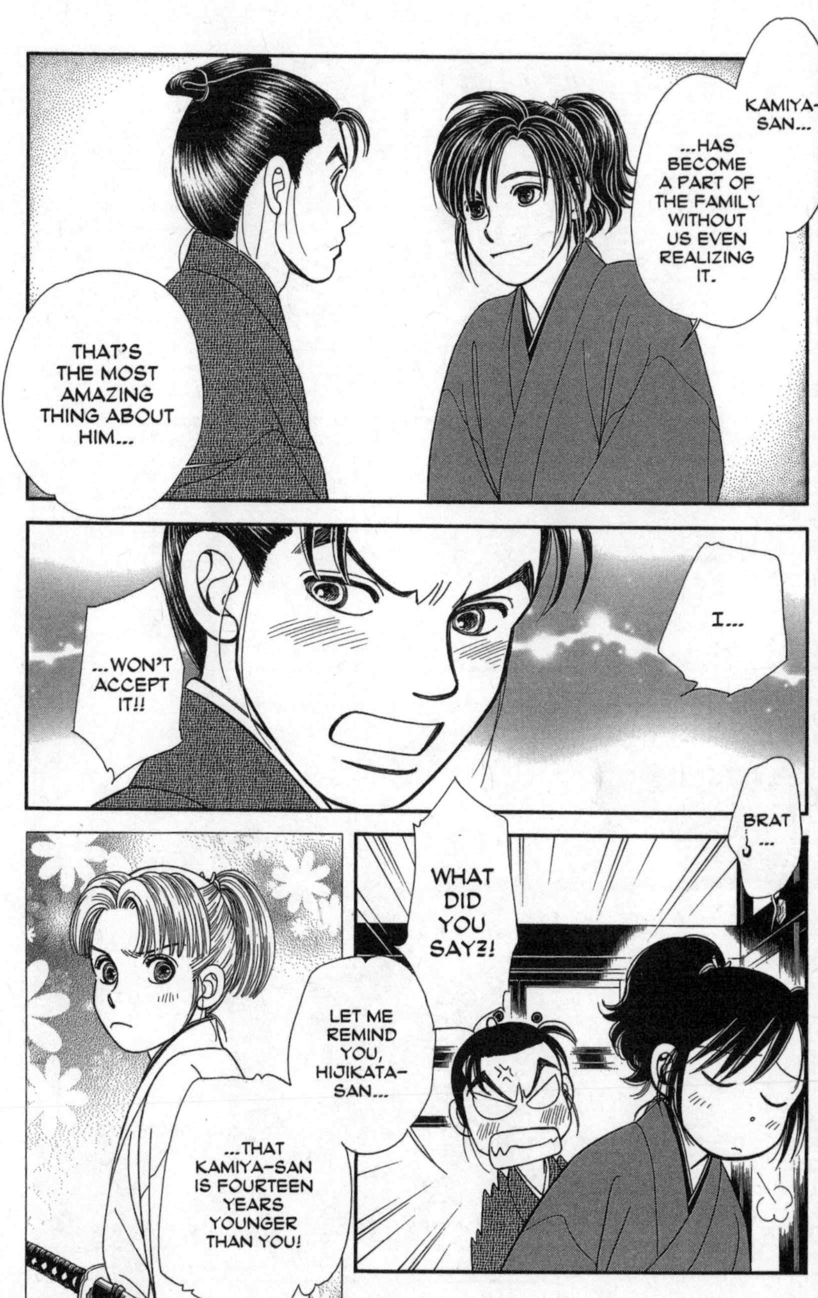
KAMIYA-SAN...
...HAS BECOME A PART OF THE FAMILY WITHOUT US EVEN REALIZING IT.
THAT'S THE MOST AMAZING THING ABOUT HIM...
I...
...WON'T ACCEPT IT!!
BRAT...
WHAT DID YOU SAY?!
LET ME REMIND YOU, HIJIKATA-SAN...
...THAT KAMIYA-SAN IS FOURTEEN YEARS YOUNGER THAN YOU!

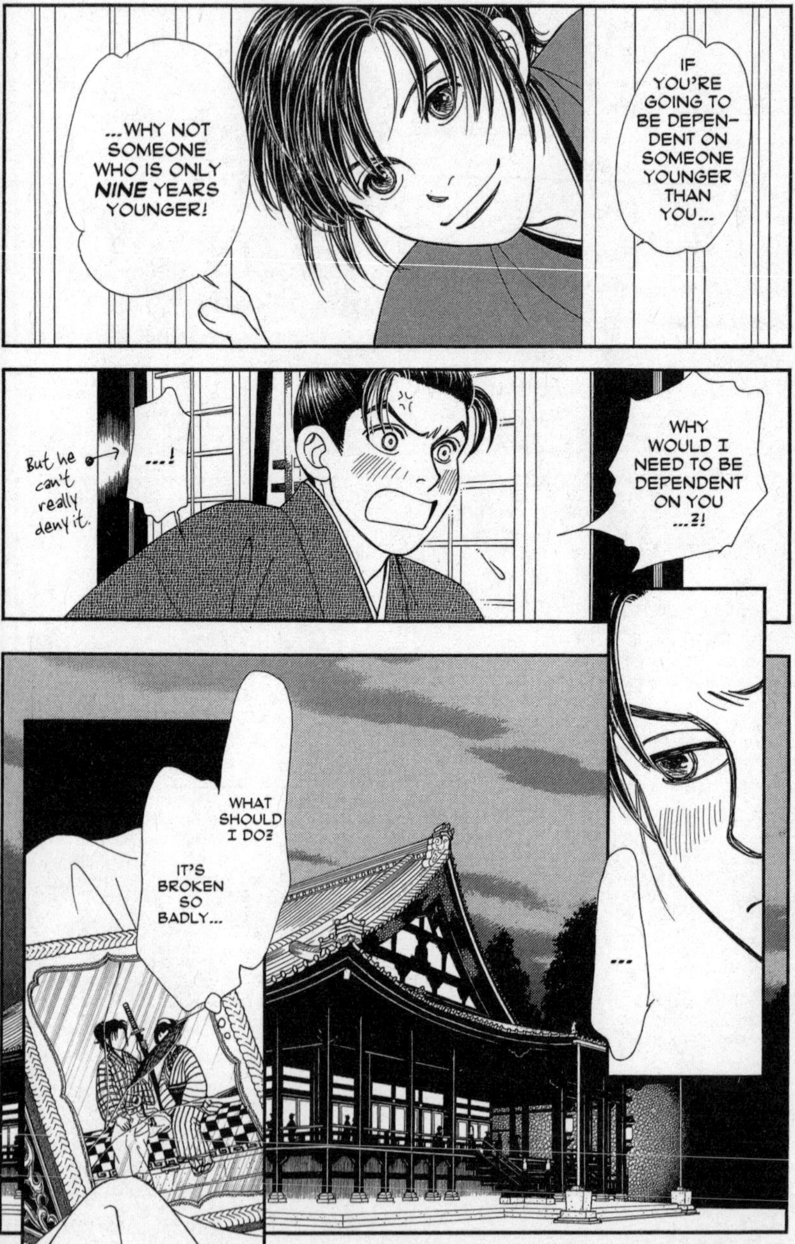
IF YOU'RE GOING TO BE DEPENDENT ON SOMEONE YOUNGER THAN YOU...
...WHY NOT SOMEONE WHO IS ONLY NINE YEARS YOUNGER!
WHY WOULD I NEED TO BE DEPENDENT ON YOU...?!
...!
But he can't really deny it.
...
WHAT SHOULD I DO?
IT'S BROKEN SO BADLY...

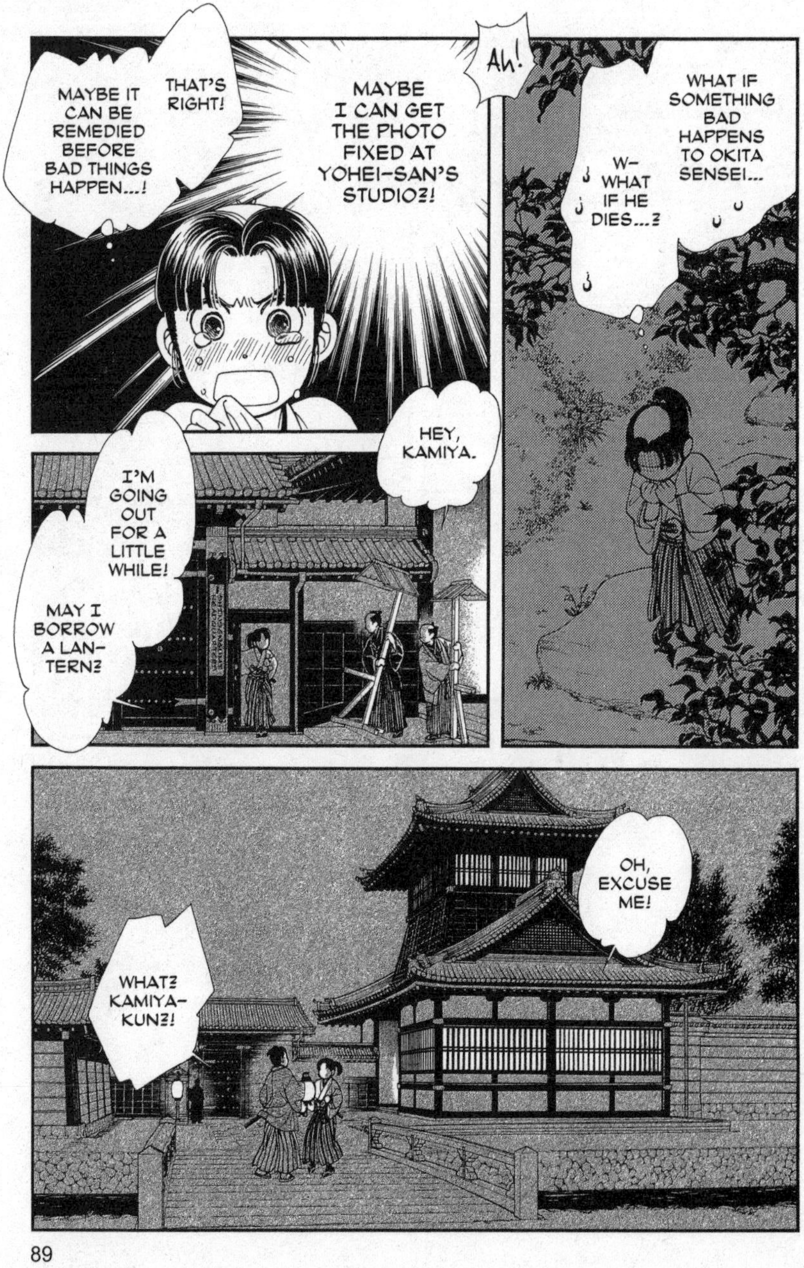
WHAT IF SOMETHING BAD HAPPENS TO OKITA SENSEI...
W-WHAT IF HE DIES...?
Ah!
MAYBE I CAN GET THE PHOTO FIXED AT YOHEI-SAN'S STUDIO?!
THAT'S RIGHT!
MAYBE IT CAN BE REMEDIED BEFORE BAD THINGS HAPPEN...!
HEY, KAMIYA.
I'M GOING OUT FOR A LITTLE WHILE!
MAY I BORROW A LAN-TERN?
OH, EXCUSE ME!
WHAT? KAMIYA-KUN?!

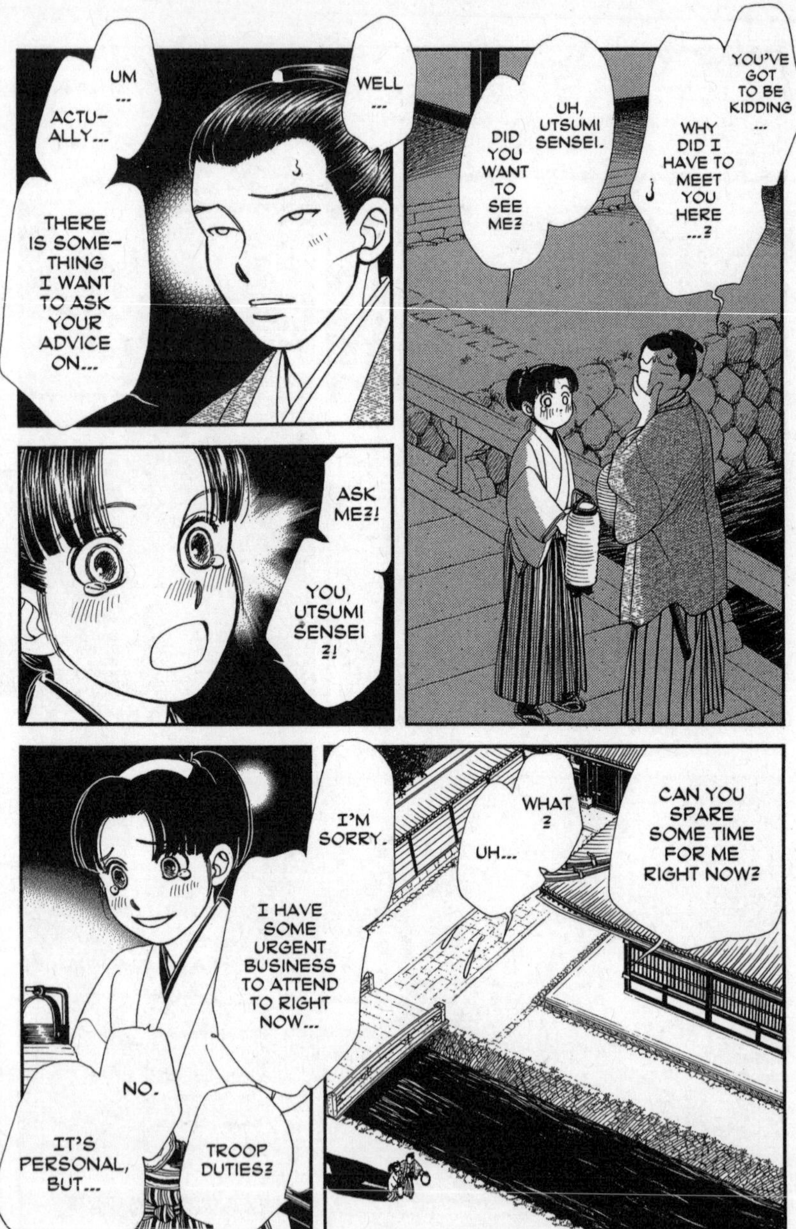
YOU'VE GOT TO BE KIDDING ...
WHY DID I HAVE TO MEET YOU HERE ...?
UH, UTSUMI SENSEI.
DID YOU WANT TO SEE ME?
WELL ...
UM ... ACTU-ALLY...
THERE IS SOME-THING I WANT TO ASK YOUR ADVICE ON...
ASK ME?!
YOU, UTSUMI SENSEI ?!
CAN YOU SPARE SOME TIME FOR ME RIGHT NOW?
WHAT ?
UH...
I'M SORRY.
I HAVE SOME URGENT BUSINESS TO ATTEND TO RIGHT NOW...
TROOP DUTIES?
NO.
IT'S PERSONAL, BUT...

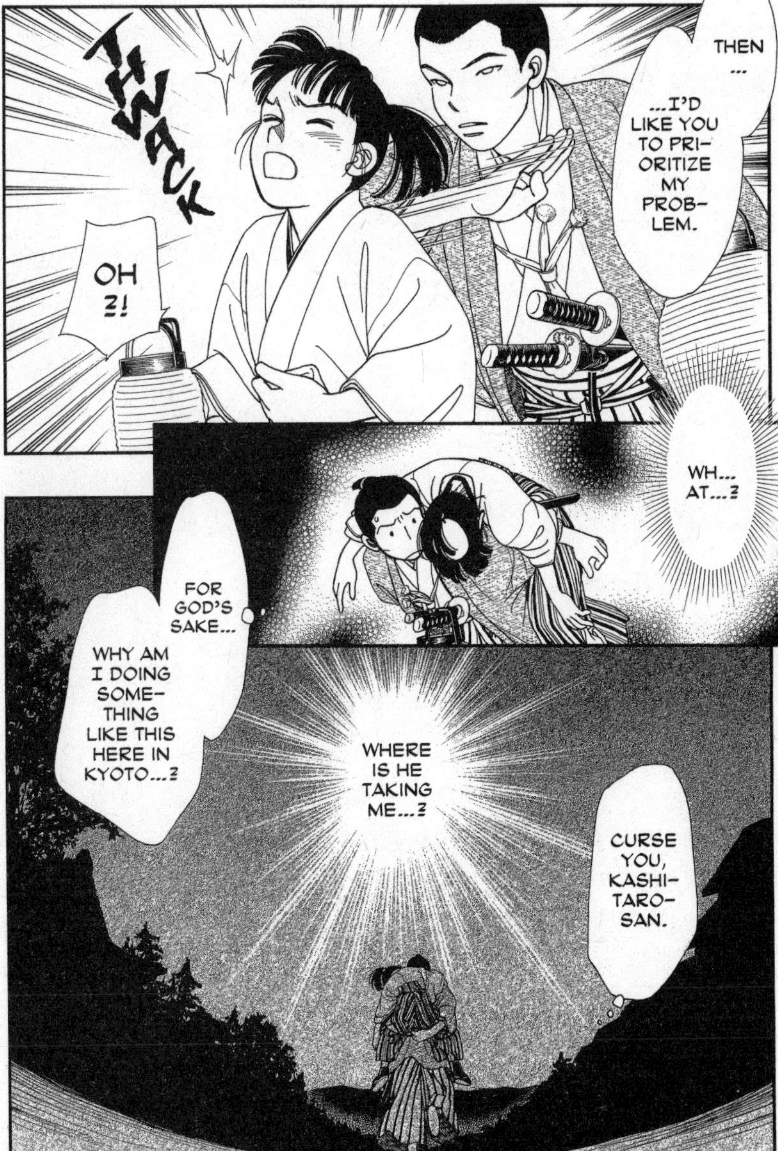
THEN ...
...I'D LIKE YOU TO PRI-ORITIZE MY PROB-LEM.
THWACK
OH ?!
WH... AT...?
FOR GOD'S SAKE...
WHY AM I DOING SOME-THING LIKE THIS HERE IN KYOTO...?
WHERE IS HE TAKING ME...?
CURSE YOU, KASHI-TARO-SAN.

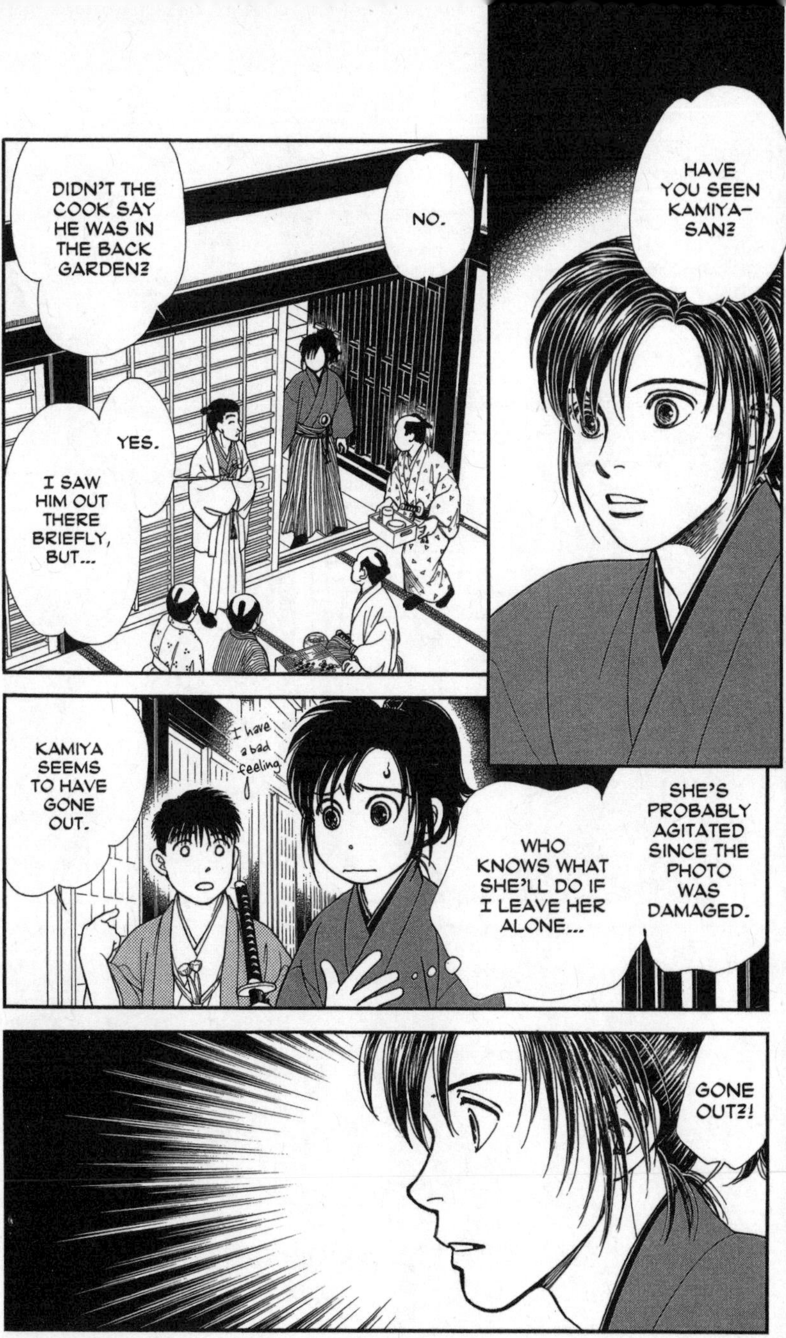
HAVE YOU SEEN KAMIYA-SAN?
NO.
DIDN'T THE COOK SAY HE WAS IN THE BACK GARDEN?
YES.
I SAW HIM OUT THERE BRIEFLY, BUT...
SHE'S PROBABLY AGITATED SINCE THE PHOTO WAS DAMAGED.
WHO KNOWS WHAT SHE'LL DO IF I LEAVE HER ALONE...
KAMIYA SEEMS TO HAVE GONE OUT.
I have a bad feeling
GONE OUT?!

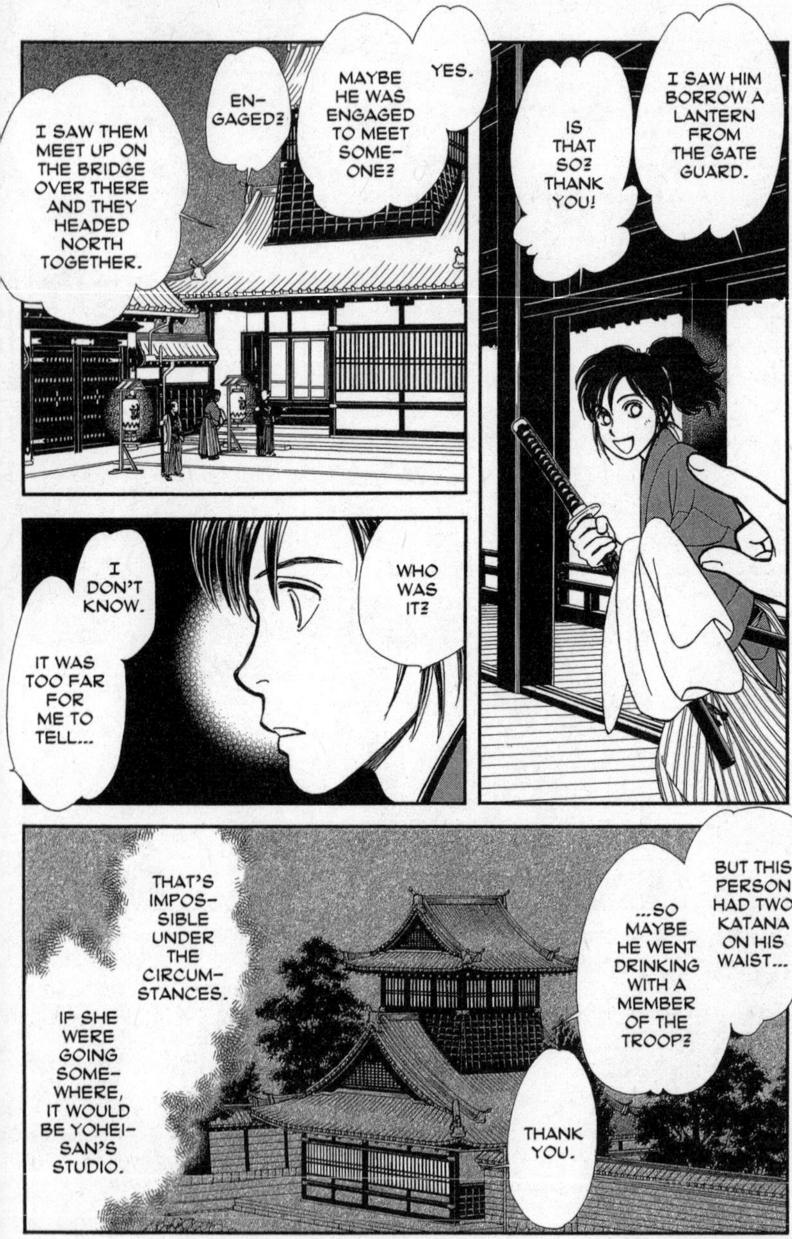

I SAW HIM BORROW A LANTERN FROM THE GATE GUARD.
IS THAT SO? THANK YOU!
YES.
MAYBE HE WAS ENGAGED TO MEET SOME-ONE?
EN-GAGED?
I SAW THEM MEET UP ON THE BRIDGE OVER THERE AND THEY HEADED NORTH TOGETHER.
WHO WAS IT?
I DON'T KNOW.
IT WAS TOO FAR FOR ME TO TELL...
BUT THIS PERSON HAD TWO KATANA ON HIS WAIST...
...SO MAYBE HE WENT DRINKING WITH A MEMBER OF THE TROOP?
THANK YOU.
THAT'S IMPOS-SIBLE UNDER THE CIRCUM-STANCES.
IF SHE WERE GOING SOME-WHERE, IT WOULD BE YOHEI-SAN'S STUDIO.

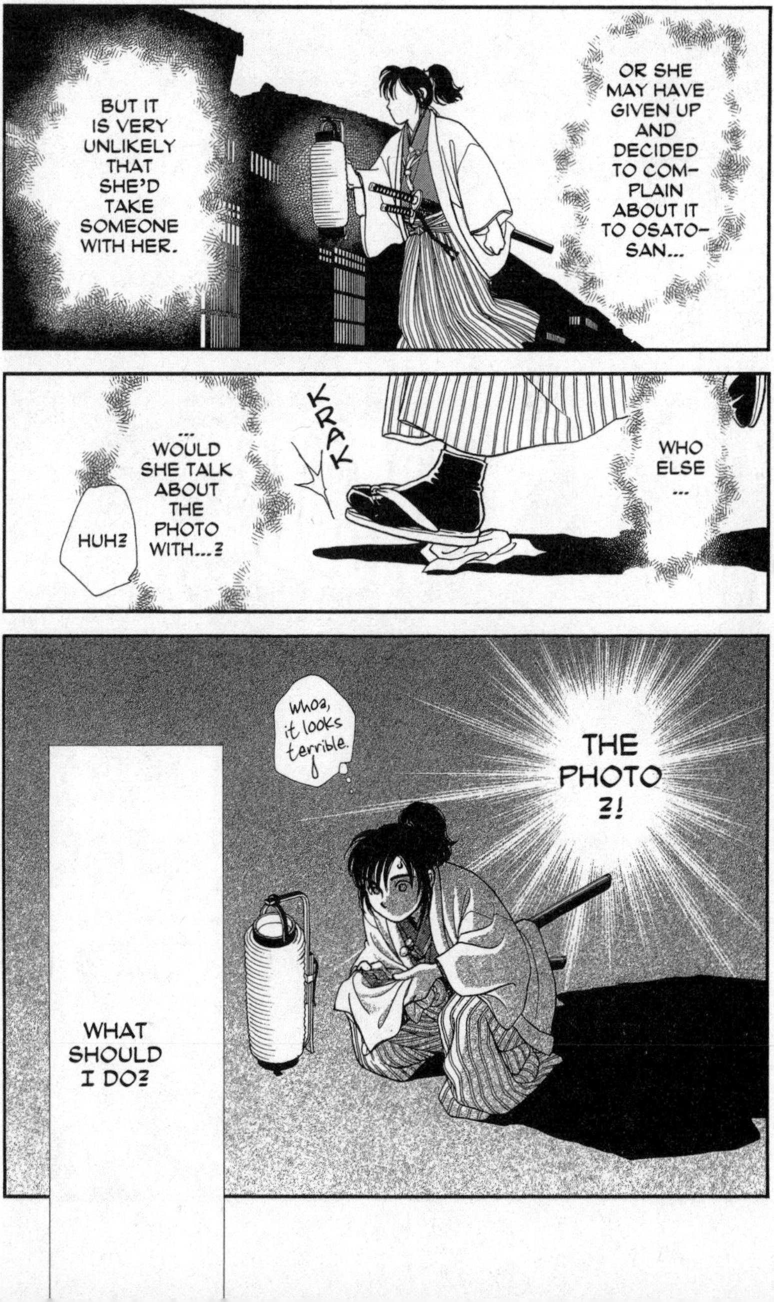
OR SHE MAY HAVE GIVEN UP AND DECIDED TO COM-PLAIN ABOUT IT TO OSATO-SAN...
BUT IT IS VERY UNLIKELY THAT SHE'D TAKE SOMEONE WITH HER.
WHO ELSE ...
KRAK
... WOULD SHE TALK ABOUT THE PHOTO WITH...?
HUH?
THE PHOTO ?!
Whoa, it looks terrible.
WHAT SHOULD I DO?

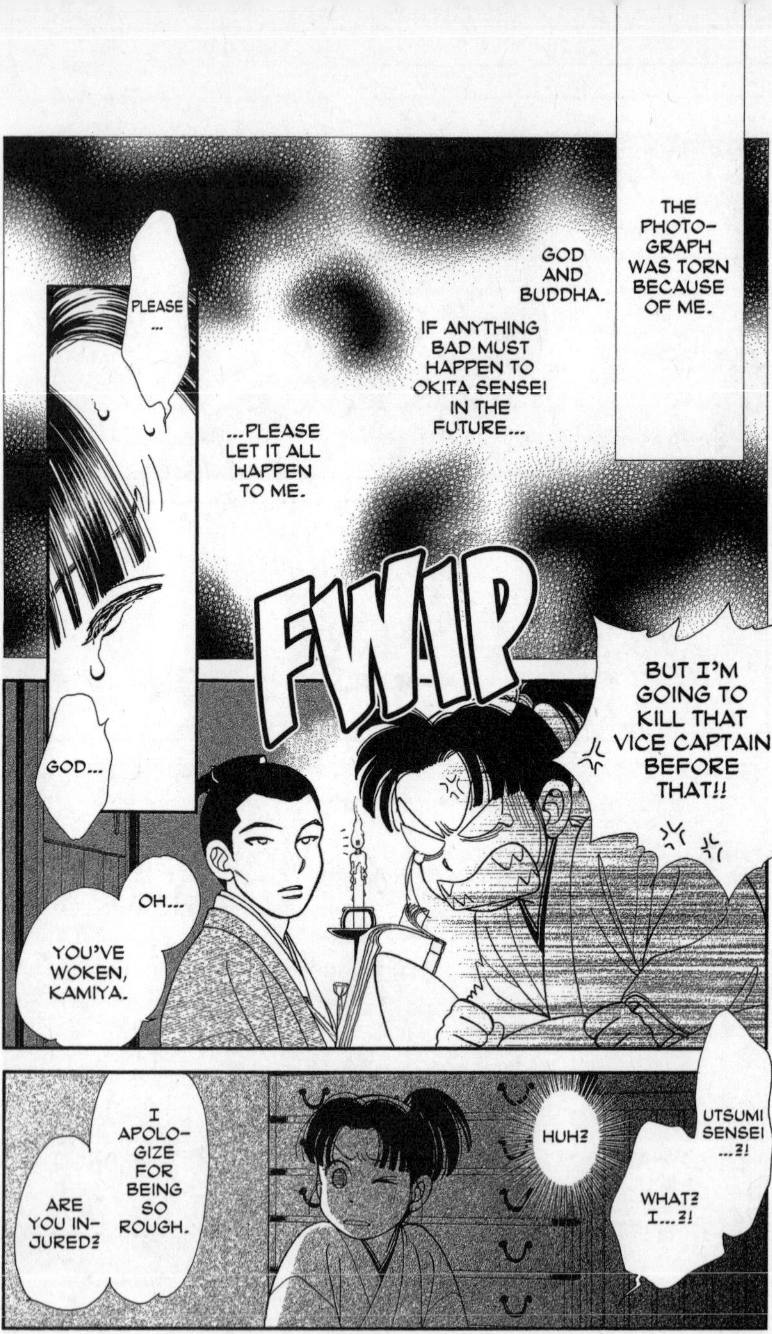

THE PHOTOGRAPH WAS TORN BECAUSE OF ME.
GOD AND BUDDHA.
IF ANYTHING BAD MUST HAPPEN TO OKITA SENSEI IN THE FUTURE...
...PLEASE LET IT ALL HAPPEN TO ME.
PLEASE ...
GOD...
FWIP
BUT I'M GOING TO KILL THAT VICE CAPTAIN BEFORE THAT!!
OH...
YOU'VE WOKEN, KAMIYA.
UTSUMI SENSEI ...?!
WHAT? I...?!
HUH?
I APOLOGIZE FOR BEING SO ROUGH.
ARE YOU INJURED?

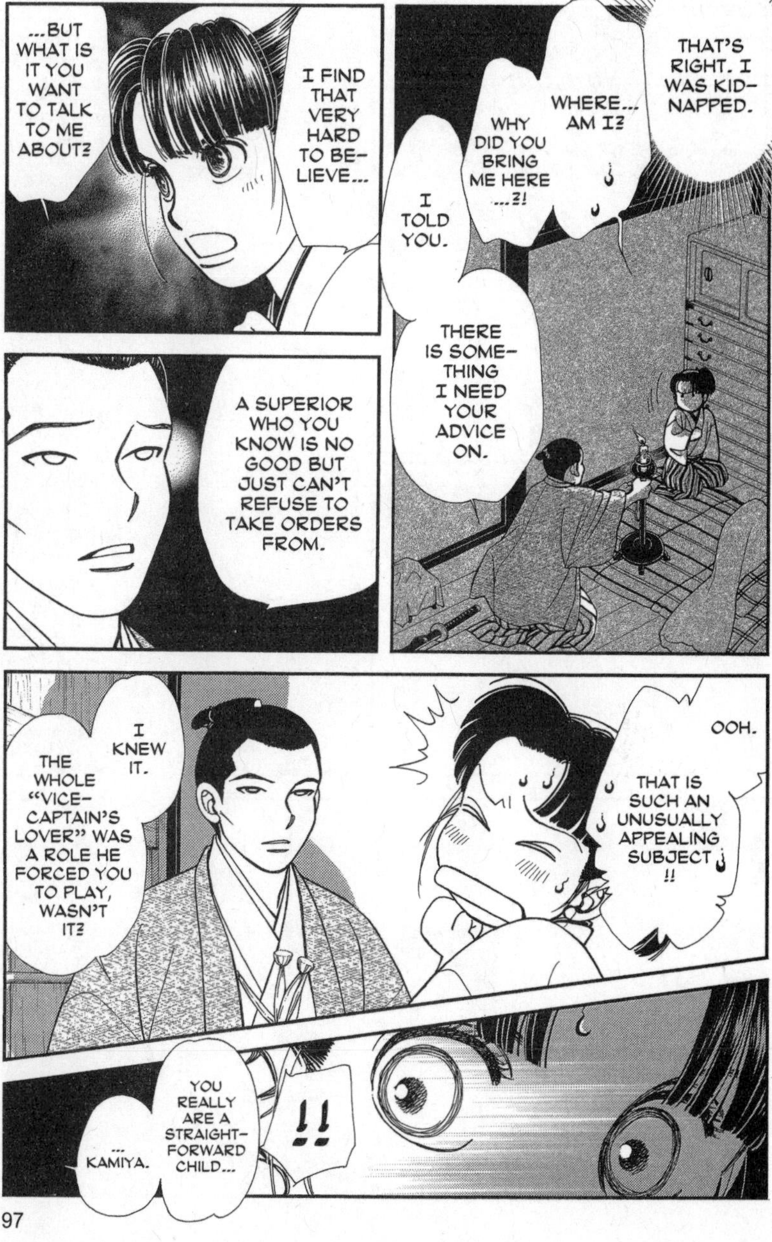
THAT'S RIGHT. I WAS KID-NAPPED.
WHERE... AM I?
WHY DID YOU BRING ME HERE ...?!
I TOLD YOU.
THERE IS SOME-THING I NEED YOUR ADVICE ON.
I FIND THAT VERY HARD TO BE-LIEVE...
...BUT WHAT IS IT YOU WANT TO TALK TO ME ABOUT?
A SUPERIOR WHO YOU KNOW IS NO GOOD BUT JUST CAN'T REFUSE TO TAKE ORDERS FROM.
OOH.
THAT IS SUCH AN UNUSUALLY APPEALING SUBJECT !!
I KNEW IT.
THE WHOLE "VICE-CAPTAIN'S LOVER" WAS A ROLE HE FORCED YOU TO PLAY, WASN'T IT?
!!
YOU REALLY ARE A STRAIGHT-FORWARD CHILD...
... KAMIYA.

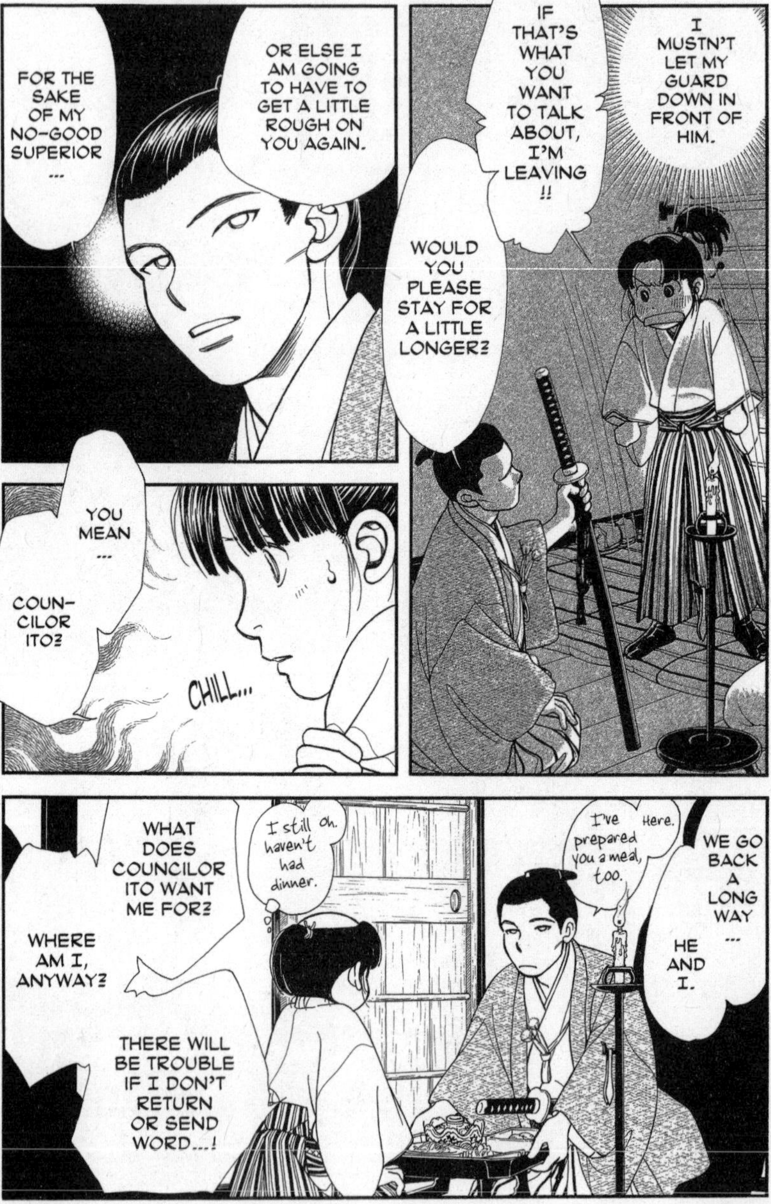

I MUSTN'T LET MY GUARD DOWN IN FRONT OF HIM.
IF THAT'S WHAT YOU WANT TO TALK ABOUT, I'M LEAVING!!
WOULD YOU PLEASE STAY FOR A LITTLE LONGER?
OR ELSE I AM GOING TO HAVE TO GET A LITTLE ROUGH ON YOU AGAIN.
FOR THE SAKE OF MY NO-GOOD SUPERIOR...
YOU MEAN... COUNCILOR ITO?
CHILL...
WE GO BACK A LONG WAY... HE AND I.
Here. I've prepared you a meal, too.
Oh. I still haven't had dinner.
WHAT DOES COUNCILOR ITO WANT ME FOR?
WHERE AM I, ANYWAY?
THERE WILL BE TROUBLE IF I DON'T RETURN OR SEND WORD...!

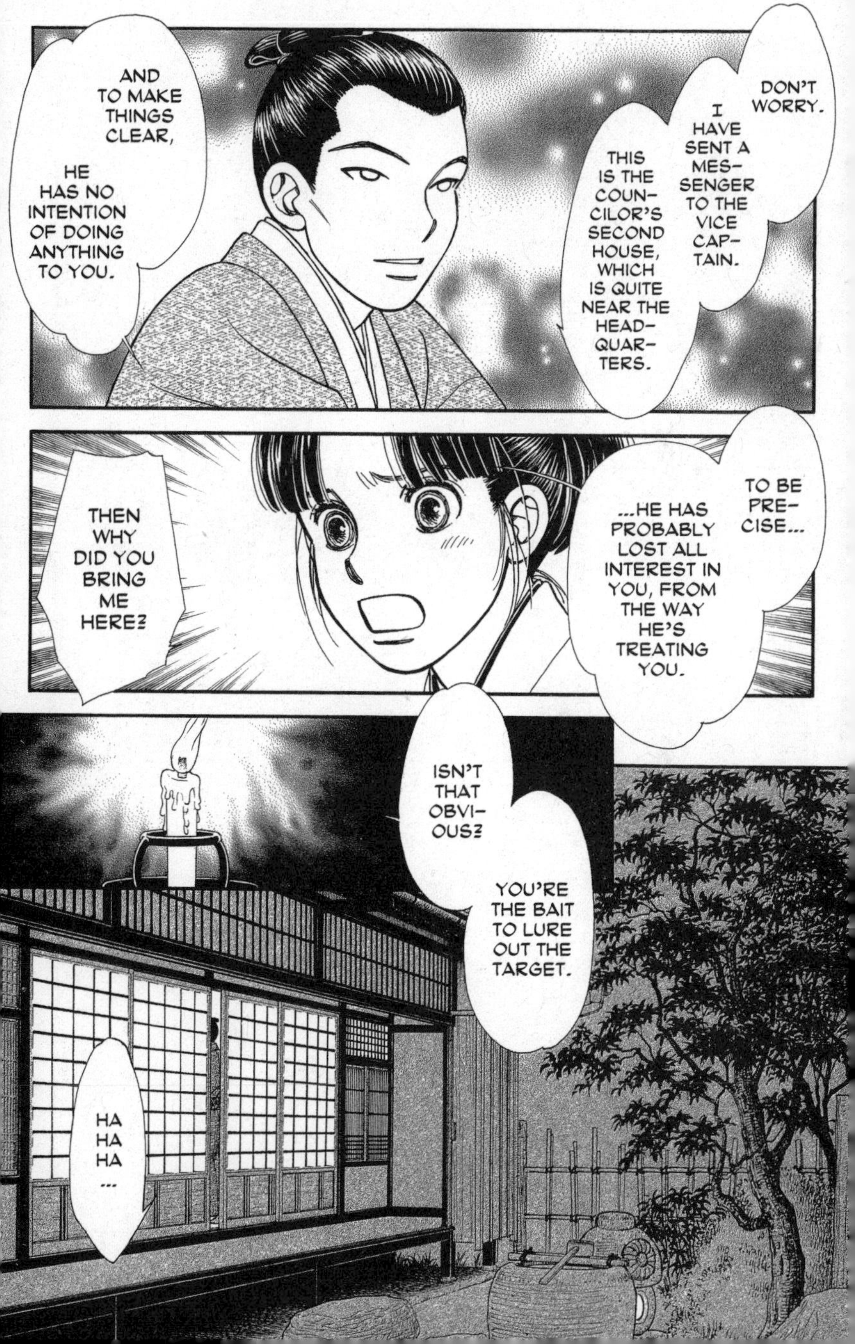
DON'T WORRY.
I HAVE SENT A MESSENGER TO THE VICE CAPTAIN.
THIS IS THE COUNCILOR'S SECOND HOUSE, WHICH IS QUITE NEAR THE HEADQUARTERS.
AND TO MAKE THINGS CLEAR,
HE HAS NO INTENTION OF DOING ANYTHING TO YOU.
TO BE PRECISE...
...HE HAS PROBABLY LOST ALL INTEREST IN YOU, FROM THE WAY HE'S TREATING YOU.
THEN WHY DID YOU BRING ME HERE?
ISN'T THAT OBVIOUS?
YOU'RE THE BAIT TO LURE OUT THE TARGET.
HA HA HA ...

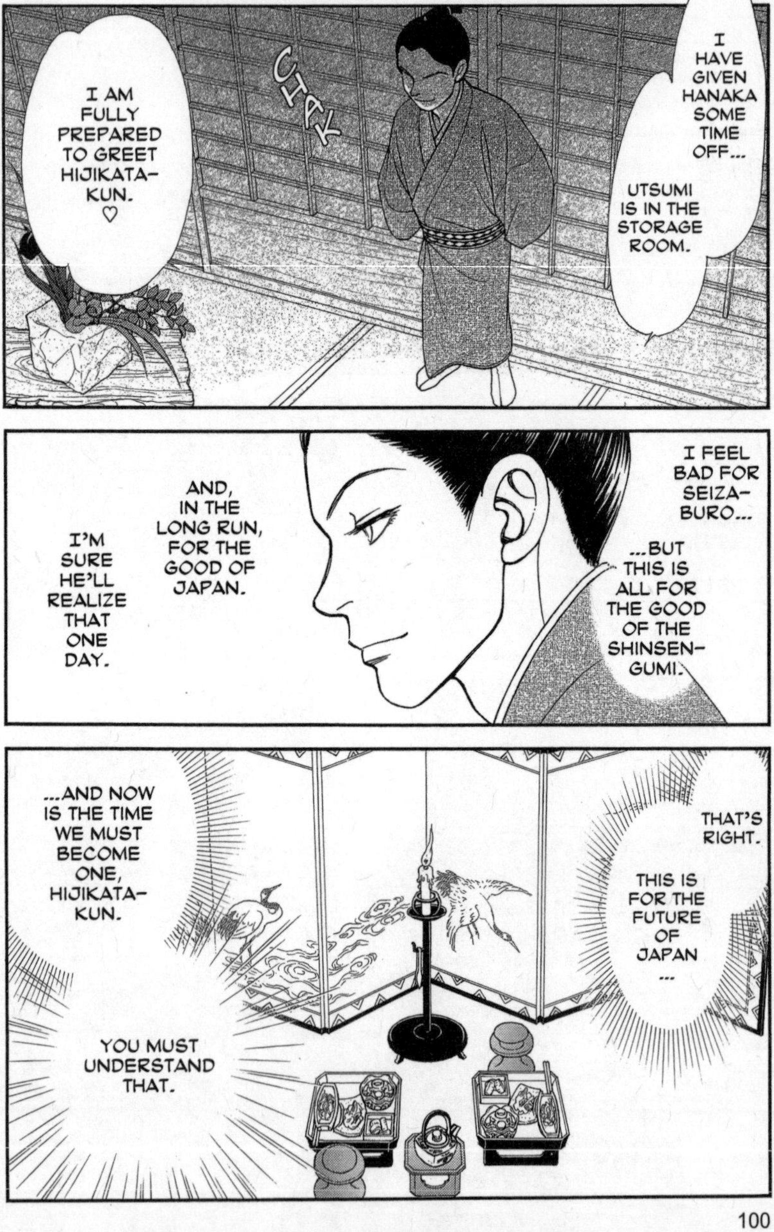
I HAVE GIVEN HANAKA SOME TIME OFF...
UTSUMI IS IN THE STORAGE ROOM.
CHAK
I AM FULLY PREPARED TO GREET HIJIKATA-KUN. ♡
I FEEL BAD FOR SEIZA-BURO...
...BUT THIS IS ALL FOR THE GOOD OF THE SHINSEN-GUMI.
AND, IN THE LONG RUN, FOR THE GOOD OF JAPAN.
I'M SURE HE'LL REALIZE THAT ONE DAY.
THAT'S RIGHT.
THIS IS FOR THE FUTURE OF JAPAN ...
...AND NOW IS THE TIME WE MUST BECOME ONE, HIJIKATA-KUN.
YOU MUST UNDERSTAND THAT.

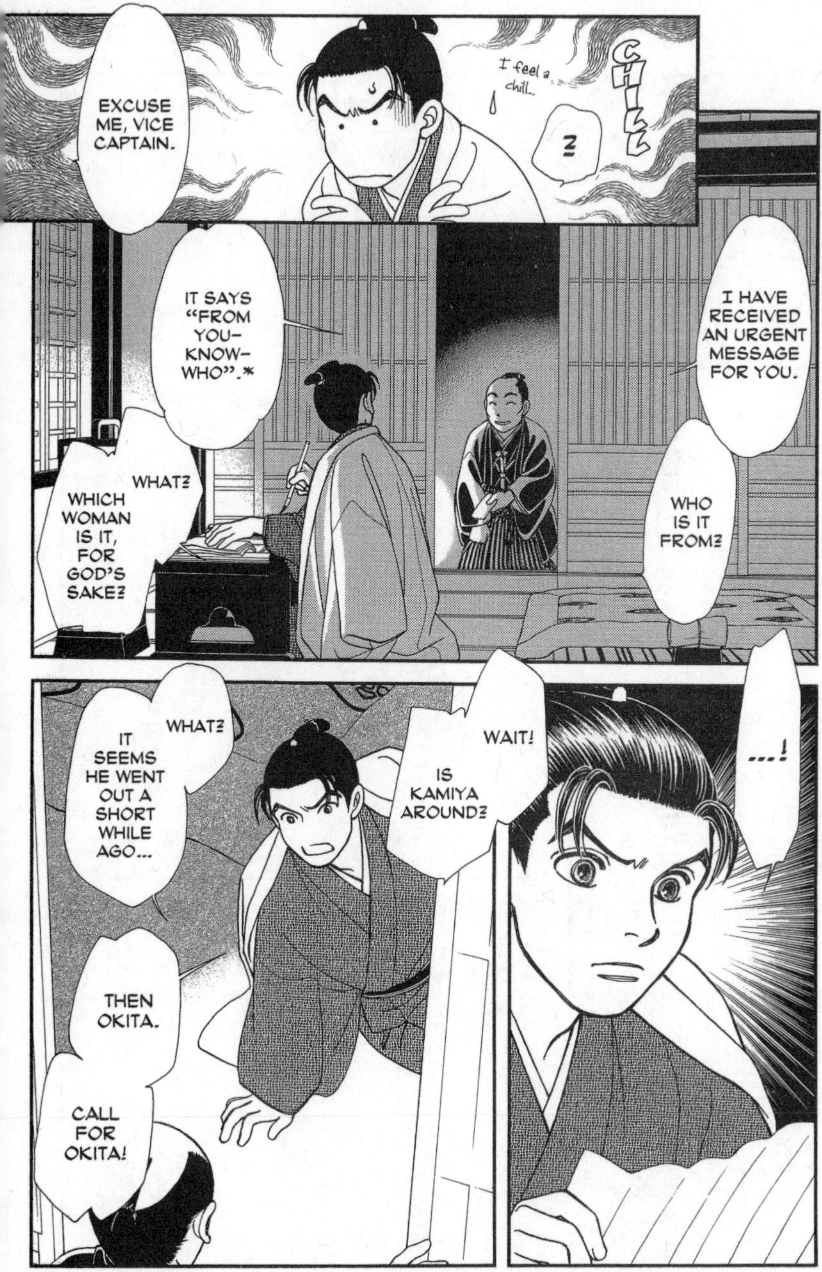
CHILL
I feel a chill..
?
EXCUSE ME, VICE CAPTAIN.
I HAVE RECEIVED AN URGENT MESSAGE FOR YOU.
WHO IS IT FROM?
IT SAYS "FROM YOU-KNOW-WHO".*
WHAT? WHICH WOMAN IS IT, FOR GOD'S SAKE?
...!
WAIT! IS KAMIYA AROUND?
WHAT? IT SEEMS HE WENT OUT A SHORT WHILE AGO...
THEN OKITA.
CALL FOR OKITA!

*"*Gozonji-yori,*" a phrase used in love letters when the sender wanted to hide their name.

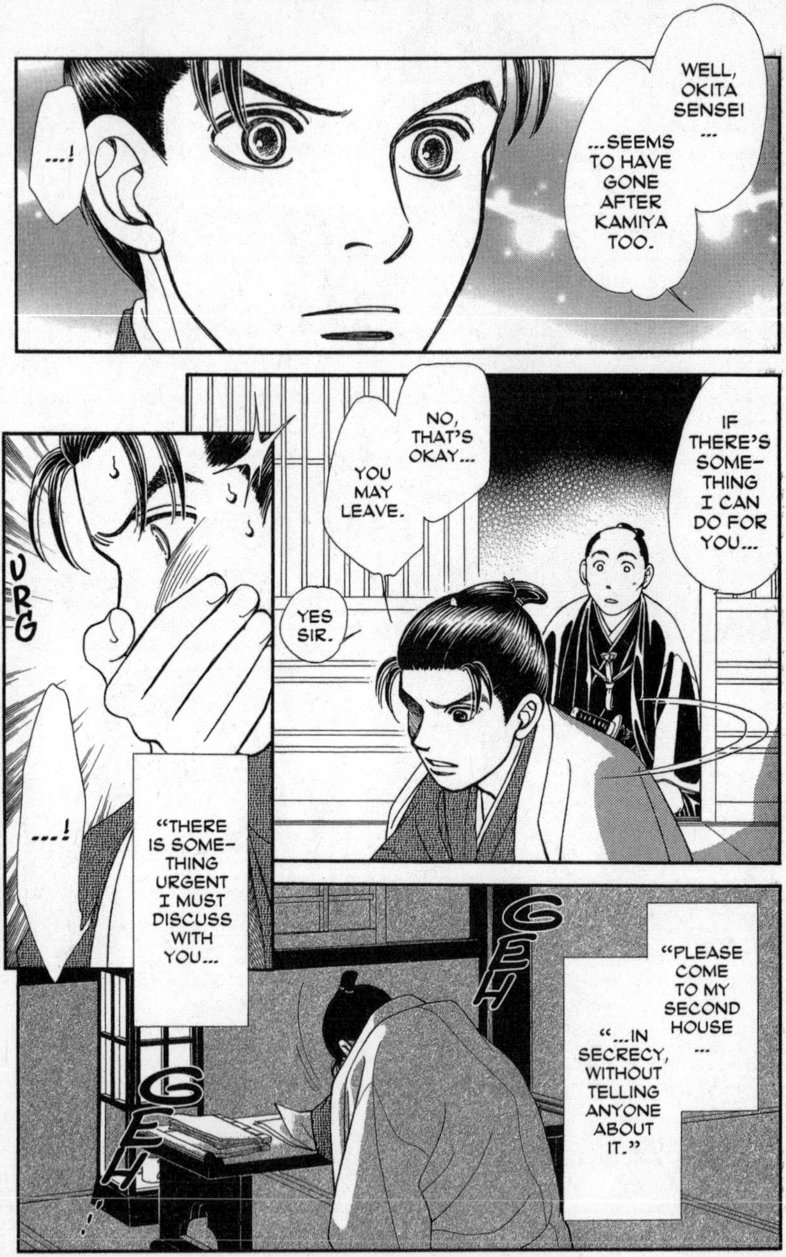
WELL, OKITA SENSEI ...
...SEEMS TO HAVE GONE AFTER KAMIYA TOO.
...!
IF THERE'S SOME-THING I CAN DO FOR YOU...
NO, THAT'S OKAY...
YOU MAY LEAVE.
YES SIR.
URG
...!
"THERE IS SOME-THING URGENT I MUST DISCUSS WITH YOU...
"PLEASE COME TO MY SECOND HOUSE ...
"...IN SECRECY, WITHOUT TELLING ANYONE ABOUT IT."
GEH
GEH

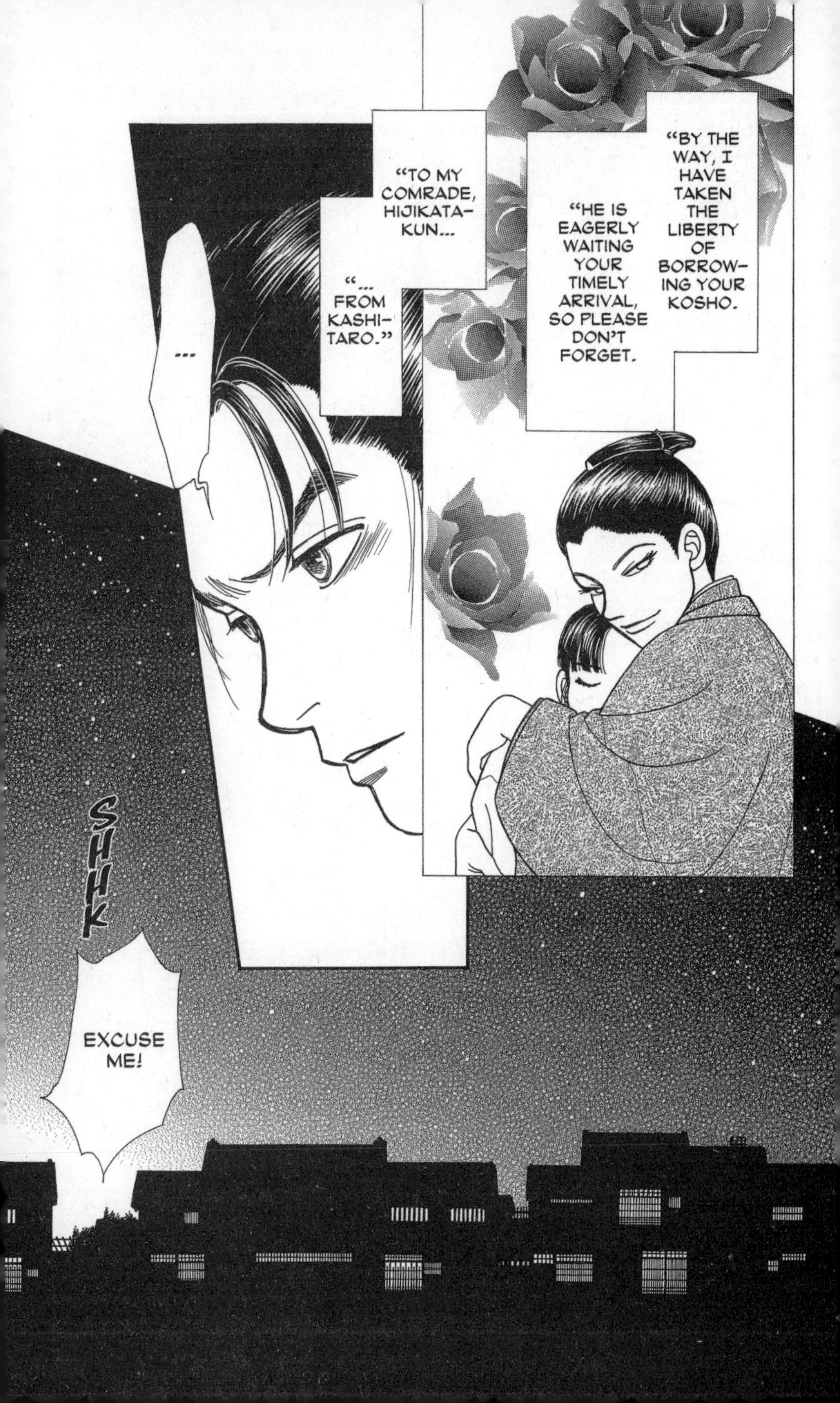
"BY THE WAY, I HAVE TAKEN THE LIBERTY OF BORROW-ING YOUR KOSHO.
"HE IS EAGERLY WAITING YOUR TIMELY ARRIVAL, SO PLEASE DON'T FORGET.
"TO MY COMRADE, HIJIKATA-KUN...
"... FROM KASHI-TARO."
...
SHHK
EXCUSE ME!

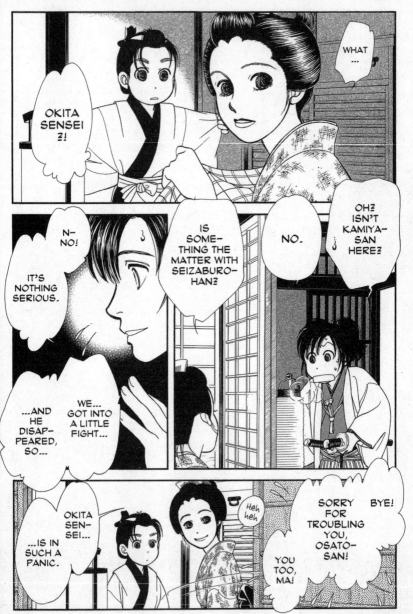

WHAT ...
OKITA SENSEI ?!
OH? ISN'T KAMIYA-SAN HERE?
NO.
IS SOMETHING THE MATTER WITH SEIZABURO-HAN?
N-NO!
IT'S NOTHING SERIOUS.
WE... GOT INTO A LITTLE FIGHT...
...AND HE DISAPPEARED, SO...
BYE!
SORRY FOR TROUBLING YOU, OSATO-SAN!
YOU TOO, MA!
Heh heh
OKITA SEN-SEI...
...IS IN SUCH A PANIC.

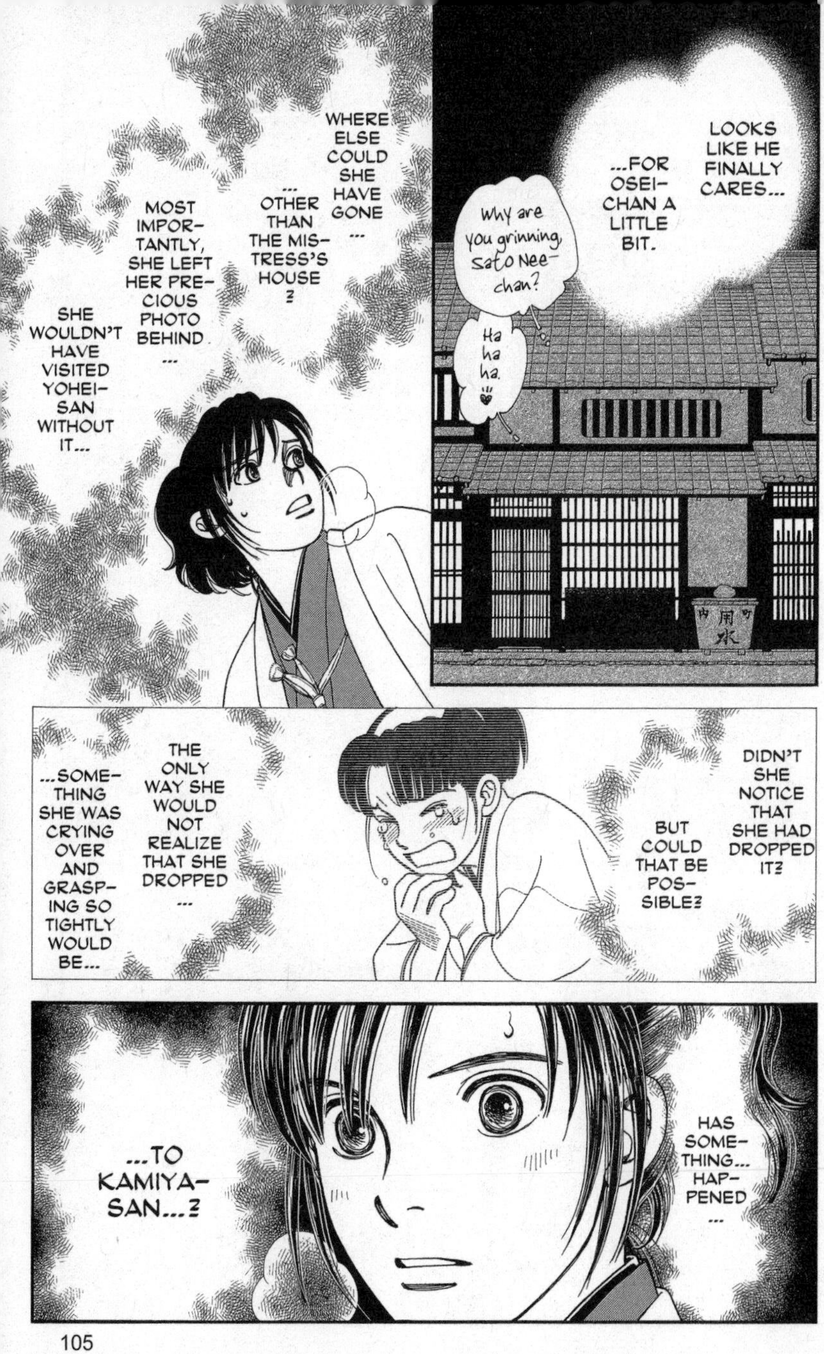
LOOKS LIKE HE FINALLY CARES...
...FOR OSEI-CHAN A LITTLE BIT.
Why are you grinning, Sato Nee-chan?
Ha ha ha.
WHERE ELSE COULD SHE HAVE GONE...
...OTHER THAN THE MISTRESS'S HOUSE?
MOST IMPORTANTLY, SHE LEFT HER PRECIOUS PHOTO BEHIND...
SHE WOULDN'T HAVE VISITED YOHEI-SAN WITHOUT IT...
DIDN'T SHE NOTICE THAT SHE HAD DROPPED IT?
BUT COULD THAT BE POSSIBLE?
THE ONLY WAY SHE WOULD NOT REALIZE THAT SHE DROPPED...
...SOMETHING SHE WAS CRYING OVER AND GRASPING SO TIGHTLY WOULD BE...
HAS SOMETHING... HAPPENED...
...TO KAMIYA-SAN...?

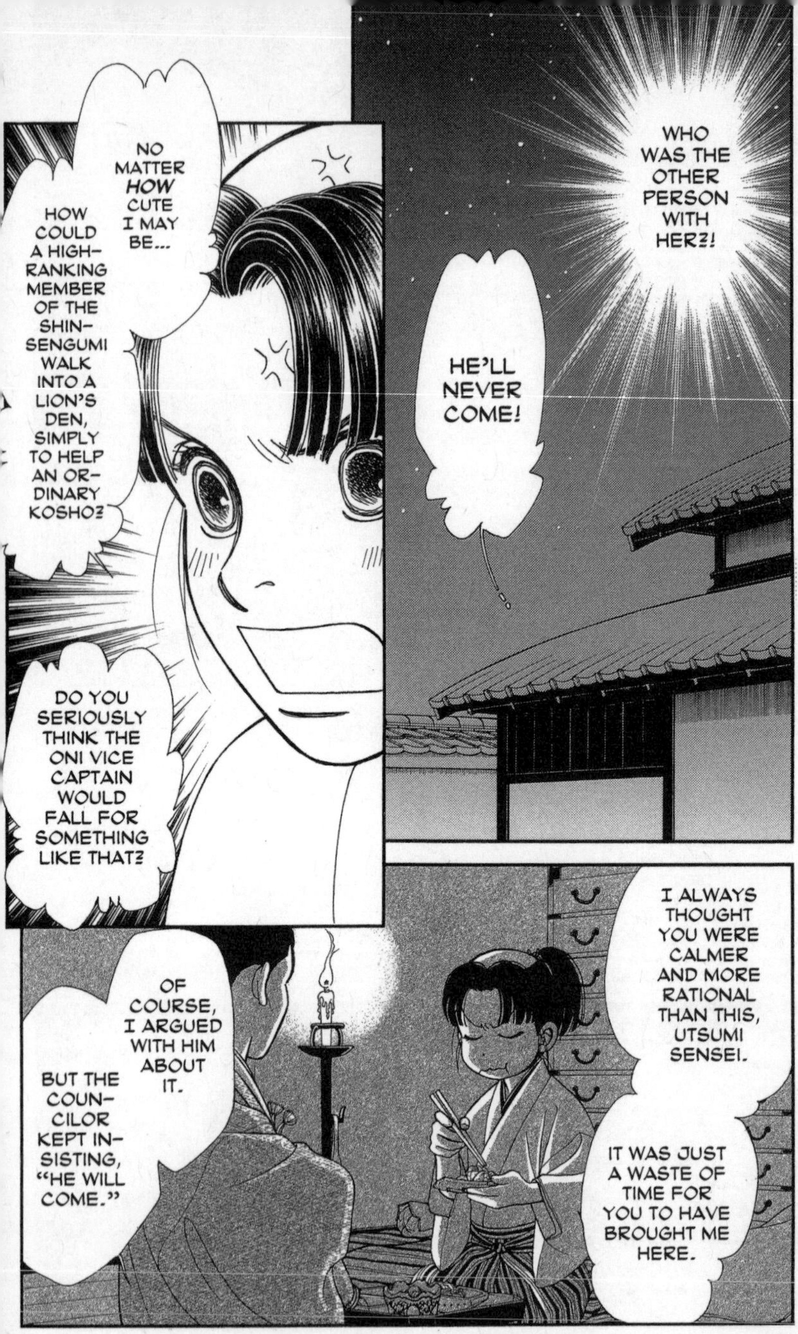
WHO WAS THE OTHER PERSON WITH HER?!
HE'LL NEVER COME!
NO MATTER *HOW* CUTE I MAY BE...
HOW COULD A HIGH-RANKING MEMBER OF THE SHINSENGUMI WALK INTO A LION'S DEN, SIMPLY TO HELP AN ORDINARY KOSHO?
DO YOU SERIOUSLY THINK THE ONI VICE CAPTAIN WOULD FALL FOR SOMETHING LIKE THAT?
I ALWAYS THOUGHT YOU WERE CALMER AND MORE RATIONAL THAN THIS, UTSUMI SENSEI.
IT WAS JUST A WASTE OF TIME FOR YOU TO HAVE BROUGHT ME HERE.
OF COURSE, I ARGUED WITH HIM ABOUT IT.
BUT THE COUNCILOR KEPT INSISTING, "HE WILL COME."

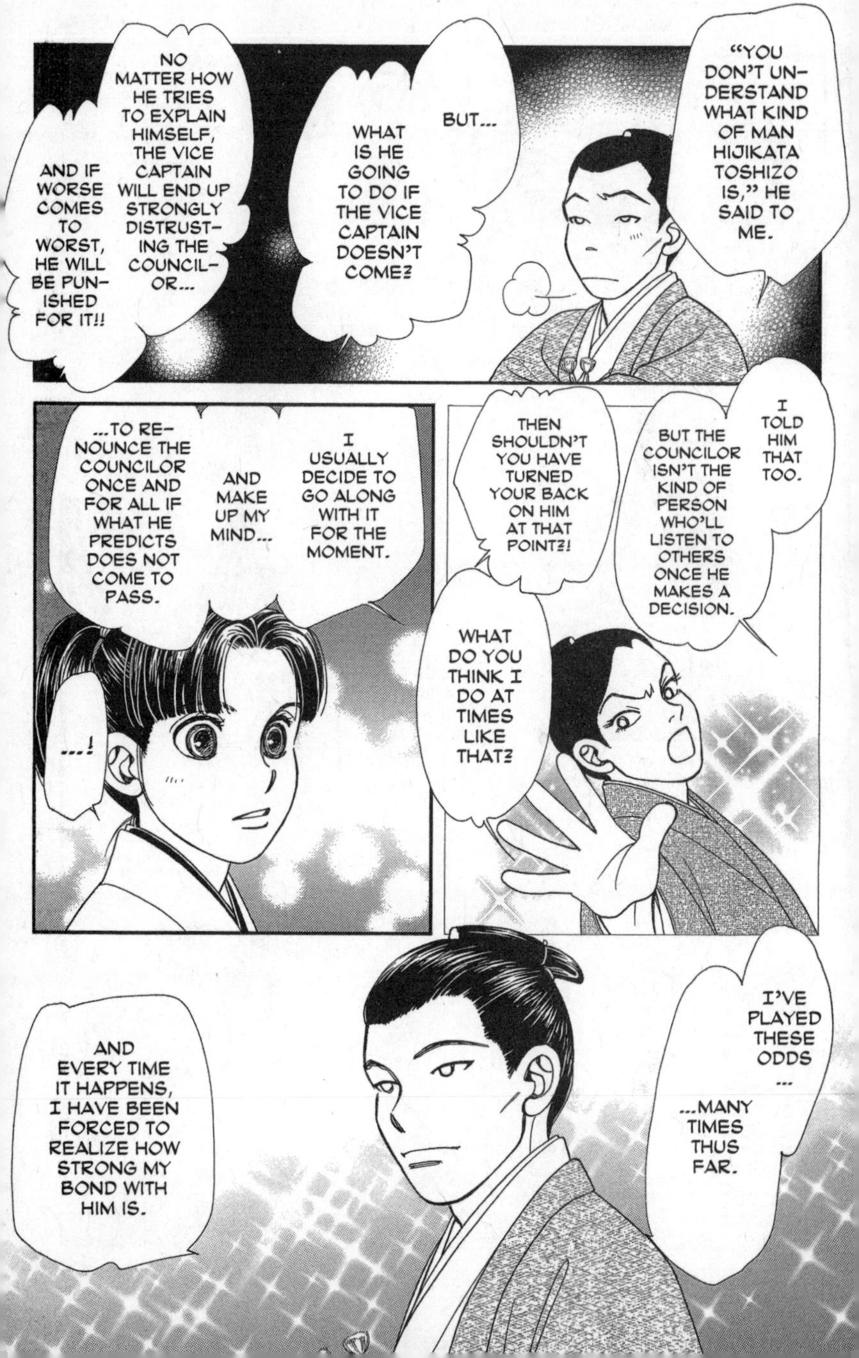
"YOU DON'T UNDERSTAND WHAT KIND OF MAN HIJIKATA TOSHIZO IS," HE SAID TO ME.
BUT...
WHAT IS HE GOING TO DO IF THE VICE CAPTAIN DOESN'T COME?
NO MATTER HOW HE TRIES TO EXPLAIN HIMSELF, THE VICE CAPTAIN WILL END UP STRONGLY DISTRUSTING THE COUNCILOR...
AND IF WORSE COMES TO WORST, HE WILL BE PUNISHED FOR IT!!
I TOLD HIM THAT TOO.
BUT THE COUNCILOR ISN'T THE KIND OF PERSON WHO'LL LISTEN TO OTHERS ONCE HE MAKES A DECISION.
THEN SHOULDN'T YOU HAVE TURNED YOUR BACK ON HIM AT THAT POINT?!
WHAT DO YOU THINK I DO AT TIMES LIKE THAT?
I USUALLY DECIDE TO GO ALONG WITH IT FOR THE MOMENT.
AND MAKE UP MY MIND...
...TO RENOUNCE THE COUNCILOR ONCE AND FOR ALL IF WHAT HE PREDICTS DOES NOT COME TO PASS.
...!
I'VE PLAYED THESE ODDS...
...MANY TIMES THUS FAR.
AND EVERY TIME IT HAPPENS, I HAVE BEEN FORCED TO REALIZE HOW STRONG MY BOND WITH HIM IS.

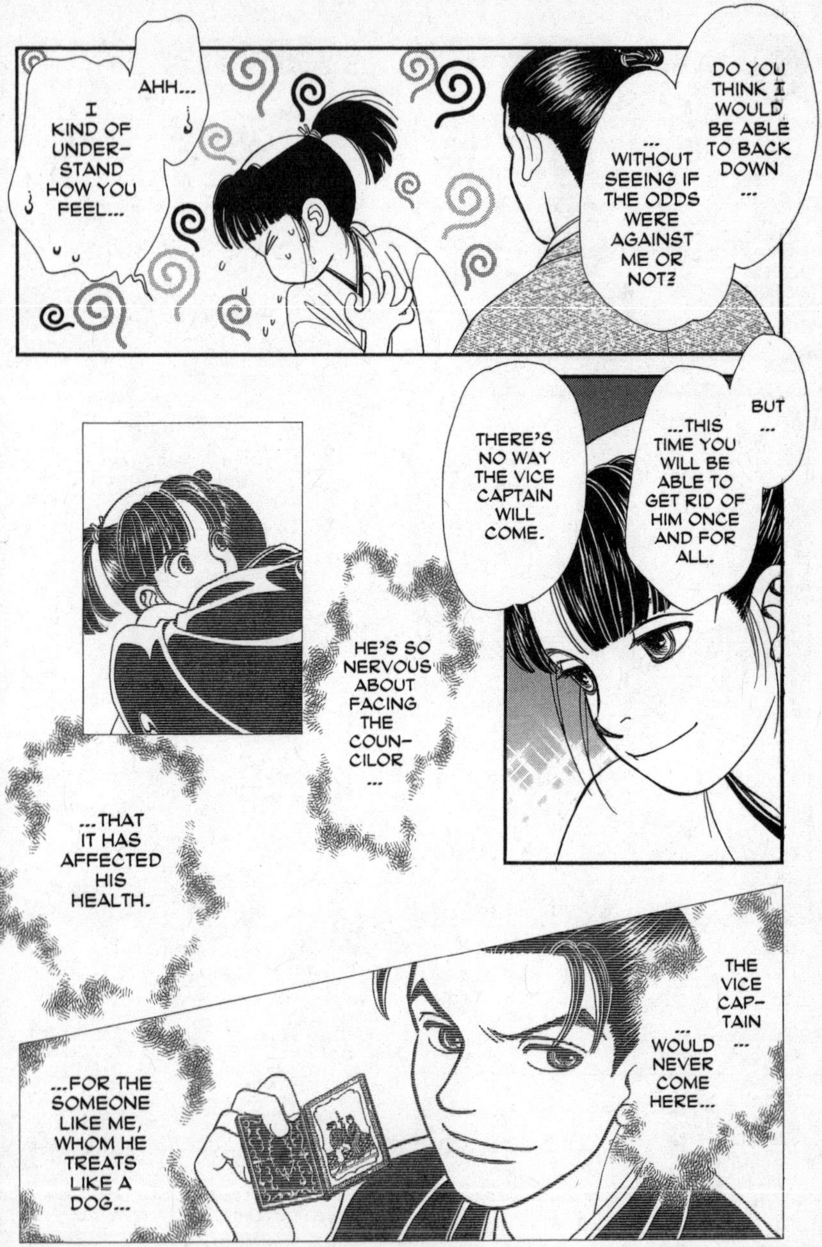
DO YOU THINK I WOULD BE ABLE TO BACK DOWN ...
... WITHOUT SEEING IF THE ODDS WERE AGAINST ME OR NOT?
AHH... I KIND OF UNDER-STAND HOW YOU FEEL...
BUT ...
...THIS TIME YOU WILL BE ABLE TO GET RID OF HIM ONCE AND FOR ALL.
THERE'S NO WAY THE VICE CAPTAIN WILL COME.
HE'S SO NERVOUS ABOUT FACING THE COUN-CILOR ...
...THAT IT HAS AFFECTED HIS HEALTH.
THE VICE CAP-TAIN ...
... WOULD NEVER COME HERE...
...FOR THE SOMEONE LIKE ME, WHOM HE TREATS LIKE A DOG...

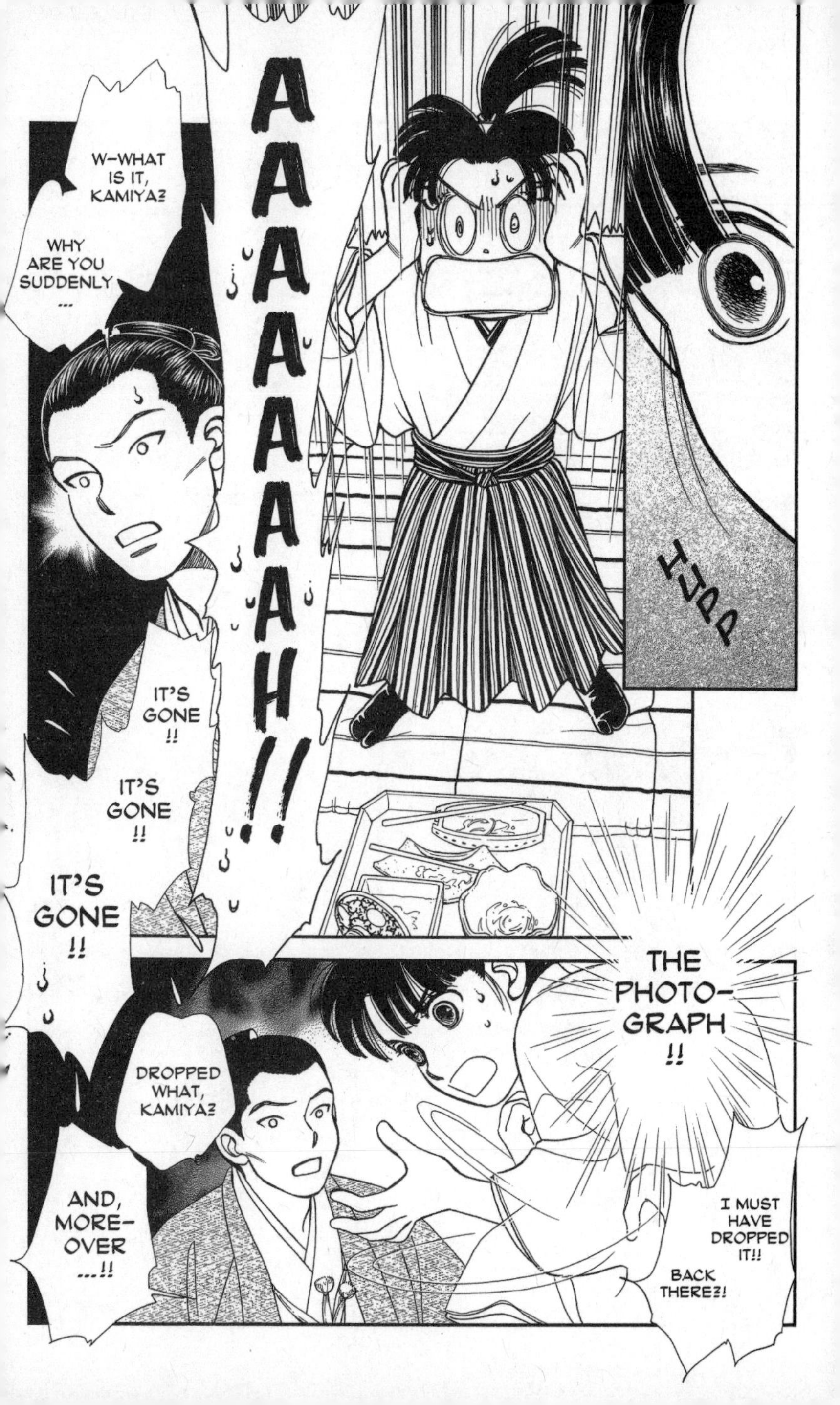

PULL
AAAAAAAH!!
W-WHAT IS IT, KAMIYA?
WHY ARE YOU SUDDENLY...
IT'S GONE!!
IT'S GONE!!
IT'S GONE!!
THE PHOTOGRAPH!!
I MUST HAVE DROPPED IT!!
BACK THERE?!
DROPPED WHAT, KAMIYA?
AND, MOREOVER...!!

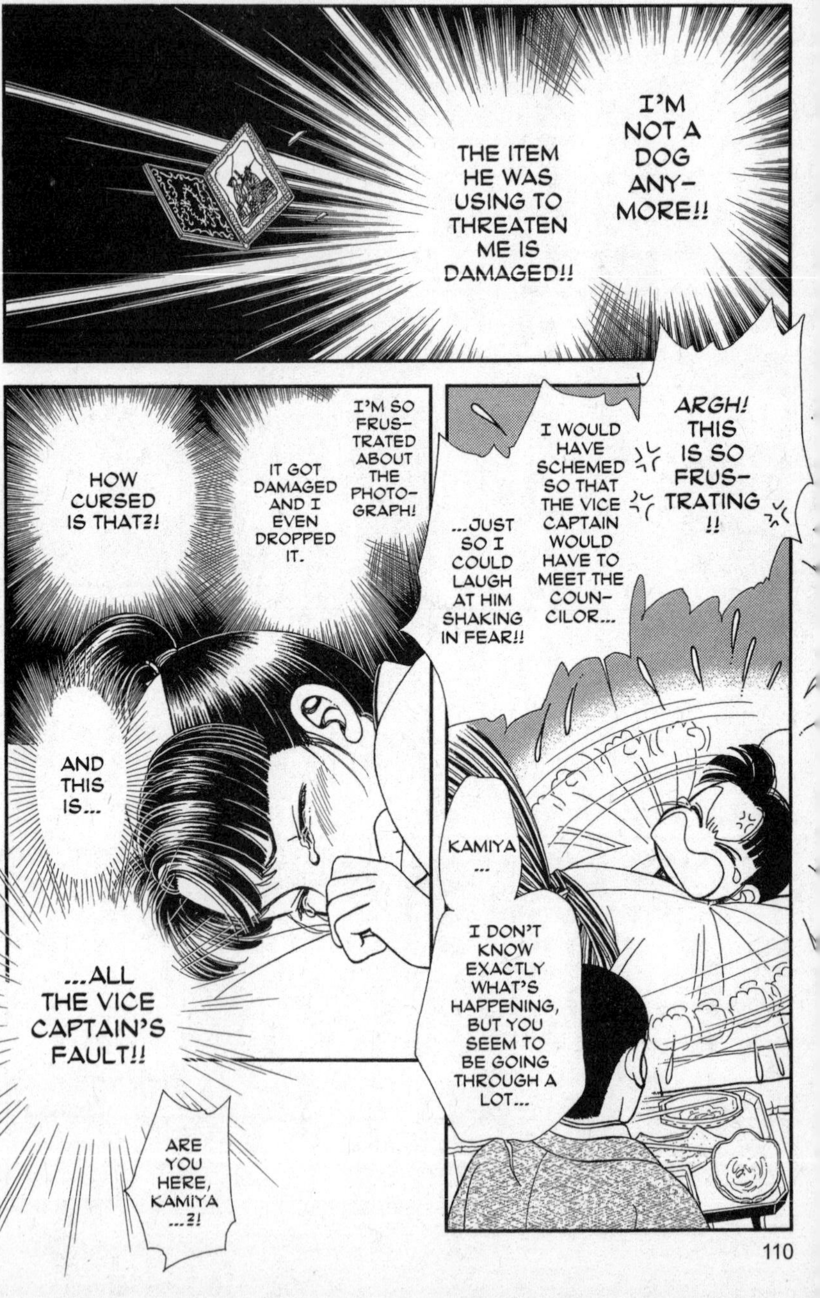
I'M NOT A DOG ANYMORE!!
THE ITEM HE WAS USING TO THREATEN ME IS DAMAGED!!
ARGH! THIS IS SO FRUSTRATING!!
I WOULD HAVE SCHEMED SO THAT THE VICE CAPTAIN WOULD HAVE TO MEET THE COUNCILOR...
...JUST SO I COULD LAUGH AT HIM SHAKING IN FEAR!!
KAMIYA...
I DON'T KNOW EXACTLY WHAT'S HAPPENING, BUT YOU SEEM TO BE GOING THROUGH A LOT...
I'M SO FRUSTRATED ABOUT THE PHOTOGRAPH!
IT GOT DAMAGED AND I EVEN DROPPED IT.
HOW CURSED IS THAT?!
AND THIS IS...
...ALL THE VICE CAPTAIN'S FAULT!!
ARE YOU HERE, KAMIYA...?!

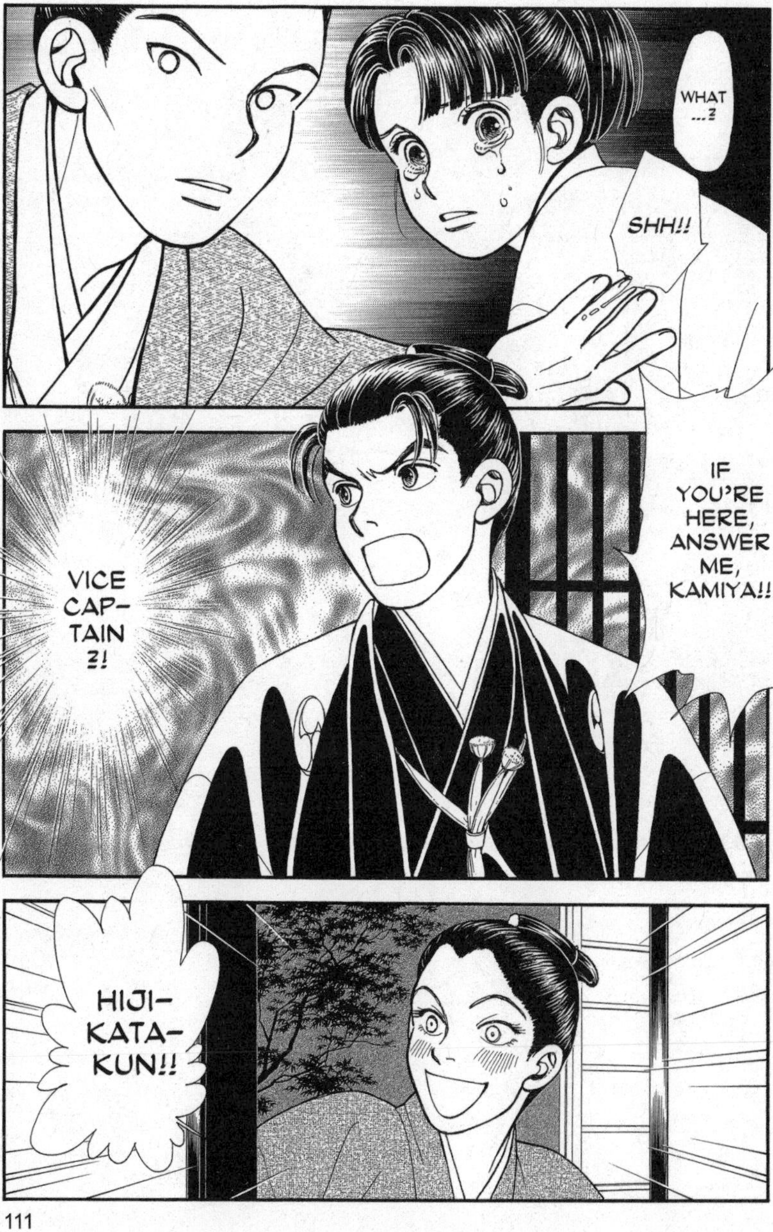
WHAT ...?
SHH!!
IF YOU'RE HERE, ANSWER ME, KAMIYA!!
VICE CAP-TAIN?!
HIJI-KATA-KUN!!

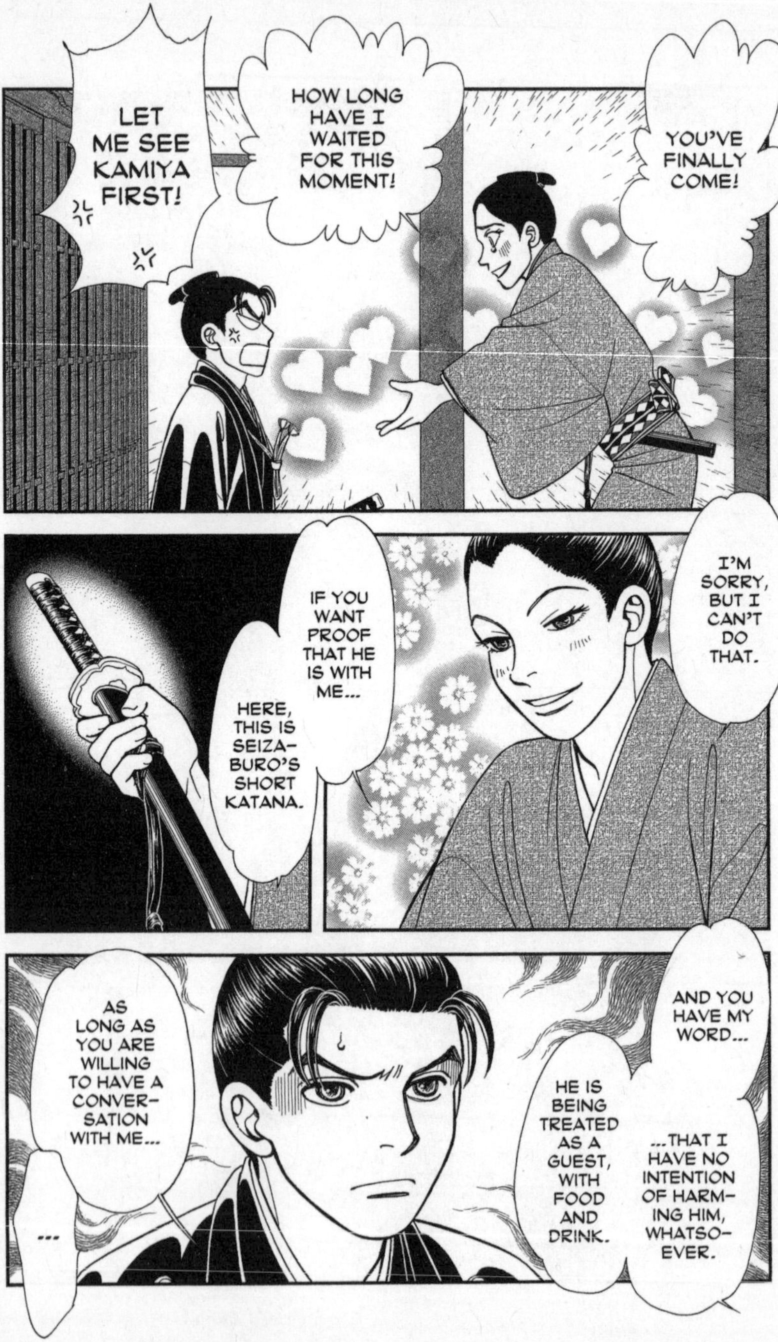
YOU'VE FINALLY COME!
HOW LONG HAVE I WAITED FOR THIS MOMENT!
LET ME SEE KAMIYA FIRST!
I'M SORRY, BUT I CAN'T DO THAT.
IF YOU WANT PROOF THAT HE IS WITH ME...
HERE, THIS IS SEIZABURO'S SHORT KATANA.
AND YOU HAVE MY WORD...
...THAT I HAVE NO INTENTION OF HARMING HIM, WHATSOEVER.
HE IS BEING TREATED AS A GUEST, WITH FOOD AND DRINK.
AS LONG AS YOU ARE WILLING TO HAVE A CONVERSATION WITH ME...
...

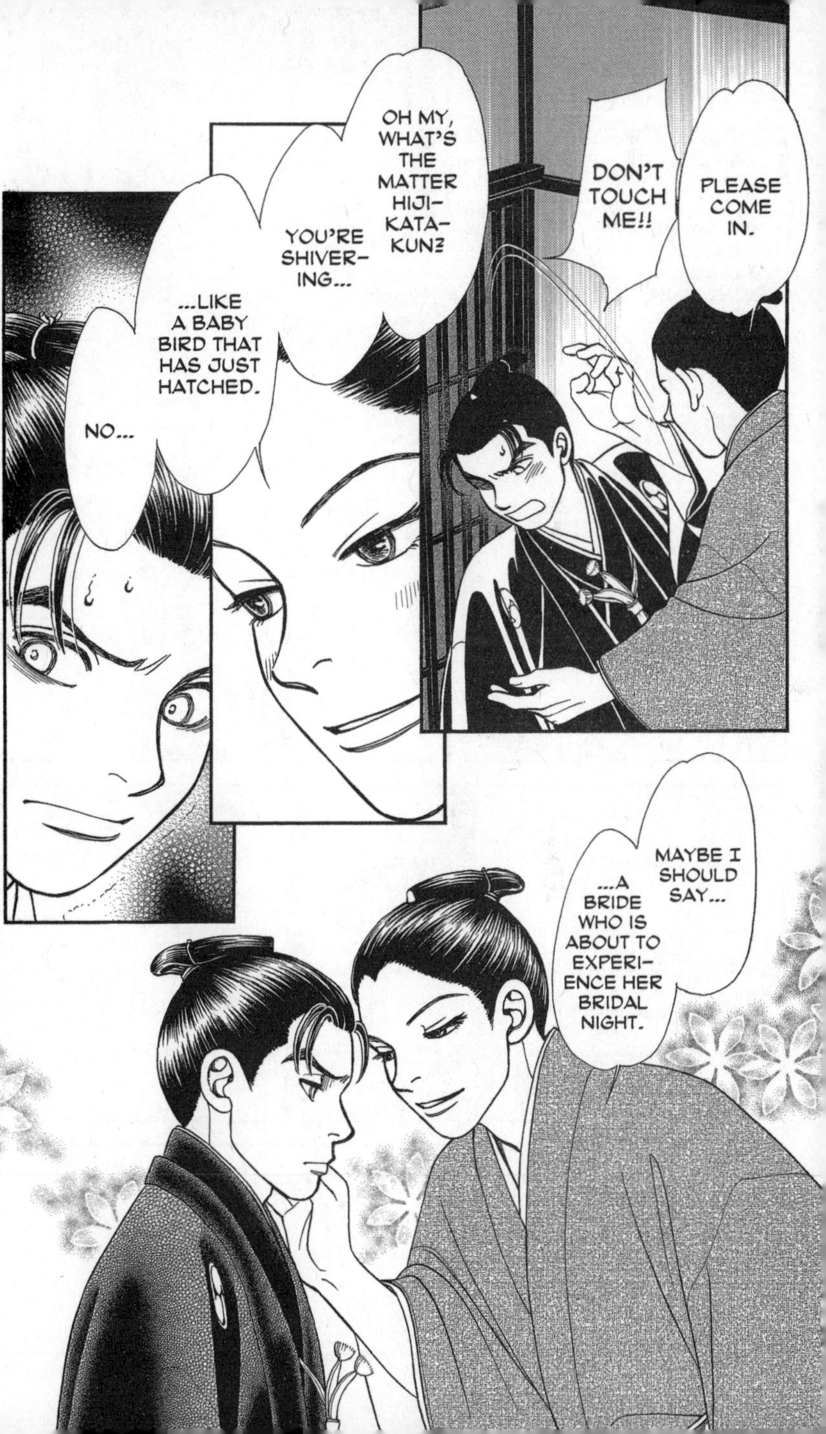
PLEASE COME IN.
DON'T TOUCH ME!!
OH MY, WHAT'S THE MATTER HIJI-KATA-KUN?
YOU'RE SHIVER-ING...
...LIKE A BABY BIRD THAT HAS JUST HATCHED.
NO...
MAYBE I SHOULD SAY...
...A BRIDE WHO IS ABOUT TO EXPERI-ENCE HER BRIDAL NIGHT.

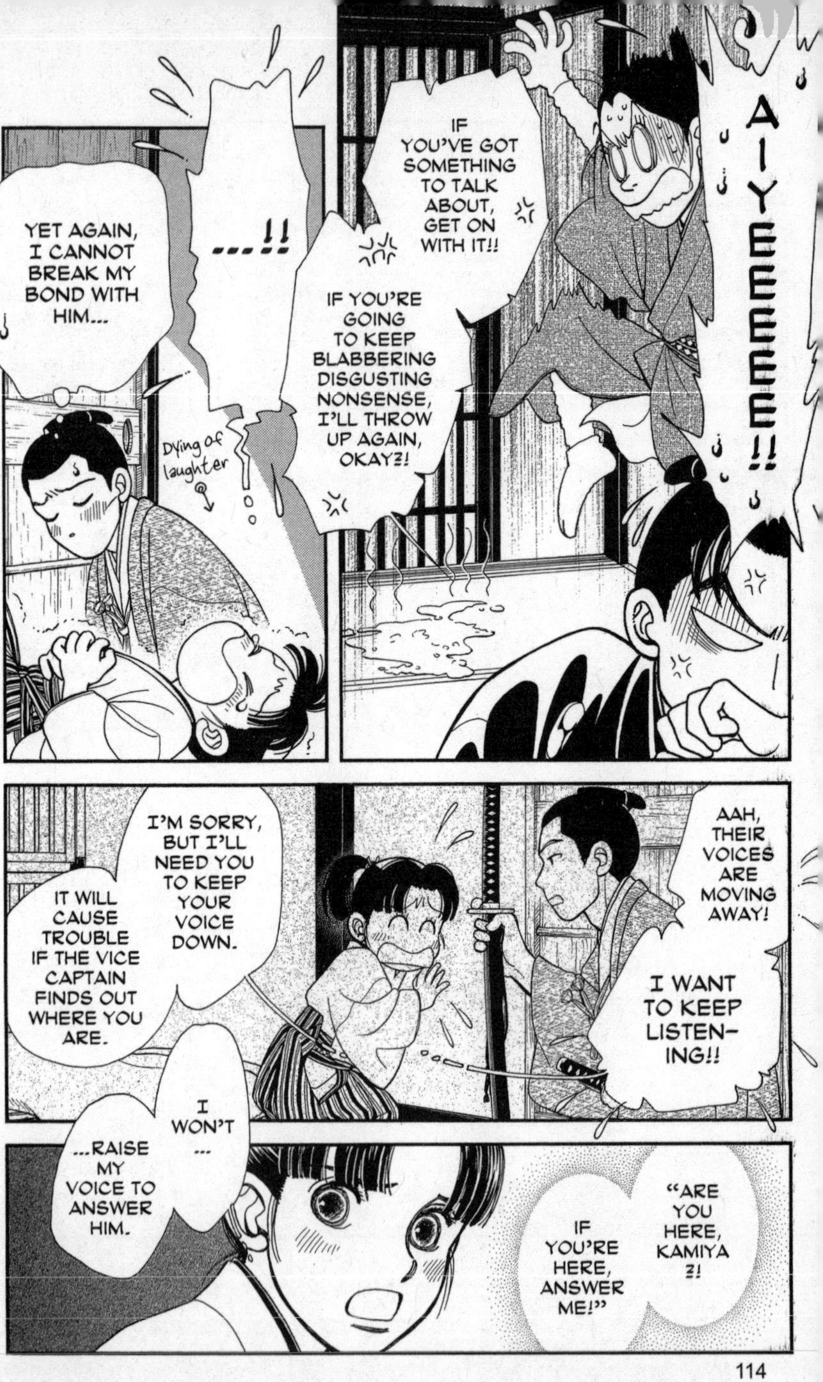
AIYEEEEE!!
IF YOU'VE GOT SOMETHING TO TALK ABOUT, GET ON WITH IT!!
IF YOU'RE GOING TO KEEP BLABBERING DISGUSTING NONSENSE, I'LL THROW UP AGAIN, OKAY?!
...!!
YET AGAIN, I CANNOT BREAK MY BOND WITH HIM...
Dying of laughter
AAH, THEIR VOICES ARE MOVING AWAY!
I WANT TO KEEP LISTEN-ING!!
I'M SORRY, BUT I'LL NEED YOU TO KEEP YOUR VOICE DOWN.
IT WILL CAUSE TROUBLE IF THE VICE CAPTAIN FINDS OUT WHERE YOU ARE.
"ARE YOU HERE, KAMIYA?!
IF YOU'RE HERE, ANSWER ME!"
I WON'T...
...RAISE MY VOICE TO ANSWER HIM.

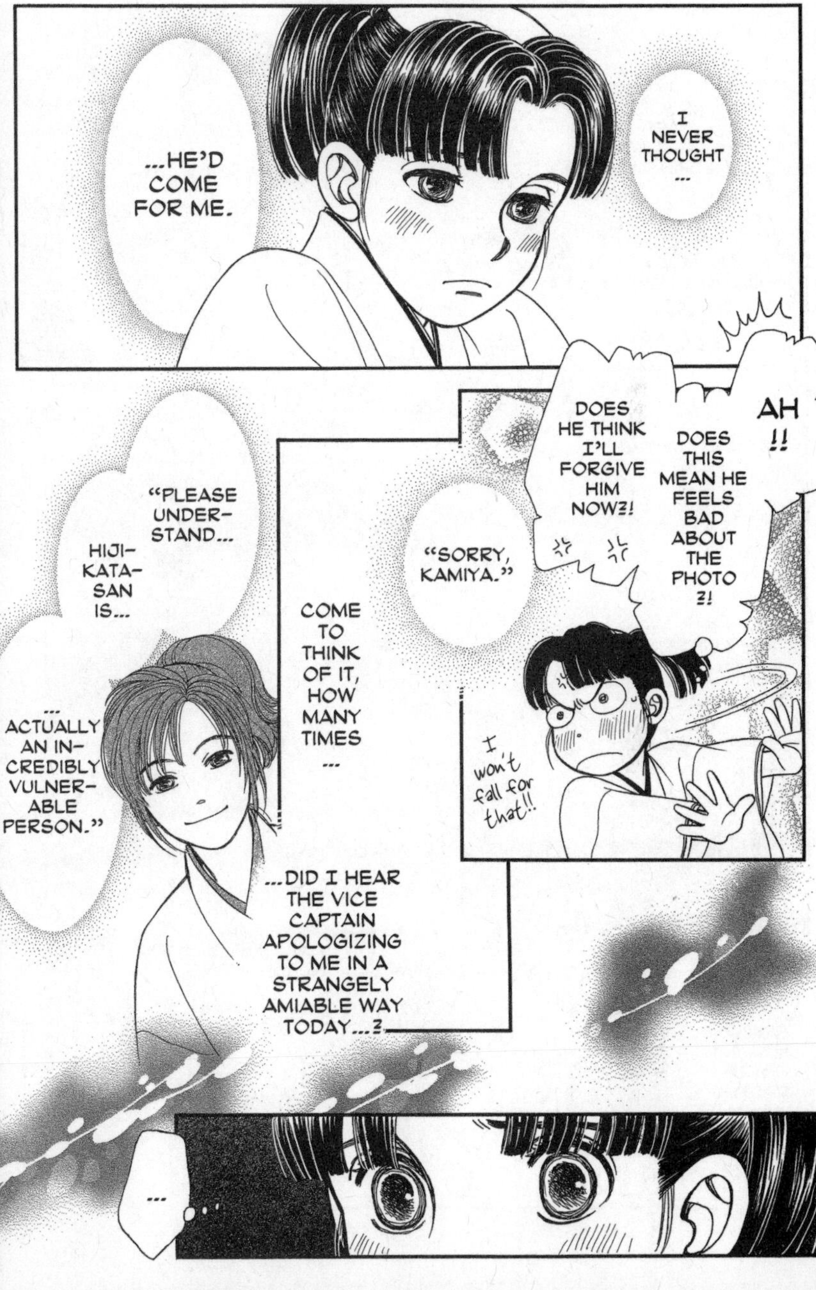
I NEVER THOUGHT ...
...HE'D COME FOR ME.
AH!!
DOES THIS MEAN HE FEELS BAD ABOUT THE PHOTO?!
DOES HE THINK I'LL FORGIVE HIM NOW?!
I won't fall for that!!
"SORRY, KAMIYA."
COME TO THINK OF IT, HOW MANY TIMES ...
...DID I HEAR THE VICE CAPTAIN APOLOGIZING TO ME IN A STRANGELY AMIABLE WAY TODAY...?
"PLEASE UNDER-STAND...
HIJI-KATA-SAN IS...
...ACTUALLY AN IN-CREDIBLY VULNER-ABLE PERSON."
...

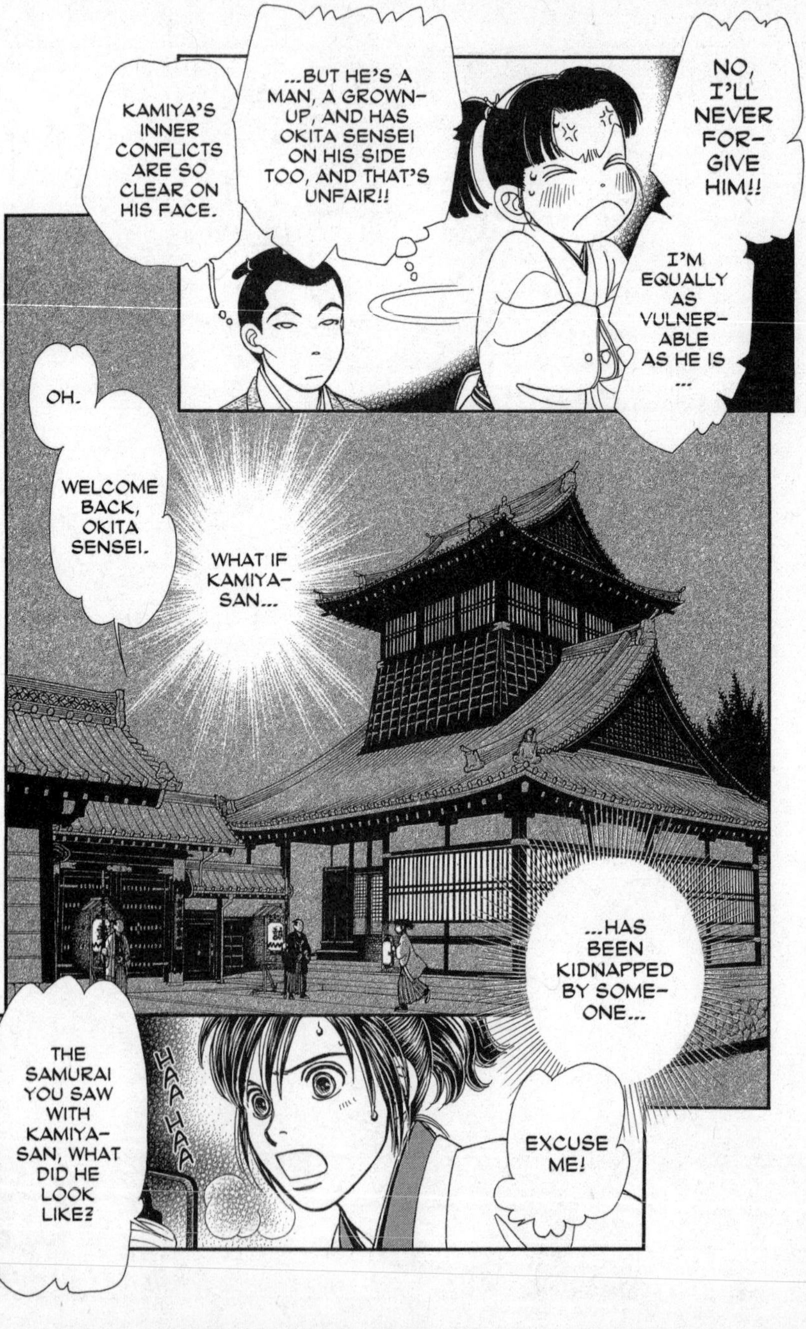
NO, I'LL NEVER FOR-GIVE HIM!!
I'M EQUALLY AS VULNER-ABLE AS HE IS ...
...BUT HE'S A MAN, A GROWN-UP, AND HAS OKITA SENSEI ON HIS SIDE TOO, AND THAT'S UNFAIR!!
KAMIYA'S INNER CONFLICTS ARE SO CLEAR ON HIS FACE.
OH.
WELCOME BACK, OKITA SENSEI.
WHAT IF KAMIYA-SAN...
...HAS BEEN KIDNAPPED BY SOME-ONE...
EXCUSE ME!
HAA HAA
THE SAMURAI YOU SAW WITH KAMIYA-SAN, WHAT DID HE LOOK LIKE?

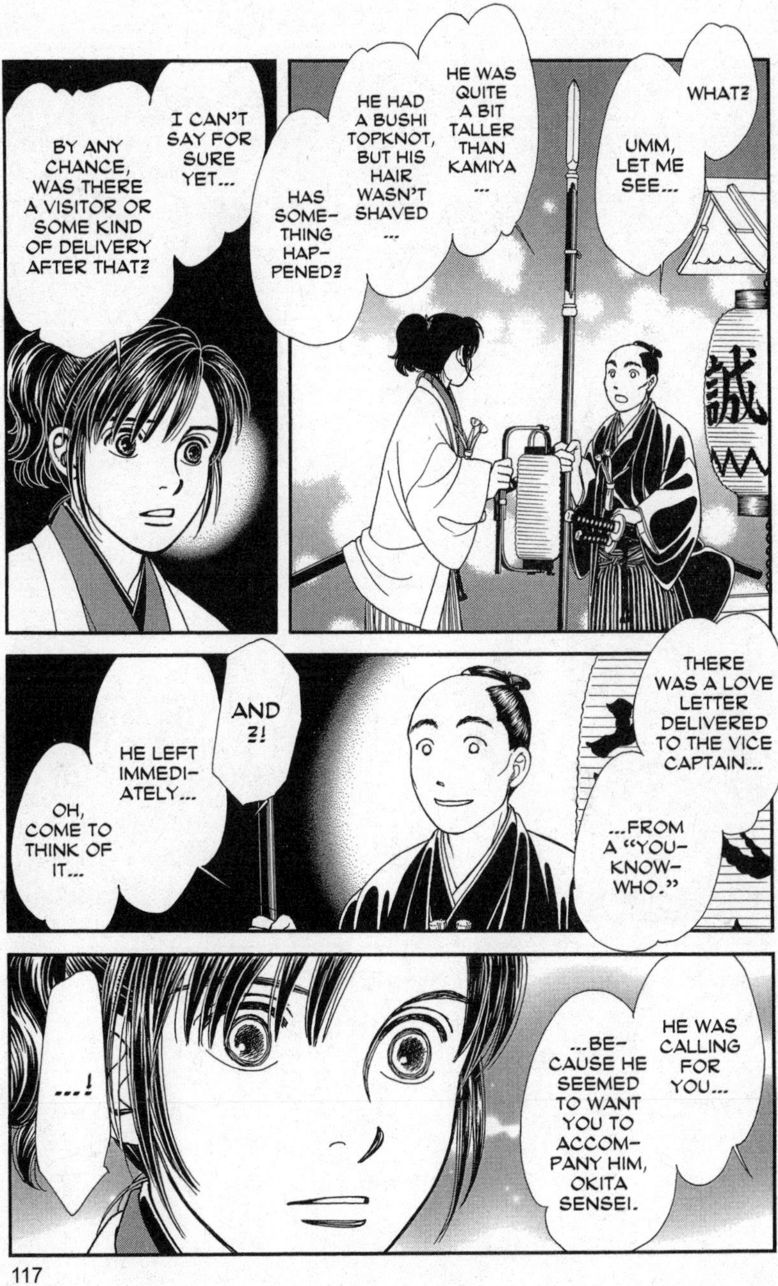
WHAT?
UMM, LET ME SEE...
HE WAS QUITE A BIT TALLER THAN KAMIYA ...
HE HAD A BUSHI TOPKNOT, BUT HIS HAIR WASN'T SHAVED ...
HAS SOMETHING HAPPENED?
I CAN'T SAY FOR SURE YET...
BY ANY CHANCE, WAS THERE A VISITOR OR SOME KIND OF DELIVERY AFTER THAT?
THERE WAS A LOVE LETTER DELIVERED TO THE VICE CAPTAIN...
...FROM A "YOU-KNOW-WHO."
AND ?!
HE LEFT IMMEDIATELY...
OH, COME TO THINK OF IT...
HE WAS CALLING FOR YOU...
...BECAUSE HE SEEMED TO WANT YOU TO ACCOMPANY HIM, OKITA SENSEI.
...!

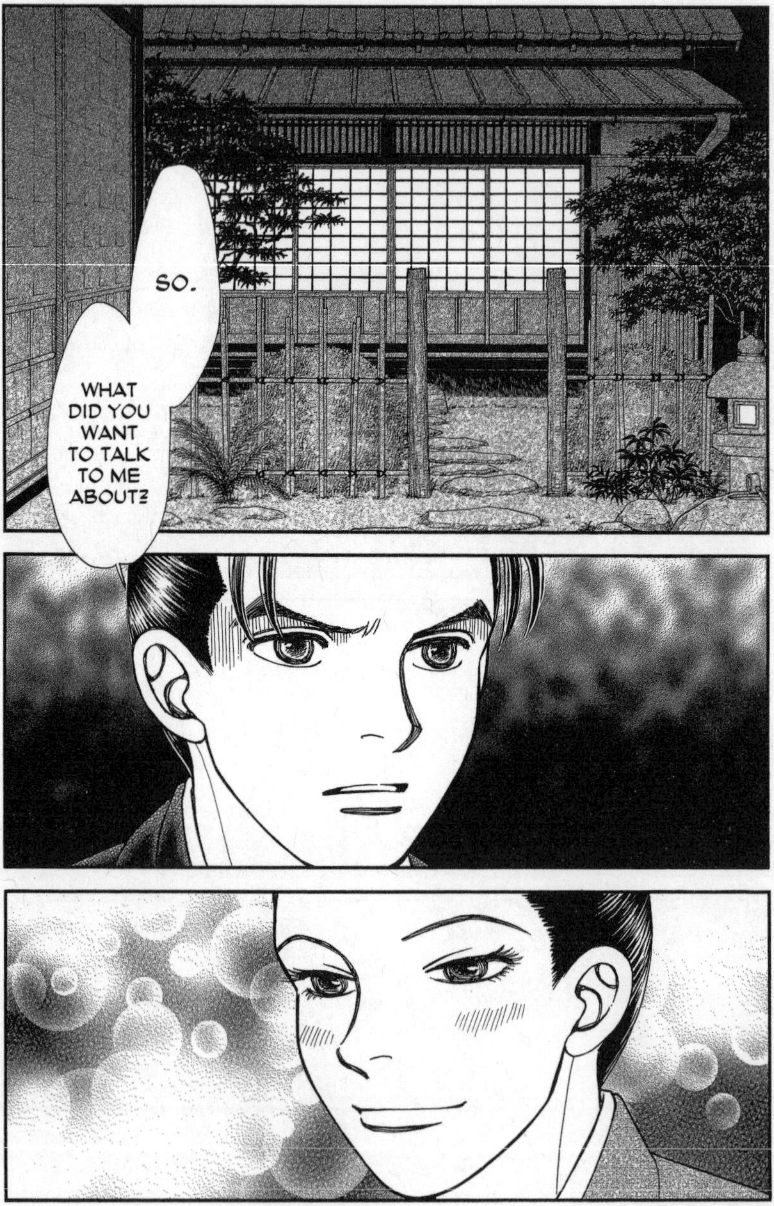
SO.
WHAT DID YOU WANT TO TALK TO ME ABOUT?

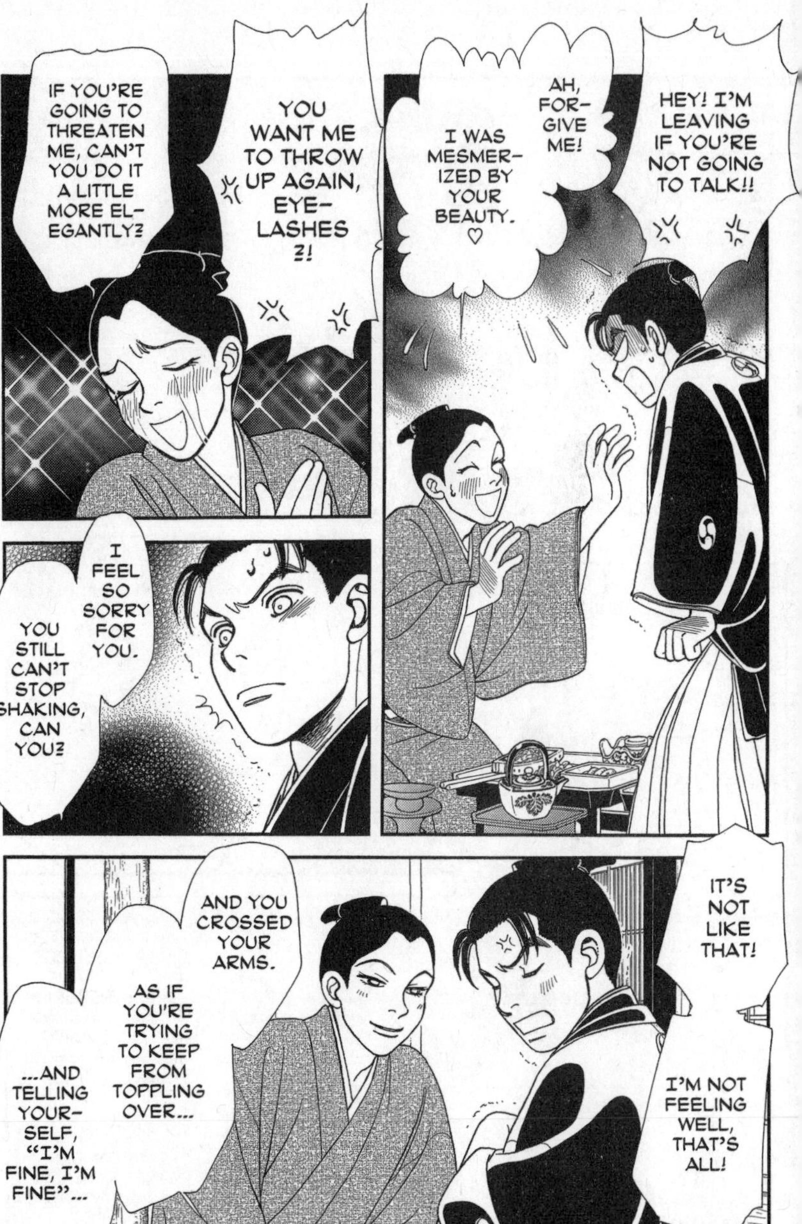
HEY! I'M LEAVING IF YOU'RE NOT GOING TO TALK!!
AH, FOR-GIVE ME!
I WAS MESMER-IZED BY YOUR BEAUTY. ♡
YOU WANT ME TO THROW UP AGAIN, EYE-LASHES ?!
IF YOU'RE GOING TO THREATEN ME, CAN'T YOU DO IT A LITTLE MORE EL-EGANTLY?
I FEEL SO SORRY FOR YOU.
YOU STILL CAN'T STOP SHAKING, CAN YOU?
IT'S NOT LIKE THAT!
I'M NOT FEELING WELL, THAT'S ALL!
AND YOU CROSSED YOUR ARMS.
AS IF YOU'RE TRYING TO KEEP FROM TOPPLING OVER...
...AND TELLING YOUR-SELF, "I'M FINE, I'M FINE"...

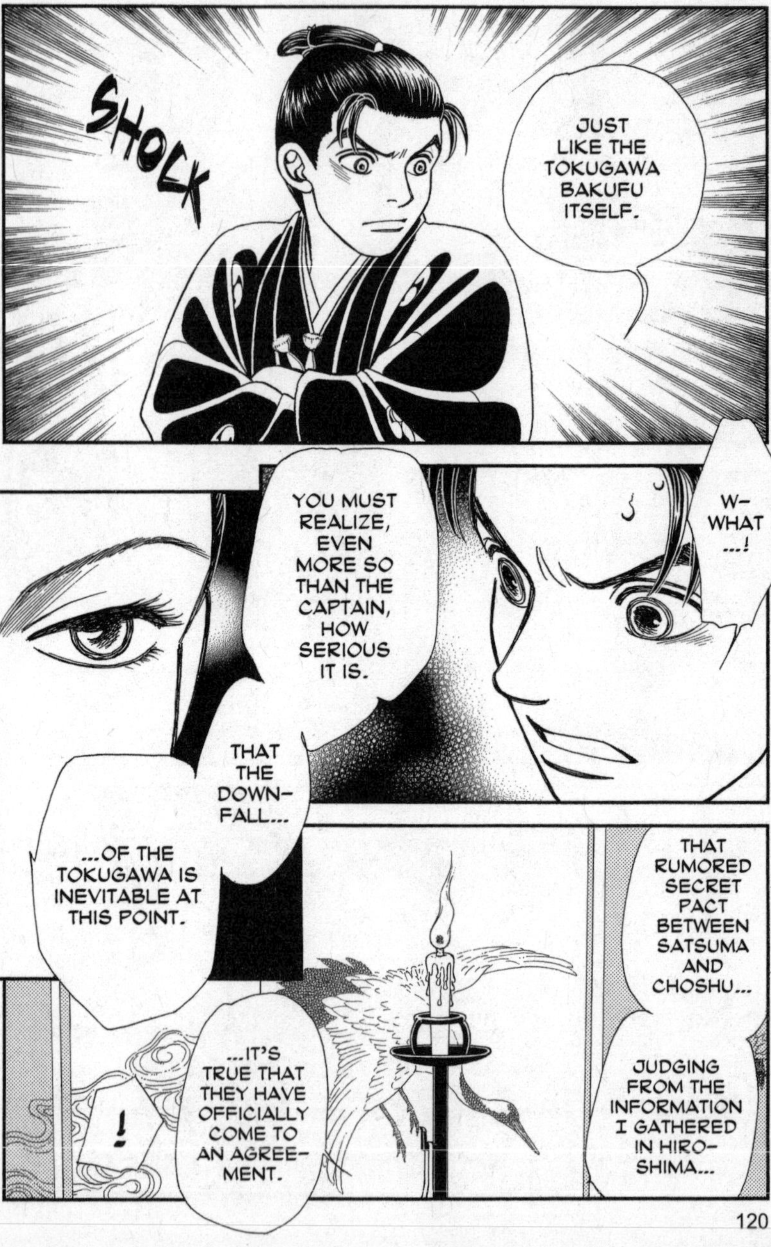
JUST LIKE THE TOKUGAWA BAKUFU ITSELF.
SHOCK
W-WHAT...!
YOU MUST REALIZE, EVEN MORE SO THAN THE CAPTAIN, HOW SERIOUS IT IS.
THAT THE DOWN-FALL...
...OF THE TOKUGAWA IS INEVITABLE AT THIS POINT.
THAT RUMORED SECRET PACT BETWEEN SATSUMA AND CHOSHU...
JUDGING FROM THE INFORMATION I GATHERED IN HIRO-SHIMA...
...IT'S TRUE THAT THEY HAVE OFFICIALLY COME TO AN AGREE-MENT.
!

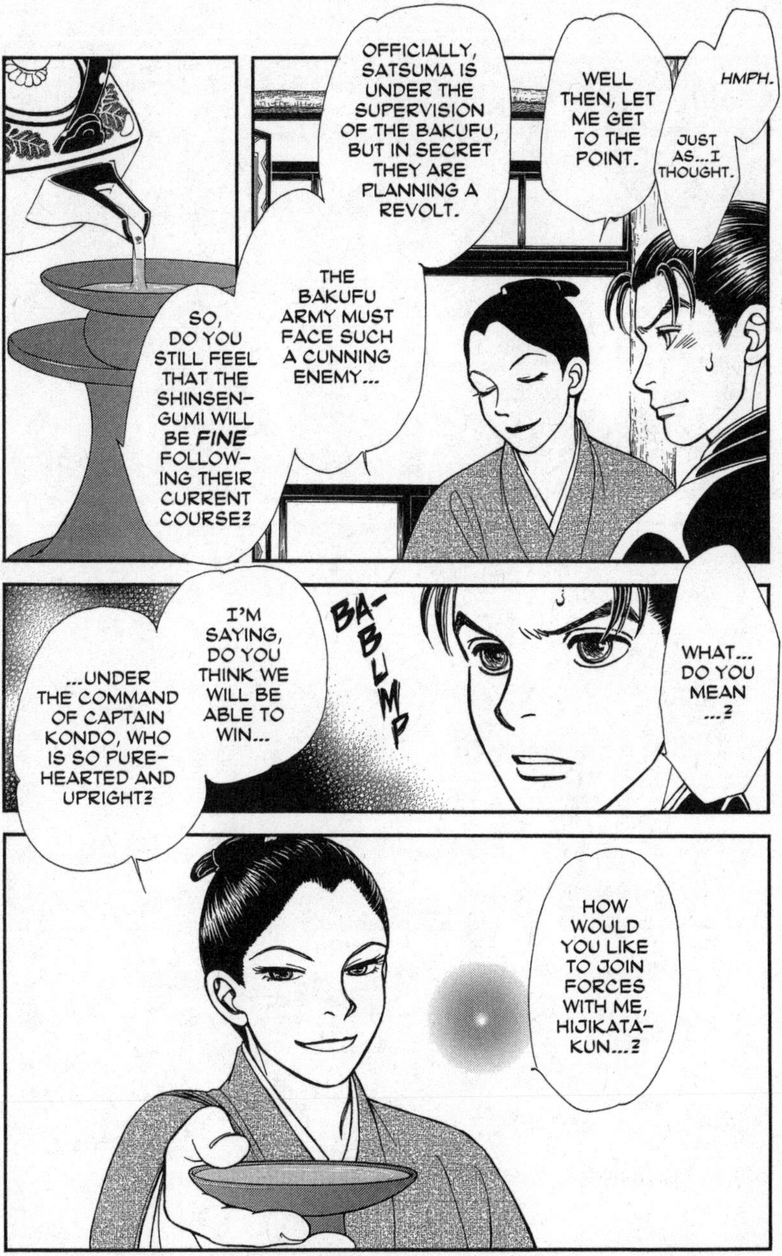
HMPH.
JUST AS...I THOUGHT.
WELL THEN, LET ME GET TO THE POINT.
OFFICIALLY, SATSUMA IS UNDER THE SUPERVISION OF THE BAKUFU, BUT IN SECRET THEY ARE PLANNING A REVOLT.
THE BAKUFU ARMY MUST FACE SUCH A CUNNING ENEMY...
SO, DO YOU STILL FEEL THAT THE SHINSEN-GUMI WILL BE *FINE* FOLLOW-ING THEIR CURRENT COURSE?
WHAT... DO YOU MEAN...?
BA-BUMP
I'M SAYING, DO YOU THINK WE WILL BE ABLE TO WIN...
...UNDER THE COMMAND OF CAPTAIN KONDO, WHO IS SO PURE-HEARTED AND UPRIGHT?
HOW WOULD YOU LIKE TO JOIN FORCES WITH ME, HIJIKATA-KUN...?

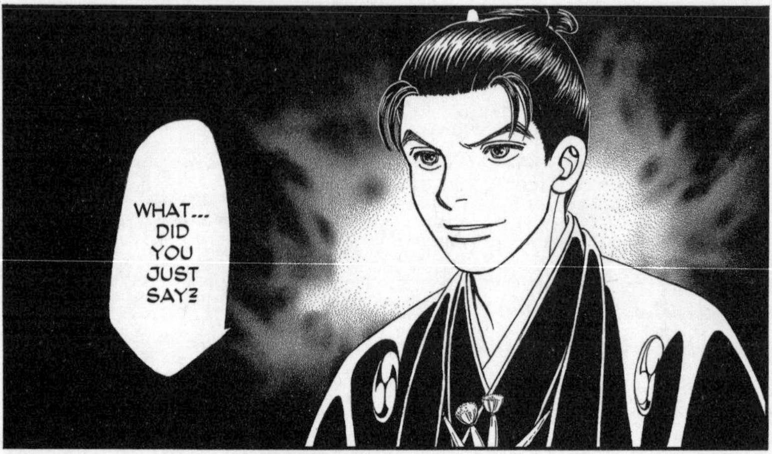
WHAT... DID YOU JUST SAY?

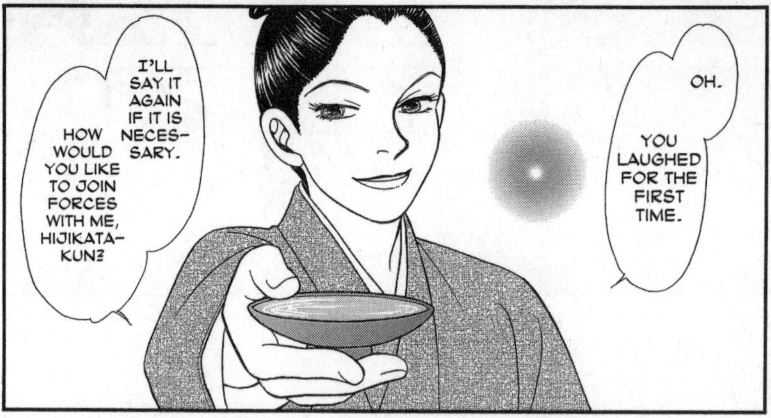
OH.
YOU LAUGHED FOR THE FIRST TIME.
I'LL SAY IT AGAIN IF IT IS NECES-SARY.
HOW WOULD YOU LIKE TO JOIN FORCES WITH ME, HIJIKATA-KUN?

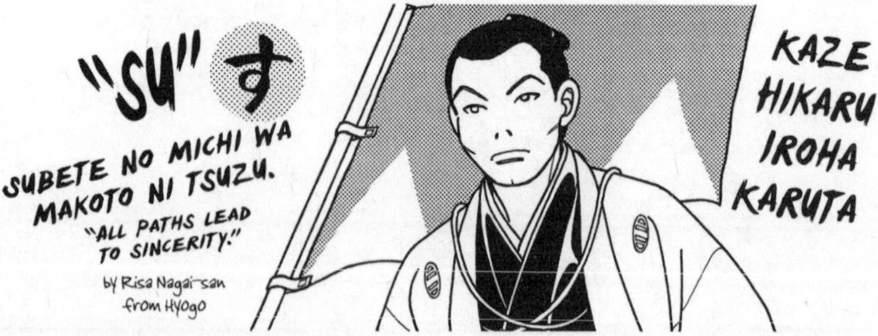
KAZE HIKARU IROHA KARUTA
"SU" す
SUBETE NO MICHI WA MAKOTO NI TSUZU.
"ALL PATHS LEAD TO SINCERITY."
by Risa Nagai-san from Hyogo

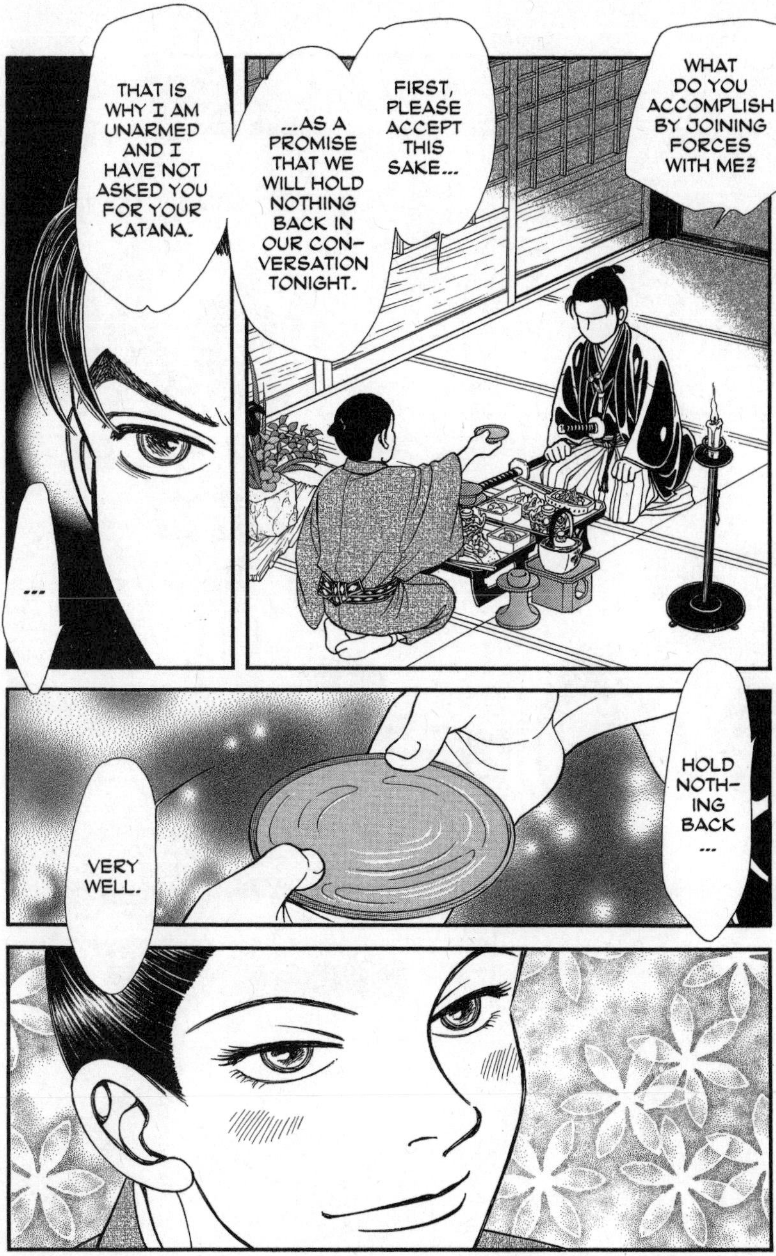

WHAT DO YOU ACCOMPLISH BY JOINING FORCES WITH ME?
FIRST, PLEASE ACCEPT THIS SAKE...
...AS A PROMISE THAT WE WILL HOLD NOTHING BACK IN OUR CON- VERSATION TONIGHT.
THAT IS WHY I AM UNARMED AND I HAVE NOT ASKED YOU FOR YOUR KATANA.
...
HOLD NOTH- ING BACK ...
VERY WELL.

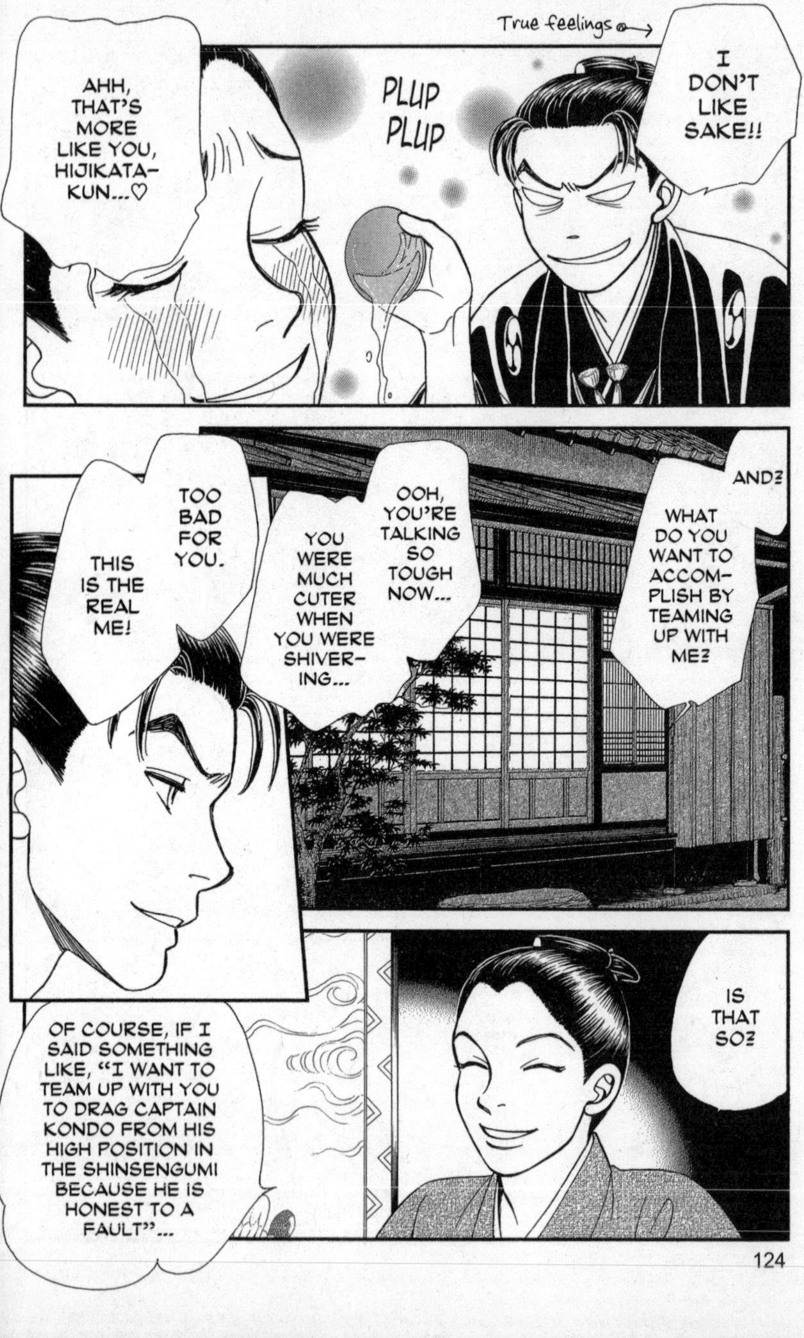
True feelings
I DON'T LIKE SAKE!!
PLUP PLUP
AHH, THAT'S MORE LIKE YOU, HIJIKATA-KUN...♡
AND?
WHAT DO YOU WANT TO ACCOMPLISH BY TEAMING UP WITH ME?
OOH, YOU'RE TALKING SO TOUGH NOW...
YOU WERE MUCH CUTER WHEN YOU WERE SHIVERING...
TOO BAD FOR YOU.
THIS IS THE REAL ME!
IS THAT SO?
OF COURSE, IF I SAID SOMETHING LIKE, "I WANT TO TEAM UP WITH YOU TO DRAG CAPTAIN KONDO FROM HIS HIGH POSITION IN THE SHINSENGUMI BECAUSE HE IS HONEST TO A FAULT"...

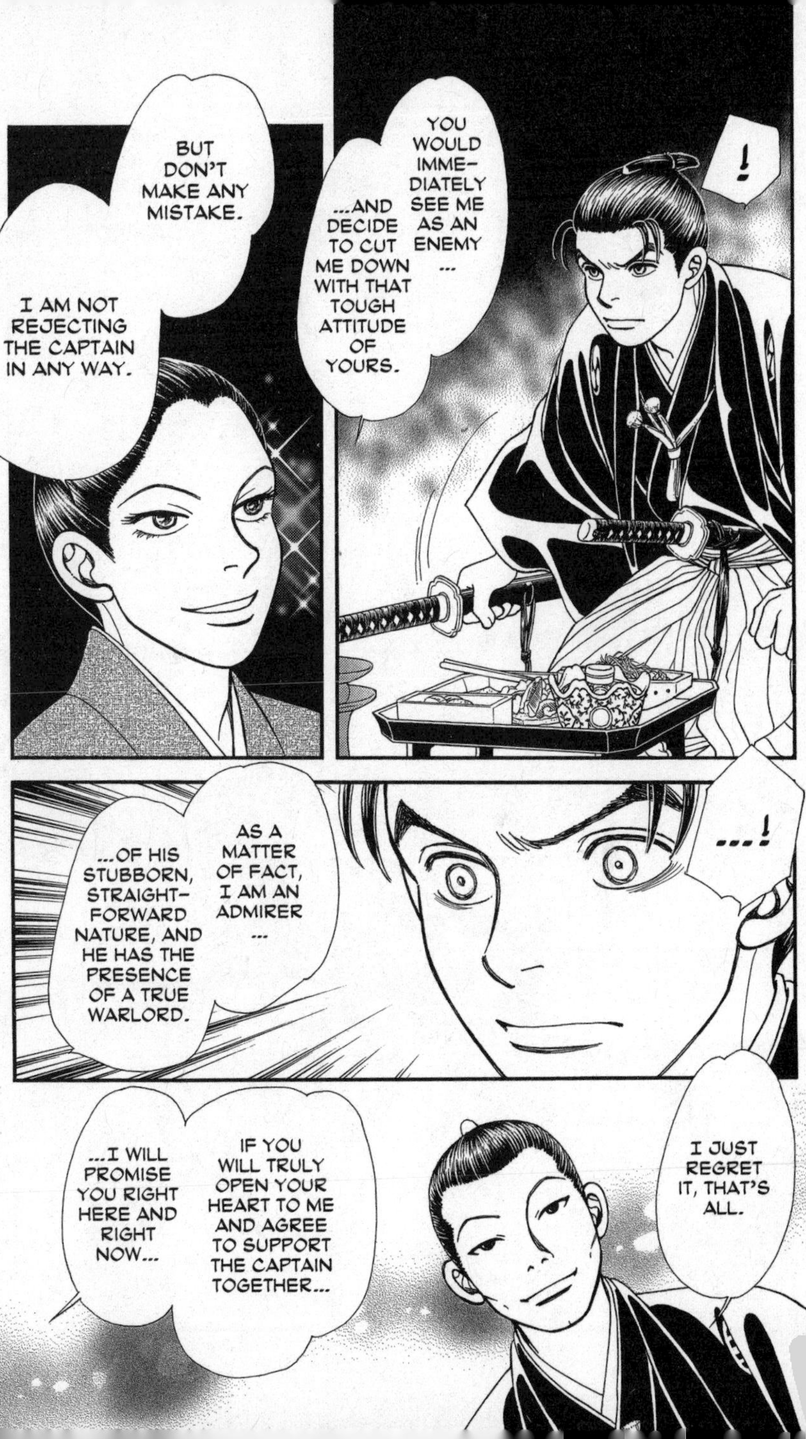
!
YOU WOULD IMMEDIATELY SEE ME AS AN ENEMY...
...AND DECIDE TO CUT ME DOWN WITH THAT TOUGH ATTITUDE OF YOURS.
BUT DON'T MAKE ANY MISTAKE.
I AM NOT REJECTING THE CAPTAIN IN ANY WAY.
...!
AS A MATTER OF FACT, I AM AN ADMIRER...
...OF HIS STUBBORN, STRAIGHTFORWARD NATURE, AND HE HAS THE PRESENCE OF A TRUE WARLORD.
I JUST REGRET IT, THAT'S ALL.
IF YOU WILL TRULY OPEN YOUR HEART TO ME AND AGREE TO SUPPORT THE CAPTAIN TOGETHER...
...I WILL PROMISE YOU RIGHT HERE AND RIGHT NOW...

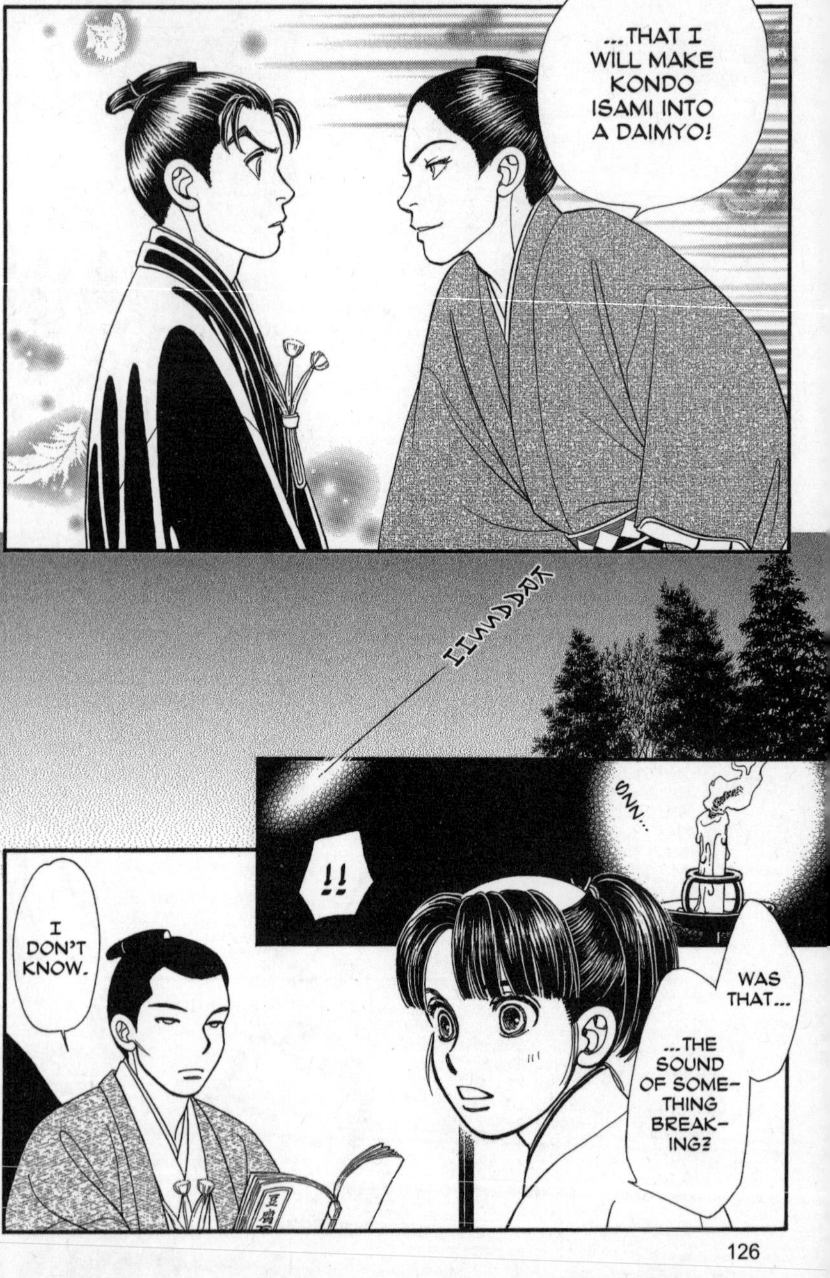
...THAT I WILL MAKE KONDO ISAMI INTO A DAIMYO!
KRRNN!!
SNN...
!!
WAS THAT...
...THE SOUND OF SOME-THING BREAK-ING?
I DON'T KNOW.

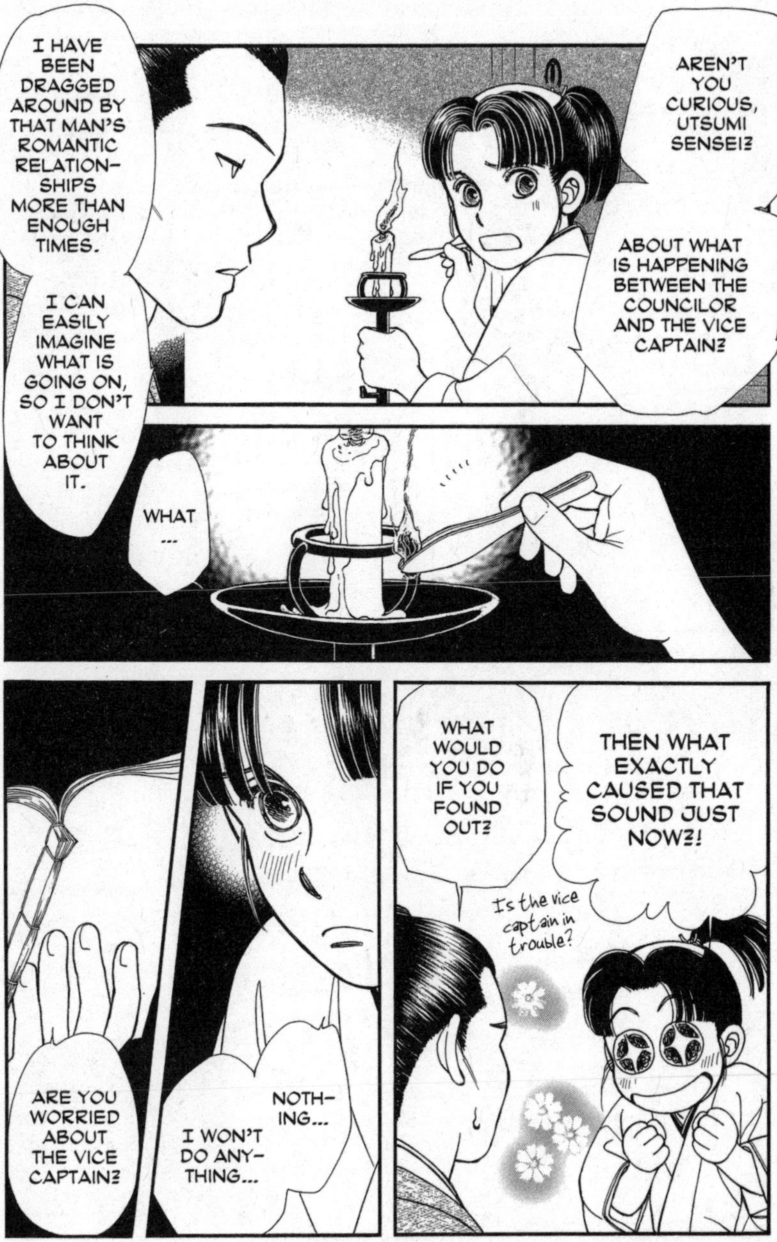

AREN'T YOU CURIOUS, UTSUMI SENSEI?
ABOUT WHAT IS HAPPENING BETWEEN THE COUNCILOR AND THE VICE CAPTAIN?
I HAVE BEEN DRAGGED AROUND BY THAT MAN'S ROMANTIC RELATION-SHIPS MORE THAN ENOUGH TIMES.
I CAN EASILY IMAGINE WHAT IS GOING ON, SO I DON'T WANT TO THINK ABOUT IT.
WHAT ...
THEN WHAT EXACTLY CAUSED THAT SOUND JUST NOW?!
WHAT WOULD YOU DO IF YOU FOUND OUT?
Is the vice captain in trouble?
NOTH-ING...
I WON'T DO ANY-THING...
ARE YOU WORRIED ABOUT THE VICE CAPTAIN?

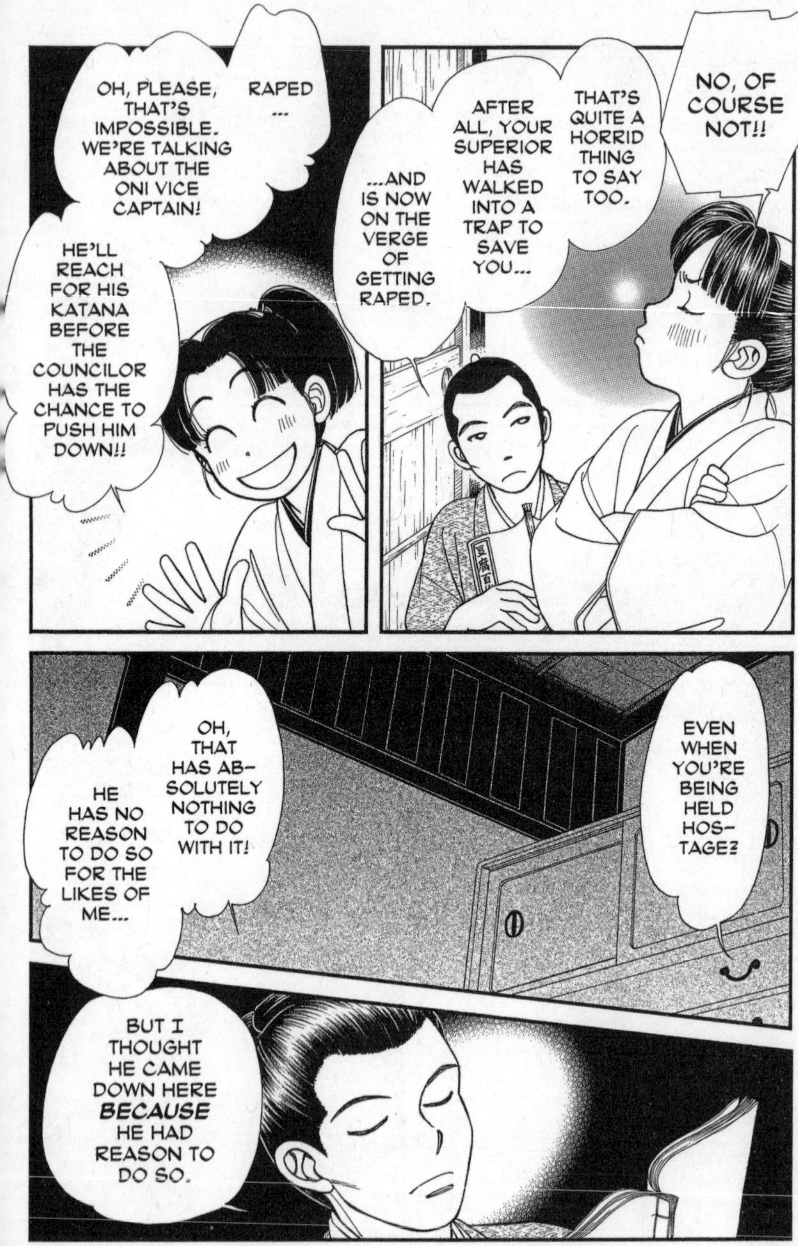
NO, OF COURSE NOT!!
THAT'S QUITE A HORRID THING TO SAY TOO.
AFTER ALL, YOUR SUPERIOR HAS WALKED INTO A TRAP TO SAVE YOU...
...AND IS NOW ON THE VERGE OF GETTING RAPED.
RAPED ...
OH, PLEASE, THAT'S IMPOSSIBLE. WE'RE TALKING ABOUT THE ONI VICE CAPTAIN!
HE'LL REACH FOR HIS KATANA BEFORE THE COUNCILOR HAS THE CHANCE TO PUSH HIM DOWN!!
EVEN WHEN YOU'RE BEING HELD HOS-TAGE?
OH, THAT HAS AB-SOLUTELY NOTHING TO DO WITH IT!
HE HAS NO REASON TO DO SO FOR THE LIKES OF ME...
BUT I THOUGHT HE CAME DOWN HERE *BECAUSE* HE HAD REASON TO DO SO.

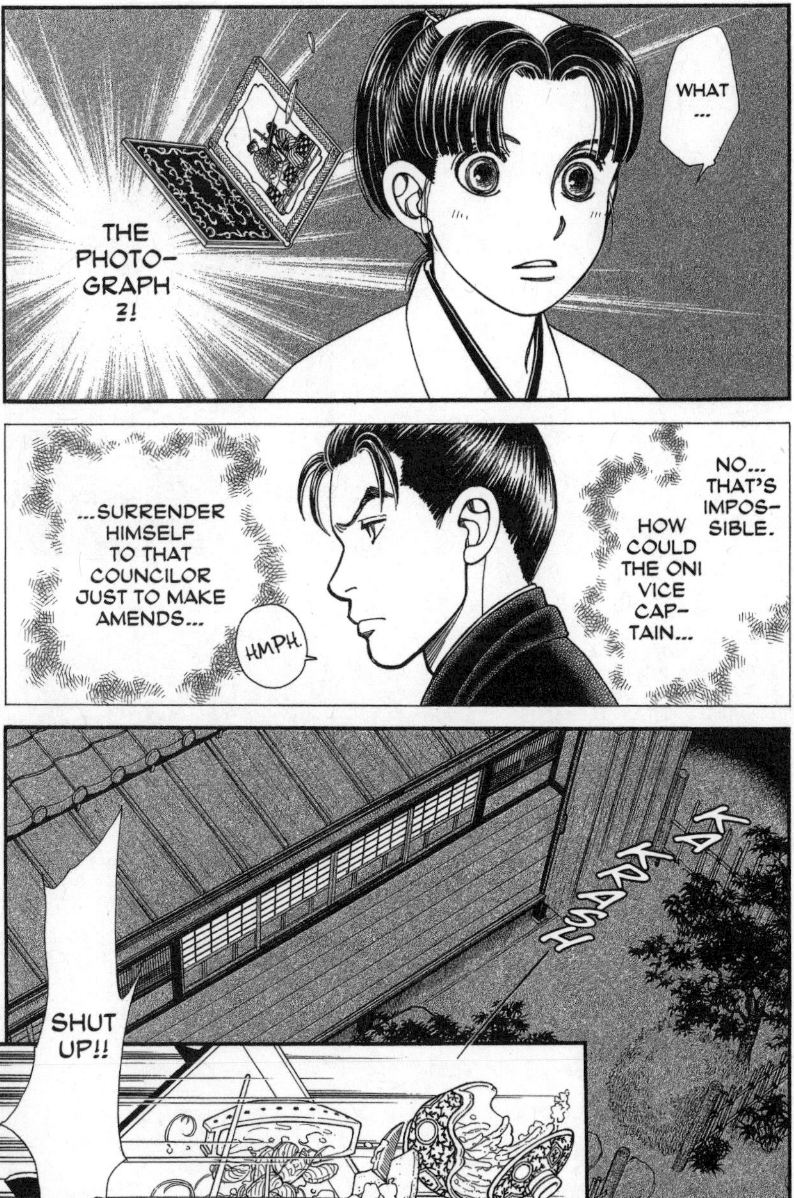
WHAT ...
THE PHOTOGRAPH ?!
NO... THAT'S IMPOSSIBLE.
HOW COULD THE ONI VICE CAPTAIN...
...SURRENDER HIMSELF TO THAT COUNCILOR JUST TO MAKE AMENDS...
HMPH.
KAKRASH
SHUT UP!!

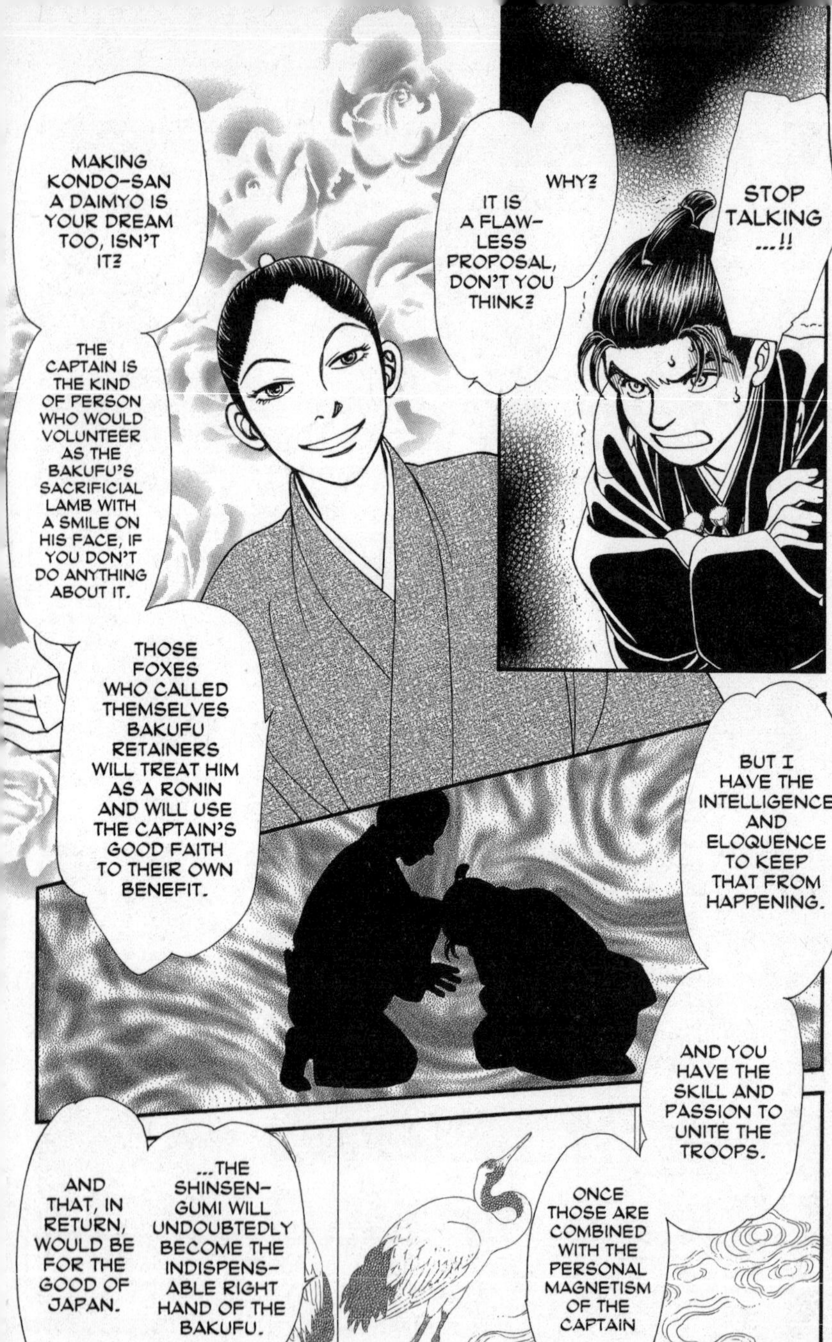

STOP TALKING ...!!
WHY? IT IS A FLAW-LESS PROPOSAL, DON'T YOU THINK?
MAKING KONDO-SAN A DAIMYO IS YOUR DREAM TOO, ISN'T IT?
THE CAPTAIN IS THE KIND OF PERSON WHO WOULD VOLUNTEER AS THE BAKUFU'S SACRIFICIAL LAMB WITH A SMILE ON HIS FACE, IF YOU DON'T DO ANYTHING ABOUT IT.
THOSE FOXES WHO CALLED THEMSELVES BAKUFU RETAINERS WILL TREAT HIM AS A RONIN AND WILL USE THE CAPTAIN'S GOOD FAITH TO THEIR OWN BENEFIT.
BUT I HAVE THE INTELLIGENCE AND ELOQUENCE TO KEEP THAT FROM HAPPENING.
AND YOU HAVE THE SKILL AND PASSION TO UNITE THE TROOPS.
ONCE THOSE ARE COMBINED WITH THE PERSONAL MAGNETISM OF THE CAPTAIN ...
...THE SHINSEN-GUMI WILL UNDOUBTEDLY BECOME THE INDISPENS-ABLE RIGHT HAND OF THE BAKUFU.
AND THAT, IN RETURN, WOULD BE FOR THE GOOD OF JAPAN.

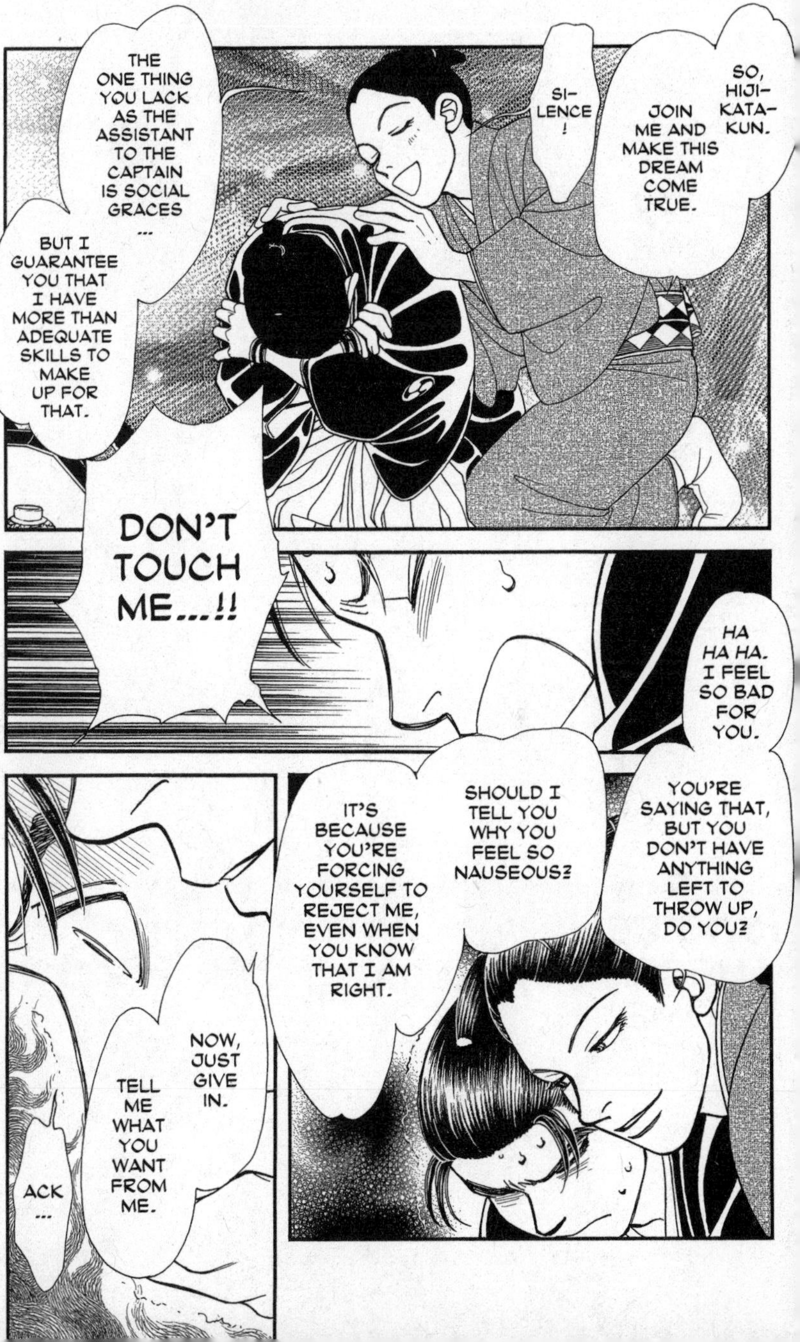
SO, HIJI-KATA-KUN.
JOIN ME AND MAKE THIS DREAM COME TRUE.
SI-LENCE!
THE ONE THING YOU LACK AS THE ASSISTANT TO THE CAPTAIN IS SOCIAL GRACES...
BUT I GUARANTEE YOU THAT I HAVE MORE THAN ADEQUATE SKILLS TO MAKE UP FOR THAT.
DON'T TOUCH ME...!!
HA HA HA. I FEEL SO BAD FOR YOU.
YOU'RE SAYING THAT, BUT YOU DON'T HAVE ANYTHING LEFT TO THROW UP, DO YOU?
SHOULD I TELL YOU WHY YOU FEEL SO NAUSEOUS?
IT'S BECAUSE YOU'RE FORCING YOURSELF TO REJECT ME, EVEN WHEN YOU KNOW THAT I AM RIGHT.
NOW, JUST GIVE IN.
TELL ME WHAT YOU WANT FROM ME.
ACK...

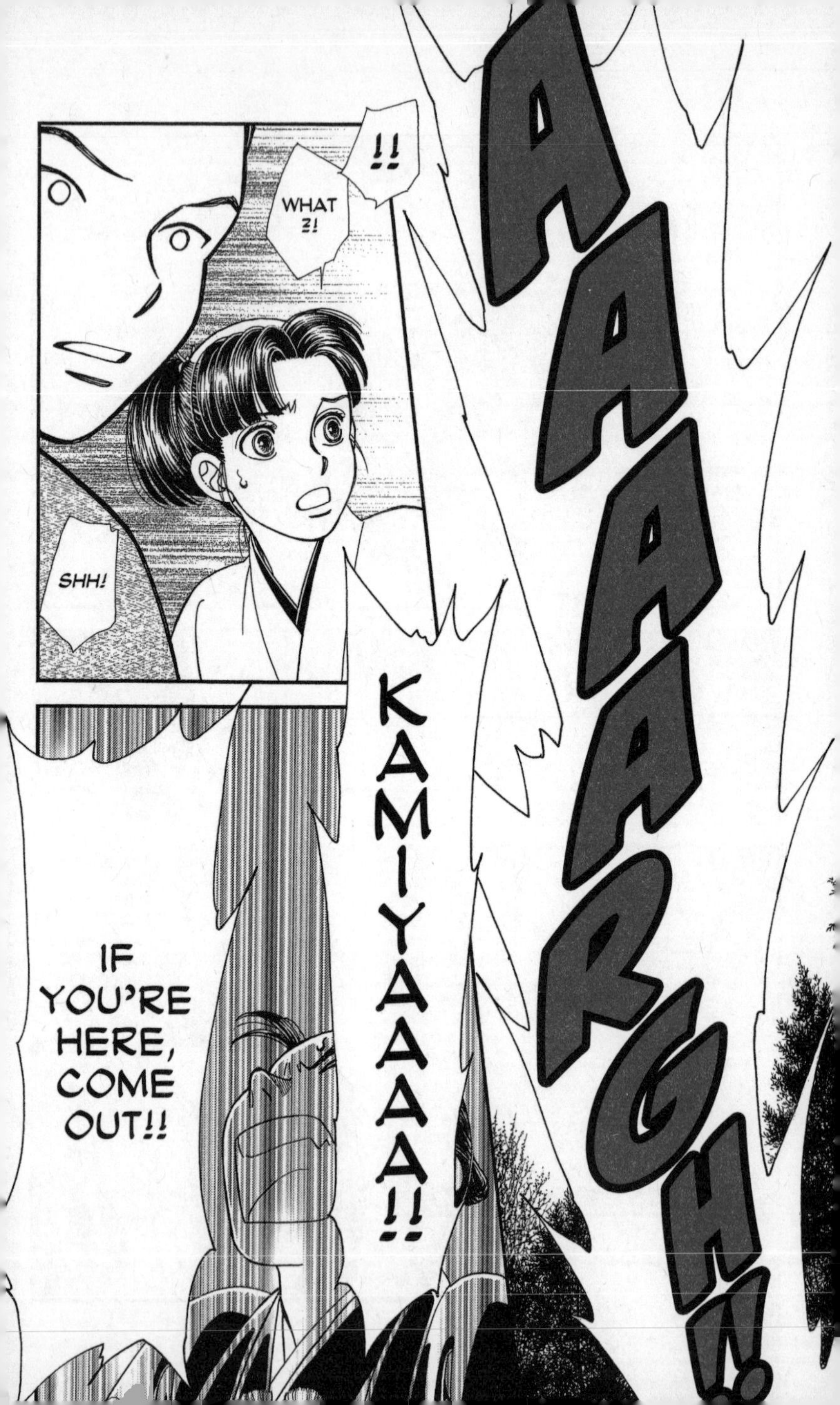
AAAARGH!!
!!
WHAT ?!
SHH!
KAMIYAAAA!!
IF YOU'RE HERE, COME OUT!!

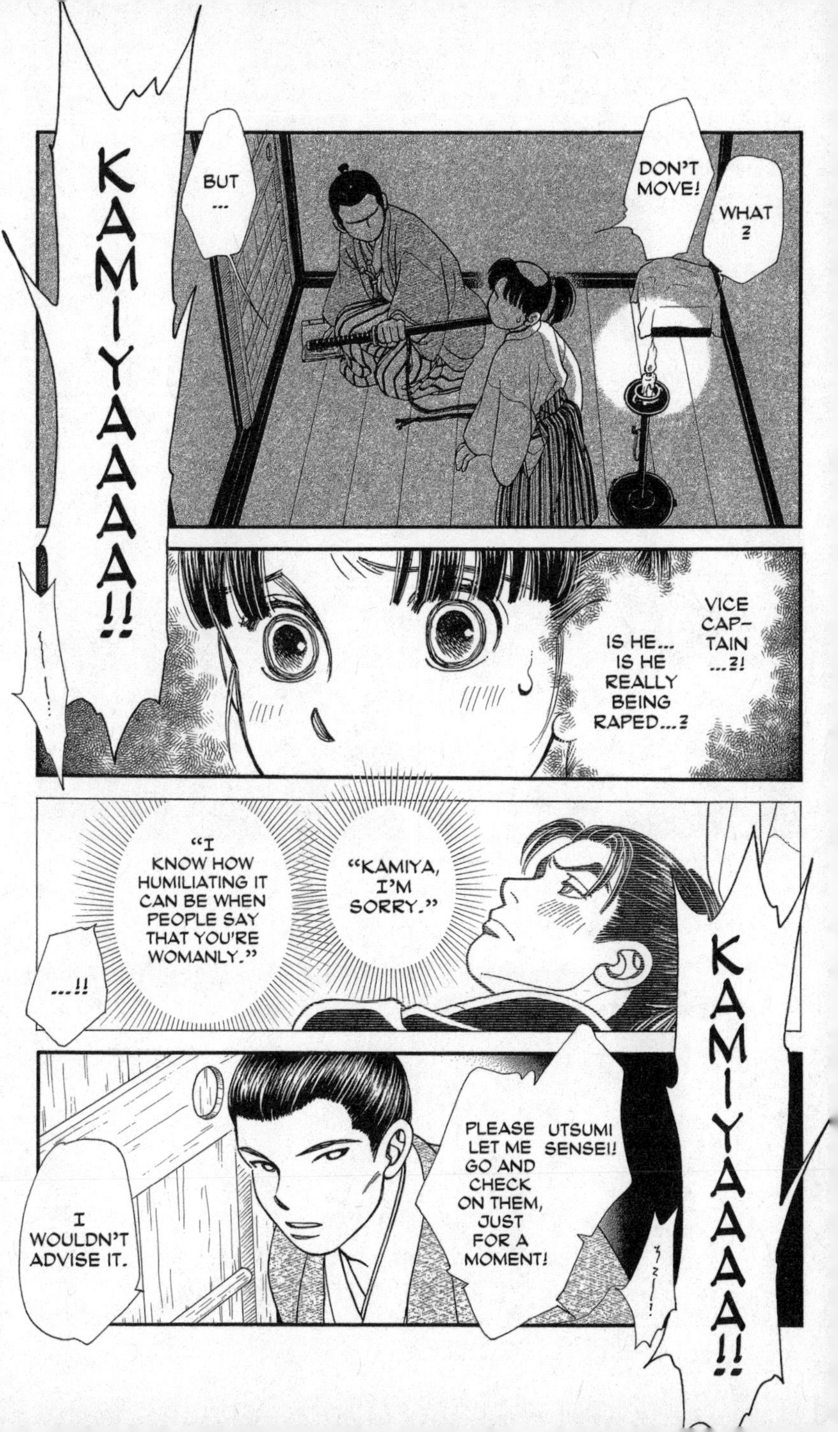
DON'T MOVE!
WHAT?
BUT ...
KAMIYAAAAA!!
VICE CAPTAIN ...?!
IS HE... IS HE REALLY BEING RAPED...?
KAMIYAAAAA!!
"KAMIYA, I'M SORRY."
"I KNOW HOW HUMILIATING IT CAN BE WHEN PEOPLE SAY THAT YOU'RE WOMANLY."
...!!
UTSUMI SENSEI!
PLEASE LET ME GO AND CHECK ON THEM, JUST FOR A MOMENT!
I WOULDN'T ADVISE IT.

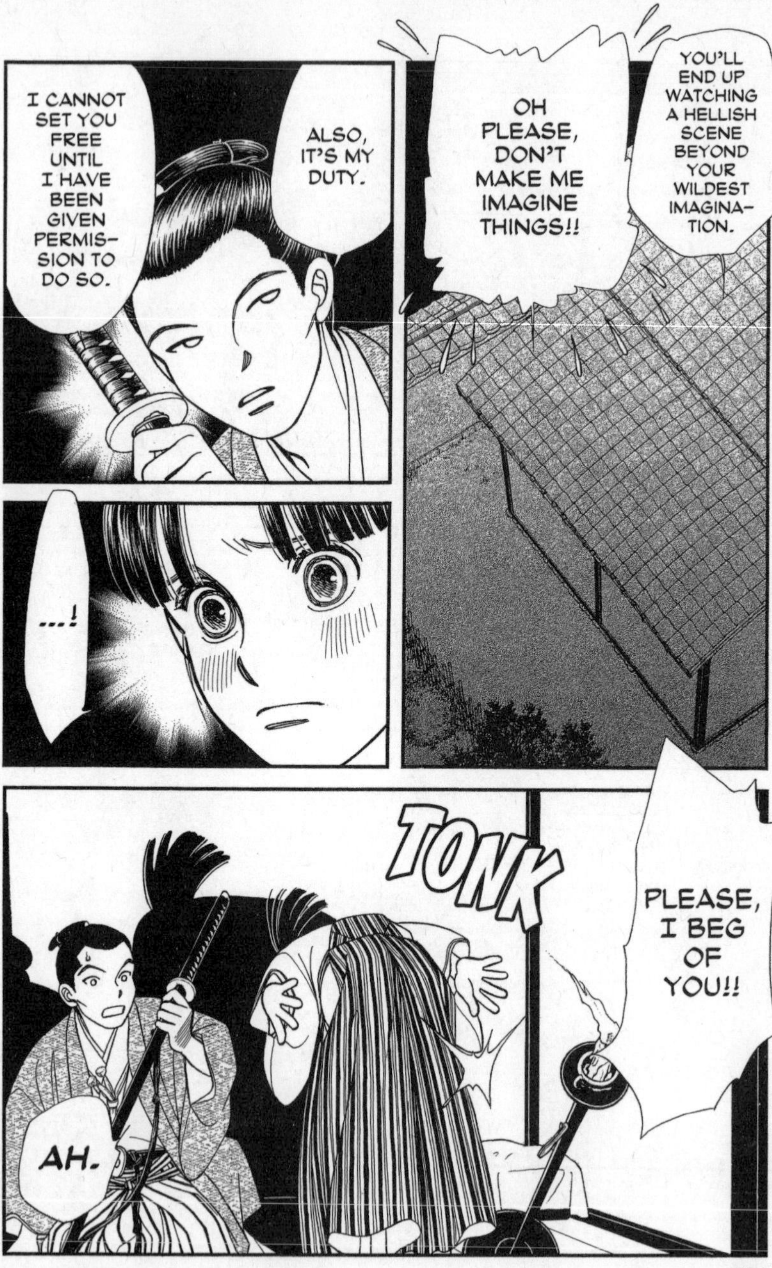
YOU'LL END UP WATCHING A HELLISH SCENE BEYOND YOUR WILDEST IMAGINA-TION.
OH PLEASE, DON'T MAKE ME IMAGINE THINGS!!
ALSO, IT'S MY DUTY.
I CANNOT SET YOU FREE UNTIL I HAVE BEEN GIVEN PERMIS-SION TO DO SO.
...!
PLEASE, I BEG OF YOU!!
TONK
AH.

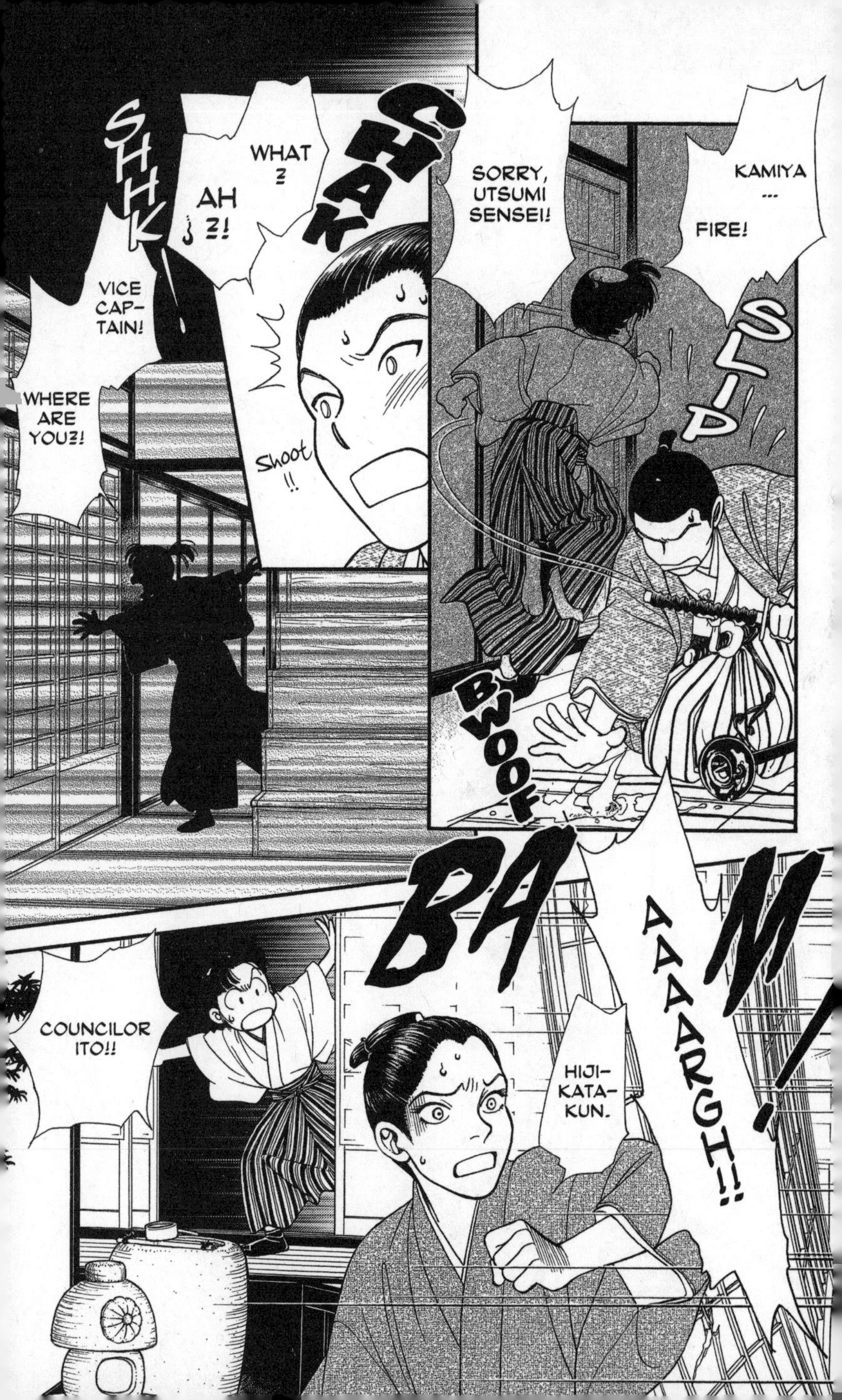

KAMIYA... FIRE!
SORRY, UTSUMI SENSEI!
SLIP
BWOOF
WHAT?
CHAK
AH?!
Shoot!!
SHHHK
VICE CAPTAIN!
WHERE ARE YOU?!
BAM!
AAAARGH!!
HIJI-KATA-KUN.
COUNCILOR ITO!!

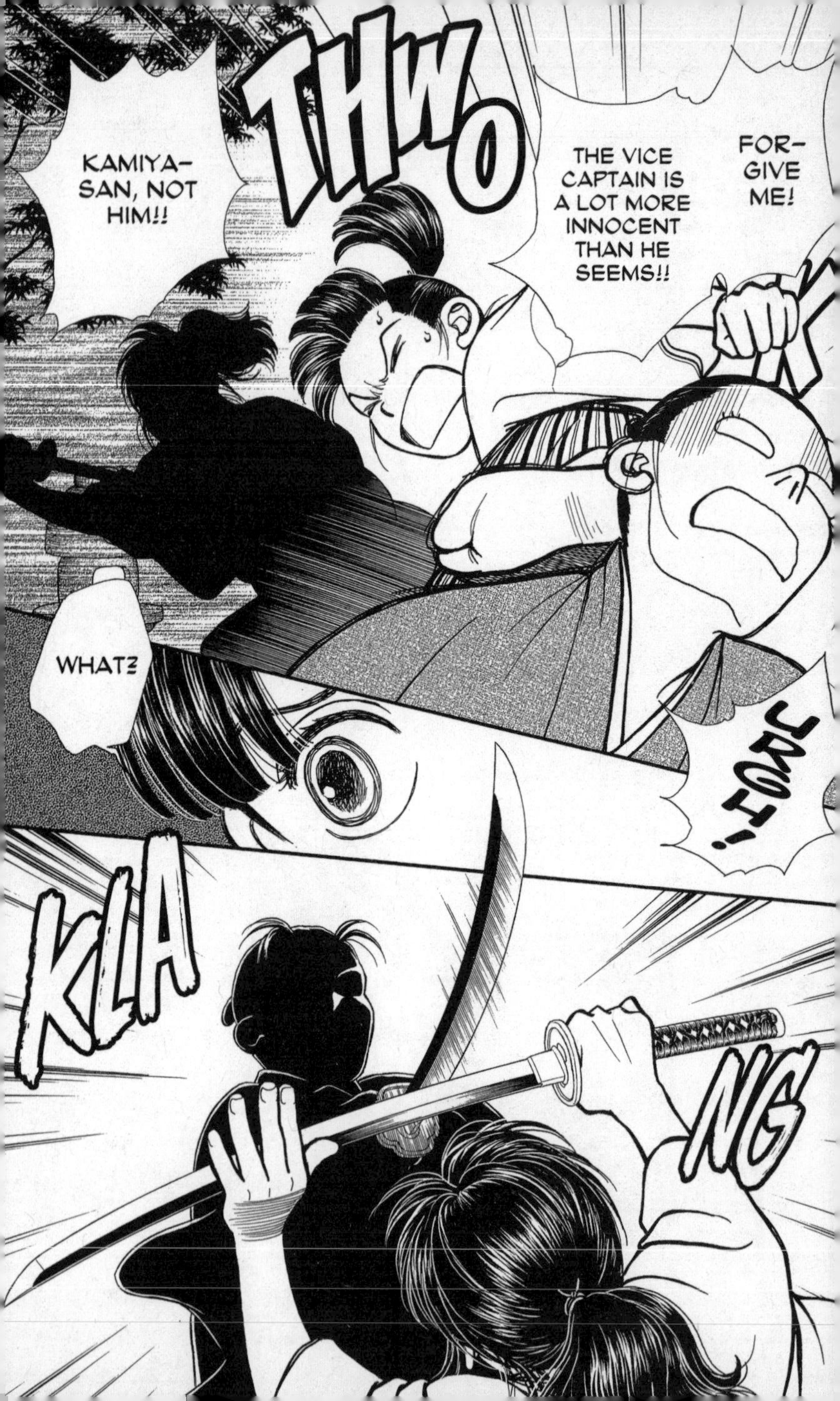
FOR-GIVE ME!
THE VICE CAPTAIN IS A LOT MORE INNOCENT THAN HE SEEMS!!
THWO
KAMIYA-SAN, NOT HIM!!
URGH!
WHAT?
KLA
NG

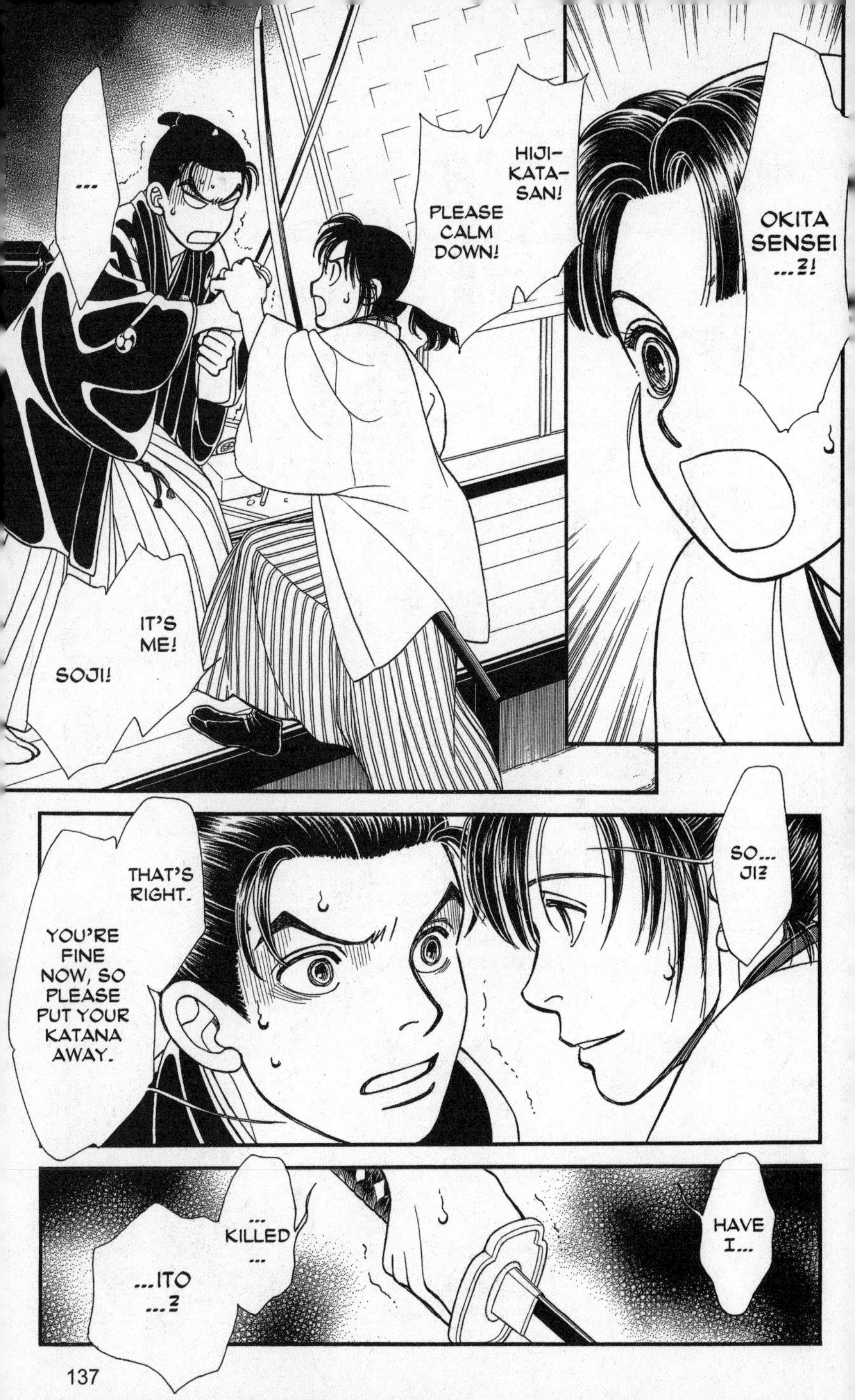
OKITA SENSEI ...?!
HIJI-KATA-SAN!
PLEASE CALM DOWN!
...
IT'S ME!
SOJI!
SO... JI?
THAT'S RIGHT.
YOU'RE FINE NOW, SO PLEASE PUT YOUR KATANA AWAY.
HAVE I...
...KILLED...
...ITO...?

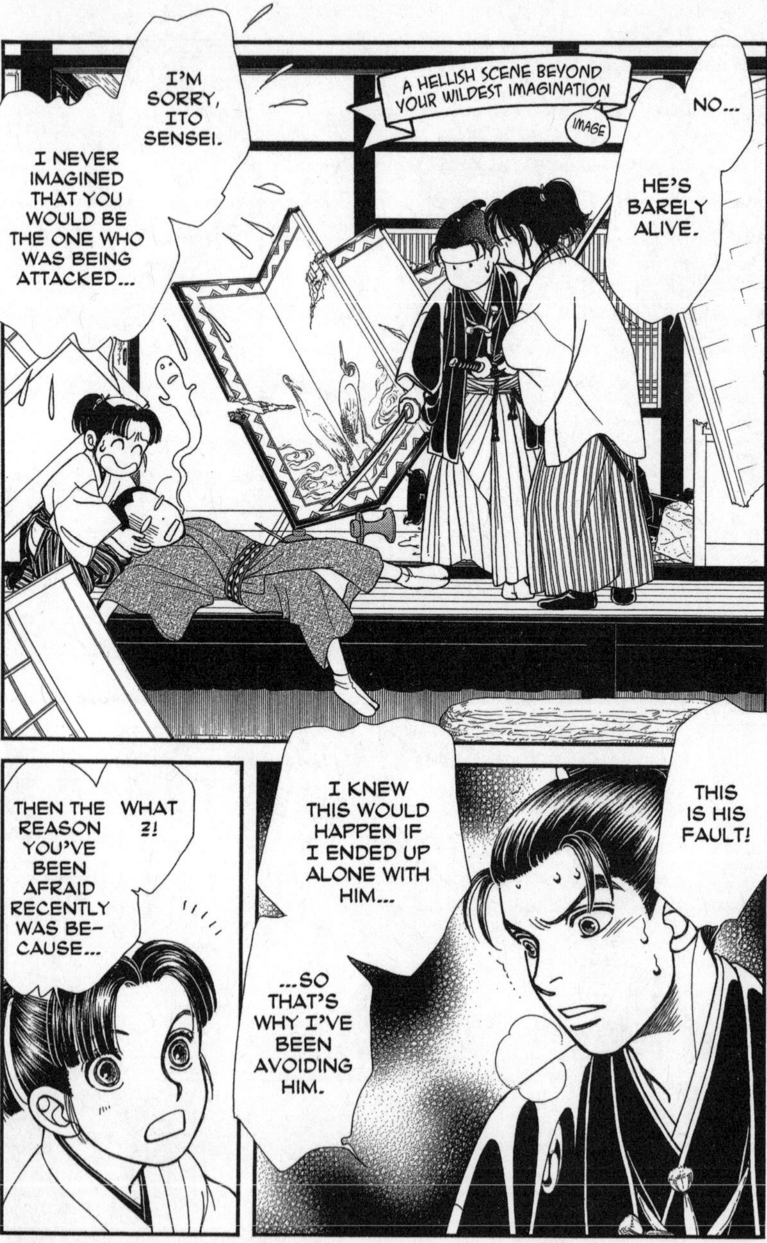
NO...
HE'S BARELY ALIVE.
A HELLISH SCENE BEYOND YOUR WILDEST IMAGINATION
IMAGE
I'M SORRY, ITO SENSEI.
I NEVER IMAGINED THAT YOU WOULD BE THE ONE WHO WAS BEING ATTACKED...
THIS IS HIS FAULT!
I KNEW THIS WOULD HAPPEN IF I ENDED UP ALONE WITH HIM...
...SO THAT'S WHY I'VE BEEN AVOIDING HIM.
WHAT ?!
THEN THE REASON YOU'VE BEEN AFRAID RECENTLY WAS BE-CAUSE...

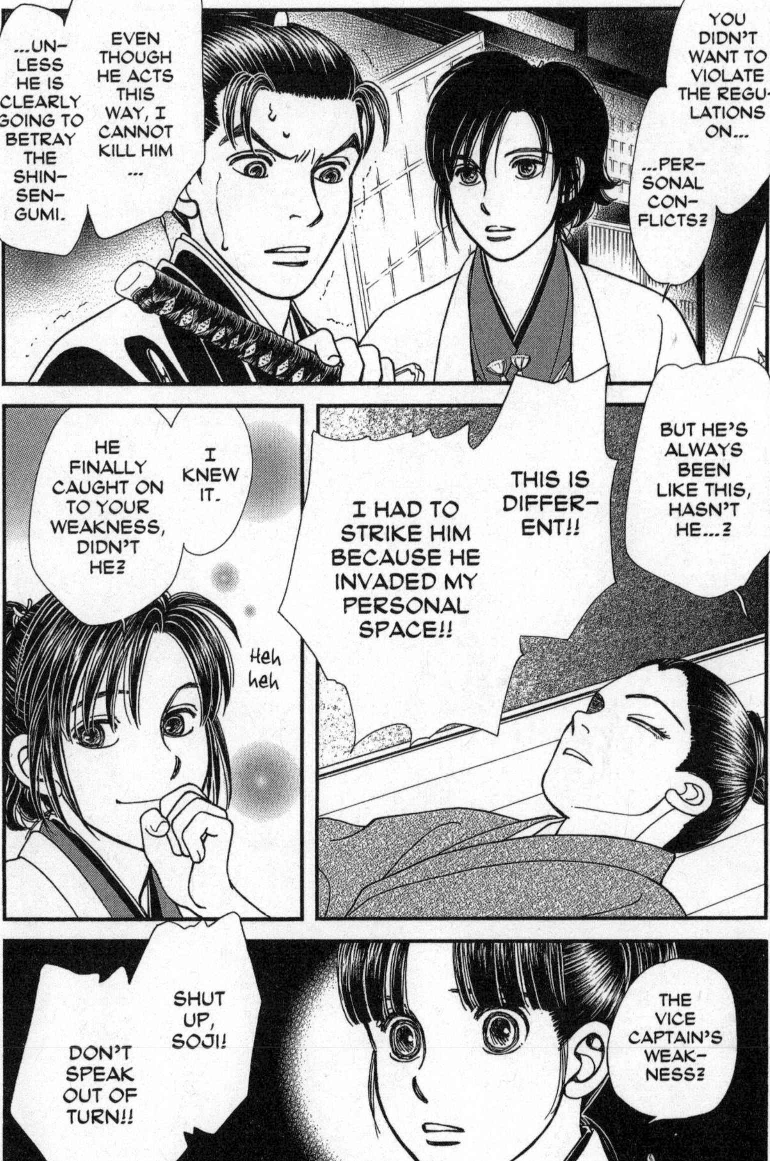
YOU DIDN'T WANT TO VIOLATE THE REGULATIONS ON...
...PERSONAL CONFLICTS?
EVEN THOUGH HE ACTS THIS WAY, I CANNOT KILL HIM...
...UNLESS HE IS CLEARLY GOING TO BETRAY THE SHINSENGUMI.
BUT HE'S ALWAYS BEEN LIKE THIS, HASN'T HE...?
THIS IS DIFFERENT!!
I HAD TO STRIKE HIM BECAUSE HE INVADED MY PERSONAL SPACE!!
I KNEW IT.
HE FINALLY CAUGHT ON TO YOUR WEAKNESS, DIDN'T HE?
Heh heh
THE VICE CAPTAIN'S WEAKNESS?
SHUT UP, SOJI!
DON'T SPEAK OUT OF TURN!!

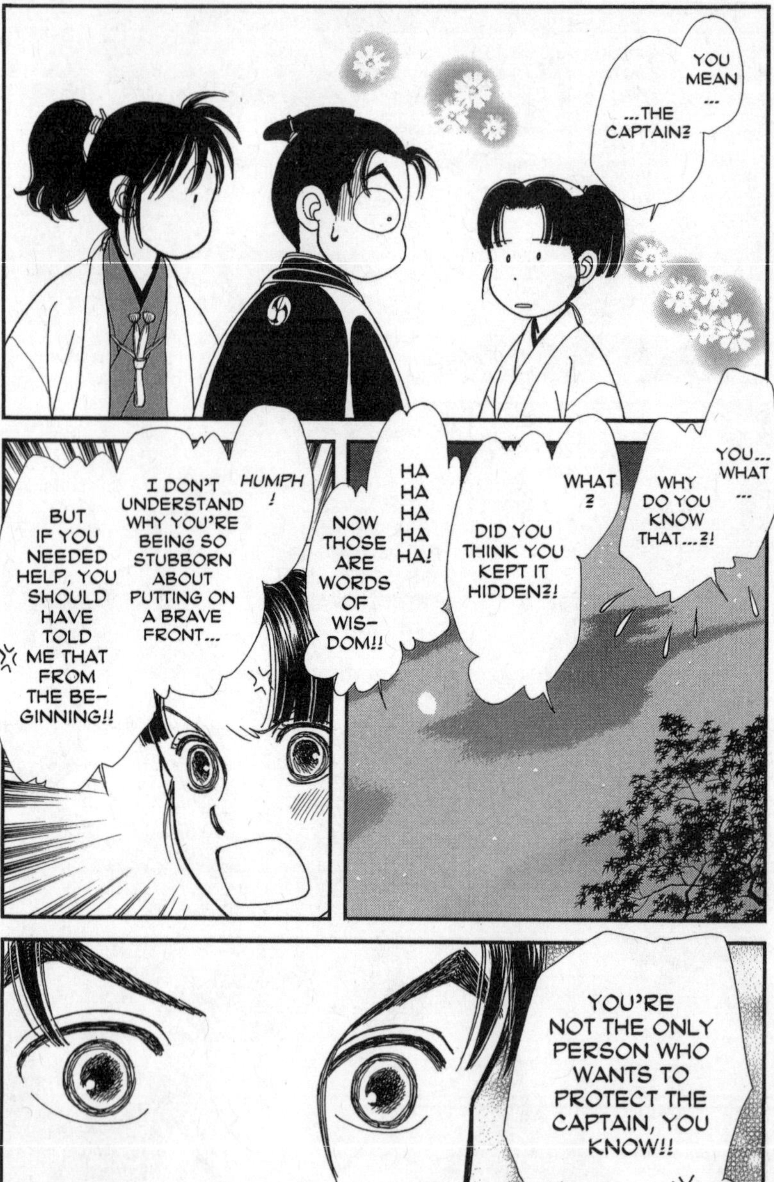
YOU MEAN ... ...THE CAPTAIN?
YOU... WHAT...
WHY DO YOU KNOW THAT...?!
WHAT?
DID YOU THINK YOU KEPT IT HIDDEN?!
HA HA HA HA HA!
NOW THOSE ARE WORDS OF WISDOM!!
HUMPH!
I DON'T UNDERSTAND WHY YOU'RE BEING SO STUBBORN ABOUT PUTTING ON A BRAVE FRONT...
BUT IF YOU NEEDED HELP, YOU SHOULD HAVE TOLD ME THAT FROM THE BEGINNING!!
YOU'RE NOT THE ONLY PERSON WHO WANTS TO PROTECT THE CAPTAIN, YOU KNOW!!

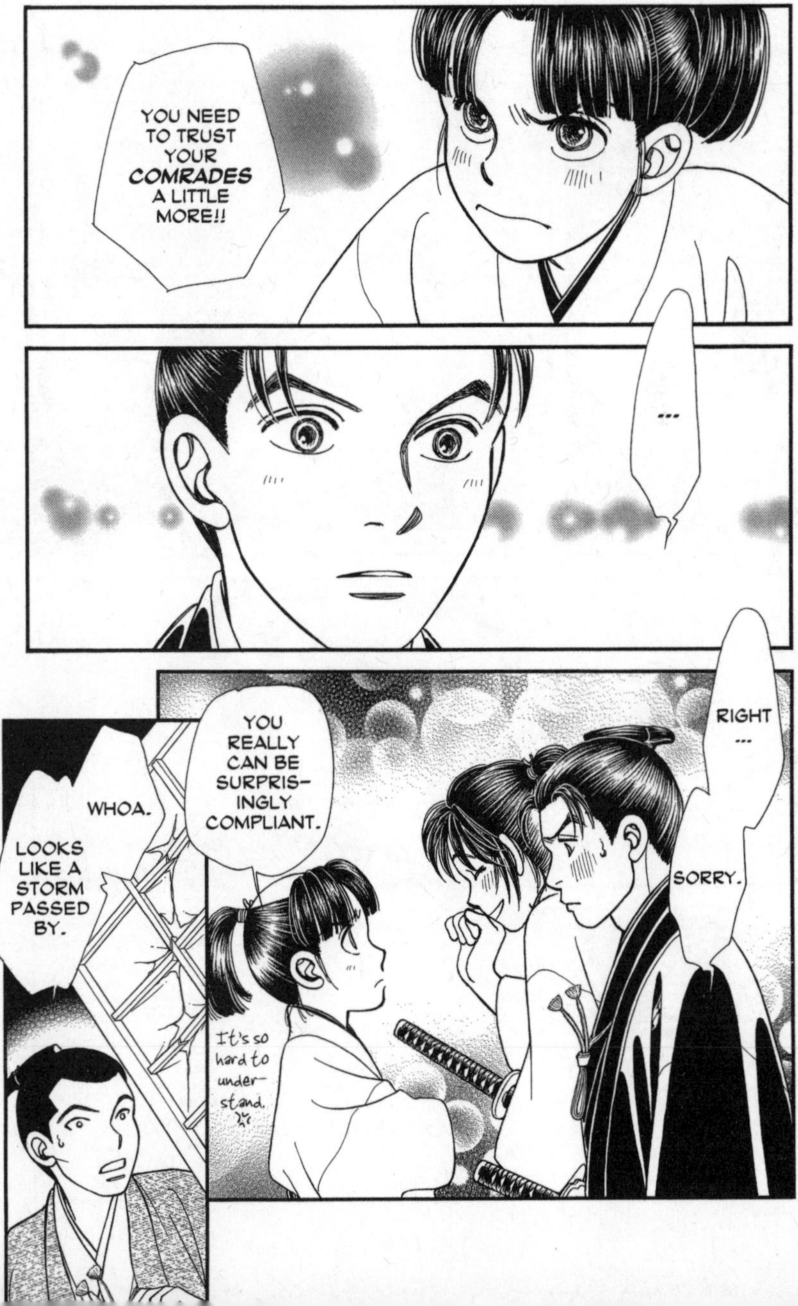
YOU NEED TO TRUST YOUR COMRADES A LITTLE MORE!!
...
RIGHT ...
SORRY.
YOU REALLY CAN BE SURPRIS-INGLY COMPLIANT.
It's so hard to under-stand.
WHOA.
LOOKS LIKE A STORM PASSED BY.

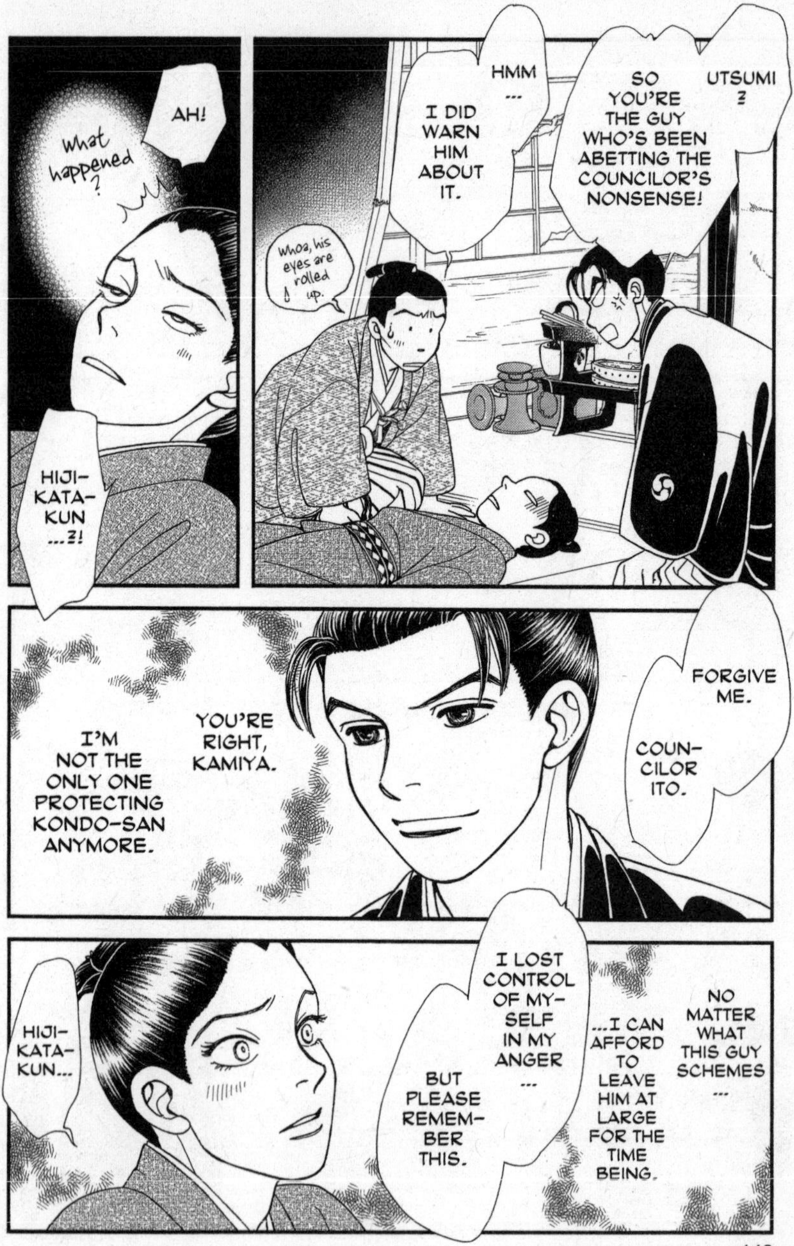

UTSUMI?
SO YOU'RE THE GUY WHO'S BEEN ABETTING THE COUNCILOR'S NONSENSE!
HMM ...
I DID WARN HIM ABOUT IT.
Whoa, his eyes are rolled up.
AH!
What happened?
HIJI-KATA-KUN ...?!
FORGIVE ME.
COUN-CILOR ITO.
YOU'RE RIGHT, KAMIYA.
I'M NOT THE ONLY ONE PROTECTING KONDO-SAN ANYMORE.
NO MATTER WHAT THIS GUY SCHEMES ...
...I CAN AFFORD TO LEAVE HIM AT LARGE FOR THE TIME BEING.
I LOST CONTROL OF MY-SELF IN MY ANGER ...
BUT PLEASE REMEM-BER THIS.
HIJI-KATA-KUN...

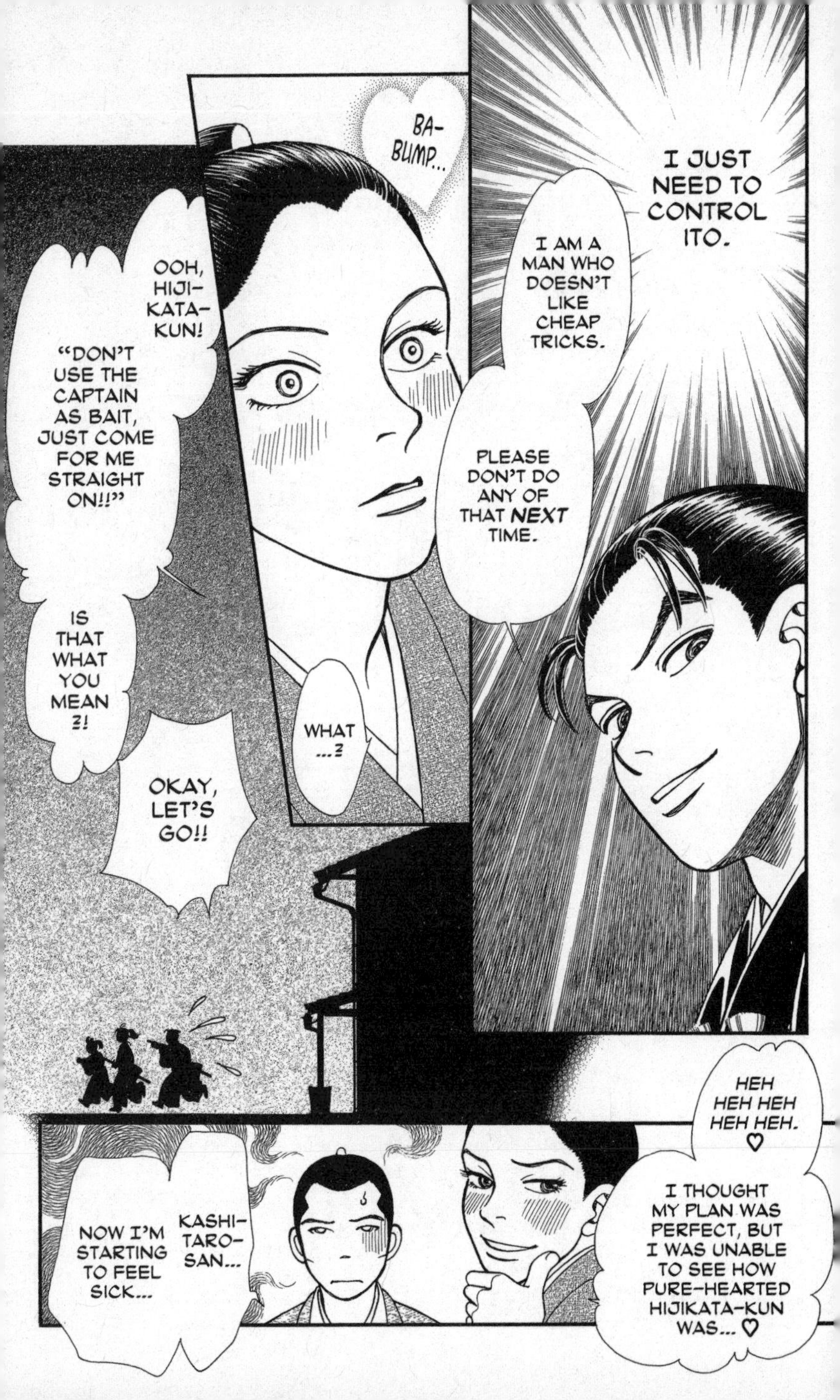
I JUST NEED TO CONTROL ITO.
I AM A MAN WHO DOESN'T LIKE CHEAP TRICKS.
PLEASE DON'T DO ANY OF THAT ***NEXT*** TIME.
BA-BUMP...
WHAT ...?
OOH, HIJI-KATA-KUN!
“DON'T USE THE CAPTAIN AS BAIT, JUST COME FOR ME STRAIGHT ON!!”
IS THAT WHAT YOU MEAN ?!
OKAY, LET'S GO!!
HEH HEH HEH HEH HEH. ♡
I THOUGHT MY PLAN WAS PERFECT, BUT I WAS UNABLE TO SEE HOW PURE-HEARTED HIJIKATA-KUN WAS... ♡
KASHI-TARO-SAN...
NOW I'M STARTING TO FEEL SICK...

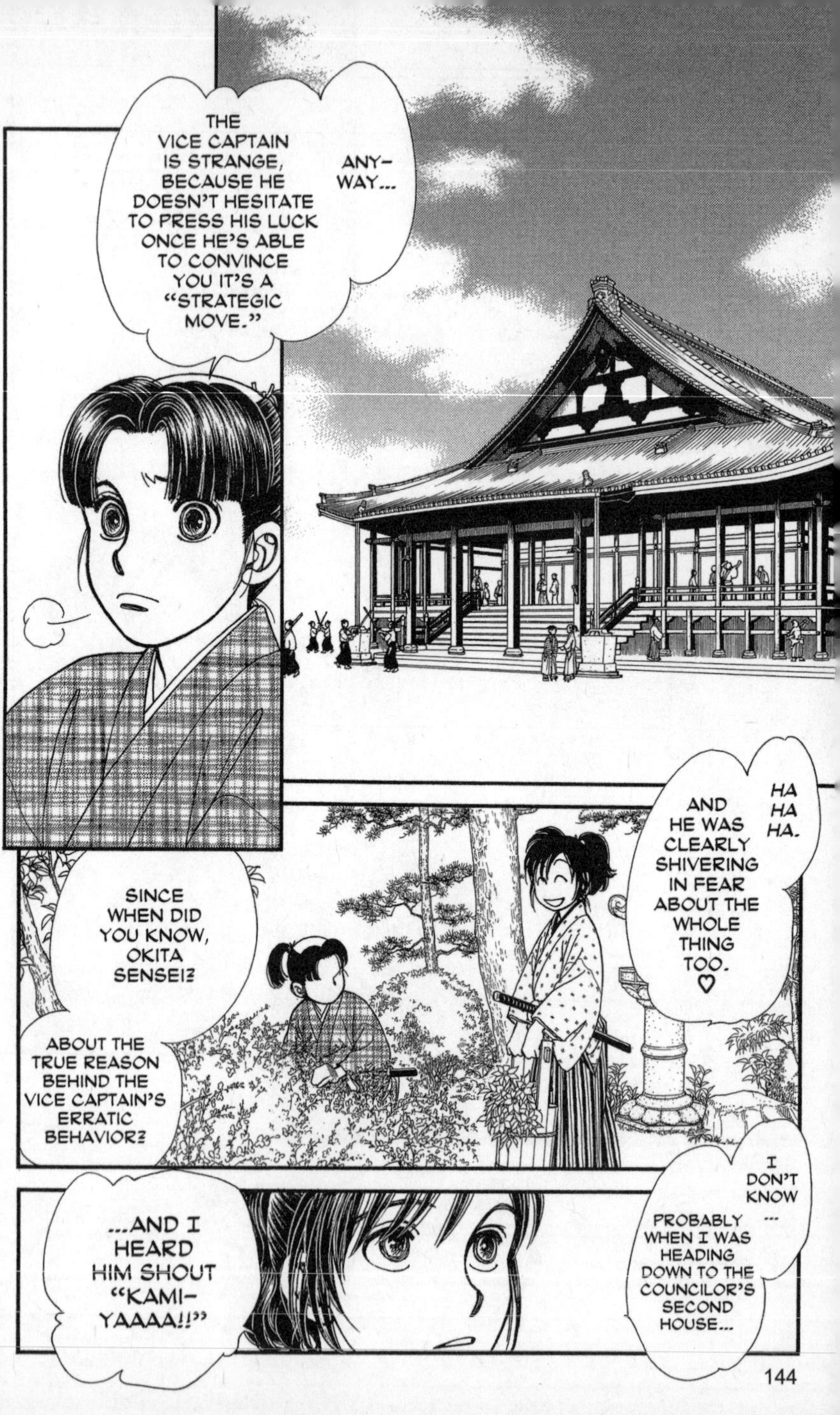
ANY- WAY...
THE VICE CAPTAIN IS STRANGE, BECAUSE HE DOESN'T HESITATE TO PRESS HIS LUCK ONCE HE'S ABLE TO CONVINCE YOU IT'S A "STRATEGIC MOVE."
HA HA HA.
AND HE WAS CLEARLY SHIVERING IN FEAR ABOUT THE WHOLE THING TOO. ♡
SINCE WHEN DID YOU KNOW, OKITA SENSEI?
ABOUT THE TRUE REASON BEHIND THE VICE CAPTAIN'S ERRATIC BEHAVIOR?
I DON'T KNOW ...
PROBABLY WHEN I WAS HEADING DOWN TO THE COUNCILOR'S SECOND HOUSE...
...AND I HEARD HIM SHOUT "KAMI-YAAAA!!"

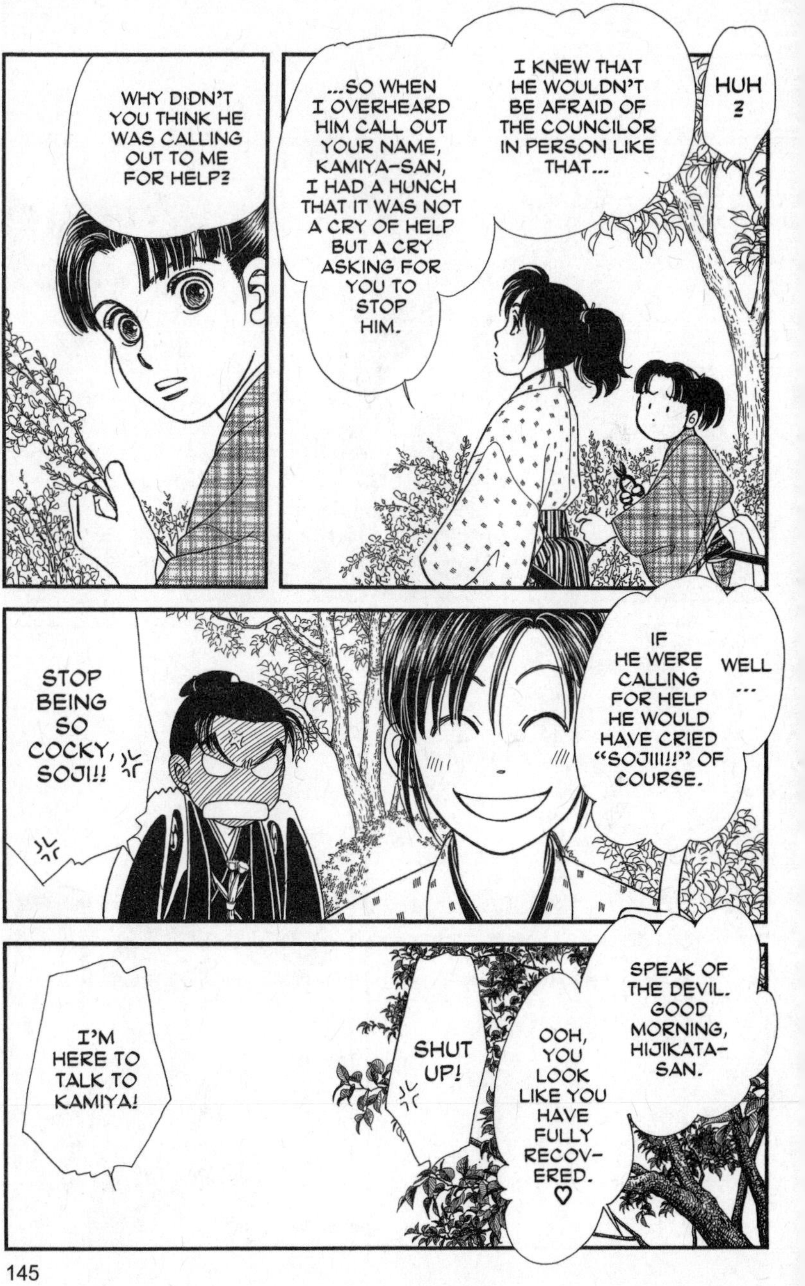
HUH?
I KNEW THAT HE WOULDN'T BE AFRAID OF THE COUNCILOR IN PERSON LIKE THAT...
...SO WHEN I OVERHEARD HIM CALL OUT YOUR NAME, KAMIYA-SAN, I HAD A HUNCH THAT IT WAS NOT A CRY OF HELP BUT A CRY ASKING FOR YOU TO STOP HIM.
WHY DIDN'T YOU THINK HE WAS CALLING OUT TO ME FOR HELP?
WELL...
IF HE WERE CALLING FOR HELP HE WOULD HAVE CRIED "SOJI!!!" OF COURSE.
STOP BEING SO COCKY, SOJI!!
SPEAK OF THE DEVIL. GOOD MORNING, HIJIKATA-SAN.
OOH, YOU LOOK LIKE YOU HAVE FULLY RECOVERED. ♡
SHUT UP!
I'M HERE TO TALK TO KAMIYA!

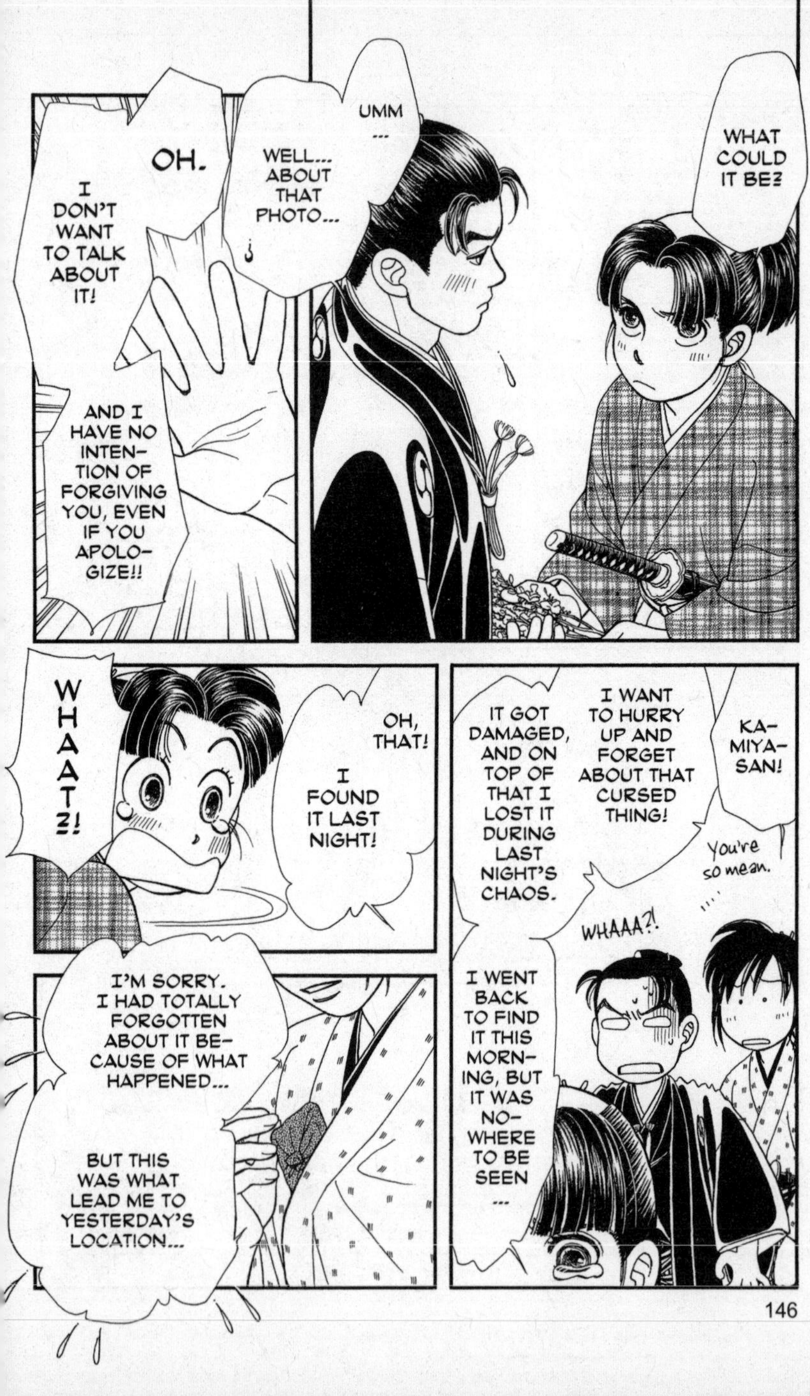
WHAT COULD IT BE?
UMM ...
WELL... ABOUT THAT PHOTO...
OH.
I DON'T WANT TO TALK ABOUT IT!
AND I HAVE NO INTENTION OF FORGIVING YOU, EVEN IF YOU APOLOGIZE!!
KA-MIYA-SAN!
I WANT TO HURRY UP AND FORGET ABOUT THAT CURSED THING!
IT GOT DAMAGED, AND ON TOP OF THAT I LOST IT DURING LAST NIGHT'S CHAOS.
You're so mean.
WHAAA?!
I WENT BACK TO FIND IT THIS MORNING, BUT IT WAS NOWHERE TO BE SEEN ...
WHAAT?!
OH, THAT!
I FOUND IT LAST NIGHT!
I'M SORRY. I HAD TOTALLY FORGOTTEN ABOUT IT BECAUSE OF WHAT HAPPENED...
BUT THIS WAS WHAT LEAD ME TO YESTERDAY'S LOCATION...

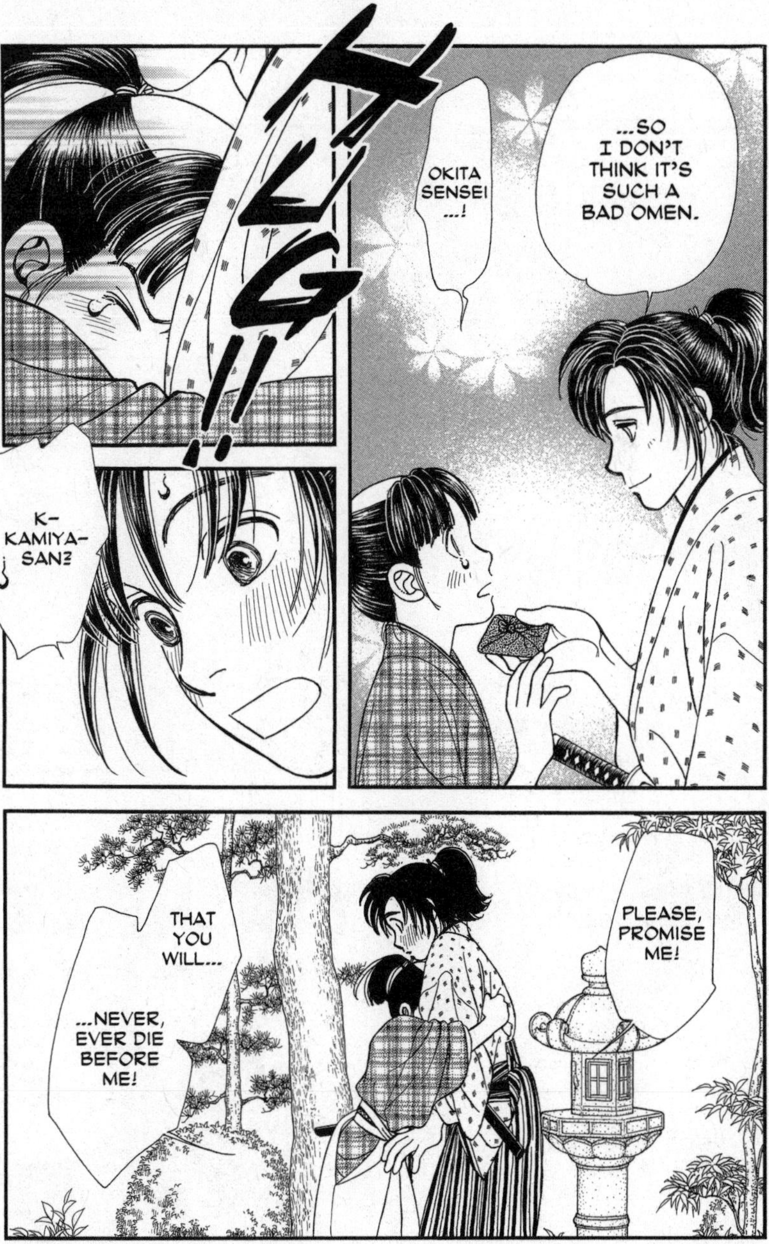

...SO I DON'T THINK IT'S SUCH A BAD OMEN.
OKITA SENSEI ...!
HUG!!
K-KAMIYA-SAN?
PLEASE, PROMISE ME!
THAT YOU WILL...
...NEVER, EVER DIE BEFORE ME!

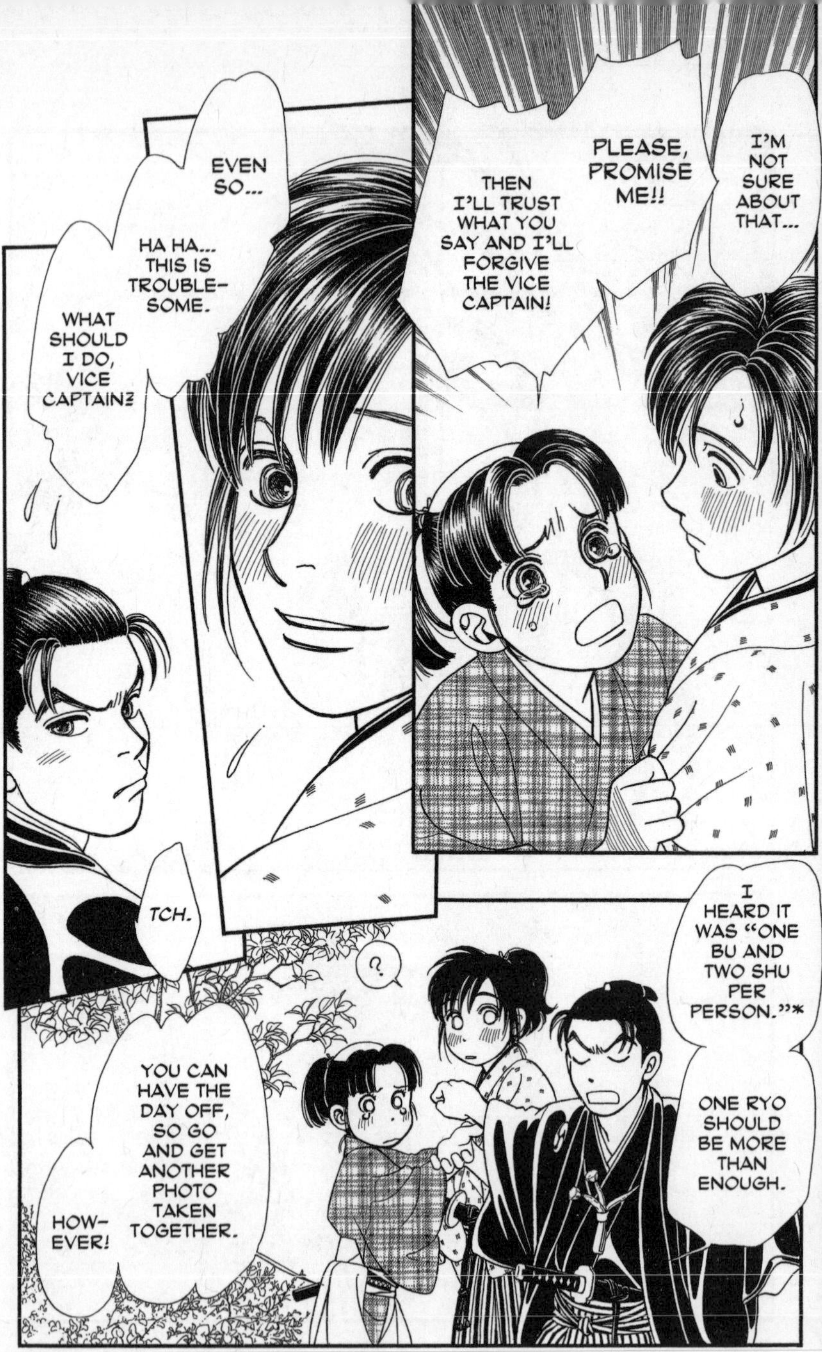
I'M NOT SURE ABOUT THAT...
PLEASE, PROMISE ME!!
THEN I'LL TRUST WHAT YOU SAY AND I'LL FORGIVE THE VICE CAPTAIN!
EVEN SO...
HA HA... THIS IS TROUBLE-SOME.
WHAT SHOULD I DO, VICE CAPTAIN?
TCH.
I HEARD IT WAS "ONE BU AND TWO SHU PER PERSON."*
ONE RYO SHOULD BE MORE THAN ENOUGH.
?
YOU CAN HAVE THE DAY OFF, SO GO AND GET ANOTHER PHOTO TAKEN TOGETHER.
HOW-EVER!

*One ryo = four bu = sixteen shu. One bu and two shu is roughly thirty thousand yen at the current rate.

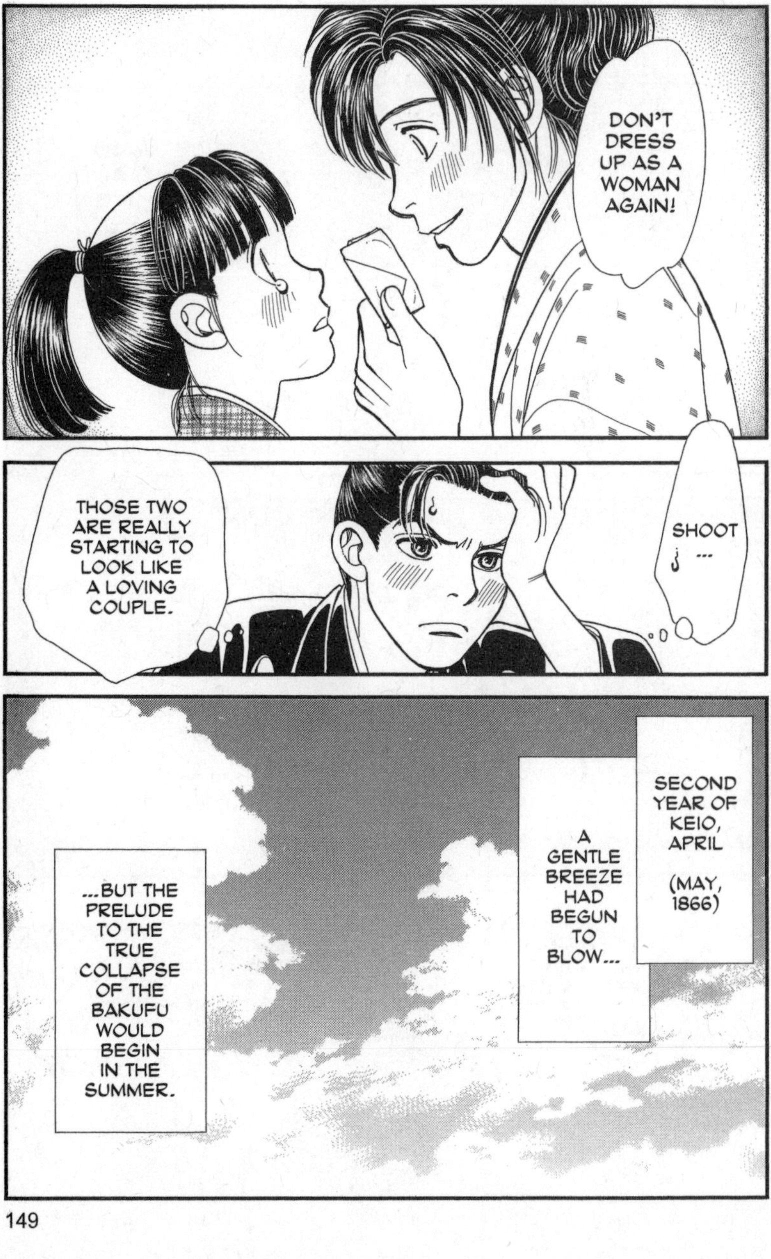
DON'T DRESS UP AS A WOMAN AGAIN!
SHOOT...
THOSE TWO ARE REALLY STARTING TO LOOK LIKE A LOVING COUPLE.
SECOND YEAR OF KEIO, APRIL (MAY, 1866)
A GENTLE BREEZE HAD BEGUN TO BLOW...
...BUT THE PRELUDE TO THE TRUE COLLAPSE OF THE BAKUFU WOULD BEGIN IN THE SUMMER.

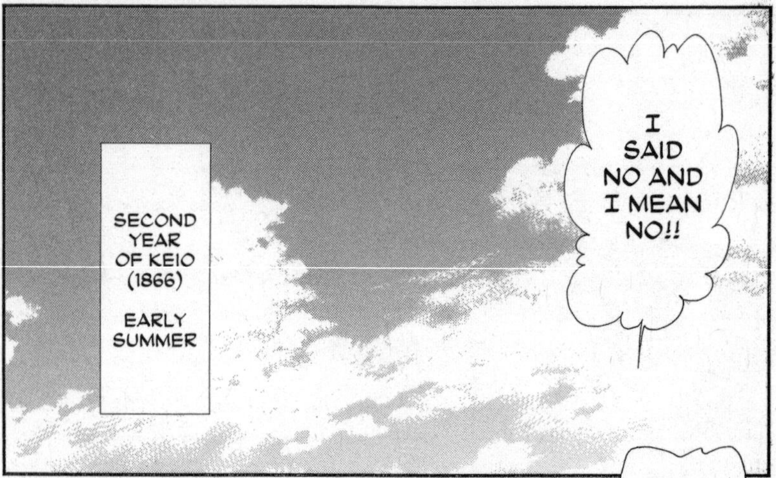
I SAID NO AND I MEAN NO!!
SECOND YEAR OF KEIO (1866)
EARLY SUMMER

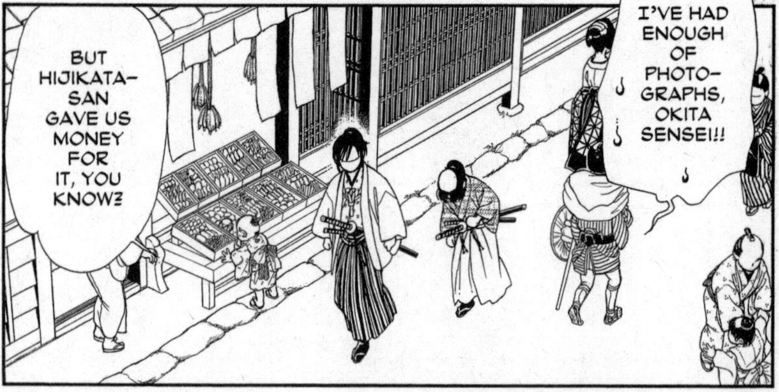
I'VE HAD ENOUGH OF PHOTO-GRAPHS, OKITA SENSEI!!
BUT HIJIKATA-SAN GAVE US MONEY FOR IT, YOU KNOW?

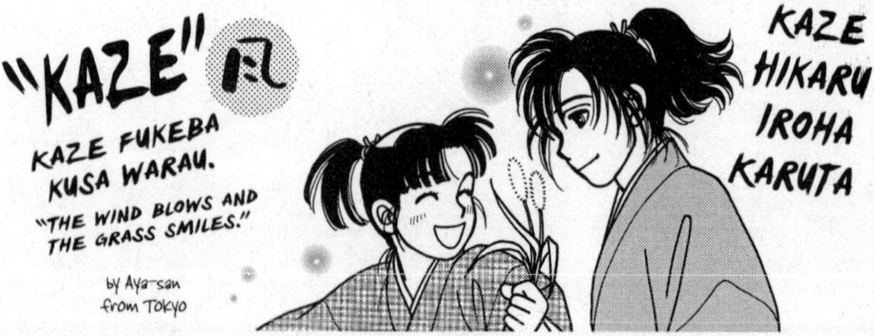
KAZE HIKARU IROHA KARUTA
"KAZE" 風
KAZE FUKEBA KUSA WARAU.
"THE WIND BLOWS AND THE GRASS SMILES."
by Aya-san from Tokyo

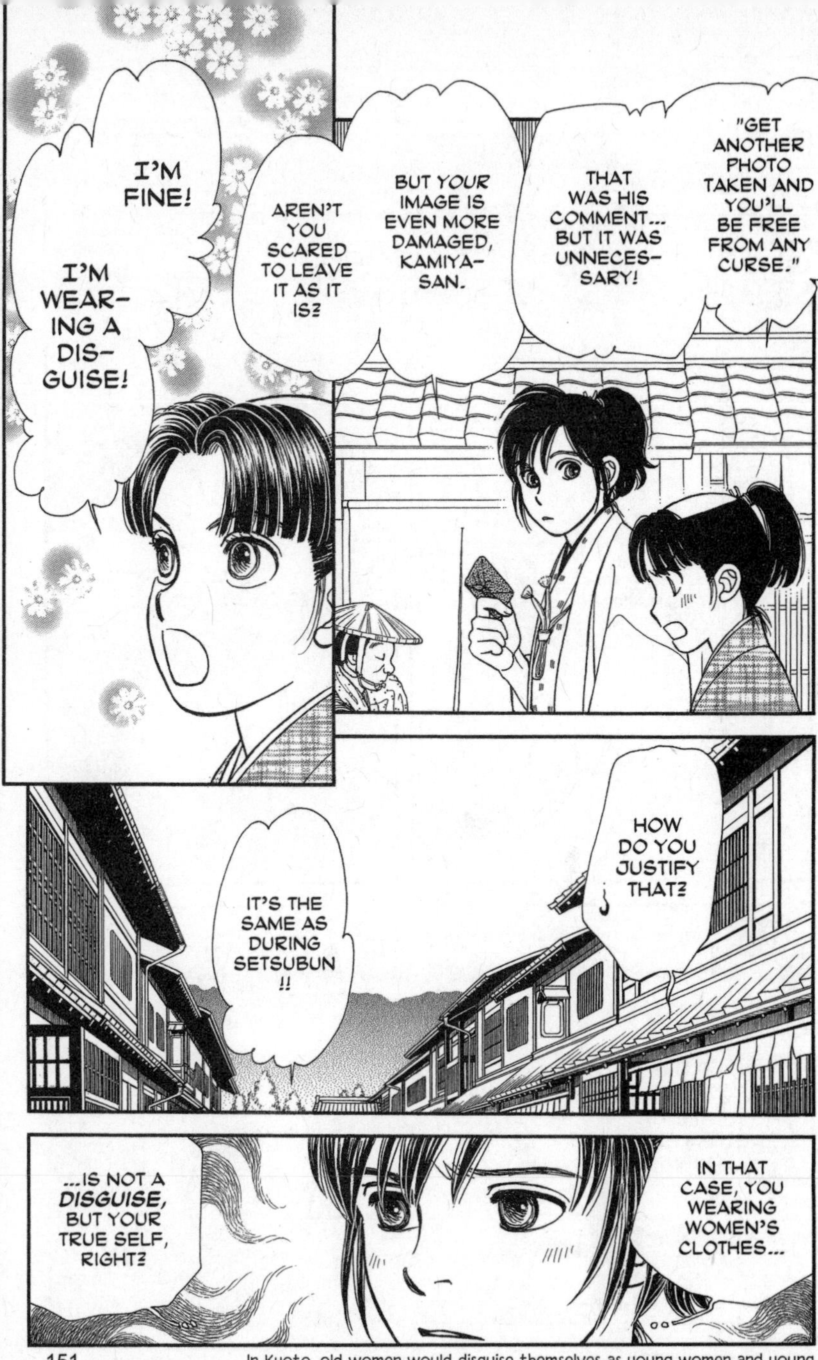
"GET ANOTHER PHOTO TAKEN AND YOU'LL BE FREE FROM ANY CURSE."
THAT WAS HIS COMMENT... BUT IT WAS UNNECES-SARY!
BUT *YOUR* IMAGE IS EVEN MORE DAMAGED, KAMIYA-SAN.
AREN'T YOU SCARED TO LEAVE IT AS IT IS?
I'M FINE!
I'M WEAR-ING A DIS-GUISE!
HOW DO YOU JUSTIFY THAT?
IT'S THE SAME AS DURING SETSUBUN !!
IN THAT CASE, YOU WEARING WOMEN'S CLOTHES...
...IS NOT A *DISGUISE,* BUT YOUR TRUE SELF, RIGHT?

In Kyoto, old women would disguise themselves as young women and young girls would dress as married women to ward off evil during Setsubun.

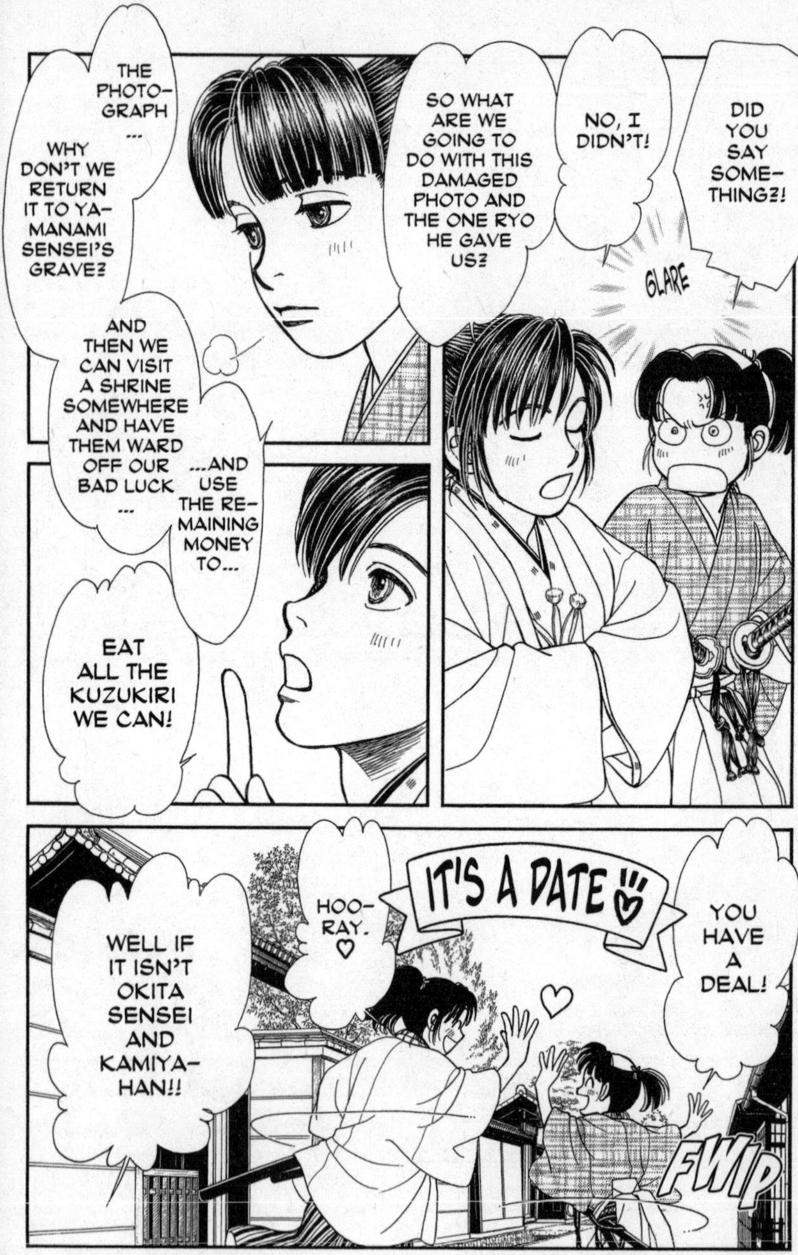
DID YOU SAY SOME-THING?!
NO, I DIDN'T!
SO WHAT ARE WE GOING TO DO WITH THIS DAMAGED PHOTO AND THE ONE RYO HE GAVE US?
GLARE
THE PHOTO-GRAPH ... WHY DON'T WE RETURN IT TO YA-MANAMI SENSEI'S GRAVE?
AND THEN WE CAN VISIT A SHRINE SOMEWHERE AND HAVE THEM WARD OFF OUR BAD LUCK ...
...AND USE THE RE-MAINING MONEY TO...
EAT ALL THE KUZUKIRI WE CAN!
YOU HAVE A DEAL!
IT'S A DATE!! ♡
HOO-RAY. ♡
WELL IF IT ISN'T OKITA SENSEI AND KAMIYA-HAN!!
FWIP
...

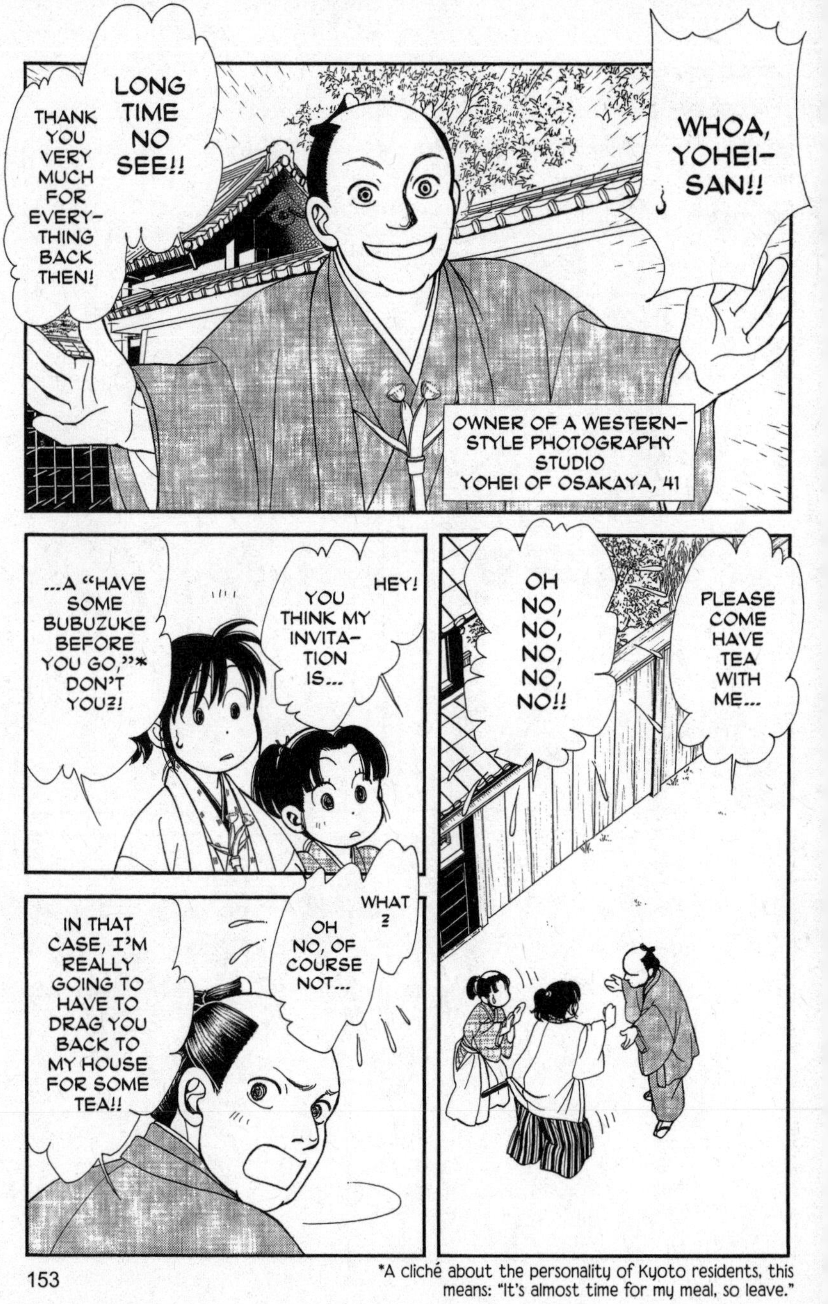
WHOA, YOHEI-SAN!!
LONG TIME NO SEE!!
THANK YOU VERY MUCH FOR EVERYTHING BACK THEN!
OWNER OF A WESTERN-STYLE PHOTOGRAPHY STUDIO YOHEI OF OSAKAYA, 41
PLEASE COME HAVE TEA WITH ME...
OH NO, NO, NO, NO, NO!!
HEY! YOU THINK MY INVITATION IS...
...A "HAVE SOME BUBUZUKE BEFORE YOU GO,"* DON'T YOU?!
WHAT?
OH NO, OF COURSE NOT...
IN THAT CASE, I'M REALLY GOING TO HAVE TO DRAG YOU BACK TO MY HOUSE FOR SOME TEA!!

*A cliché about the personality of Kyoto residents, this means: "It's almost time for my meal, so leave."

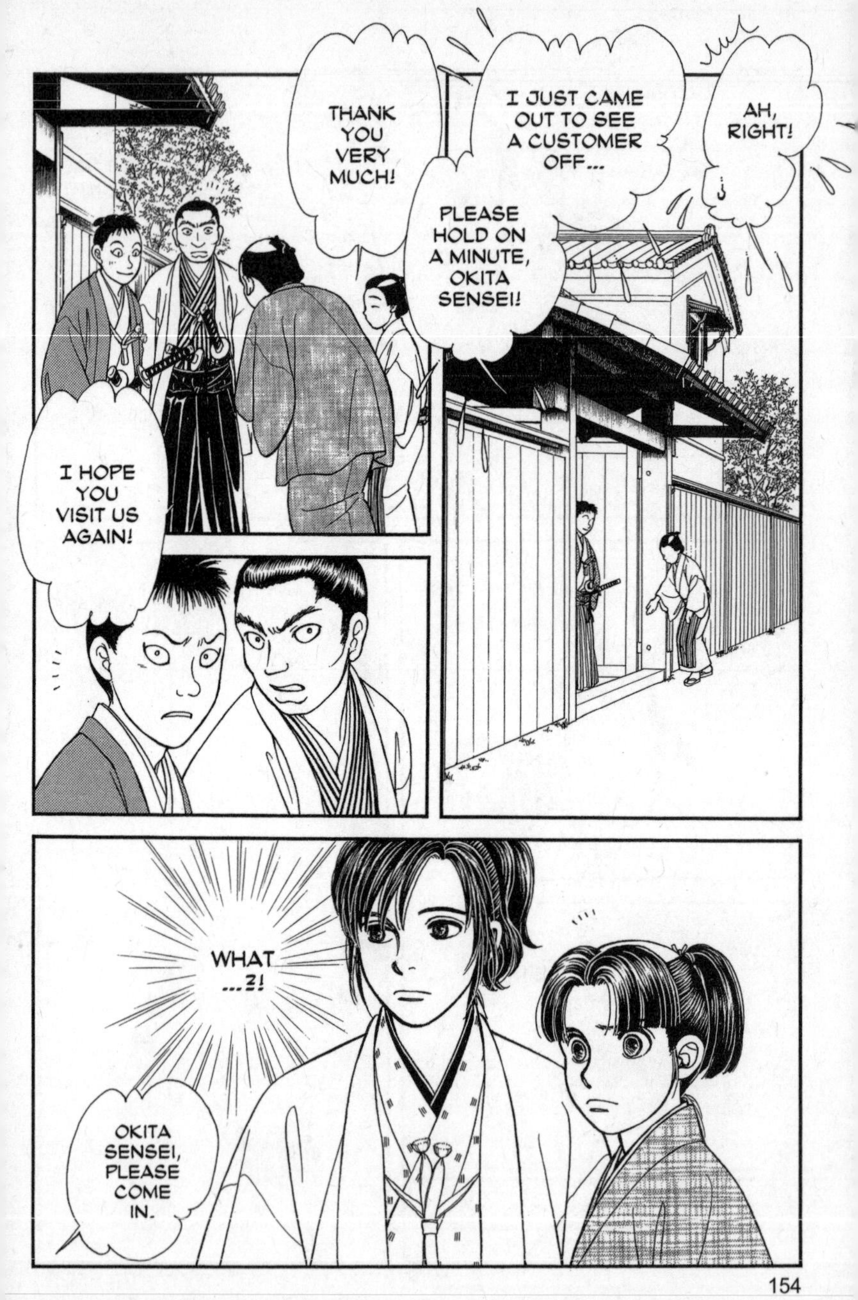
AH, RIGHT!
I JUST CAME OUT TO SEE A CUSTOMER OFF...
PLEASE HOLD ON A MINUTE, OKITA SENSEI!
THANK YOU VERY MUCH!
I HOPE YOU VISIT US AGAIN!
WHAT ...?!
OKITA SENSEI, PLEASE COME IN.

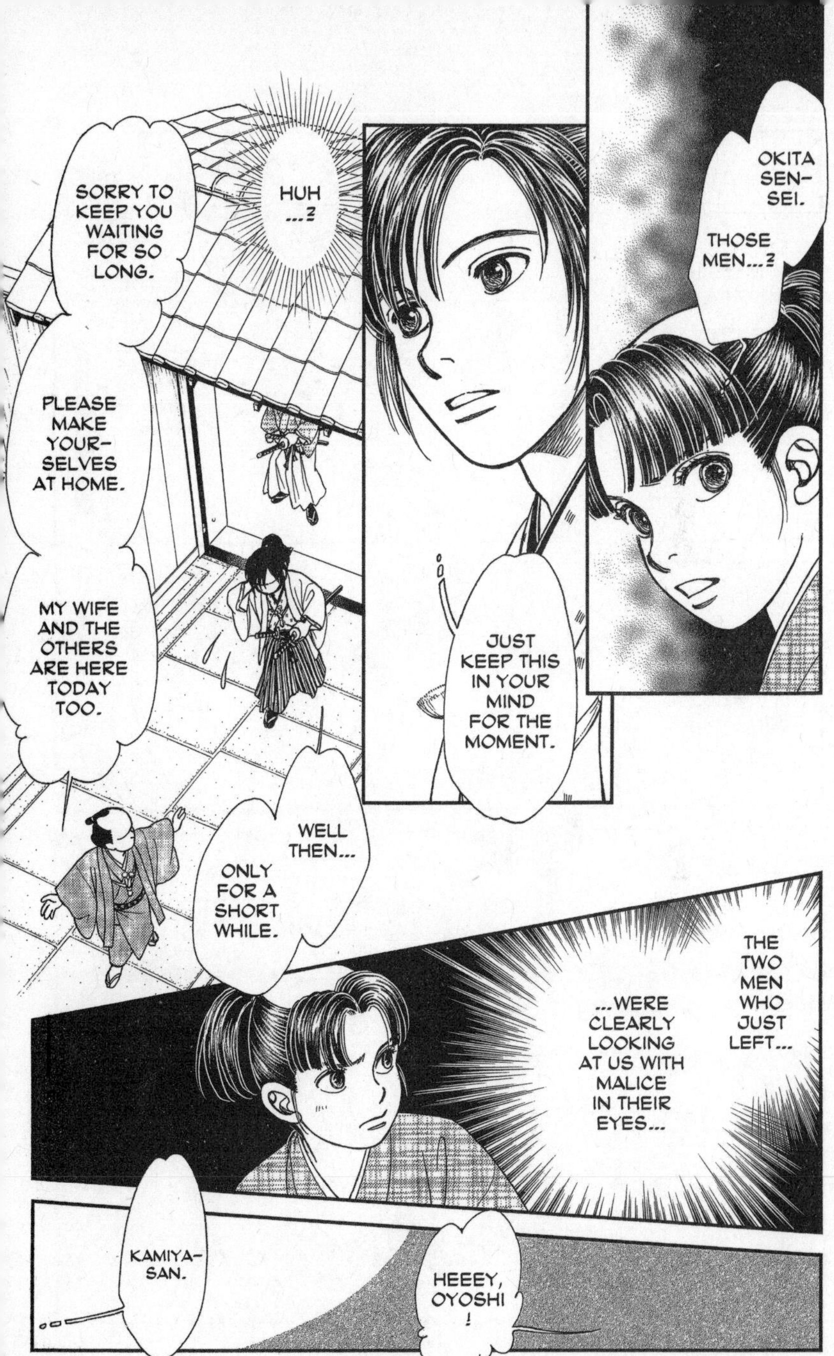

OKITA SEN-SEI.
THOSE MEN...?
JUST KEEP THIS IN YOUR MIND FOR THE MOMENT.
HUH ...?
SORRY TO KEEP YOU WAITING FOR SO LONG.
PLEASE MAKE YOUR-SELVES AT HOME.
MY WIFE AND THE OTHERS ARE HERE TODAY TOO.
WELL THEN...
ONLY FOR A SHORT WHILE.
THE TWO MEN WHO JUST LEFT...
...WERE CLEARLY LOOKING AT US WITH MALICE IN THEIR EYES...
HEEEY, OYOSHI !
KAMIYA-SAN.

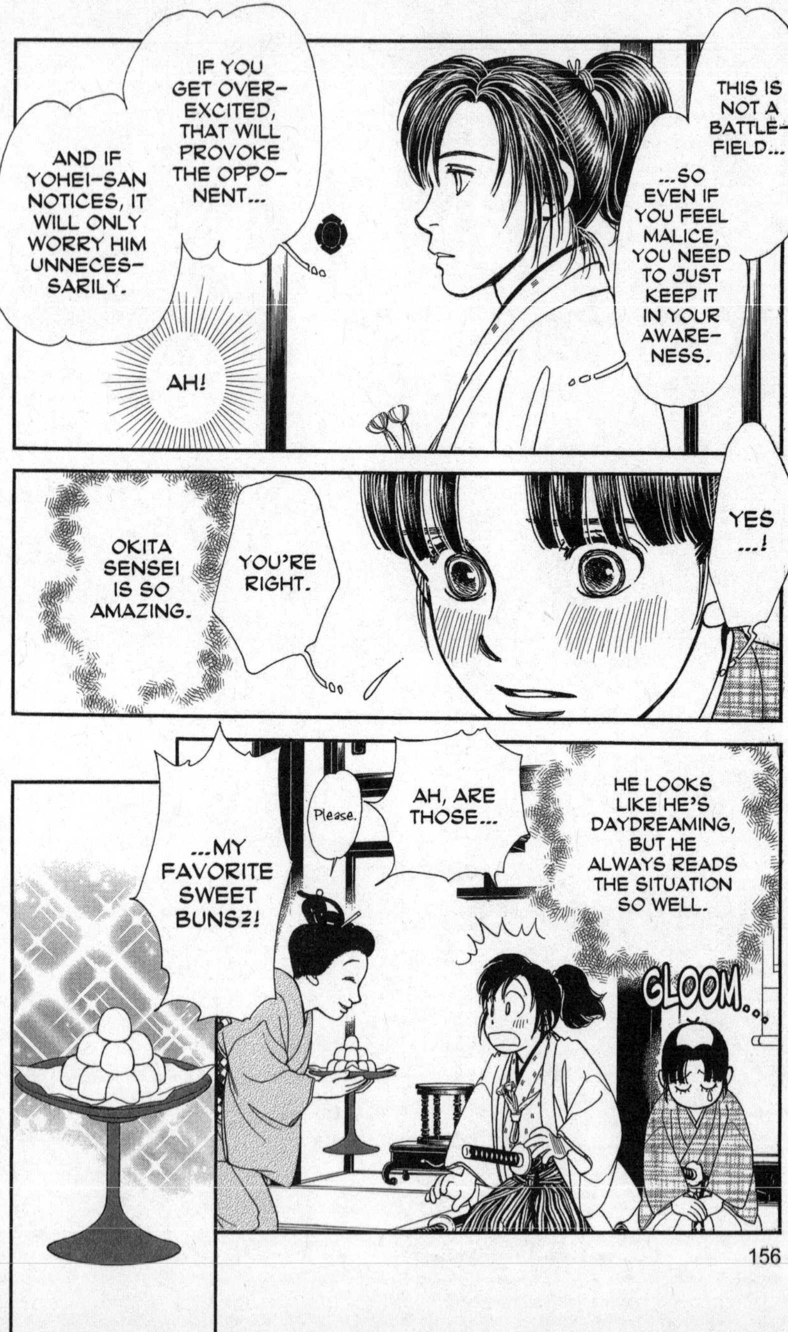
THIS IS NOT A BATTLEFIELD...
...SO EVEN IF YOU FEEL MALICE, YOU NEED TO JUST KEEP IT IN YOUR AWARENESS.
IF YOU GET OVER-EXCITED, THAT WILL PROVOKE THE OPPONENT...
AND IF YOHEI-SAN NOTICES, IT WILL ONLY WORRY HIM UNNECESSARILY.
AH!
YES ...!
YOU'RE RIGHT.
OKITA SENSEI IS SO AMAZING.
HE LOOKS LIKE HE'S DAYDREAMING, BUT HE ALWAYS READS THE SITUATION SO WELL.
AH, ARE THOSE...
Please.
...MY FAVORITE SWEET BUNS?!
GLOOM...

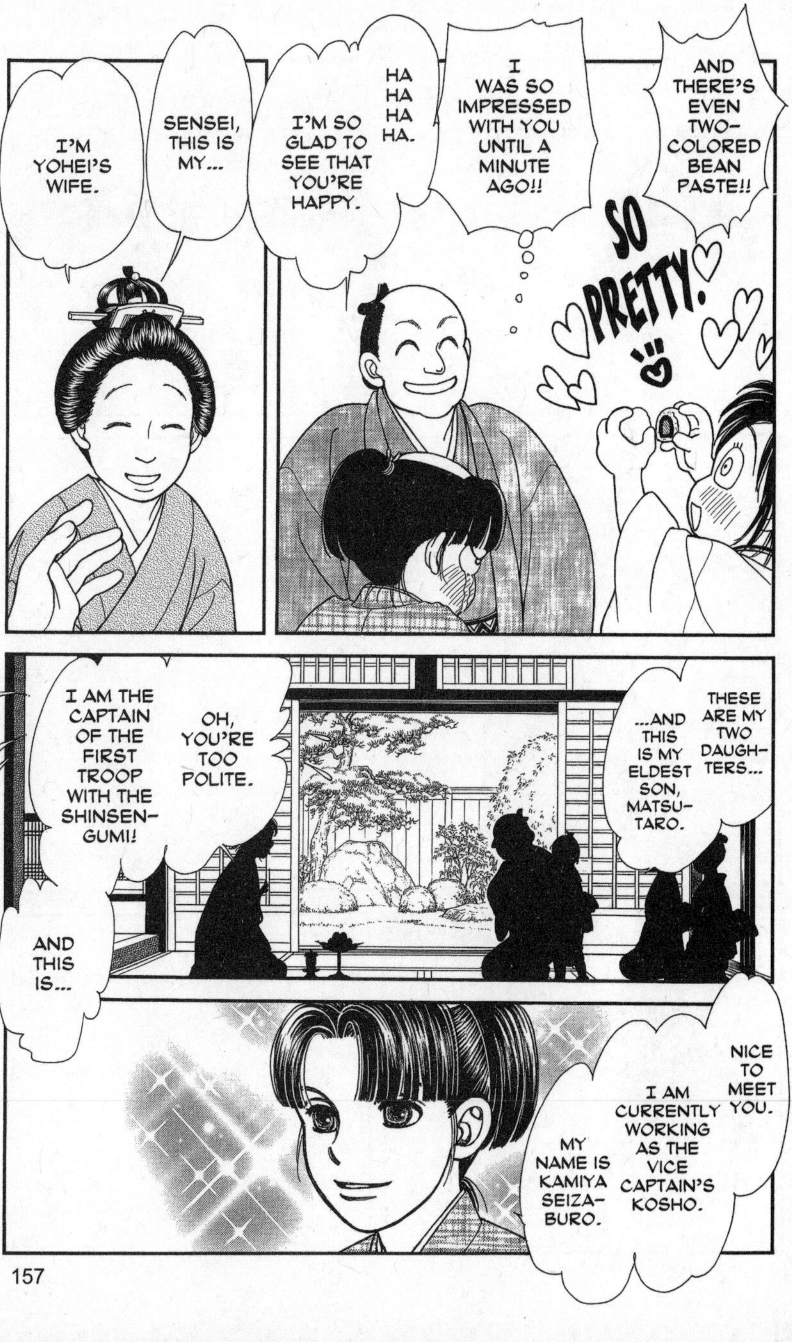
AND THERE'S EVEN TWO-COLORED BEAN PASTE!!
SO PRETTY.
I WAS SO IMPRESSED WITH YOU UNTIL A MINUTE AGO!!
HA HA HA HA.
I'M SO GLAD TO SEE THAT YOU'RE HAPPY.
SENSEI, THIS IS MY...
I'M YOHEI'S WIFE.
THESE ARE MY TWO DAUGH-TERS...
...AND THIS IS MY ELDEST SON, MATSU-TARO.
OH, YOU'RE TOO POLITE.
I AM THE CAPTAIN OF THE FIRST TROOP WITH THE SHINSEN-GUMI!
AND THIS IS...
NICE TO MEET YOU.
I AM CURRENTLY WORKING AS THE VICE CAPTAIN'S KOSHO.
MY NAME IS KAMIYA SEIZA-BURO.

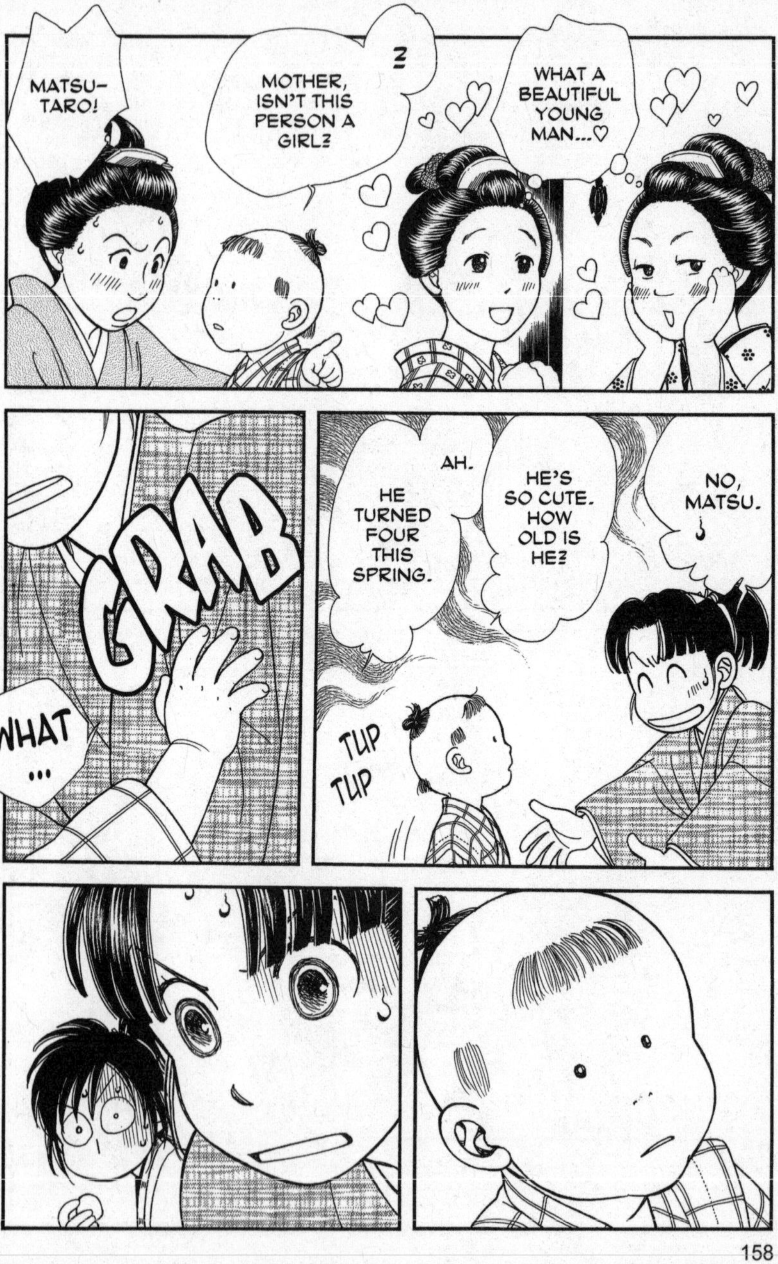
WHAT A BEAUTIFUL YOUNG MAN...♡
MOTHER, ISN'T THIS PERSON A GIRL?
MATSU-TARO!
NO, MATSU.
HE'S SO CUTE. HOW OLD IS HE?
AH.
HE TURNED FOUR THIS SPRING.
TUP TUP
GRAB
WHAT...

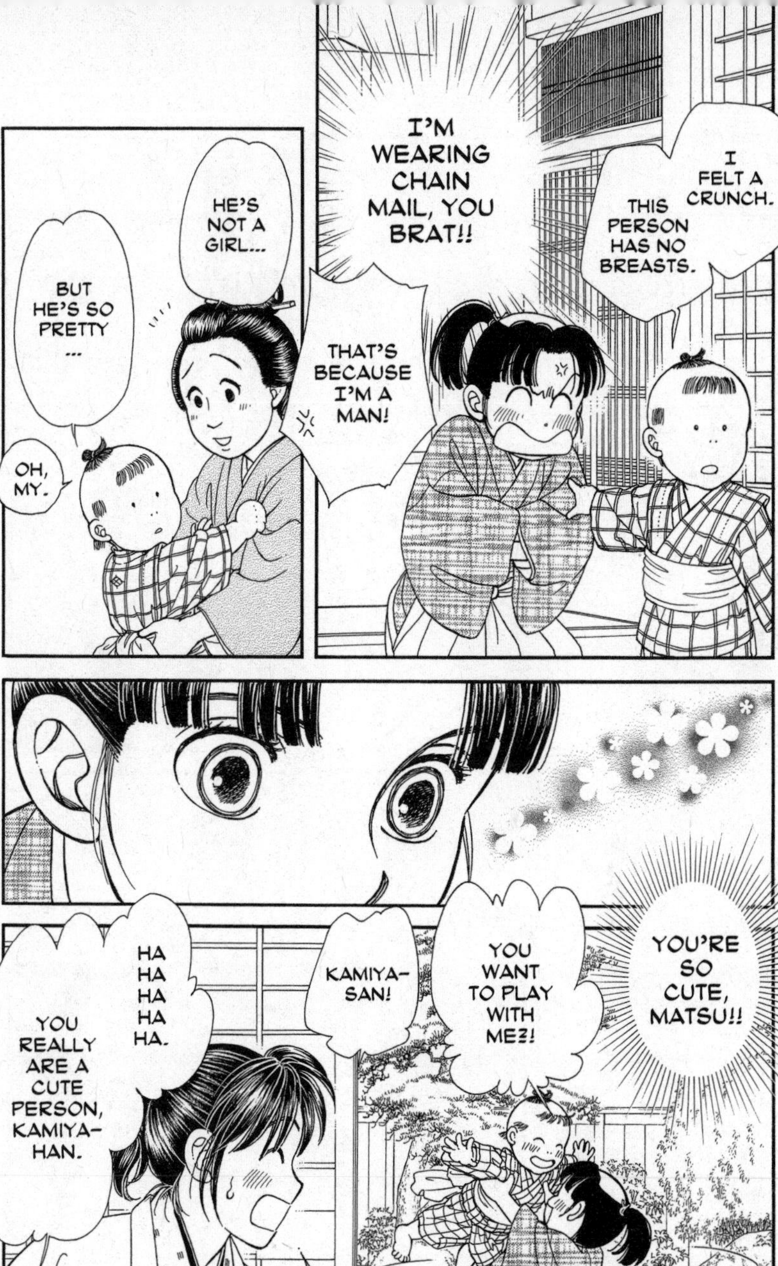
I FELT A CRUNCH.
THIS PERSON HAS NO BREASTS.
I'M WEARING CHAIN MAIL, YOU BRAT!!
THAT'S BECAUSE I'M A MAN!
HE'S NOT A GIRL...
BUT HE'S SO PRETTY ...
OH, MY.
YOU'RE SO CUTE, MATSU!!
YOU WANT TO PLAY WITH ME?!
KAMIYA-SAN!
HA HA HA HA HA.
YOU REALLY ARE A CUTE PERSON, KAMIYA-HAN.

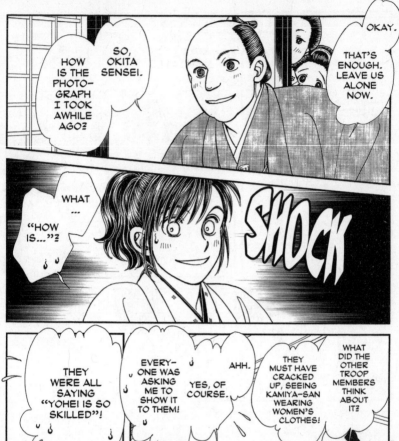

OKAY. THAT'S ENOUGH. LEAVE US ALONE NOW.
SO, OKITA SENSEI. HOW IS THE PHOTOGRAPH I TOOK AWHILE AGO?
SHOCK
WHAT ... "HOW IS..."?
WHAT DID THE OTHER TROOP MEMBERS THINK ABOUT IT?
THEY MUST HAVE CRACKED UP, SEEING KAMIYA-SAN WEARING WOMEN'S CLOTHES!
AHH. YES, OF COURSE.
EVERYONE WAS ASKING ME TO SHOW IT TO THEM!
THEY WERE ALL SAYING "YOHEI IS SO SKILLED"!
IS THAT SO?
I'M SO HAPPY TO HEAR IT!
Both talking through their teeth out of guilt about damaging the photo.

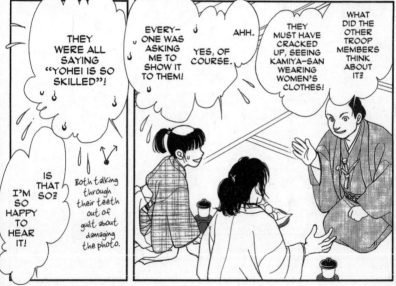

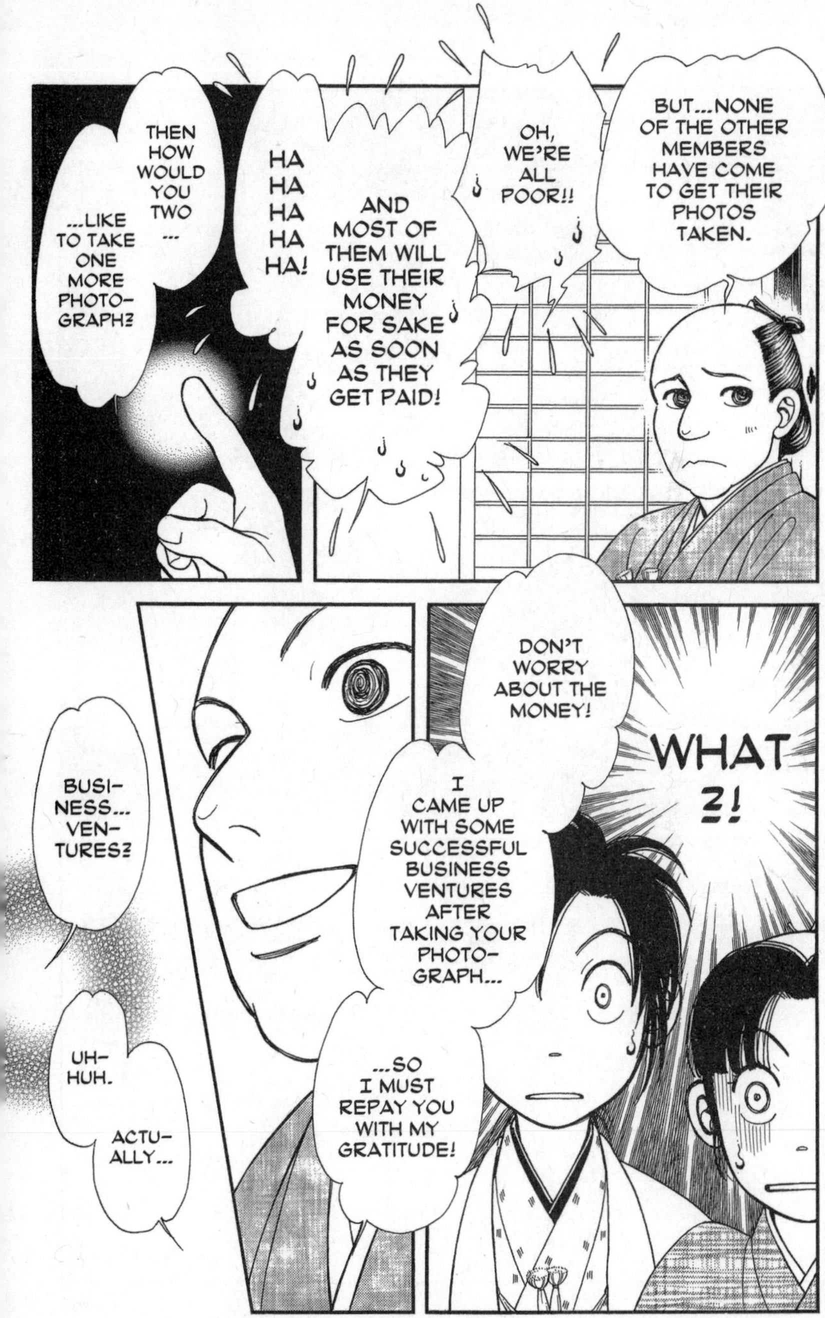
BUT...NONE OF THE OTHER MEMBERS HAVE COME TO GET THEIR PHOTOS TAKEN.
OH, WE'RE ALL POOR!!
AND MOST OF THEM WILL USE THEIR MONEY FOR SAKE AS SOON AS THEY GET PAID!
HA HA HA HA HA!
THEN HOW WOULD YOU TWO ...
...LIKE TO TAKE ONE MORE PHOTOGRAPH?
DON'T WORRY ABOUT THE MONEY!
WHAT?!
I CAME UP WITH SOME SUCCESSFUL BUSINESS VENTURES AFTER TAKING YOUR PHOTOGRAPH...
...SO I MUST REPAY YOU WITH MY GRATITUDE!
BUSINESS... VENTURES?
UH-HUH.
ACTUALLY...

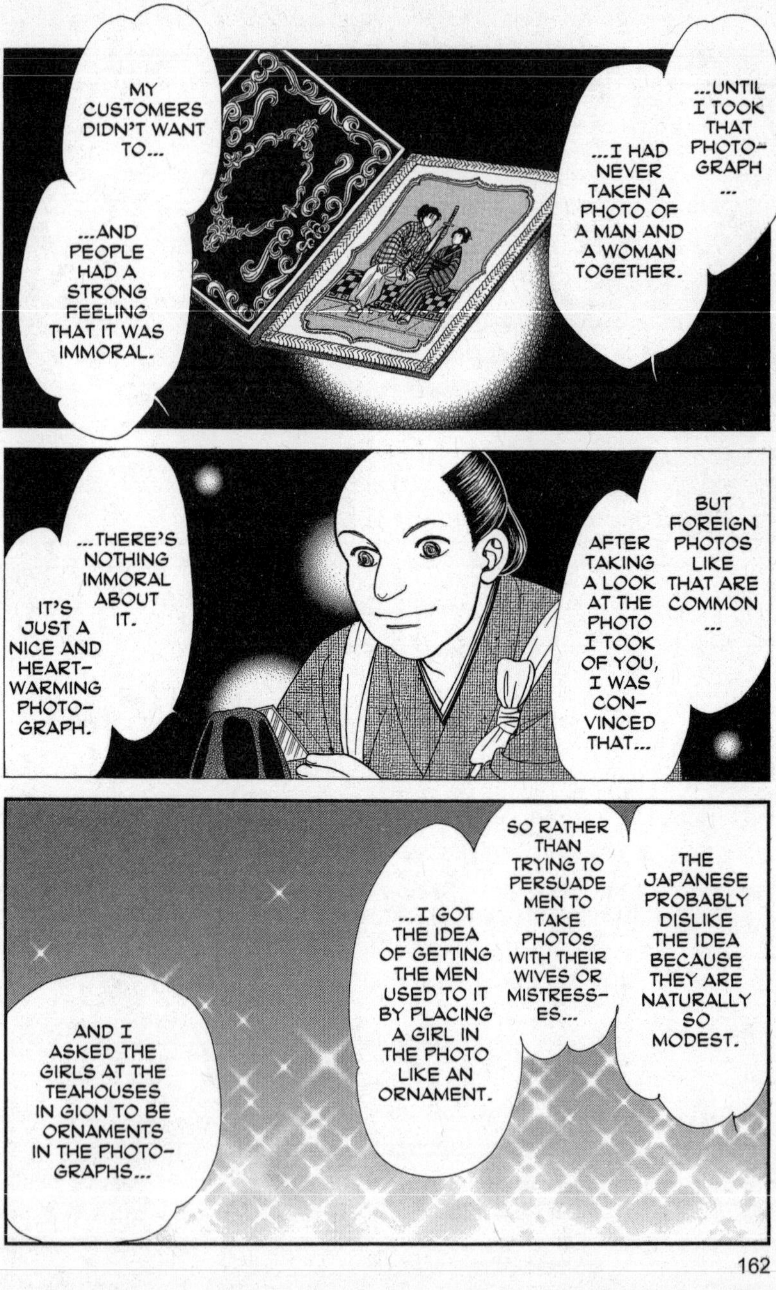
...UNTIL I TOOK THAT PHOTOGRAPH...
...I HAD NEVER TAKEN A PHOTO OF A MAN AND A WOMAN TOGETHER.
MY CUSTOMERS DIDN'T WANT TO...
...AND PEOPLE HAD A STRONG FEELING THAT IT WAS IMMORAL.
BUT FOREIGN PHOTOS LIKE THAT ARE COMMON...
AFTER TAKING A LOOK AT THE PHOTO I TOOK OF YOU, I WAS CONVINCED THAT...
...THERE'S NOTHING IMMORAL ABOUT IT.
IT'S JUST A NICE AND HEARTWARMING PHOTOGRAPH.
THE JAPANESE PROBABLY DISLIKE THE IDEA BECAUSE THEY ARE NATURALLY SO MODEST.
SO RATHER THAN TRYING TO PERSUADE MEN TO TAKE PHOTOS WITH THEIR WIVES OR MISTRESSES...
...I GOT THE IDEA OF GETTING THE MEN USED TO IT BY PLACING A GIRL IN THE PHOTO LIKE AN ORNAMENT.
AND I ASKED THE GIRLS AT THE TEAHOUSES IN GION TO BE ORNAMENTS IN THE PHOTOGRAPHS...

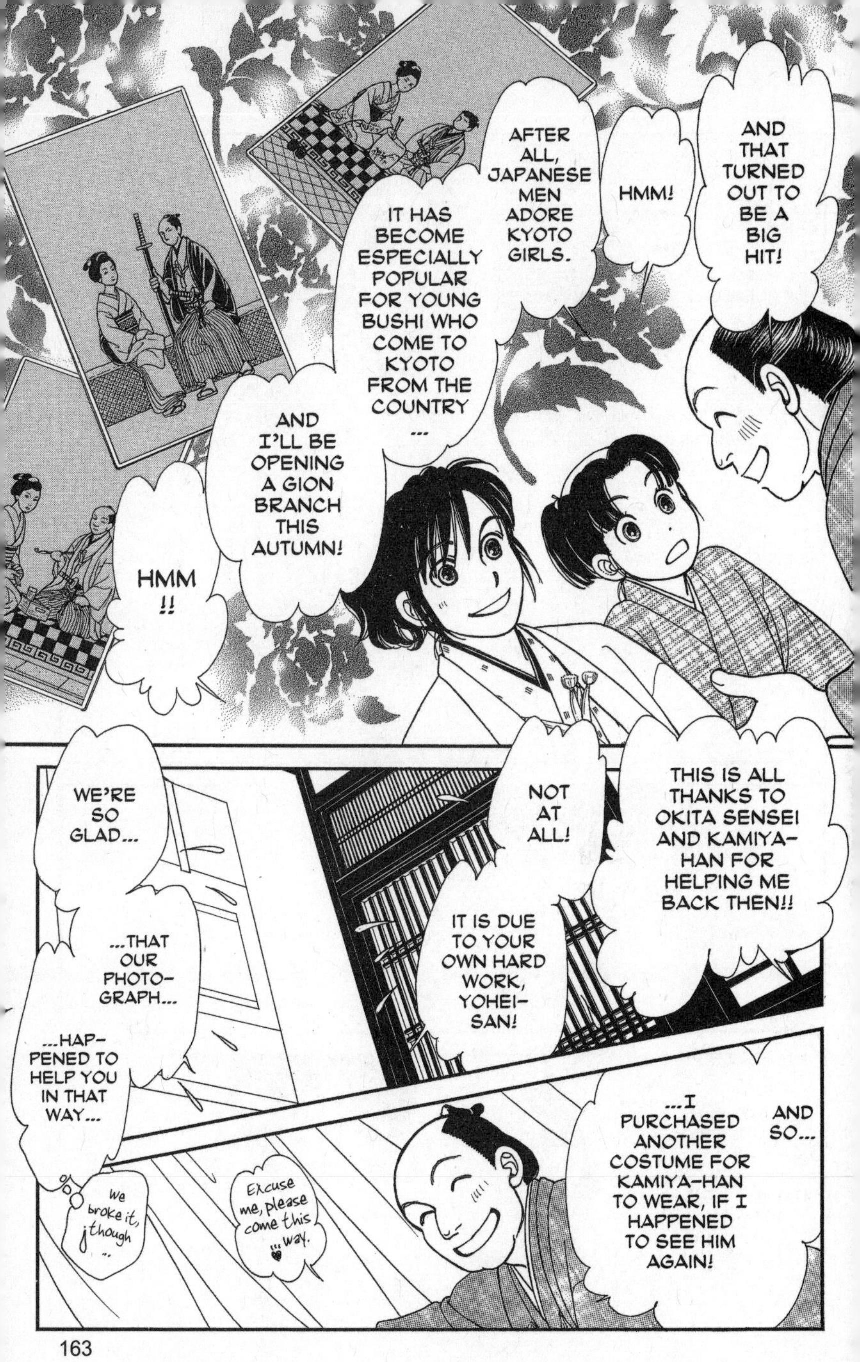

AND THAT TURNED OUT TO BE A BIG HIT!
HMM!
AFTER ALL, JAPANESE MEN ADORE KYOTO GIRLS.
IT HAS BECOME ESPECIALLY POPULAR FOR YOUNG BUSHI WHO COME TO KYOTO FROM THE COUNTRY ...
AND I'LL BE OPENING A GION BRANCH THIS AUTUMN!
HMM !!
THIS IS ALL THANKS TO OKITA SENSEI AND KAMIYA-HAN FOR HELPING ME BACK THEN!!
NOT AT ALL!
IT IS DUE TO YOUR OWN HARD WORK, YOHEI-SAN!
WE'RE SO GLAD...
...THAT OUR PHOTOGRAPH...
...HAPPENED TO HELP YOU IN THAT WAY...
We broke it, though ...
AND SO...
...I PURCHASED ANOTHER COSTUME FOR KAMIYA-HAN TO WEAR, IF I HAPPENED TO SEE HIM AGAIN!
Excuse me, please come this way.

WHAT DO YOU THINK?
I'M SURE IT'LL LOOK GOOD ON YOU.
...!!
PFFT ...
HAR HAR HAR!
YOU'LL LOOK LOVELY IN IT, KAMIYA-SAN!
YOU THINK SO TOO?!
ONCE I SHOW EVERYONE THE PHOTO OF KAMIYA-HAN WEARING THIS...
...PHOTOGRAPHS OF GIRLS IN WESTERN CLOTHES WILL BE THE NEXT BIG HIT ...

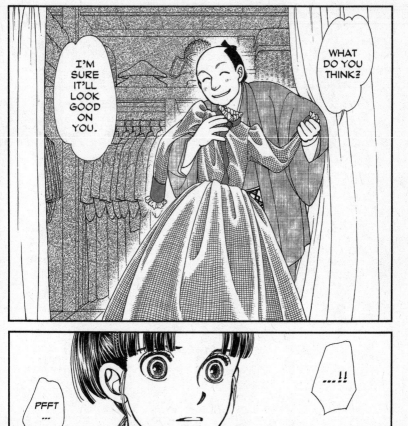

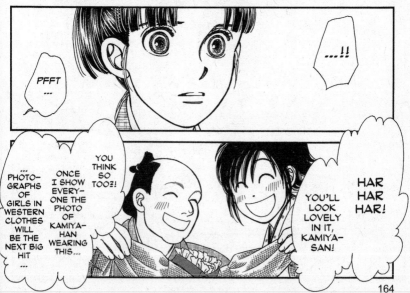

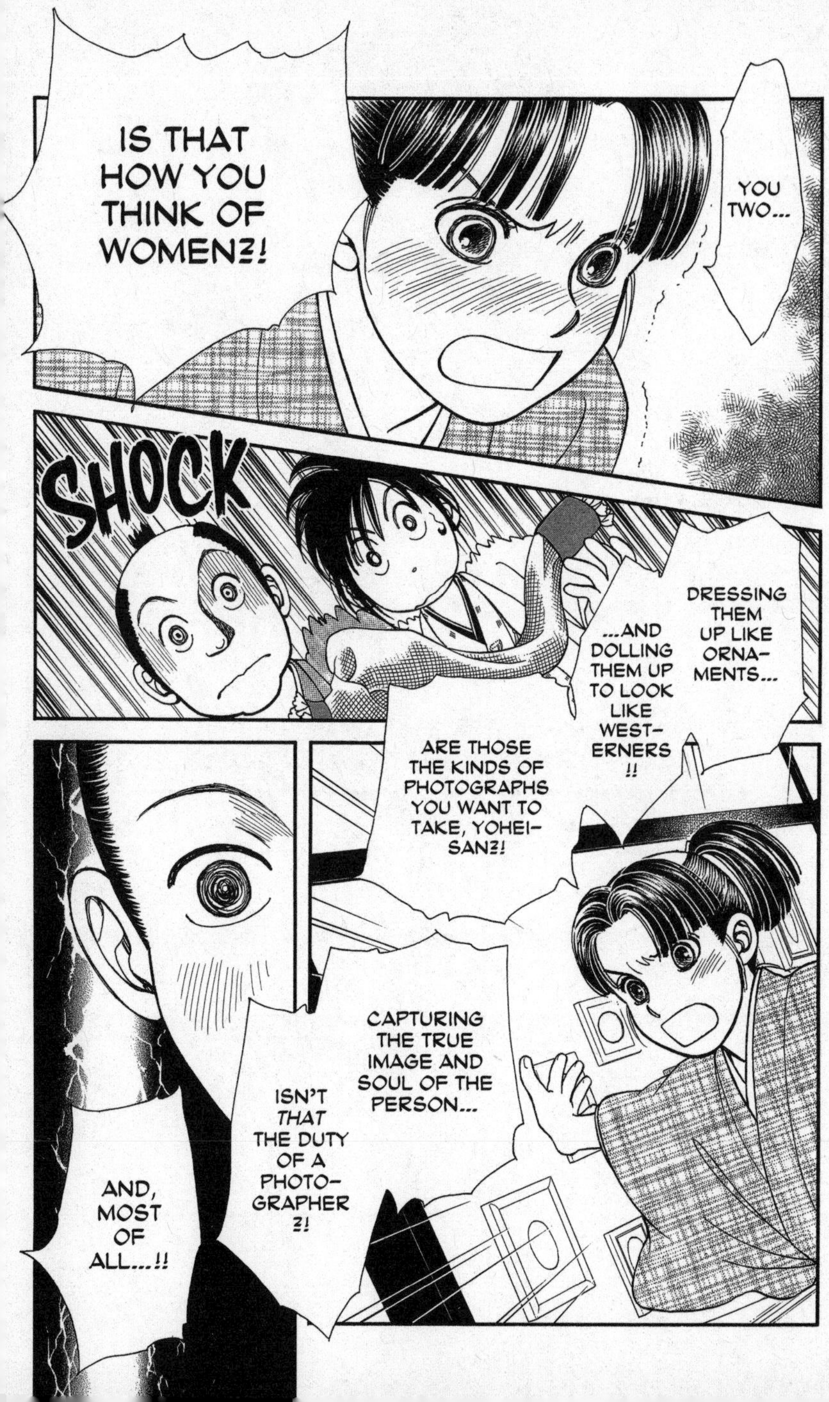
YOU TWO...
IS THAT HOW YOU THINK OF WOMEN?!
DRESSING THEM UP LIKE ORNAMENTS...
...AND DOLLING THEM UP TO LOOK LIKE WESTERNERS!!
SHOCK
ARE THOSE THE KINDS OF PHOTOGRAPHS YOU WANT TO TAKE, YOHEI-SAN?!
CAPTURING THE TRUE IMAGE AND SOUL OF THE PERSON...
ISN'T *THAT* THE DUTY OF A PHOTOGRAPHER?!
AND, MOST OF ALL...!!

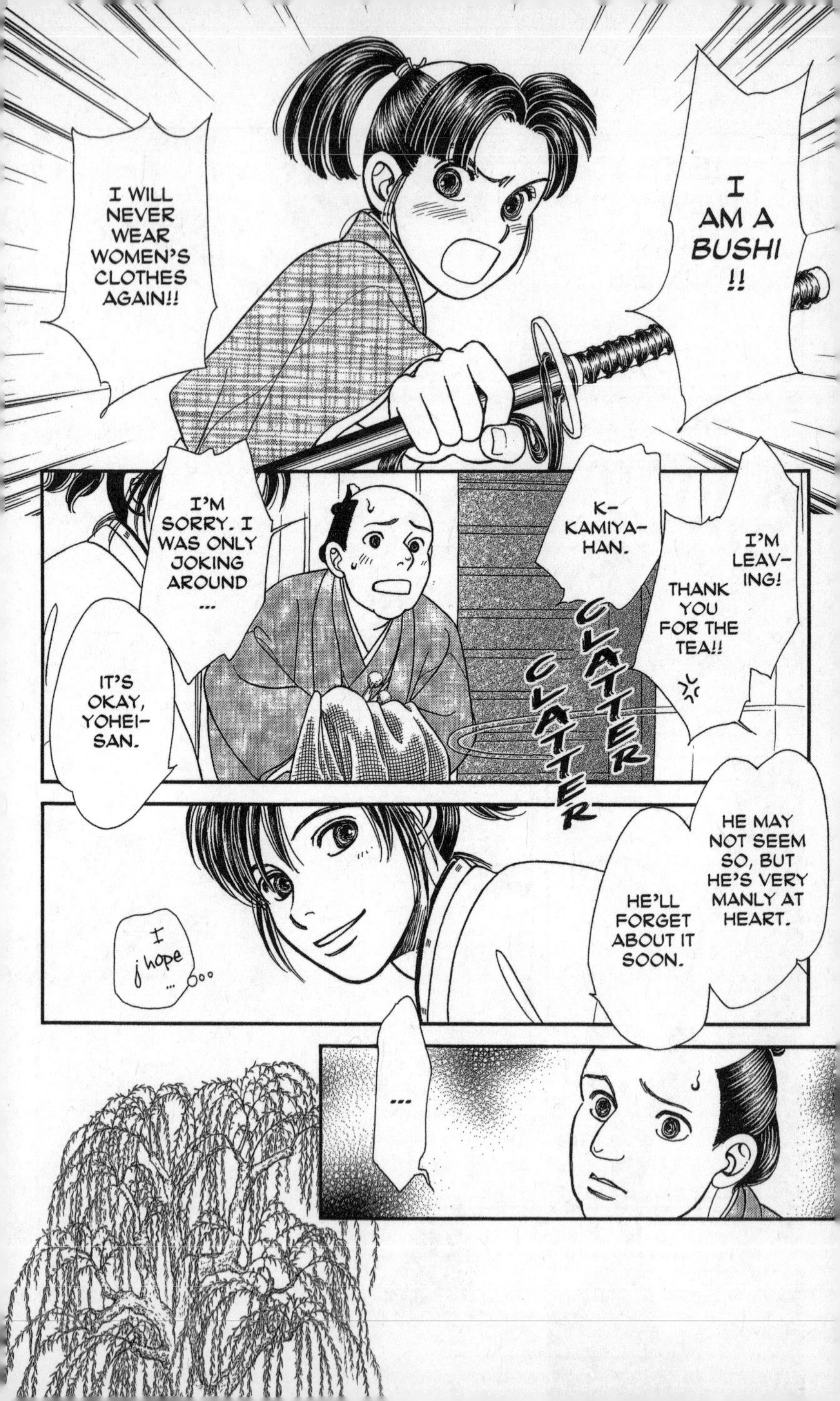
I AM A BUSHI !!
I WILL NEVER WEAR WOMEN'S CLOTHES AGAIN!!
I'M LEAVING!
THANK YOU FOR THE TEA!!
K-KAMIYA-HAN.
CLATTER CLATTER
I'M SORRY. I WAS ONLY JOKING AROUND ...
IT'S OKAY, YOHEI-SAN.
HE MAY NOT SEEM SO, BUT HE'S VERY MANLY AT HEART.
HE'LL FORGET ABOUT IT SOON.
I hope ...
...

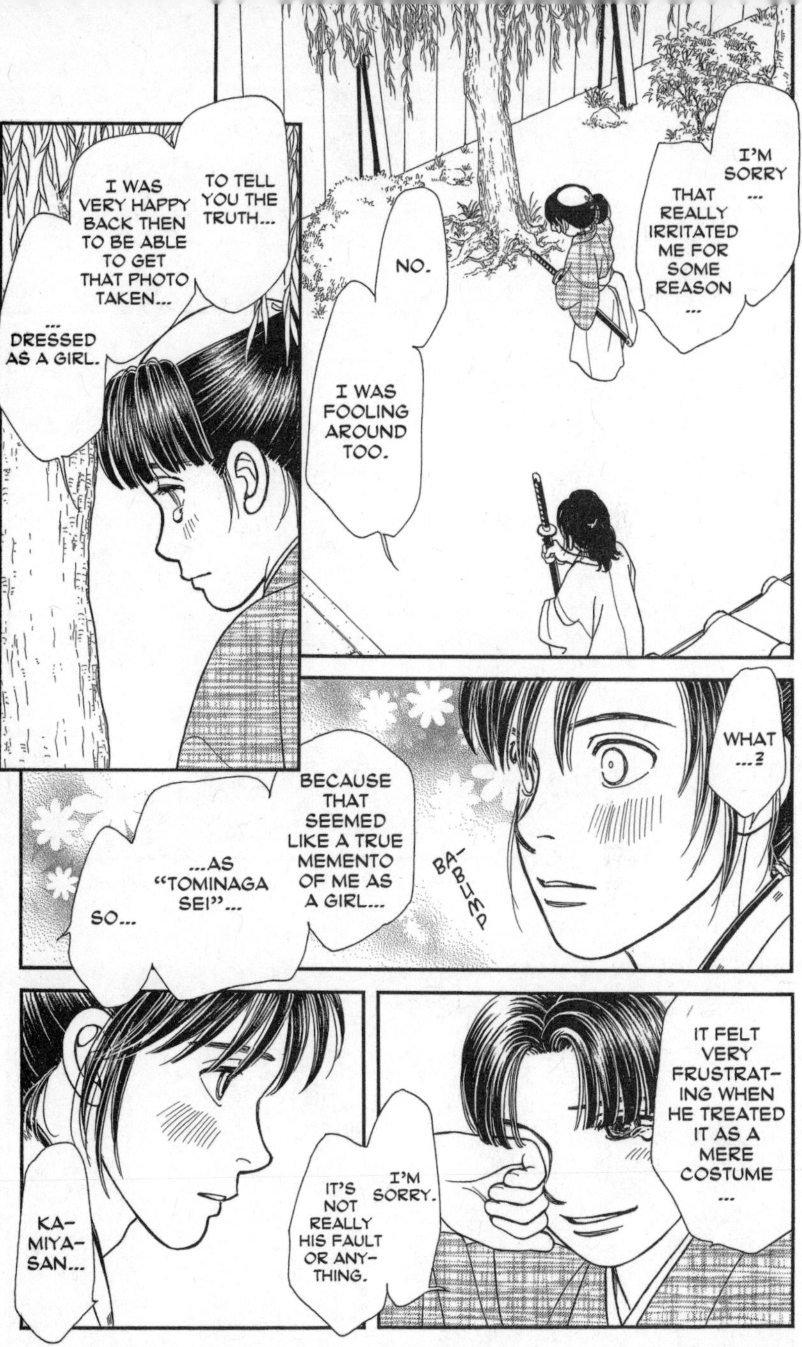

I'M SORRY...
THAT REALLY IRRITATED ME FOR SOME REASON...
NO.
I WAS FOOLING AROUND TOO.
TO TELL YOU THE TRUTH...
I WAS VERY HAPPY BACK THEN TO BE ABLE TO GET THAT PHOTO TAKEN...
...DRESSED AS A GIRL.
WHAT...?
BA-BUMP
BECAUSE THAT SEEMED LIKE A TRUE MEMENTO OF ME AS A GIRL...
...AS "TOMINAGA SEI"...
SO...
IT FELT VERY FRUSTRAT-ING WHEN HE TREATED IT AS A MERE COSTUME...
I'M SORRY.
IT'S NOT REALLY HIS FAULT OR ANY-THING.
KA-MIYA-SAN...

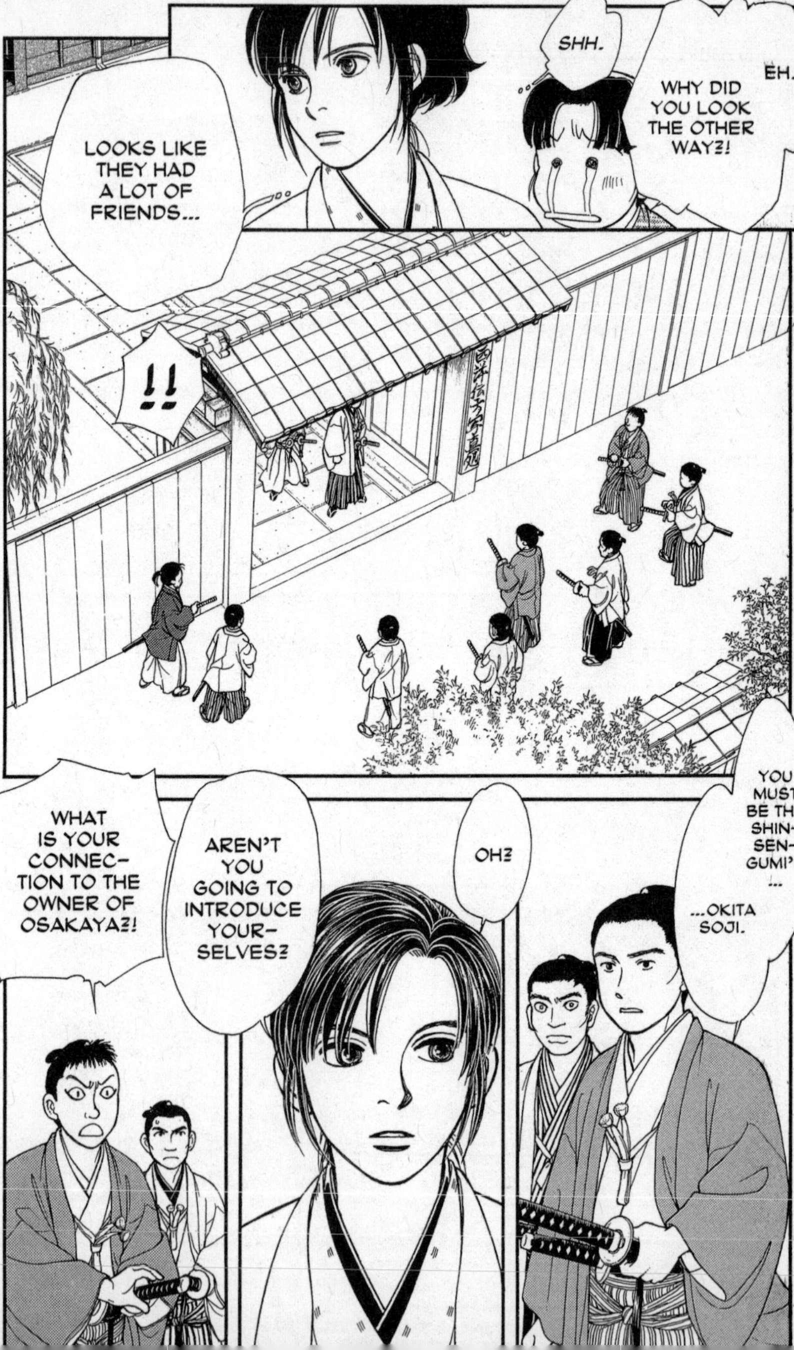
EH...
WHY DID YOU LOOK THE OTHER WAY?!
SHH.
LOOKS LIKE THEY HAD A LOT OF FRIENDS...
!!
YOU MUST BE THE SHINSENGUMI'S ...
...OKITA SOJI.
OH?
AREN'T YOU GOING TO INTRODUCE YOURSELVES?
WHAT IS YOUR CONNECTION TO THE OWNER OF OSAKAYA?!

Sign: Osakaya Western-Style Photo Studio

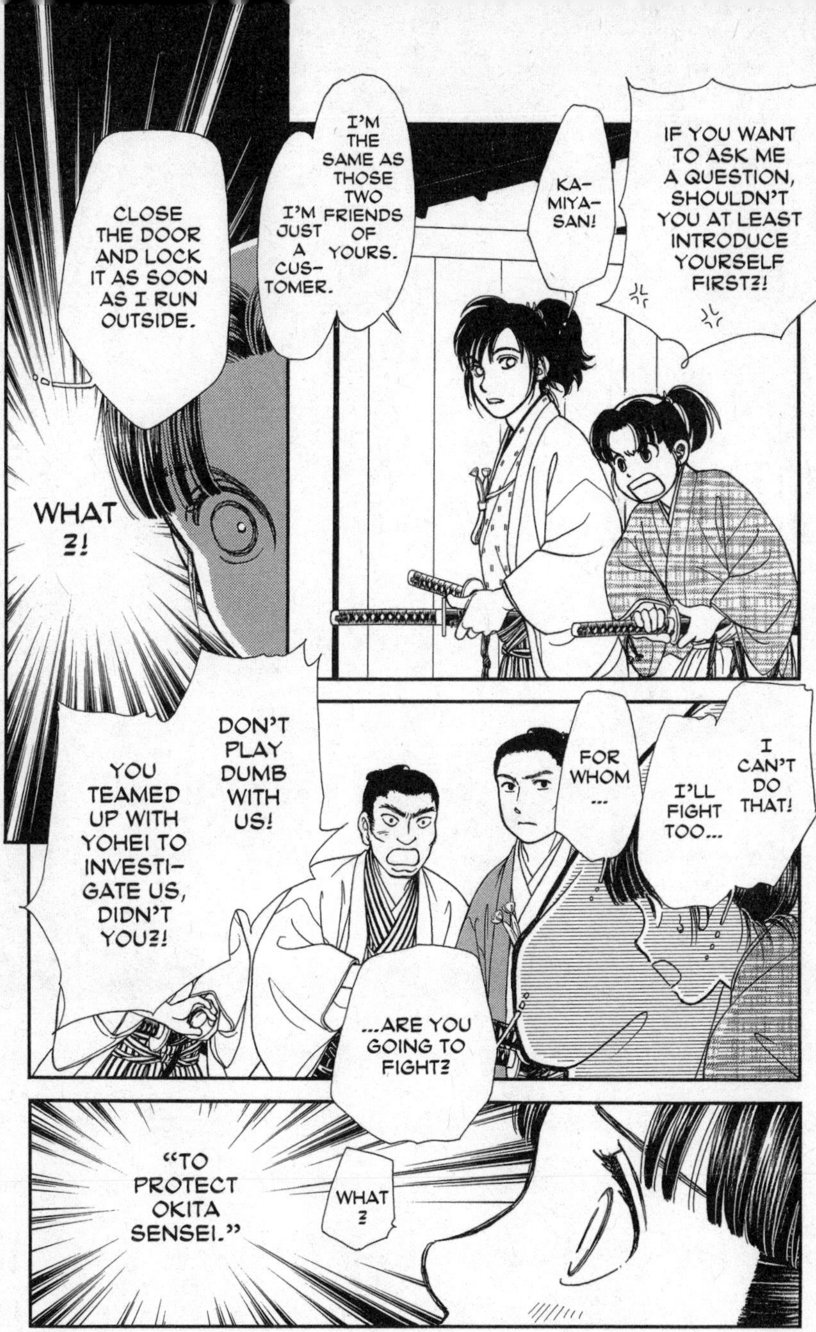
IF YOU WANT TO ASK ME A QUESTION, SHOULDN'T YOU AT LEAST INTRODUCE YOURSELF FIRST?!
KA-MIYA-SAN!
I'M THE SAME AS THOSE TWO FRIENDS OF YOURS.
I'M JUST A CUS-TOMER.
CLOSE THE DOOR AND LOCK IT AS SOON AS I RUN OUTSIDE.
WHAT?!
I CAN'T DO THAT!
I'LL FIGHT TOO...
FOR WHOM...
...ARE YOU GOING TO FIGHT?
DON'T PLAY DUMB WITH US!
YOU TEAMED UP WITH YOHEI TO INVESTI-GATE US, DIDN'T YOU?!
WHAT?
"TO PROTECT OKITA SENSEI."

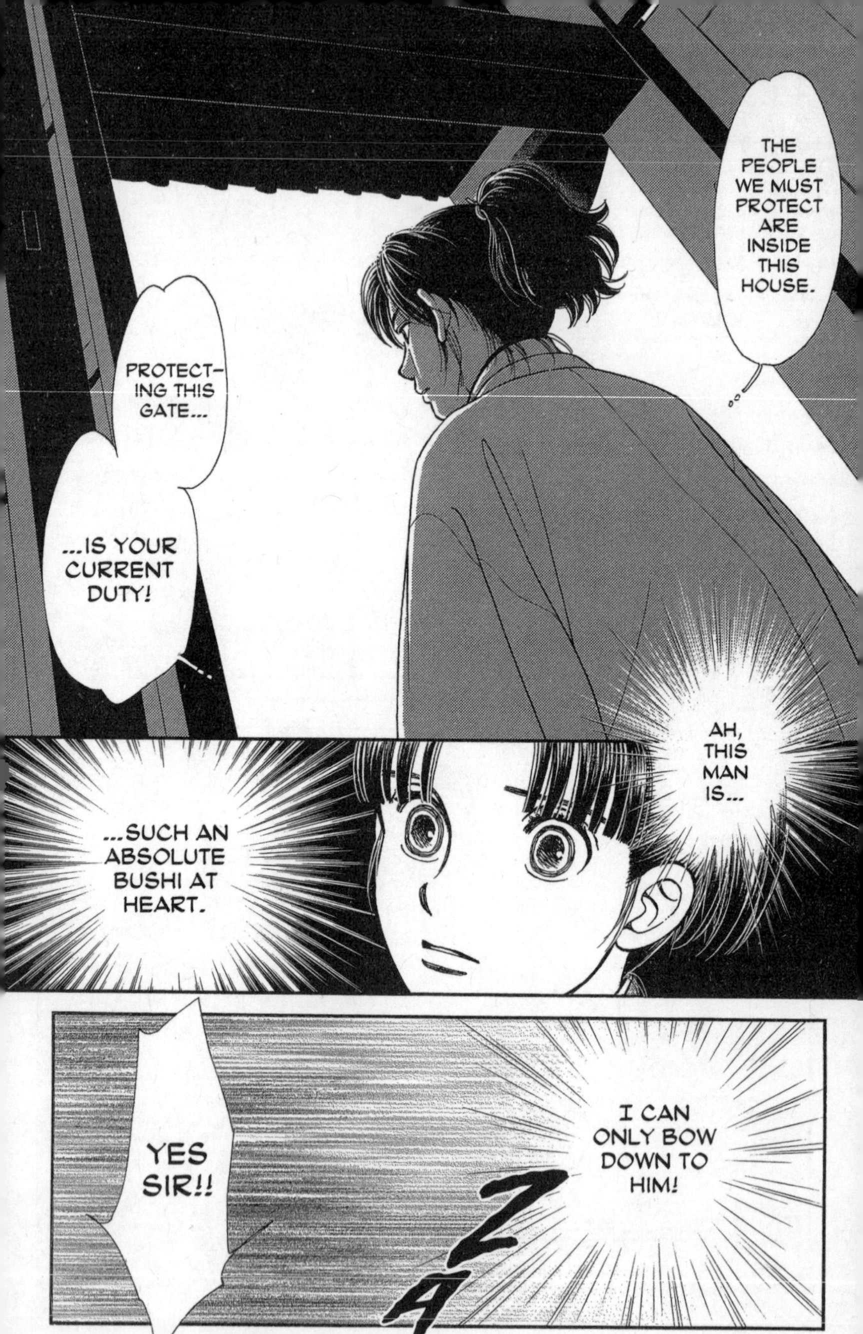
THE PEOPLE WE MUST PROTECT ARE INSIDE THIS HOUSE.
PROTECT-ING THIS GATE...
...IS YOUR CURRENT DUTY!
AH, THIS MAN IS...
...SUCH AN ABSOLUTE BUSHI AT HEART.
I CAN ONLY BOW DOWN TO HIM!
YES SIR!!
ZA

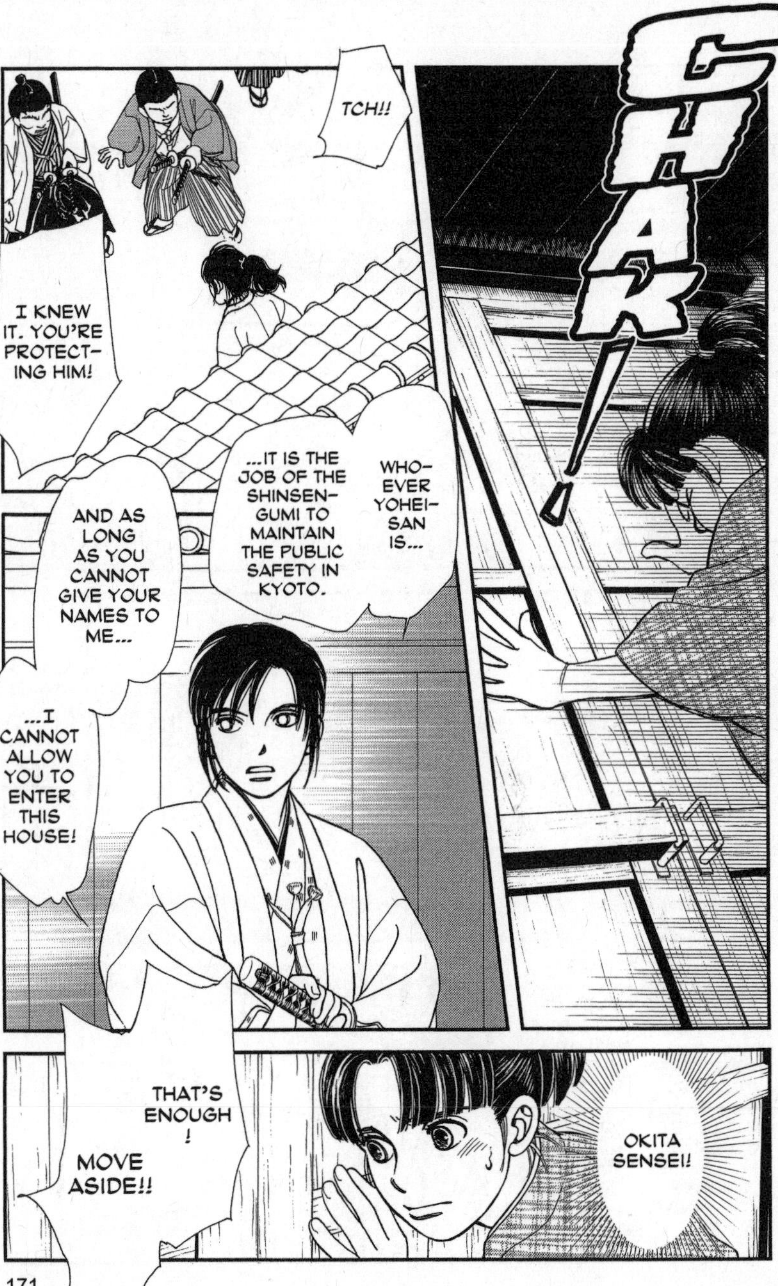
CHAK!
TCH!!
I KNEW IT. YOU'RE PROTECTING HIM!
WHOEVER YOHEI-SAN IS...
...IT IS THE JOB OF THE SHINSENGUMI TO MAINTAIN THE PUBLIC SAFETY IN KYOTO.
AND AS LONG AS YOU CANNOT GIVE YOUR NAMES TO ME...
...I CANNOT ALLOW YOU TO ENTER THIS HOUSE!
OKITA SENSEI!
THAT'S ENOUGH!
MOVE ASIDE!!

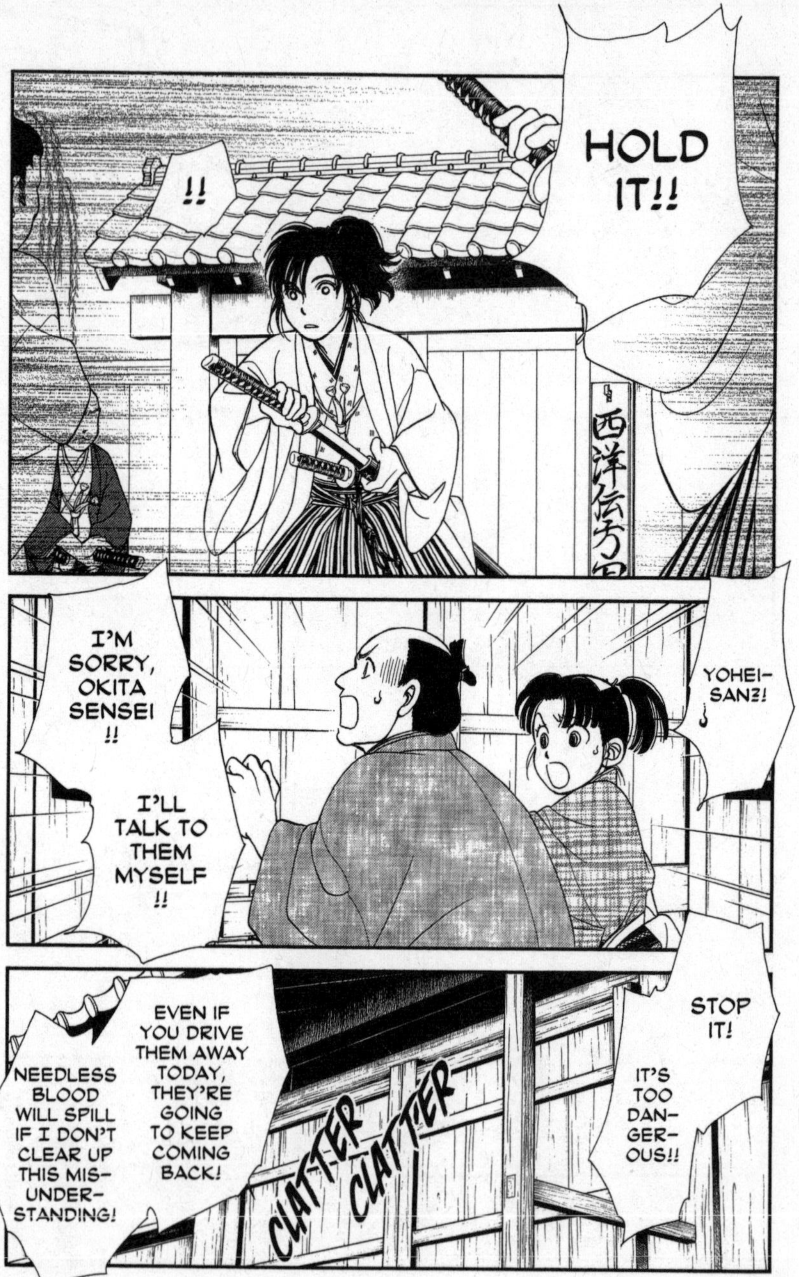
HOLD IT!!
!!
YOHEI-SAN?!
I'M SORRY, OKITA SENSEI!!
I'LL TALK TO THEM MYSELF!!
STOP IT!
IT'S TOO DAN-GER-OUS!!
EVEN IF YOU DRIVE THEM AWAY TODAY, THEY'RE GOING TO KEEP COMING BACK!
NEEDLESS BLOOD WILL SPILL IF I DON'T CLEAR UP THIS MIS-UNDER-STANDING!
CLATTER CLATTER

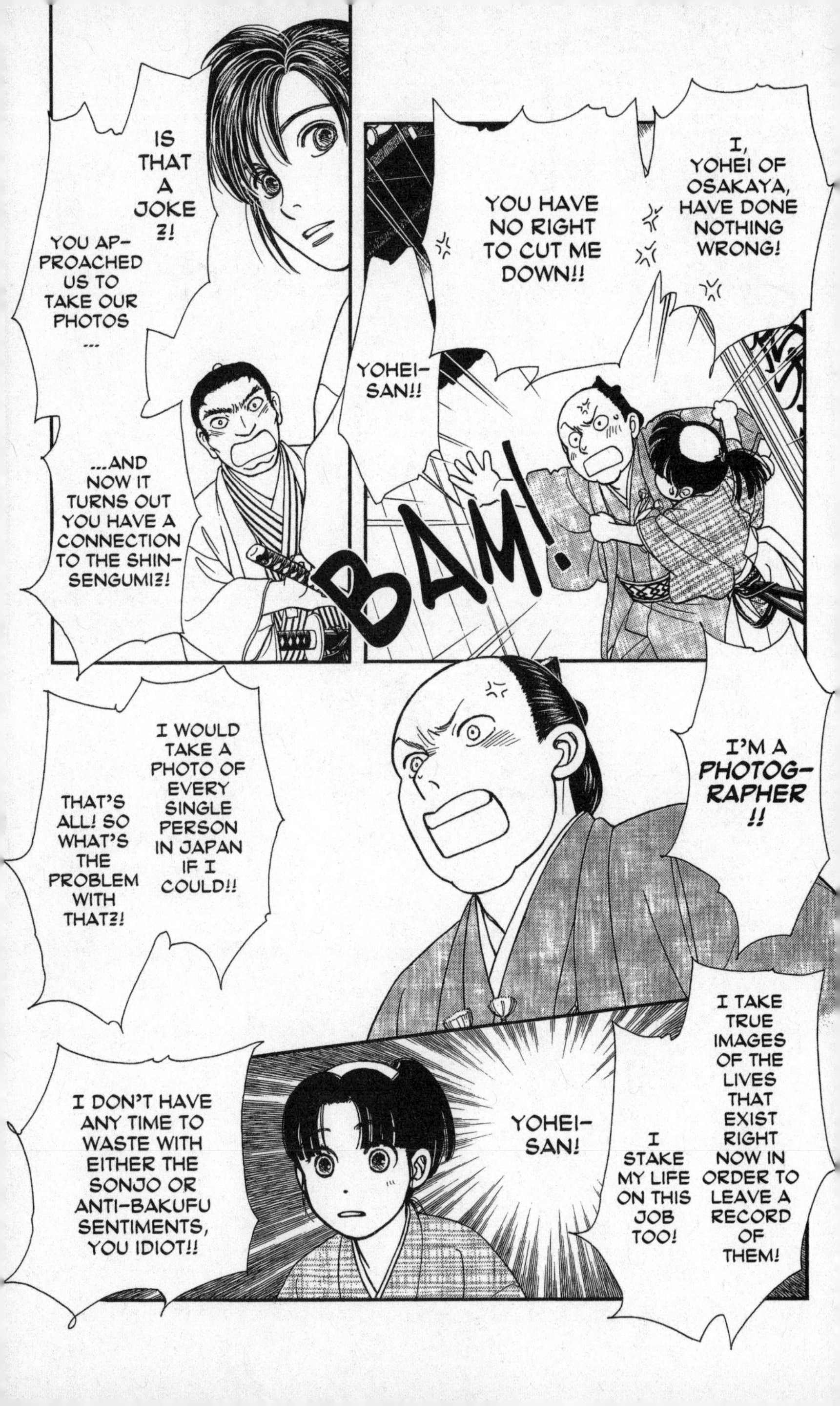
I, YOHEI OF OSAKAYA, HAVE DONE NOTHING WRONG!
YOU HAVE NO RIGHT TO CUT ME DOWN!!
YOHEI-SAN!!
BAM!
IS THAT A JOKE?!
YOU APPROACHED US TO TAKE OUR PHOTOS...
...AND NOW IT TURNS OUT YOU HAVE A CONNECTION TO THE SHINSENGUMI?!
I'M A *PHOTOGRAPHER*!!
I WOULD TAKE A PHOTO OF EVERY SINGLE PERSON IN JAPAN IF I COULD!!
THAT'S ALL! SO WHAT'S THE PROBLEM WITH THAT?!
I TAKE TRUE IMAGES OF THE LIVES THAT EXIST RIGHT NOW IN ORDER TO LEAVE A RECORD OF THEM!
I STAKE MY LIFE ON THIS JOB TOO!
YOHEI-SAN!
I DON'T HAVE ANY TIME TO WASTE WITH EITHER THE SONJO OR ANTI-BAKUFU SENTIMENTS, YOU IDIOT!!

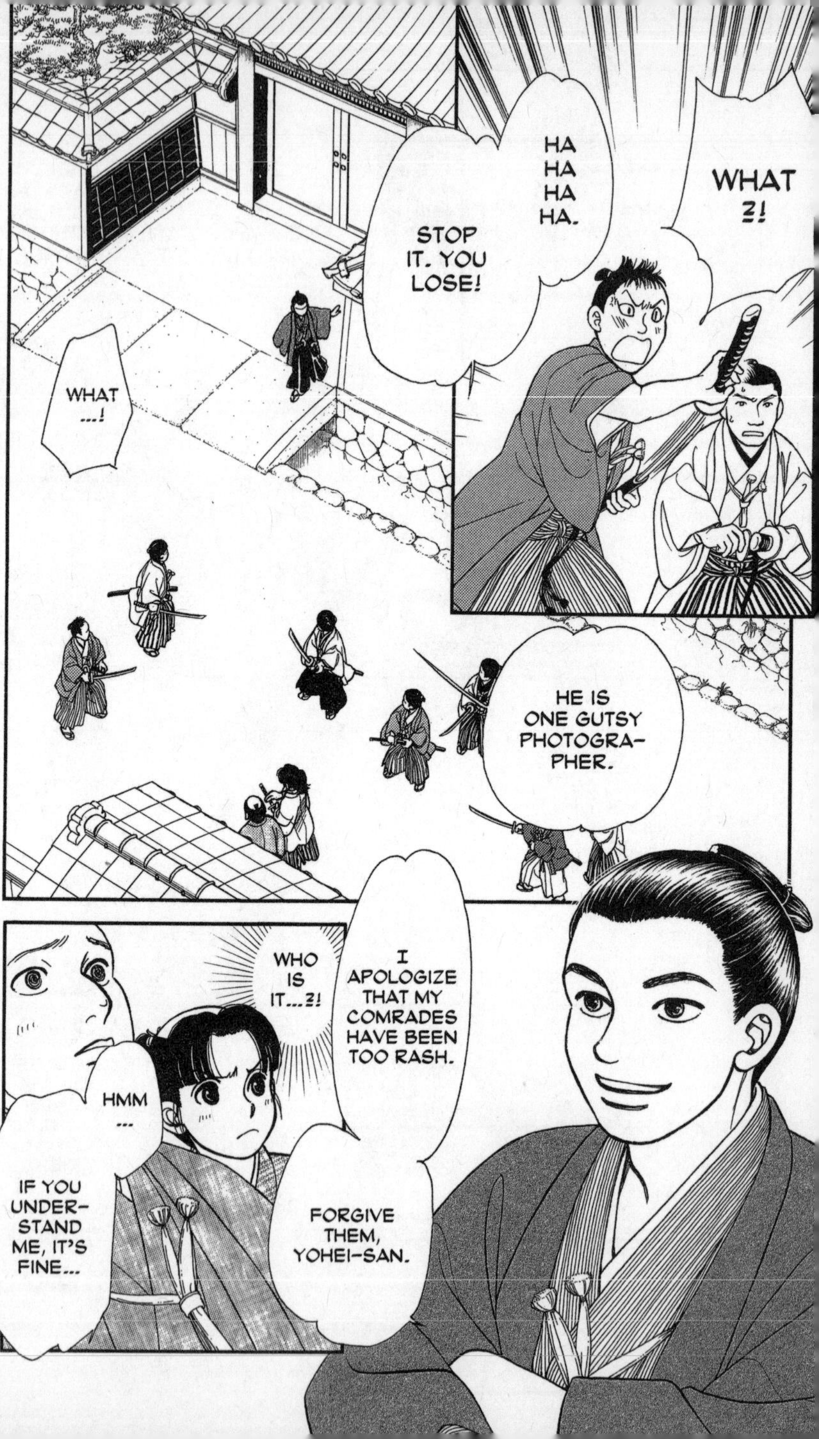
WHAT ?!
HA HA HA HA.
STOP IT. YOU LOSE!
WHAT ...!
HE IS ONE GUTSY PHOTOGRA-PHER.
I APOLOGIZE THAT MY COMRADES HAVE BEEN TOO RASH.
FORGIVE THEM, YOHEI-SAN.
WHO IS IT...?!
HMM ...
IF YOU UNDER-STAND ME, IT'S FINE...

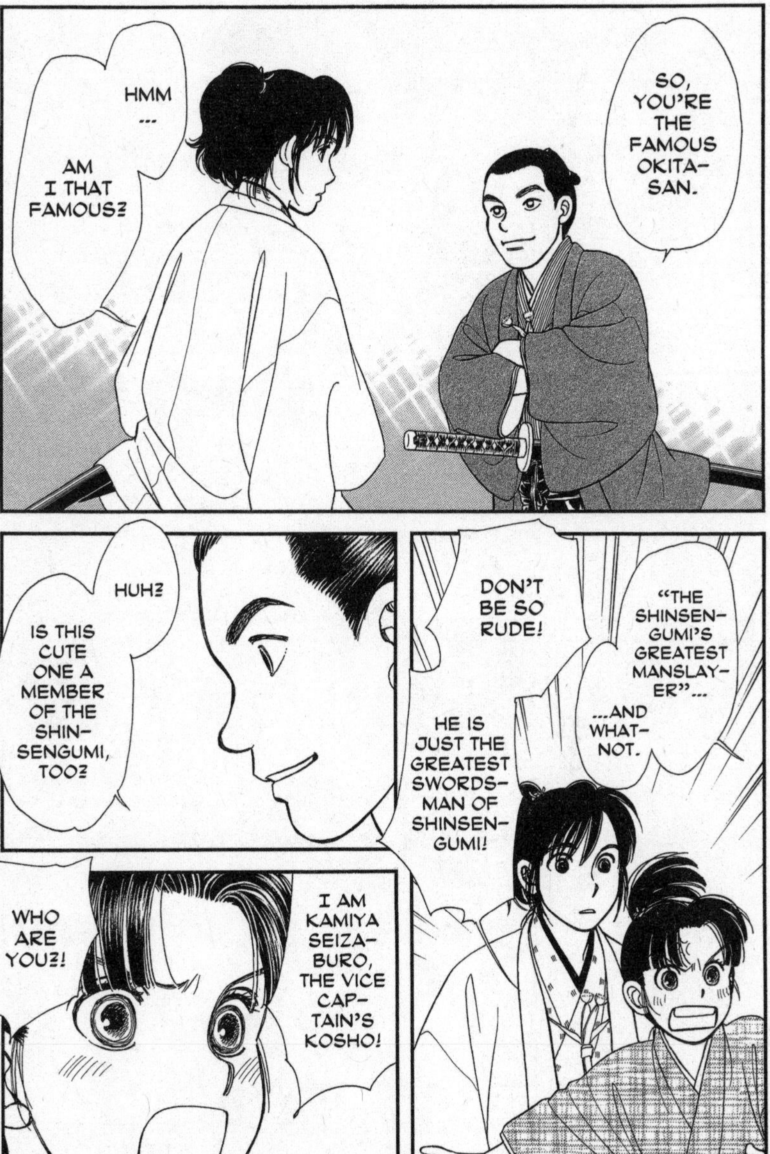
SO, YOU'RE THE FAMOUS OKITA-SAN.
HMM ... AM I THAT FAMOUS?
"THE SHINSEN-GUMI'S GREATEST MANSLAY-ER"... ...AND WHAT-NOT.
DON'T BE SO RUDE!
HE IS JUST THE GREATEST SWORDS-MAN OF SHINSEN-GUMI!
HUH? IS THIS CUTE ONE A MEMBER OF THE SHIN-SENGUMI, TOO?
I AM KAMIYA SEIZA-BURO, THE VICE CAP-TAIN'S KOSHO!
WHO ARE YOU?!

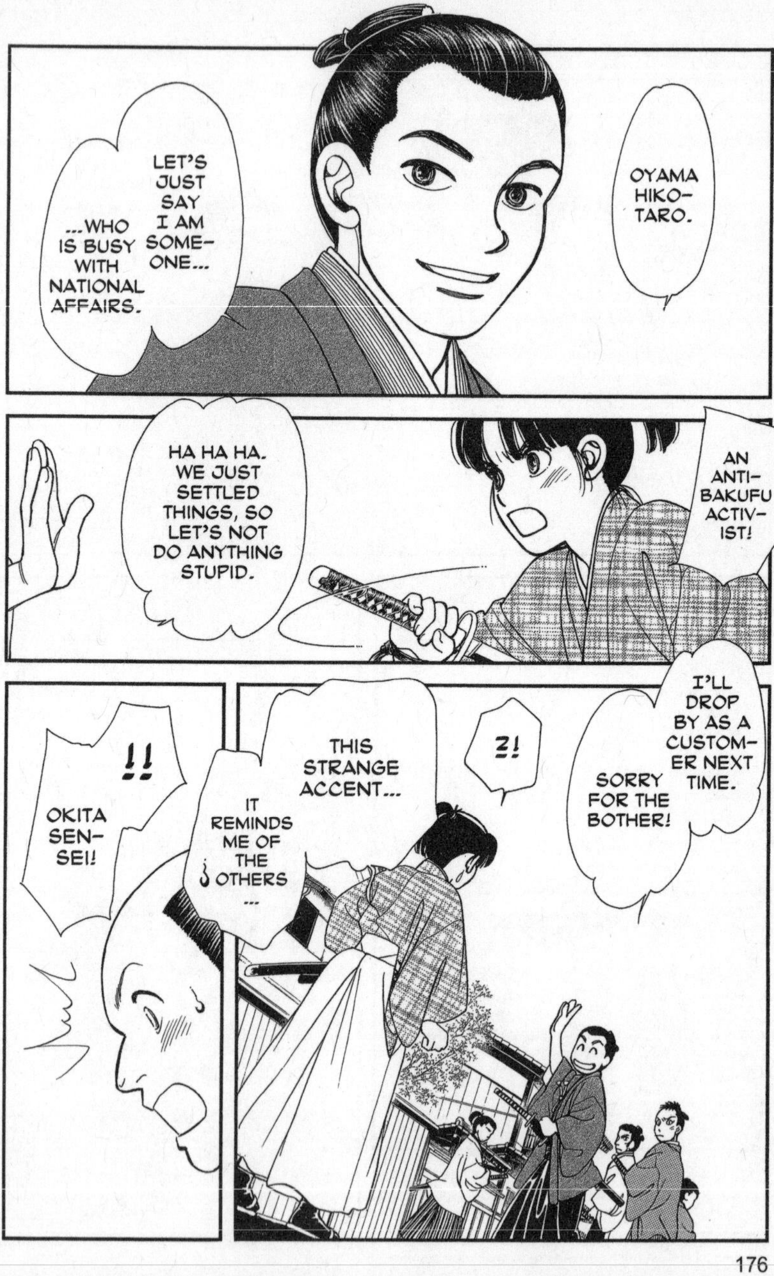

OYAMA HIKO-TARO.
LET'S JUST SAY I AM SOME-ONE...
...WHO IS BUSY WITH NATIONAL AFFAIRS.
AN ANTI-BAKUFU ACTIVIST!
HA HA HA. WE JUST SETTLED THINGS, SO LET'S NOT DO ANYTHING STUPID.
I'LL DROP BY AS A CUSTOMER NEXT TIME.
SORRY FOR THE BOTHER!
?!
THIS STRANGE ACCENT...
IT REMINDS ME OF THE OTHERS...
!!
OKITA SEN-SEI!

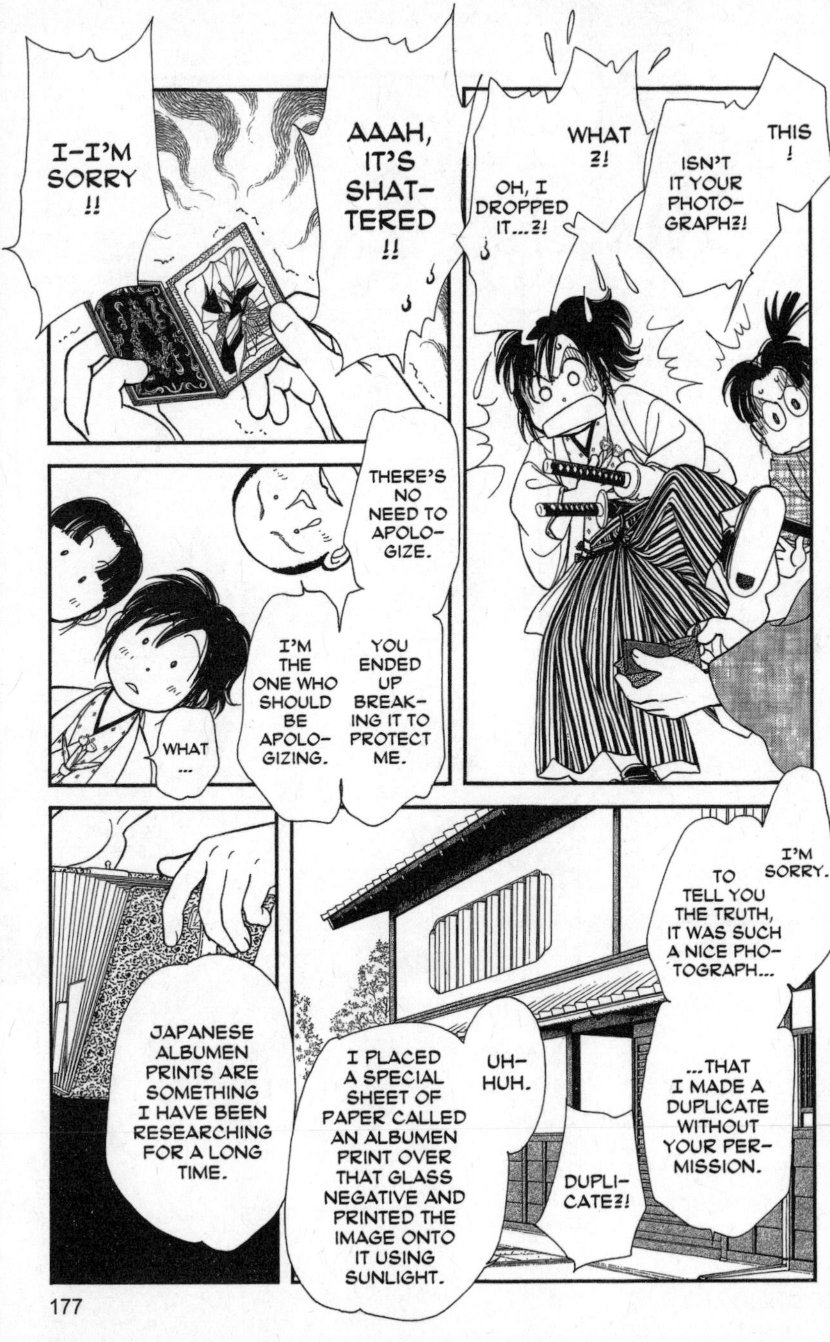
THIS!
ISN'T IT YOUR PHOTOGRAPH?!
WHAT?!
OH, I DROPPED IT...?!
AAAH, IT'S SHATTERED!!
I-I'M SORRY!!
THERE'S NO NEED TO APOLOGIZE.
YOU ENDED UP BREAKING IT TO PROTECT ME.
I'M THE ONE WHO SHOULD BE APOLOGIZING.
WHAT...
I'M SORRY.
TO TELL YOU THE TRUTH, IT WAS SUCH A NICE PHOTOGRAPH...
...THAT I MADE A DUPLICATE WITHOUT YOUR PERMISSION.
DUPLICATE?!
UH-HUH.
I PLACED A SPECIAL SHEET OF PAPER CALLED AN ALBUMEN PRINT OVER THAT GLASS NEGATIVE AND PRINTED THE IMAGE ONTO IT USING SUNLIGHT.
JAPANESE ALBUMEN PRINTS ARE SOMETHING I HAVE BEEN RESEARCHING FOR A LONG TIME.

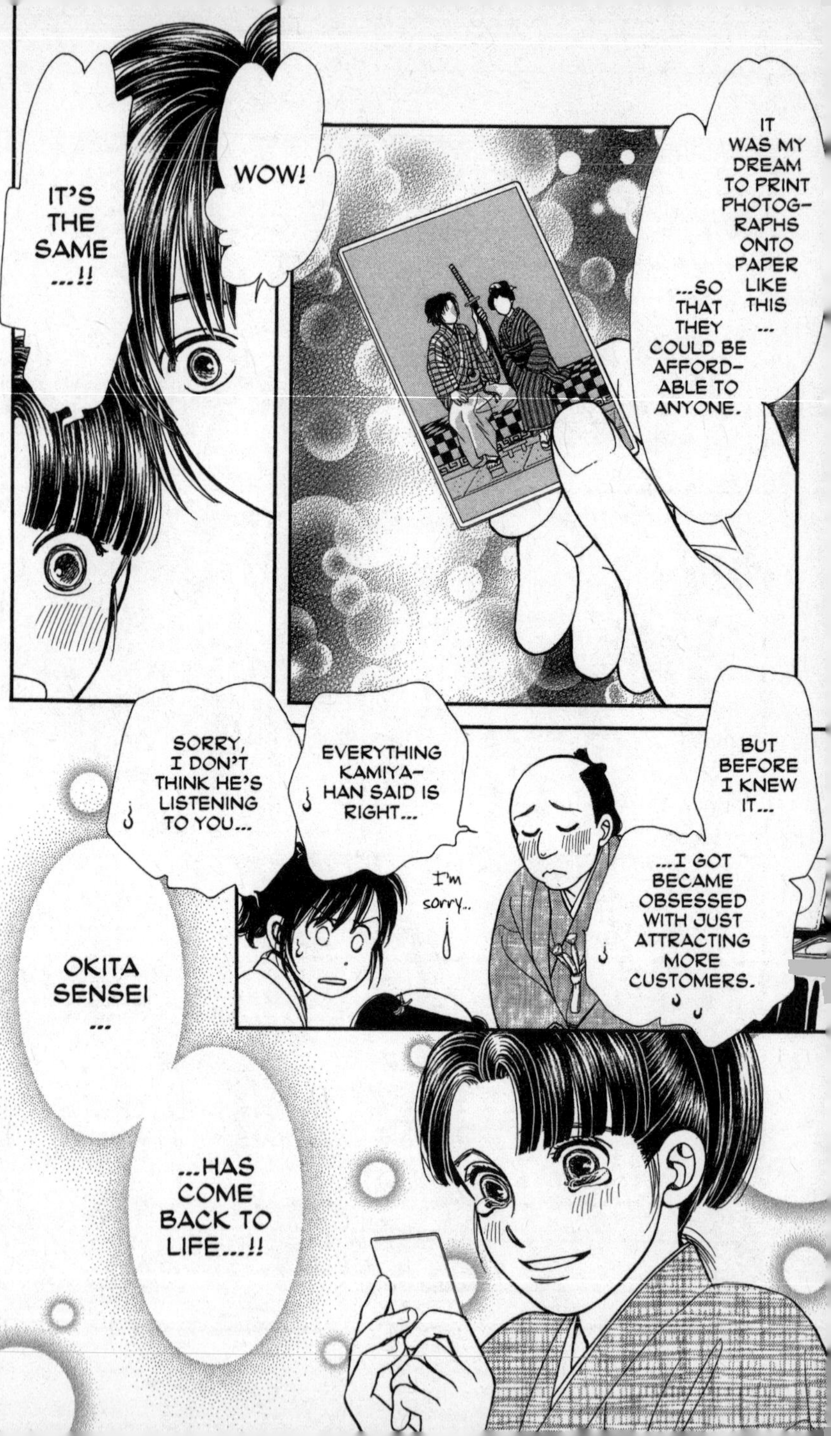
IT WAS MY DREAM TO PRINT PHOTOG-RAPHS ONTO PAPER LIKE THIS...
...SO THAT THEY COULD BE AFFORD-ABLE TO ANYONE.
WOW!
IT'S THE SAME...!!
BUT BEFORE I KNEW IT...
...I GOT BECAME OBSESSED WITH JUST ATTRACTING MORE CUSTOMERS.
I'm sorry...
EVERYTHING KAMIYA-HAN SAID IS RIGHT...
SORRY, I DON'T THINK HE'S LISTENING TO YOU...
OKITA SENSEI...
...HAS COME BACK TO LIFE...!!

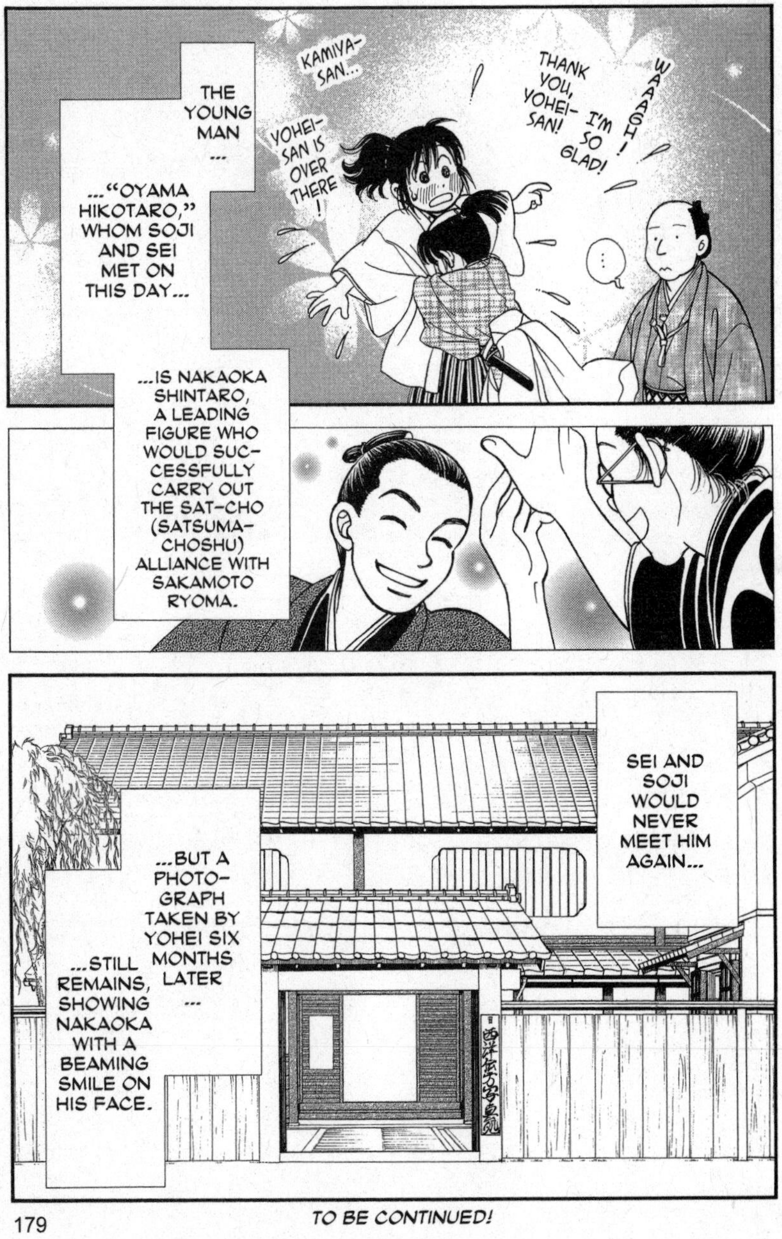
WAAAGH!
THANK YOU, YOHEI-SAN!
I'M SO GLAD!
KAMIYA-SAN...
!
YOHEI-SAN IS OVER THERE!
...
THE YOUNG MAN...
..."OYAMA HIKOTARO," WHOM SOJI AND SEI MET ON THIS DAY...
...IS NAKAOKA SHINTARO, A LEADING FIGURE WHO WOULD SUCCESSFULLY CARRY OUT THE SAT-CHO (SATSUMA-CHOSHU) ALLIANCE WITH SAKAMOTO RYOMA.
SEI AND SOJI WOULD NEVER MEET HIM AGAIN...
...BUT A PHOTOGRAPH TAKEN BY YOHEI SIX MONTHS LATER...
...STILL REMAINS, SHOWING NAKAOKA WITH A BEAMING SMILE ON HIS FACE.

TO BE CONTINUED!

TAEKO WATANABE PRESENTS

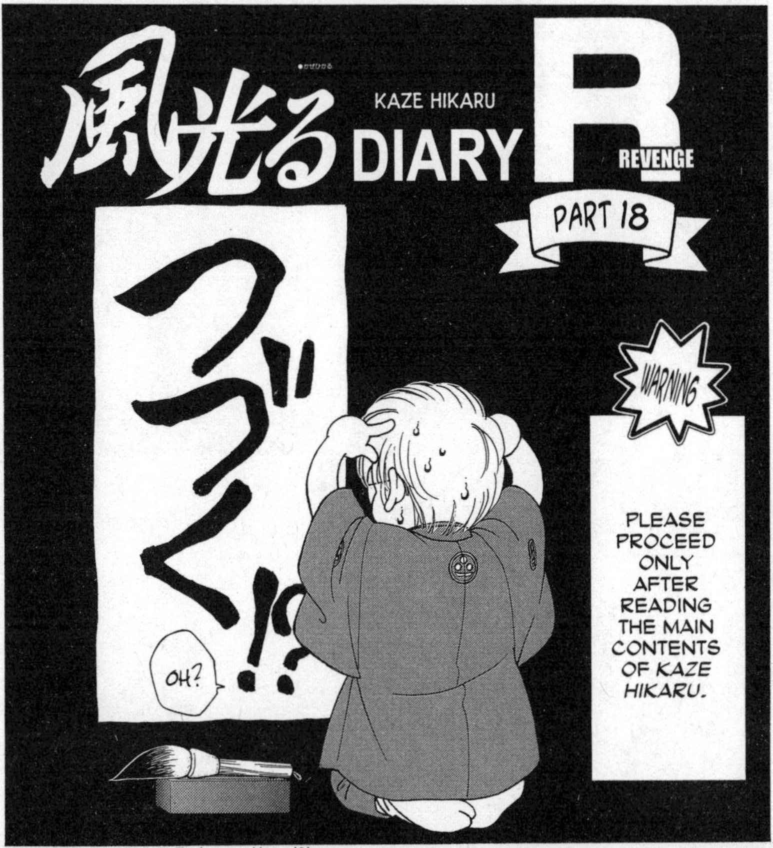

風光る
KAZE HIKARU
DIARY R
REVENGE
PART 18
WARNING
PLEASE PROCEED ONLY AFTER READING THE MAIN CONTENTS OF KAZE HIKARU.
つづく!?
OH?

Scroll: To be continued?!

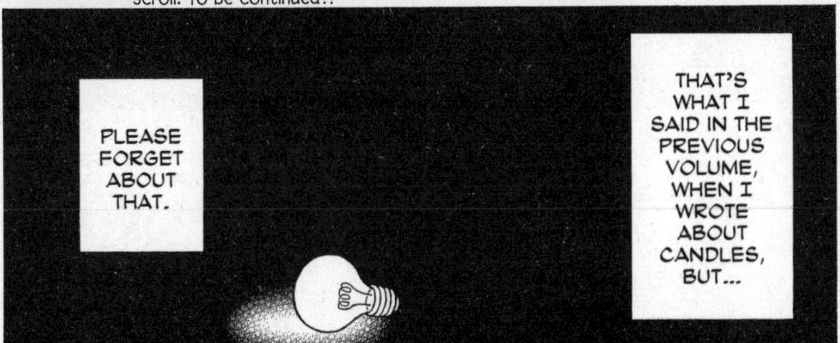

THAT'S WHAT I SAID IN THE PREVIOUS VOLUME, WHEN I WROTE ABOUT CANDLES, BUT...
PLEASE FORGET ABOUT THAT.

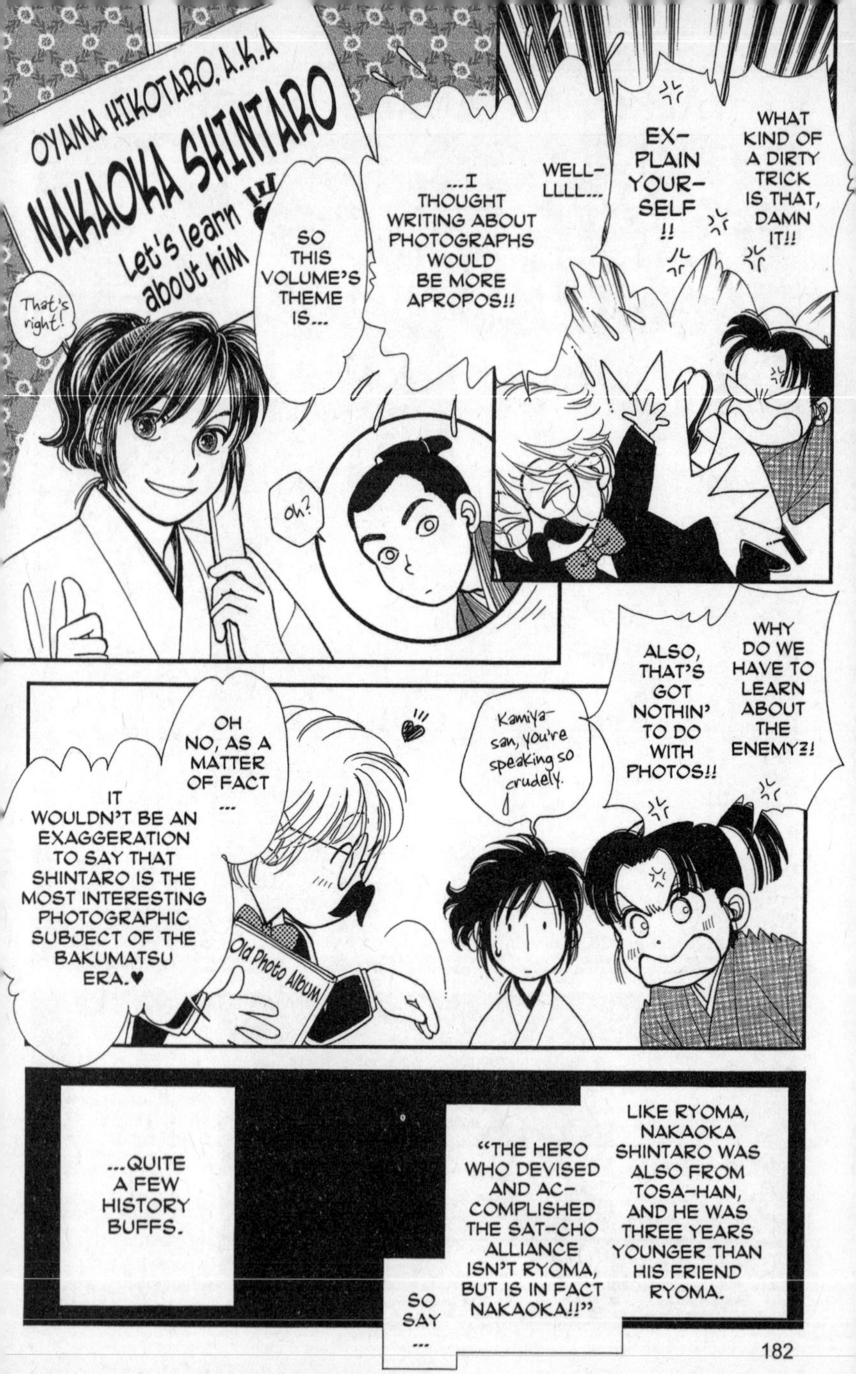

WHAT KIND OF A DIRTY TRICK IS THAT, DAMN IT!!
EX-PLAIN YOUR-SELF!!
WELL-LLLL...
...I THOUGHT WRITING ABOUT PHOTOGRAPHS WOULD BE MORE APROPOS!!
OYAMA HIKOTARO, A.K.A NAKAOKA SHINTARO Let's learn about him
SO THIS VOLUME'S THEME IS...
That's right!
Oh?
WHY DO WE HAVE TO LEARN ABOUT THE ENEMY?!
ALSO, THAT'S GOT NOTHIN' TO DO WITH PHOTOS!!
Kamiya-san, you're speaking so crudely.
OH NO, AS A MATTER OF FACT...
IT WOULDN'T BE AN EXAGGERATION TO SAY THAT SHINTARO IS THE MOST INTERESTING PHOTOGRAPHIC SUBJECT OF THE BAKUMATSU ERA.♥
Old Photo Album
LIKE RYOMA, NAKAOKA SHINTARO WAS ALSO FROM TOSA-HAN, AND HE WAS THREE YEARS YOUNGER THAN HIS FRIEND RYOMA.
"THE HERO WHO DEVISED AND AC-COMPLISHED THE SAT-CHO ALLIANCE ISN'T RYOMA, BUT IS IN FACT NAKAOKA!!"
SO SAY...
...QUITE A FEW HISTORY BUFFS.

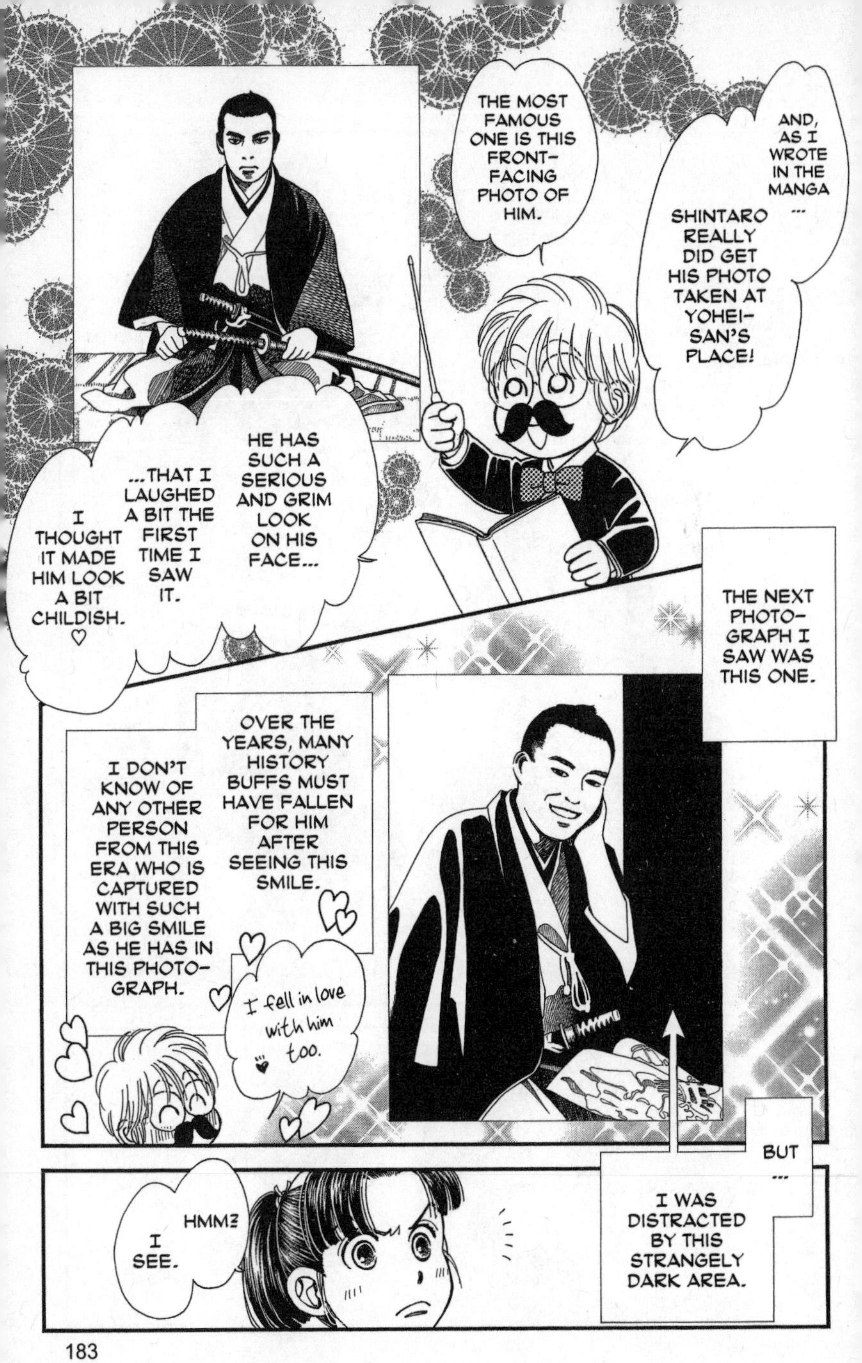
AND, AS I WROTE IN THE MANGA ...
SHINTARO REALLY DID GET HIS PHOTO TAKEN AT YOHEI-SAN'S PLACE!
THE MOST FAMOUS ONE IS THIS FRONT-FACING PHOTO OF HIM.
HE HAS SUCH A SERIOUS AND GRIM LOOK ON HIS FACE...
...THAT I LAUGHED A BIT THE FIRST TIME I SAW IT.
I THOUGHT IT MADE HIM LOOK A BIT CHILDISH. ♡
THE NEXT PHOTOGRAPH I SAW WAS THIS ONE.
OVER THE YEARS, MANY HISTORY BUFFS MUST HAVE FALLEN FOR HIM AFTER SEEING THIS SMILE.
I DON'T KNOW OF ANY OTHER PERSON FROM THIS ERA WHO IS CAPTURED WITH SUCH A BIG SMILE AS HE HAS IN THIS PHOTOGRAPH.
I fell in love with him too.
BUT ...
I WAS DISTRACTED BY THIS STRANGELY DARK AREA.
HMM?
I SEE.

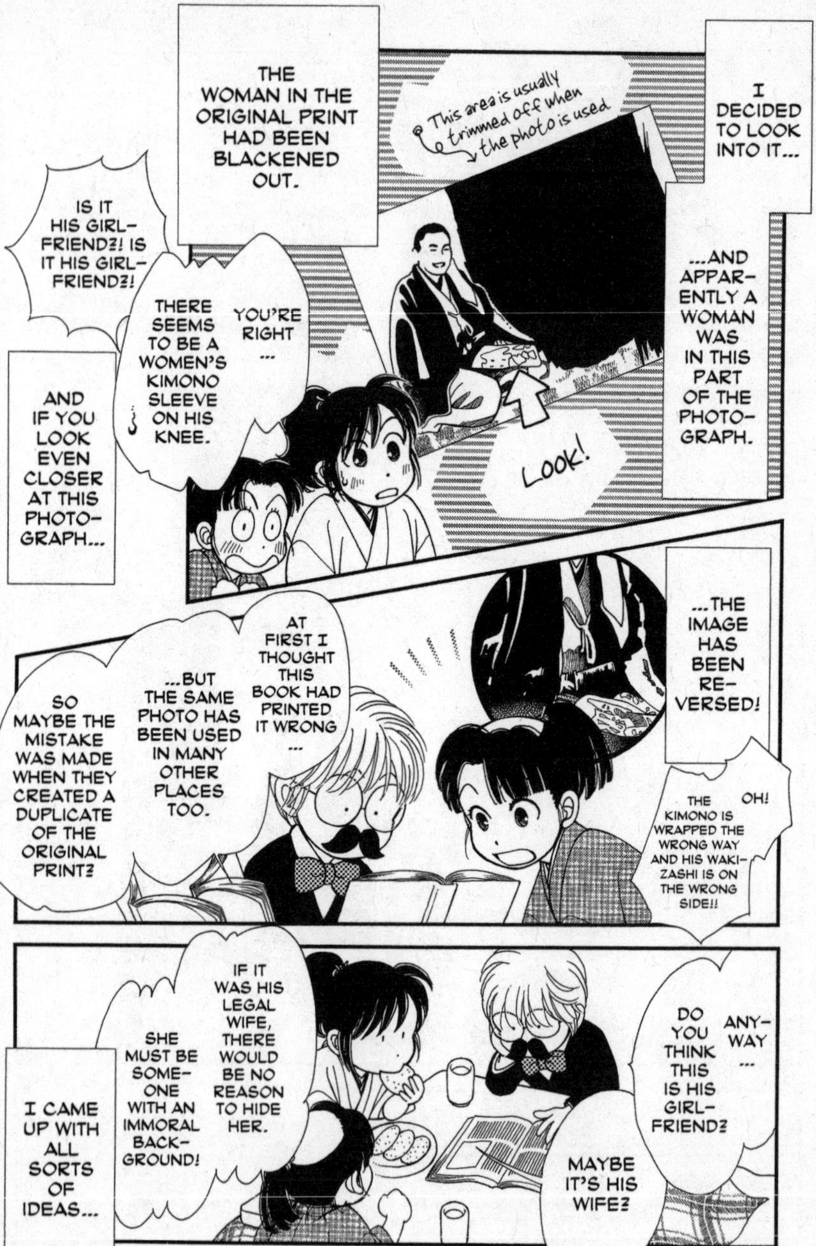
I DECIDED TO LOOK INTO IT...
...AND APPARENTLY A WOMAN WAS IN THIS PART OF THE PHOTOGRAPH.
LOOK!
THE WOMAN IN THE ORIGINAL PRINT HAD BEEN BLACKENED OUT.
This area is usually trimmed off when the photo is used.
YOU'RE RIGHT...
THERE SEEMS TO BE A WOMEN'S KIMONO SLEEVE ON HIS KNEE.
IS IT HIS GIRLFRIEND?! IS IT HIS GIRLFRIEND?!
AND IF YOU LOOK EVEN CLOSER AT THIS PHOTOGRAPH...
...THE IMAGE HAS BEEN REVERSED!
OH!
THE KIMONO IS WRAPPED THE WRONG WAY AND HIS WAKIZASHI IS ON THE WRONG SIDE!!
AT FIRST I THOUGHT THIS BOOK HAD PRINTED IT WRONG...
...BUT THE SAME PHOTO HAS BEEN USED IN MANY OTHER PLACES TOO.
SO MAYBE THE MISTAKE WAS MADE WHEN THEY CREATED A DUPLICATE OF THE ORIGINAL PRINT?
ANYWAY...
DO YOU THINK THIS IS HIS GIRLFRIEND?
MAYBE IT'S HIS WIFE?
IF IT WAS HIS LEGAL WIFE, THERE WOULD BE NO REASON TO HIDE HER.
SHE MUST BE SOMEONE WITH AN IMMORAL BACKGROUND!
I CAME UP WITH ALL SORTS OF IDEAS...

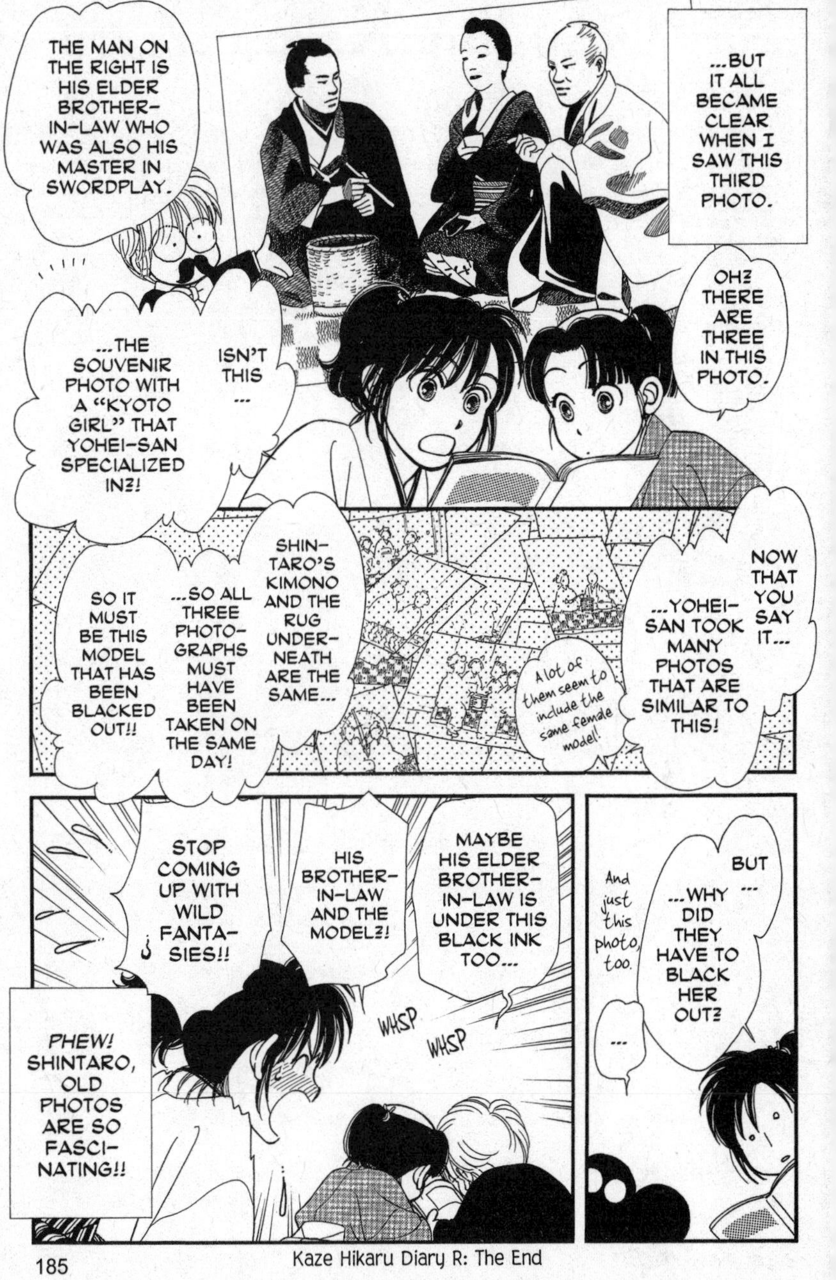
...BUT IT ALL BECAME CLEAR WHEN I SAW THIS THIRD PHOTO.
THE MAN ON THE RIGHT IS HIS ELDER BROTHER-IN-LAW WHO WAS ALSO HIS MASTER IN SWORDPLAY.
OH? THERE ARE THREE IN THIS PHOTO.
ISN'T THIS ...
...THE SOUVENIR PHOTO WITH A "KYOTO GIRL" THAT YOHEI-SAN SPECIALIZED IN?!
NOW THAT YOU SAY IT...
...YOHEI-SAN TOOK MANY PHOTOS THAT ARE SIMILAR TO THIS!
A lot of them seem to include the same female model!
SHIN-TARO'S KIMONO AND THE RUG UNDER-NEATH ARE THE SAME...
...SO ALL THREE PHOTO-GRAPHS MUST HAVE BEEN TAKEN ON THE SAME DAY!
SO IT MUST BE THIS MODEL THAT HAS BEEN BLACKED OUT!!
BUT ...WHY DID THEY HAVE TO BLACK HER OUT?
And just this photo, too.
...
MAYBE HIS ELDER BROTHER-IN-LAW IS UNDER THIS BLACK INK TOO...
HIS BROTHER-IN-LAW AND THE MODEL?!
STOP COMING UP WITH WILD FANTA-SIES!!
WHSP
WHSP
PHEW! SHINTARO, OLD PHOTOS ARE SO FASCI-NATING!!

Kaze Hikaru Diary R: The End

Decoding Kaze Hikaru

Kaze Hikaru is a historical drama based in 19th century Japan and thus contains some fairly mystifying terminology. In this glossary we'll break down archaic phrases, terms and other linguistic curiosities for you so that you can move through life with the smug assurance that you are indeed a know-it-all.

First and foremost, because *Kaze Hikaru* is a period story, we kept all character names in their traditional Japanese form—that is, family name followed by first name. For example, the character Okita Soji's family name is Okita and his personal name is Soji.

BAKUFU:
Literally, "tent government." Shogunate; the feudal, military government that dominated Japan for more than 200 years.

BAKUMATSU:
The final 15 years of bakufu rule.

BONBORI:
A Japanese paper lantern that often plays a role in traditional festivals.

BUBUZUKE:
Name used in Kyoto for ochazuke, a dish of rice with tea.

BUSHI:
A samurai or warrior (part of the compound word *bushido*, which means "way of the warrior").

-CHAN:
A diminutive suffix that conveys endearment.

DAIMYO:
A landholding feudal lord.

-DAYU:
An honorific suffix indicating the highest-ranking courtesan (*yujo*).

DOJO:
A school of martial arts.

EDO:
The former name of Tokyo.

GION:
Kyoto's entertainment district.

HAN:
A feudal domain of Japan during the Tokugawa period.

-HAN:
The same as the honorific *-san*, pronounced in the dialect of southern Japan.

KATANA:
A traditional longsword used by samurai.

KOSHO:
A Shinsengumi captain's personal assistant.

-KUN:
An honorific suffix that indicates a difference in rank and title. The use of *-kun* is also a way of indicating familiarity and friendliness between students or compatriots.

KUZUKIRI:
A sweet noodle dish traditionally eaten in the summer.

MIBU ROSHI or MIBURO:
A group of warriors that supports the Bakufu.

NEE-CHAN:
An affectionate term for a sister or female relative.

OBI:
Belt worn with a kimono.

ONI:
Literally, "ogre."

ROGAI:
A term used for tuberculosis.

RONIN:
Masterless samurai.

RYO:

At the time of this story, one and a half *ryo* was enough currency to support a family of five for an entire month.

-SAMA:

An honorific suffix used for one of higher rank; a more respectful version of *-san*.

-SAN:

An honorific suffix that carries the meaning of "Mr." or "Ms."

SENSEI:

A teacher, master or instructor.

SHUDO:

A romantic relationship between a younger samurai and his older mentor.

SONJO-HA:

Those loyal to the emperor and dedicated to the expulsion of foreigners from the country.

TEN'NEN RISHIN-RYU:

The form of martial art practiced by members of the Shinsengumi.

TOKUGAWA BAKUFU:

The last feudal military government of Japan's pre-modern period, directed by hereditary leaders—shoguns—of the Tokugawa clan.

WAKIZASHI:

A short katana.

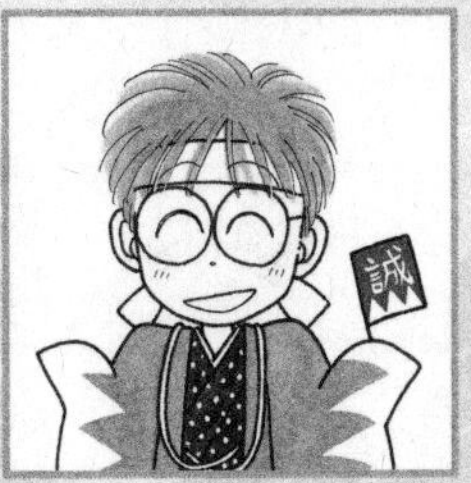
誠

An-chan, who wrote the promotional copy for this volume,* is a longtime, second-generation fan of mine who has been following the series with her mother, who is almost my age. So seeing An-chan's success is like seeing my own child grow up, and it's very touching. Of course, that doesn't only go for An-chan. I love receiving letters from readers telling me that they've been following this series since they were students and now they're working or raising children! I haven't been married, but I get to feel like I've raised my own children. I just can't get enough of this job (*ha ha*). Well then, this volume's seasonal term is "autumn gingko leaves." Obviously it's an autumn word, but this will become "falling gingko leaves" in winter and "gingko flowers" in spring, to represent each season. I guess we can't get enough of gingko as a theme, huh? (*Ha ha.*)

*Included in the original Japanese release in 2009.

Taeko Watanabe debuted as a manga artist in 1979 with her story *Waka-chan no Netsuai Jidai* (Love Struck Days of Waka). *Kaze Hikaru* is her longest-running series, but she has created a number of other popular series. Watanabe is a two-time winner of the prestigious Shogakukan Manga Award in the girls' category—her manga *Hajime-chan ga Ichiban!* (Hajime-chan Is Number One!) claimed the award in 1991, and *Kaze Hikaru* took it in 2003.

Watanabe read hundreds of historical sources to create *Kaze Hikaru*. She is from Tokyo.

KAZE HIKARU
VOL. 27
Shojo Beat Edition

STORY AND ART BY
TAEKO WATANABE

KAZE HIKARU Vol. 27
by Taeko WATANABE
© 1997 Taeko WATANABE
All rights reserved.
Original Japanese edition published by SHOGAKUKAN.
English translation rights in the United States of America and Canada arranged with
SHOGAKUKAN.

Translation & English Adaptation/Tetsuichiro Miyaki
Touch-up Art & Lettering/Rina Mapa
Design/Veronica Casson
Editor/Megan Bates

Printed in the U.S.A.

Published by VIZ Media, LLC
P.O. Box 77010
San Francisco, CA 94107

10 9 8 7 6 5 4 3 2 1
First printing, October 2019

VIZ MEDIA
viz.com

shojobeat.com

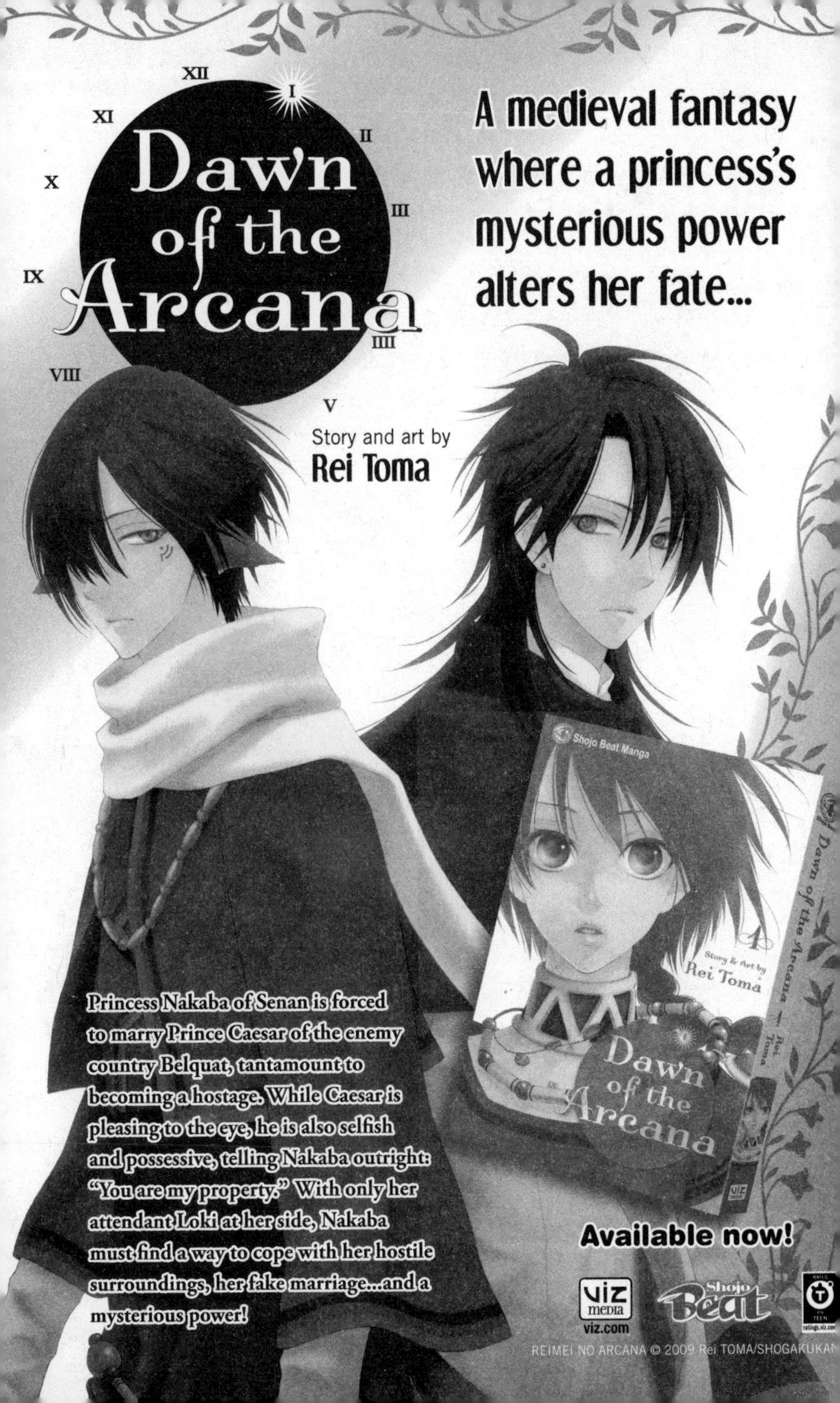
XII
I
II
III
IIII
V
VIII
IX
X
XI
Dawn of the Arcana
A medieval fantasy where a princess's mysterious power alters her fate...
Story and art by
Rei Toma
Shojo Beat Manga
Dawn of the Arcana
1
Story & Art by
Rei Toma
Princess Nakaba of Senan is forced to marry Prince Caesar of the enemy country Belquat, tantamount to becoming a hostage. While Caesar is pleasing to the eye, he is also selfish and possessive, telling Nakaba outright: "You are my property." With only her attendant Loki at her side, Nakaba must find a way to cope with her hostile surroundings, her fake marriage...and a mysterious power!
Available now!
VIZ MEDIA
viz.com
Shojo Beat
TEEN
REIMEI NO ARCANA © 2009 Rei TOMA/SHOGAKUKAN

SURPRISE!

You may be reading the wrong way!

It's true: In keeping with the original Japanese comic format, this book reads from right to left—so action, sound effects, and word balloons are completely reversed. This preserves the orientation of the original artwork—plus, it's fun! Check out the diagram shown here to get the hang of things, and then turn to the other side of the book to get started!

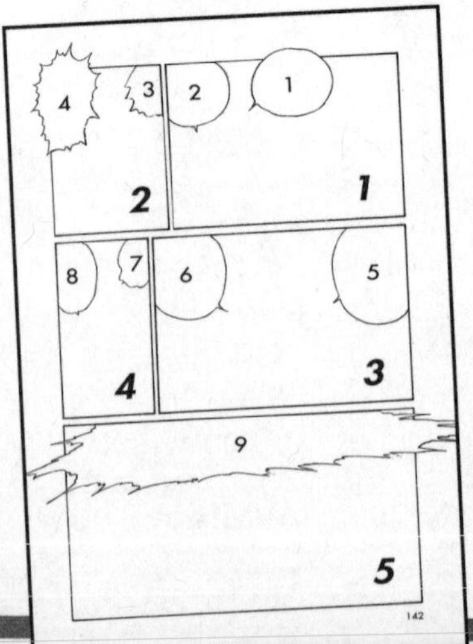

1
2
1
3
4
2
5
6
3
7
8
4
9
5
142

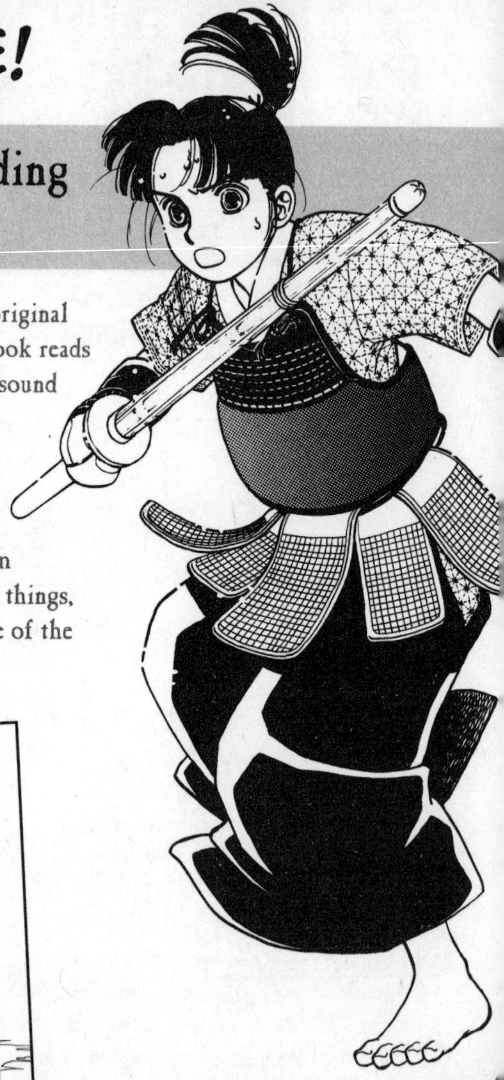